The Power of Human Rights
International Norms and Domestic Change

On the fiftieth anniversary of the Universal Declaration of Human Rights, this book evaluates the impact of these norms on the behavior of national governments in many regions of the world. Have the principles articulated in the Declaration had any effect at all on the actual behavior of states towards their citizens? What are the conditions under which international human rights norms are internalized in domestic practices? And what can we learn from this case about why, how, and under what conditions international norms in general influence the actions of states? This book tackles these questions. A five-phase "spiral model" of human rights change is developed to suggest a socialization process by which international norms are internalized in the domestic practices of states. The model links the interactions among transnationally operating advocacy networks, international organizations, Western states, domestic opposition groups, and norm-violating national governments in one unified concept. The book applies the model in the various empirical chapters to eleven countries representing five different world regions – Northern Africa, Sub-Saharan Africa, Southeast Asia, Latin America, and Eastern Europe. Finally, practical lessons are drawn from the analysis that provides fresh perspectives for activists and policy makers concerned with preserving and extending the human rights gains made during the past fifty years.

Thomas Risse is Chair of International Relations at the Robert Schuman Centre and the Department of Social and Political Sciences of the European University Institute, Florence. He is the author of *Cooperation among Democracies: The European Influence on US Foreign Policy* (1995), editor of *Bringing Transnational Relations Back In* (1995), and co-editor (with Richard N. Lebow) of *International Relations Theory and the End of the Cold War* (1995).

Stephen C. Ropp is Professor of Political Science at the University of Wyoming. He is the author of *Panamanian Politics: From Guarded Nation to National Guard* (1982) and *The Latin American Military Institution* (1986), and co-editor of *Central America: Crisis and Adaptation* (1984).

Kathryn Sikkink is Professor of Political Science at the University of Minnesota. She is the author of *Ideas and Institutions: Developmentalism in Brazil and Argentina* (1991), and co-author (with Margaret Keck) of *Activists Beyond Borders: Advocacy Networks in International Politics* (1998).

The power of human rights

CAMBRIDGE STUDIES IN INTERNATIONAL RELATIONS

Series list continues after index

The Power of Human Rights
International Norms and Domestic Change

edited by
Thomas Risse, Stephen C. Ropp,
and Kathryn Sikkink

CAMBRIDGE
UNIVERSITY PRESS

PUBLISHED BY THE PRESS SYNDICATE OF THE UNIVERSITY OF CAMBRIDGE
The Pitt Building, Trumpington Street, Cambridge, United Kingdom

CAMBRIDGE UNIVERSITY PRESS
The Edinburgh Building, Cambridge CB2 2RU, UK   http://www.cup.cam.ac.uk
40 West 20th Street, New York, NY 10011–4211, USA   http://www.cup.org
10 Stamford Road, Oakleigh, Melbourne 3166, Australia
Ruiz de Alarcón 13, 28014 Madrid, Spain

First published 1999
Reprinted 2000

Printed in the United Kingdom at the University Press, Cambridge

Typeset in Palatino 10/12.5pt [VN]

A catalogue record for this book is available from the British Library

Library of Congress Cataloguing in Publication Data

The power of human rights: international norms and domestic change /
edited by Thomas Risse. Stephen C. Ropp, Kathryn Sikkink.
       p.   cm. – (Cambridge studies in international relations: 66)
Includes bibliographical referrences and index.
ISBN 0 521 65093 3 hbk   ISBN 65882 9 pbk
    1. Human rights.   I. Risse-Kappen. Thomas.   II. Ropp, Stephen C.
III. Sikkink, Kathryn, 1955–   . IV. Series.
JC571.H769673   1999   323 – dc21   98-42345   CIP

ISBN 0 521 65093 3 hardback
ISBN 0 521 65882 9 paperback

Contents

Contents

Contributors

David Black   Associate Professor of Political Science,
                     Department of Political Science, Dalhousie
                     University, Halifax, Nova Scotia, Canada
Sieglinde Gränzer   PhD Candidate and Research Associate,
                     Department of Social and Political Sciences,
                     European University Institute, Florence, Italy
Anja Jetschke   PhD Candidate and Research Associate,
                     Department of Social and Political Sciences,
                     European University Institute, Florence, Italy
Thomas Risse   International Relations Chair, Robert Schuman
                     Centre and Department of Social and Political
                     Sciences, European University Institute,
                     Florence, Italy
Stephen C. Ropp   Professor of Political Science, Department of
                     Political Science, University of Wyoming,
                     Laramie, Wyoming, USA
Kathryn Sikkink   Professor of Political Science, Department of
                     Political Science, University of Minnesota,
                     Minneapolis, Minnesota, USA
Hans Peter Schmitz   PhD Candidate and Research Associate,
                     Department of Social and Political Sciences,
                     European University Institute, Florence, Italy
Daniel C. Thomas   Assistant Professor, Department of Political
                     Science, University of Illinois at Chicago,
                     Chicago, Illinois, USA

Preface

This book results from a sustained transatlantic cooperation over more than five years. It all began in 1993 when Thomas Risse and Steve Ropp were both teaching at the University of Wyoming and started developing some common research interests in the area of human rights and democratization. Thomas then left Wyoming and returned to Germany to teach at the University of Konstanz. But he and Steve kept in touch and held a first German–American workshop on international human rights norms and their domestic effects at Laramie, Wyoming, in the spring of 1994. At about the same time, Thomas ran into Kathryn Sikkink at the annual meeting of the American Political Science Association and they started talking about transnational relations, principled issue networks, and the like. At this point, the three of us joined forces, with an extraordinary team of young German scholars gathered together by Thomas at the University of Konstanz: Sieglinde Gränzer, Anja Jetschke, and Hans Peter Schmitz. We held a second workshop on how to study the domestic impact of international norms in the human rights area in June 1995, this time in Germany, at the Catholic Academy of the Diocese of Rottenburg-Stuttgart, in the beautiful town of Weingarten. We then decided to work on an edited volume. Drafts of the chapters were presented at a third workshop in equally beautiful Jackson, Wyoming, in March 1997. We also presented the draft chapters at the 1997 Annual Convention of the International Studies Association in Toronto, Canada. This book is the product of our previous collective work in a variety of areas such as human rights, transnational relations, and domestic regime change in developing nations (cf. Risse-Kappen 1995; Ropp 1992; Sikkink 1993a and b; Keck and Sikkink 1998).

We received a lot of support and helpful suggestions from many people along the way. First, Marty Finnemore read the entire manuscript and provided excellent comments that improved the final product considerably. We also thank an anonymous reviewer from Cambridge University Press for constructive suggestions. Second, we received crucial input from many people at the various workshops and conferences. In particular, we wish to thank Stephanie Anderson, Mike Barnett, Henning Boekle, Tanja Börzel, Lothar Brock, Ann Clark, Andrea Czepek, Francois Debrix, Brigitte Hamm, Wolfgang Heinz, David Holiday, Patrick Ireland, Douglas Johnson, Margaret Keck, Beth Kier, Audie Klotz, Elizabeth Lira, Michael Marks, Rainer Öhlschläger, David Patton, Frank Schimmelfennig, Siegmar Schmidt, Joachim Schmitt, Philippe Schmitter, Thomas Seitz, Michael Shifter, Nina Tannenwald, Ann Towns, Cornelia Ulbert, and many others. John Haslam and Steve Smith agreed to take the book in the Cambridge International Relations series and helped steer it through the production process. Last but not least, special thanks go to Martin Marcussen who did a tremendous job in producing the list of references at the end of the book, and to Jean Field for her splendid copy-editing work.

The empirical findings reported in this book mostly result from extensive (and expensive!) field research over many years. The "German team" (Sieglinde Gränzer, Anja Jetschke, Thomas Risse, Hans Peter Schmitz) received funding from the Deutsche Forschungsgemeinschaft (German Research Association). The "US team" was supported by the McKnight-Land Grant Professorship at the University of Minnesota and the University of Wyoming's International Studies Program. Finally, we are particularly grateful to the Transcoop Program of the German–American Academic Council for co-funding our joint conferences.

We dedicate this book to the many thousands of human rights activists working in and with international organizations, national governments, political parties, foundations, churches, trade unions, and other non-governmental organizations around the globe. This book is ultimately about their work. We show that their efforts and their frustrations have not been futile, but have contributed to substantial improvements in human rights conditions all over the world. This is what the "Power of Human Rights" is all about.

1 The socialization of international human rights norms into domestic practices: introduction

Thomas Risse and Kathryn Sikkink

Fifty years ago, on December 10, 1948, the United Nations General Assembly adopted the Universal Declaration of Human Rights (UDHR). At the time, the delegates clearly noted that the Declaration was not a binding treaty, but rather a statement of principles. Eleanor Roosevelt said that the Declaration "set up a common standard of achievement for all peoples and all nations," and "might well become an international Magna Carta of all mankind" (Humphrey 1984). On the fiftieth anniversary of the Declaration, it seems appropriate to evaluate the impact of these norms, now embodied in diverse international agreements and treaties.[1] Have the principles articulated in the Declaration had any effect at all on the actual behavior of states towards their citizens? What are the conditions under which international human rights norms are internalized in domestic practices? In other words, what accounts for the variation in the degree to which human rights norms are implemented? And what can we learn from this case about why, how, and under what conditions international norms in general influence the actions of states? This book tries to tackle these questions.

Our project relates to broader theoretical debates in the social sciences and law about the influence of ideas and norms on the behav-

We thank the participants of the transatlantic workshops and the 1997 ISA panel for their helpful and insightful comments. We are particularly grateful for critical remarks by Michael Barnett, Sieglinde Gränzer, Anja Jetschke, Audie Klotz, Stephen Ropp, Philippe Schmitter, and Hans Peter Schmitz.
[1] The main general international treaties that embody the rights in the Universal Declaration of Human Rights are the International Covenant on Civil and Political Rights and the International Covenant on Economic, Social, and Cultural Rights. Both entered into force in 1976. There are also specific international treaties elaborating certain rights with the UDHR such as the Convention Against Torture and Other Cruel, Inhuman or Degrading Treatment or Punishment, which entered into force in 1987.

1

ior of individuals and states. Scholars of international relations are increasingly interested in studying norms and ideas, but few have yet demonstrated the actual impact that international norms can have on domestic politics. Using case studies that explore the linkages between international human rights norms and changing human rights practices, we develop and present a theory of the stages and mechanisms through which international norms can lead to changes in behavior. We believe this theory will be useful in understanding the general impact of norms in international politics.

To carry out this evaluation, we chose to look at paired cases of countries with serious human rights situations from each region of the world. In addition to the well-publicized "success stories" of international human rights like Chile, South Africa, the Philippines, Poland, and the former Czechoslovakia, we also examine a series of more obscure and apparently intractable cases of human rights violations in such places as Guatemala, Kenya, Uganda, Morocco, Tunisia, and Indonesia. We reason that these countries with less propitious domestic and international situations would be hard cases for understanding the conditions under which international human rights norms could lead to changing domestic practices. Much of the research on international norms has looked at their international diffusion, or examined their impact in a single country or region. The design of this project allows us to explore the influence that a set of international human rights norms has in a wide variety of states with very different cultures and institutions. By examining the similarities and differences in the impact of human rights norms in these diverse settings, we can see the variation of norm effects across states.

The Universal Declaration of Human Rights contains thirty articles detailing diverse rights from the right to life, to the right to work, and the right to rest and leisure. Because we could not evaluate progress on all these rights, we chose a central core of rights – the right to life (which we define as the right to be free from extrajudicial execution and disappearance) and the freedom from torture and arbitrary arrest and detention.[2] By choosing to focus on these rights we do not suggest that other rights in the Declaration are unimportant. But these basic "rights of the person" have been most accepted as universal rights, and not simply rights associated with a particular political ideology or system.

---

[2] There are two exceptions in this book. Chapter 7 on Eastern Europe concentrates on freedom of expression and freedom to assemble rights, while chapter 3 on South Africa focuses on racial equality.

Also, these basic rights have been widely institutionalized in international treaties that countries around the world have ratified. In this sense, it is around this core of rights that we would most expect human rights norms to have made an impact on human rights practices. If there is no progress here, we would not expect it in other less consensual areas. In addition, due to the work of Amnesty International, various United Nations human rights bodies and missions, and domestic truth commissions, there is now ample data dating back to the mid-1970s on changing levels of human rights practices for these basic rights. These data allow us to be more systematic in our evaluation of the impact of human rights norms.

As we began to complete our research, some of our cases took us by surprise. In late 1998, British officials arrested General Augusto Pinochet, former Chilean dictator, in a response to a request by Spanish judges. They asked that Pinochet be extradited to stand trial for human rights violations during his regime. In Guatemala, where security forces had killed over 100,000 people between 1966 and 1986, by 1997 forensic anthropology teams were exhuming mass graves, and truth commissions were publishing their reports on past human rights violations. In Indonesia in 1998, massive student demonstrations forced Suharto to step down from power, and a National Commission on Human Rights, set up in 1993, has developed a positive, if low-key, track record for documenting some human rights abuses and recommending changes in government policy. Despite the geographic, cultural, and political diversity of the countries represented in our cases, we saw similar patterns and processes in very different settings. On the other hand, in some countries like Tunisia and Kenya, the human rights situation, never as severe as in some of the cases discussed above, worsened or stabilized during the same period. How could we account for these changes, similarities, and differences?

This book serves two purposes, one empirical, the other theoretical. First, we want to understand the conditions under which international human rights regimes and the principles, norms, and rules embedded in them are internalized and implemented domestically and, thus, affect political transformation processes. We propose a five-phase "spiral model" of human rights change which explains the variation in the extent to which states have internalized these norms. We argue that the enduring implementation of human rights norms requires political systems to establish the rule of law. Stable improvements in human rights conditions usually require some measure of political transformation and can be regarded as one aspect of liberalization processes. Enduring human rights changes, therefore, go hand in hand with domestic structural changes.

We engage questions that are of interest both to academics and to activists and policy makers. Activists and policy makers have long debated the efficacy of human rights policies and pressures, but rarely had time for systematic study and analysis. Political scientists and other social scientists are increasingly interested in questions about the diffusion of international norms and principled ideas (see, for example, Finnemore 1996a, b; Finnemore and Sikkink 1998; Jepperson, Wendt, and Katzenstein 1996; Katzenstein 1996b; Klotz 1995; Kowert and Legro 1996). However, this literature is underspecified with regard to the causal mechanisms by which these ideas spread (Yee 1996) and, more important, rarely accounts for the variation in the impact of international norms (Checkel 1998). Such norms and principled ideas "do not float freely" (Risse-Kappen 1994) but affect domestic institutional change in a differential manner. The wide variety of cases examined in this volume is uniquely suited to permit a more in-depth understanding of how international norms interact with very different domestic structures.

International human rights norms provide an excellent opportunity to explore these theoretical issues for a number of reasons. First, because international human rights norms challenge state rule over society and national sovereignty, any impact on domestic change would be counter-intuitive. Second, human rights norms are well institutionalized in international regimes and organizations, and finally, they are contested and compete with other principled ideas.

This book also builds upon our earlier work on the subject. Risse-Kappen's book on transnational relations (Risse-Kappen 1995) argued that the policy impact of transnationally operating non-state actors on state policies varies according to differences in domestic institutional-structures which determine both their access to political systems and their ability to link up with domestic actors. This book goes one step further and explores the conditions under which networks of domestic and transnational actors are able to change these domestic structures themselves. Sikkink and Keck established the importance of "principled-issue" or "transnational advocacy networks" for the diffusion of international norms in the human rights and environmental issue-areas (Sikkink 1993a; Keck and Sikkink 1998). This book further elaborates the conditions under which principled ideas and international norms

4

affect domestic institutional change and presents a causal argument about the effects of transnational advocacy networks in processes of norm diffusion.

In sum, we argue that the diffusion of international norms in the human rights area crucially depends on the establishment and the sustainability of networks among domestic and transnational actors who manage to link up with international regimes, to alert Western public opinion and Western governments. We argue that these advocacy networks serve three purposes, which constitute necessary conditions for sustainable domestic change in the human rights area:

1   They put norm-violating states on the international agenda in terms of moral consciousness-raising. In doing so, they also remind liberal states of their own identity as promoters of human rights.
2   They empower and legitimate the claims of domestic opposition groups against norm-violating governments, and they partially protect the physical integrity of such groups from government repression. Thus, they are crucial in mobilizing *domestic* opposition, social movements, and non-governmental organizations (NGOs) in target countries.
3   They challenge norm-violating governments by creating a transnational structure pressuring such regimes simultaneously "from above" and "from below" (Brysk 1993). The more these pressures can be sustained, the fewer options are available to political rulers to continue repression.

This process by which international norms are internalized and implemented domestically can be understood as a process of *socialization*. We distinguish between three types of causal mechanisms which are necessary for the enduring internalization of norms:

- processes of instrumental adaptation and strategic bargaining;
- processes of moral consciousness-raising, argumentation, dialogue, and persuasion;
- processes of institutionalization and habitualization.

The significance of each process varies with different stages of the socialization process. In general, we argue that instrumental adaptation usually prevails in early stages of norms socialization. Later on, argumentation, persuasion, and dialogue become more significant, while institutionalization and habitualization mark the final steps in the so-

5

cialization processes. We develop a five-phase "spiral model" of norms socialization which specifies the causal mechanisms and the prevailing logic of action in each phase of the process. The model also contains hypotheses about the conditions under which we expect progress toward the implementation of human rights norms. Thus, the "spiral model" accounts for the variation in the domestic effects of international norms.

This chapter presents the research design of the book, in particular the "spiral model." The empirical chapters evaluate the theoretical propositions on the basis of paired comparisons of countries in different regions of the world. We show that the model is generalizable across cases irrespective of cultural, political, or economic differences among countries. These differences matter in terms of timing and duration of socialization processes; but they do not affect the overall validity of our explanatory model. Thus, the empirical chapters examine African (Hans Peter Schmitz on Kenya and Uganda; David Black on South Africa), Arab (Sieglinde Gränzer on Tunisia and Morocco), East European (Daniel Thomas on Poland and the former Czechoslovakia), Latin American (Stephen C. Ropp and Kathryn Sikkink on Chile and Guatemala), and South East Asian cases (Anja Jetschke on Indonesia and the Philippines). Together, these chapters represent a fairly comprehensive overview of the conditions of sustainable change in the human rights area. They allow for comparisons across regions which Stephen C. Ropp and Thomas Risse discuss in the concluding chapter.

Conceptualizing the impact of principled ideas and international norms on identities and interests

This book is part of a growing literature on the impact of ideas and norms in international politics (Adler 1987; Finnemore 1993, 1996a; Goldstein and Keohane 1993b; E. Haas 1990; P. Haas 1992; P. A. Hall 1989; Jacobson 1995; Katzenstein 1996a, b; Klotz 1995; Odell 1982; Sikkink 1991; Yee 1996). This new emphasis has resulted from the empirical failure of approaches emphasizing material structures as the primary determinants of state identities, interests, and preferences. We do not mean to ignore material conditions. Rather, the causal relationship between material and ideational factors is at stake. While materialist theories emphasize economic or military conditions or interests as determining the impact of ideas in international and domestic politics, social constructivists emphasize that ideas and communicative processes define in the first place which material factors are perceived as relevant and how they influence understandings of interests, preferences, and political decisions (Adler 1991, 1997; Checkel 1998; Katzenstein 1996a, b; Kratochwil 1989; Müller 1994; Schaber and Ulbert 1994; Wendt 1992, 1995, forthcoming). In other words, material factors and conditions matter through cognitive and communicative processes, the "battleground of ideas," by which actors try to determine their identities and interests and to develop collective understandings of the situation in which they act and of the moral values and norms guiding their interactions.

We are concerned about the process through which principled ideas ("beliefs about right and wrong held by individuals") become norms ("collective expectations about proper behavior for a given identity," Jepperson, Wendt, and Katzenstein 1996: 54) which in turn influence the behavior and domestic structure of states. While ideas are about cognitive commitments, norms make behavioral claims on individuals (Katzenstein 1996b). To endorse a norm not only expresses a belief, but also creates impetus for behavior consistent with the belief. While ideas are usually individualistic, norms have an explicit intersubjective quality because they are *collective* expectations. The very idea of "proper" behavior presupposes a community able to pass judgments on appropriateness.

At the same time, the state is not a black box, but is composed of different institutions and individuals. Once ideas have become norms, we still need to understand how those norms in turn influence individual behavior of state actors:

- How and why does a member of the military who has ordered extrajudicial executions in the past decide to stop ordering executions?
- Do human rights abuses end because perpetrators are persuaded they are wrong?
- Do they end because leaders care about their international image and want other countries to think well of them? Or can we explain this behavior with more instrumental factors?
- Do perpetrators come to believe that they will be held accountable, and so they change behavior to avoid punishment?
- Do countries want to renew international military and economic aid that has been cut?

It is often not possible to do the precise research to answer these questions completely, but in this book we work to document the change (or lack thereof) in human rights practices, and then we trace the process of domestic and international normative, political, and institutional developments to try to explain the changes we observe. We also consider alternative explanations for human rights behavior to see which explanation fits the patterns we observe in each country.

In the cases studied, we find many examples of some human rights changes occurring apparently because leaders of countries care about what leaders of other countries think of them. Norms have a different quality from other rules or maxims. James Fearon argues that while rules take the form "Do X to get Y," norms take a different form: "Good people do X." Thus people sometimes follow norms because they want others to think well of them, and because they want to think well of themselves (Fearon 1997). People's ability to think well of themselves is influenced by norms held by a relevant community of actors. Scholars in international law have long recognized this intersubjective nature of norms by referring to international law as relevant within a community of "civilized nations." Today the idea of "civilized" nations has gone out of fashion, but international law and international organizations are still the primary vehicles for stating community norms and for collective legitimation. Some legal scholars now discuss a community of "liberal states" seen as a sphere of peace, democracy, and human rights, and distinguish between relations among liberal states, and those between liberal and nonliberal states (Franck 1990; Slaughter 1995). Human rights norms have a special status because they both prescribe rules for appropriate behavior, and help define identities of liberal states. Human rights norms have constitutive effects because good human rights performance is one crucial signal to others to identify a member of the community of liberal states (on definitions of norms and their constitutive effects see Finnemore and Sikkink 1998; Jepperson, Wendt, and Katzenstein 1996; Katzenstein 1996a, b; Kowert and Legro 1996; Thomson 1993).

Our approach to the constitutive and behavioral effects of principled ideas and norms draws on social constructivism (for applications to international relations see Katzenstein 1996a; Kratochwil 1989; Wendt 1992, forthcoming). Actors' interests and preferences are not given outside social interaction or deduced from structural constraints in the international or domestic environment. Social constructivism does not take the interests of actors for granted, but problematizes and relates them to the identities of actors. What I want depends to a large degree on who I am. Identities then define the range of interests of actors considered as both possible and appropriate. Identities also provide a measure of inclusion and exclusion by defining a social "we" and delineating the boundaries against the "others." Norms become relevant and causally consequential during the process by which actors define and refine their collective identities and interests.

In our case, human rights norms help define a category of states – "liberal democratic states." Many (but certainly not all) of the interests these states have are quite different from those of the "others" – the authoritarian or "norm-violating" states. In some cases, these liberal "clubs" are quite specific; in the case of the European Union, for example, the formal and informal rules and norms specify that only democratic states with good human rights records can join the club. In the Inter-American system, such norms are just now emerging. The Organization of American States (OAS)'s Managua Declaration of 1993, for example, is very explicit about this process of stating norms that contribute to identity formation of member states. In it the OAS members declare "the need to consolidate, as part of the cultural identity of each nation in the Hemisphere, democratic structures and systems which encourage freedom and social justice, safeguard human rights, and favor progress" (Vaky and Muñoz, 1993).

But emphasizing the contribution of international norms to identity formation is not to suggest a "fair-weather" model of norm-induced domestic change whereby power, political struggles, and instrumental interests of actors are somehow absent from the story. We do not argue in terms of simple dichotomies such as "power versus norms" or "norms versus interests." Instead, we are interested in the interaction among these various factors. For example, we explore the "power of principles," that is, the use of principled ideas and international norms in domestic struggles among political actors. To the extent that human rights norms have become consensual, they can be used instrumentally in such power struggles. In the case of South Africa, the "power of principles" resulted in a sanctions regime which had powerful effects on the availability of material resources to the South African government (see chapter 3; Klotz 1995).[3]

Moreover, we also do not suggest that the causal arrows always point in one direction, as in "norms lead to a change in interests." There are

[3] Audie Klotz refers to "normative power" in this context.

9

ample examples in this book where national governments changed their human rights practices only to gain access to the material benefits of foreign aid or to be able to stay in power in the face of strong domestic opposition. In fact, the process of human rights change almost always begins with some instrumentally or strategically motivated adaptation by national governments to growing domestic and transnational pressures. But we also argue that this is rarely the end of the story. Even instrumental adoption of human rights norms, if it leads to domestic structural change such as redemocratization, sets into motion a process of identity transformation, so that norms initially adopted for instrumental reasons, are later maintained for reasons of belief and identity. While the old leadership is not persuaded, the new leadership has internalized human rights norms and shows a desire to take its place in a community of human rights abiding states. The Philippine president, Ferdinand Marcos, for example, adopted some human rights norms for instrumental reasons, but once democratization occurred and Corazon Aquino took office, the very identity of the Philippine state changed.

A similar process might explain the Reagan administration's pro-democracy policy. When the principled position in favor of democracy was first adopted by the Reagan administration, most interpreted it as a vehicle for an aggressive foreign policy against leftist regimes, such as the USSR, Nicaragua, and Cuba. (This would be consistent with the instrumental use of a principled idea.) But because democracy as a principled idea had achieved consensus among political elites and the general public in the United States, the Reagan administration found itself obliged to a minimal consistency in its foreign policy, and thus eventually actively encouraged democracy in authoritarian regimes which the Republicans viewed as loyal allies, such as Chile and Uruguay.

In the end, the precise direction of the causal arrows – whether norms lead to a change in (collective) identities which in turn leads to a change in (instrumental) interests or whether interests lead to a change in norms which in turn lead to a change in identities – has to be determined through careful empirical process-tracing. This book does not have a preconceived notion of the way in which the causal mechanisms work in general. But we do suggest that instrumental and material interests, processes of norm-guided identity formation, as well as argumentation, persuasion, and dialogue, on the one hand, and strategic bargaining, on the other, differ in significance during the various stages of norms socialization.

A theoretical framework of norms socialization processes

The process by which principled ideas held by individuals become norms in the sense of collective understandings about appropriate behavior which then lead to changes in identities, interests, and behavior is conceptualized in this book as a process of *socialization* (Finnemore 1993; Ikenberry and Kupchan 1990; Müller 1993; Schimmelfennig 1994). Socialization can be defined as the "induction of new members ... into the ways of behavior that are preferred in a society" (Barnes, Carter, and Skidmore 1980: 35). What is crucial to this definition is that socialization presupposes a society. Internationally, it makes sense only within the bounds of an international system defined as a society of states (Bull 1977). Contrary to some conceptions of international society, however, this definition suggests that international society is a smaller group than the total number of states in the international system, and that socialization to international norms is the crucial process through which a state becomes a member of the international society. The goal of socialization is for actors to internalize norms, so that external pressure is no longer needed to ensure compliance. The classic social science literature on socialization recognized that much socialization occurs among peer groups and social groups. "Political socialization produces a political self ... It is political socialization which molds and shapes the citizen's relation to the political community" (Dawson and Prewitt 1969). Because a state's political identity emerges not in isolation but in relation to and in interaction with other groups of states and international non-state actors, the concept of socialization may be useful in understanding how the international society transmits norms to its members.

We distinguish in this book three types of socialization processes which are necessary for enduring change in the human rights area:

1   processes of adaptation and strategic bargaining;
2   processes of moral consciousness-raising, "shaming," argumentation, dialogue, and persuasion;
3   processes of institutionalization and habitualization.

These processes constitute ideal types which differ according to their underlying logic or mode of social action and interaction. In reality, these processes usually take place simultaneously. Our task in this book

11

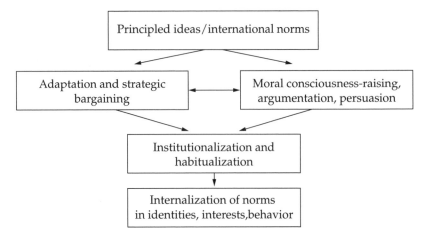

Figure 1.1   The process of norms socialization

is to identify which mode of interaction dominates in which phase of the socialization process. We suggest a rough order, which is depicted in figure 1.1.

The first type of socialization process concerns the *instrumental adaptation* to pressures – both domestic and international. Governments accused of violating human rights norms frequently adjust to pressures by making some tactical concessions. They might release political prisoners or sign some international agreements, for example, in order to regain foreign aid, to overcome international sanctions, or to strengthen their rule *vis-à-vis* domestic opposition. They might also engage in bargaining processes with the international community and/ or the domestic opposition. They might even start "talking the talk" of human rights in international fora such as the United Nations (UN) Human Rights Commission. Such activities are essentially compatible with rational choice arguments about human beings as expected utility-maximizers. Actors – norm-violating governments in this case – pursue exogenously defined and primarily instrumental or material interests and change their behavior in order to reach their goals. They adjust their behavior to the international human rights discourse without necessarily believing in the validity of the norms. We argue in this book that instrumental adaptation to growing international and domestic pressures is a typical reaction of norm-violating governments in early stages of the socialization process.

The second type of socialization process which we investigate in this book, concerns *argumentative discourses* in the Habermasian sense (Habermas 1981, 1992, 1995b; for applications to international relations see Müller 1994; Prittwitz 1996; Risse 1997). While adaptation refers to an instrumental adjustment to international norms irrespective of discursive practices, socialization through moral discourse emphasizes processes of communication, argumentation, and persuasion. Actors accept the validity and significance of norms in their discursive practices. The notion of "moral discourse" needs to be strictly distinguished from daily communicative practices. We can differentiate between two ideal types of communicative behavior: the first focuses on the exchange of information through verbal utterances. In these instances, speakers know what they want and how they see the situation in which they act and communicate this to others. Information exchanges through communicative behavior can well be incorporated in rational choice models (see, for example, Morrow 1994; Schneider 1994). This is not what we have in mind.

The other type of communicative behavior which we identify with the notion of "discourse" in this volume, challenges the validity claims entailed in these "informations." At a most basic level, actors might try to clarify whether they understood correctly the information submitted. Do we understand you correctly that you accept the validity of international human rights norms, but claim that the alleged violations did not occur? More significant are discourses arguing over whether the situation is defined correctly. You claim that these actions are part of a fight against terrorism, but we think that they constitute human rights violations. What are they an instance of? In this case, actors might actually agree on the moral validity of the norm, but disagree whether certain behavior is covered by it.

Finally, there are moral discourses which challenge the validity claims of the norm itself. You argue that human rights are universal, but we think that our culture and way of life are alien to these individualistic norms. We argue in this book that such discourses challenging validity claims inherent in definitions of the situation as well as in principled beliefs and norms are all-pervasive in the human rights area and need to be analyzed in order to explain socialization processes leading to sustainable domestic change. Moral discourses in particular not only challenge and seek justifications of norms, they also entail identity-related arguments. What I find morally appropriate depends to some degree on who I am and how I see myself. As argued above, for

13

example, human rights define a certain category of states and, thus, relate to collective identities. The logic of discursive behavior and of processes of argumentation and persuasion rather than instrumental bargaining and the exchange of fixed interests prevails when actors develop collective understandings that form part of their identities and lead them to determine their interests. Those principled beliefs carry the day when they persuade actors in potentially winning coalitions to interpret their material and political interests and preferences in light of the idea and to accept its social obligations as appropriate. Coalitions are formed not just through the convergence of pre-existing actors' interests, but also through argumentative consensus. People become convinced and persuaded to change their instrumental interests, or to see their interests in new ways, following the principled ideas.

This is not to argue that moral discourses and discursive practices in general resemble "ideal speech" situations in the Habermasian sense, where power and hierarchies are absent and nothing but the better argument counts. In real-life situations, relationships of power and interest-based arguments are rarely completely out of the picture. Nor do communicative processes always involve the exchange of logical arguments. Actors rely on a variety of techniques to persuade, including appeals to emotion, evoking symbols, as well as the use and extension of logical arguments. Although some authors privilege the role of logic in the extension of norms (Crawford 1993), psychological research suggests that both emotion and cognition operate synergistically to produce and change attitudes (Eagly and Chaiken 1993). In the area of human rights, persuasion and socialization often involve processes such as shaming and denunciations, not aimed at producing changing minds with logic, but on changing minds by isolating or embarassing the target. Persuasion is also not devoid of conflict. It often involves not just reasoning with opponents, but also pressures, arm-twisting, and sanctions. For example, Audie Klotz's work on norms and apartheid discusses coercion, incentive, and legitimation effects that are often part of a socialization process (Klotz 1995; see also chapter 3 in this book).

Nevertheless, we claim that the logic of persuasion and of discourse is conceptually different from a logic of information exchange based on fixed preferences, definitions of the situations, and collective identities. Discursive processes are precisely the types of human interaction in which at least one of these properties of actors is being challenged.

We expect to find a mix of instrumental and argumentative rationalities governing the process by which domestic and transnational actors,

14

states, and international institutions impact upon the human rights performance of particular regimes. We are particularly interested in investigating the characteristic patterns in the mix of the instrumental and the communicative, and the conditions under which actors change from one mode of action to the other. Here are a few examples taken from the human rights area of how argumentative rationality and policy deliberation, on the one hand, and instrumental adaptation, on the other, might relate to each other:

1. Repressive governments often adapt to normative pressures for purely instrumental reasons. When the pressure decreases, they return to repression, as was the case in Kenya in the early 1990s (see chapter 2). Sometimes, however, they start institutionalizing human rights norms into domestic law and change their discursive practices. This in turn opens space for the domestic opposition to catch the government in its own rhetoric. At this point, instrumental and communicative rationality intertwine. It becomes very hard for the government to deny the validity of human rights norms. Political psychology talks about "self-persuasion" in this context. Over time people come to believe what they say, particularly if they say it publicly (Chaiken, Wood, and Eagly 1996: 703–705).

2. Moral consciousness-raising by the international human rights community often involves a process of "shaming." Norm-violating states are denounced as pariah states which do not belong to the community of civilized nations, as was the case with South Africa (chapter 3). Shaming then constructs categories of "us" and "them', that is, in-groups and out-groups, thus re-affirming particular state identities. Some repressive governments might not care. Others, however, feel deeply offended, because they want to belong to the "civilized community" of states. In other words, shaming then implies a process of persuasion, since it convinces leaders that their behavior is inconsistent with an identity to which they aspire. This was the case with the Moroccan king, as Sieglinde Gränzer shows in chapter 4.

3. Domestic opposition groups might rally around human rights issues for purely instrumental reasons at first, for example, to be able to communicate and to link up with international and transnational networks or to broaden the basis of

domestic opposition by bringing in ideologically diverse groups. If they succeed in overthrowing the oppressive regime, however, there is less instrumental need to act upon their opposition rhetoric and to implement the human rights norms. It is, therefore, noteworthy that, in all cases of successful human rights change documented in this book, the new regimes matched their opposition words with deeds, although the fit was often less than perfect. This suggests a communicative process of identity change which leads actors to behave in ways consistent with their identity when they acquire the means to do so.

The three examples suggest that socialization processes start when actors adapt their behavior in accordance with the norm for initially instrumental reasons. Governments want to remain in power, while domestic NGOs seek the most effective means to rally the opposition. The more they "talk the talk," however, the more they entangle themselves in a moral discourse which they cannot escape in the long run. In the beginning, they might use arguments in order to further their instrumentally defined interests, that is, they engage in rhetoric (on rhetorical action see Schimmelfennig 1995, 1997). The more they justify their interests, however, the more others will start challenging their arguments and the validity claims inherent in them. At this point, governments need to respond by providing further arguments. They become entangled in arguments and the logic of argumentative rationality slowly but surely takes over. It follows that we expect argumentative rationality, dialogue, and processes of persuasion to prevail in later stages of the socialization process.

But argumentative processes are still not sufficient in order to socialize states into norm-abiding practices. Human rights norms can only be regarded as internalized in domestic practices, when actors comply with them *irrespective* of individual beliefs about their validity. In the case of Uganda (see chapter 2), for example, national leader Yoweri Museveni can probably be regarded as a "true believer" in human rights. But it is less clear whether the drastic improvement in human rights conditions will survive his presidency. This points to a final type of socialization process emphasizing the gradual institutionalization of norms as theorized by sociological and historical institutionalism (P. A. Hall and Taylor 1996; Jepperson 1991; March and Olsen 1989; Powell and DiMaggio 1991; Steinmo, Thelen, and Longstreth 1992). Actors incrementally adapt to norms in response to external pressures, initially for purely instrumental reasons. National governments might then change their rhetoric, gradually accept the validity of international human rights norms, and start engaging in an argumentative process with their opponents, both domestically and abroad. The more they accept the validity of the norms and the more they engage in a dialogue about norm implementation, the more they are likely to institutionalize human rights in domestic practices. Human rights norms are then incorporated in the "standard operating procedures" of domestic institutions. This type of internalization process can be conceptualized as independent from changes in individual belief systems. Actors follow the norm, because "it is the normal thing to do." Whether they are convinced of its moral validity and appropriateness or not is largely irrelevant for habitualization processes. When we stop at a red traffic light, we usually do not question the normative implications of the rule we are just following. Once human rights norms are institutionalized in this sense, changes in government and in individual leaders matter less and less. Norms are implemented independently from the moral consciousness of actors. They are simply "taken for granted" which marks the final stage in a socialization process (see Finnemore and Sikkink 1998). Institutionalization and habitualization are necessary to "depersonalize" norm compliance and to insure their implementation irrespective of individual beliefs.

Transnational advocacy networks and human rights socialization: the "spiral model"

So far, we have developed a theoretical argument about socialization processes by identifying three ideal types of social action: instrumental adaptation, argumentative discourse, and institutionalization. To guide our empirical analysis, however, this conceptual framework needs to be operationalized and applied to the human rights area more specifically. In the following, we develop a five-phase "spiral model" of human rights change which incorporates simultaneous activities at four levels into one framework:

- the international–transnational interactions among transnationally operating international non-governmental organizations (INGOs), international human rights regimes and organizations, and Western states;

17

- the *domestic society* in the norm-violating state;
- the links between the societal opposition and the transnational networks;
- the *national government* of the norm-violating state.

The "spiral model" builds upon previous work on "principled issue or transnational advocacy networks" in the human rights area. A transnational advocacy network includes those relevant actors working internationally on an issue, who are bound together by shared values, a common discourse, and dense exchanges of information and services (Keck and Sikkink 1998; see also Risse-Kappen 1995). We follow various studies on the impact of human rights norms in Latin America emphasizing how domestic and transnational social movements and networks have united to bring pressure "from above" and "from below" to accomplish human rights change (Brysk 1993; Osiel 1986; Sikkink 1993a). Keck and Sikkink have referred to this process as the "boomerang effect" (Keck and Sikkink 1998).

A "boomerang" pattern of influence exists when domestic groups in a repressive state bypass their state and directly search out international allies to try to bring pressure on their states from outside. National opposition groups, NGOs, and social movements link up with transnational networks and INGOs who then convince international human rights organizations, donor institutions, and/or great powers to pressure norm-violating states. Networks provide access, leverage, and information (and often money) to struggling domestic groups. International contacts can "amplify" the demands of domestic groups, prise open space for new issues, and then echo these demands back into the domestic arena (see figure 1.2).

The "boomerang model" can be integrated in a more dynamic conceptualization of the effects which these domestic-transnational-international linkages have on domestic political change. The "spiral model" which will be explored in the empirical chapters consists of several "boomerang throws" with diverging effects on the human rights situation in the target country (see figure 1.3). It is a causal model which attempts to explain the variation in the extent to which national governments move along the path toward improvement of human rights conditions. We do not assume evolutionary progress. Rather, below we identify those stages in the model where governments might return to repressive practices. We develop hypotheses about the conditions under which we expect movement from one phase of the "spiral

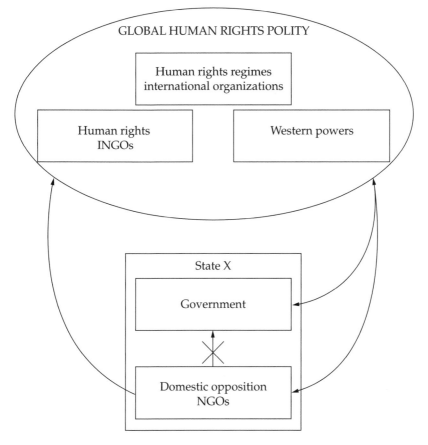

Figure 1.2   The "boomerang effect"

model" to the next. These phases are distinguished by the dominant response from the norm-violating state to the societal and transnational activities. Thus, the "spiral model" serves to operationalize the theoretical framework of norm socialization developed above, to identify the dominant mode of social interaction in each phase (adaptation, arguing, institutionalization), and, ultimately, to specify the causal mechanisms by which international norms affect domestic structural change.

"World time"

Our dynamic model is based on the prior existence of international institutions which regulate human rights norms (a social structure) and

19

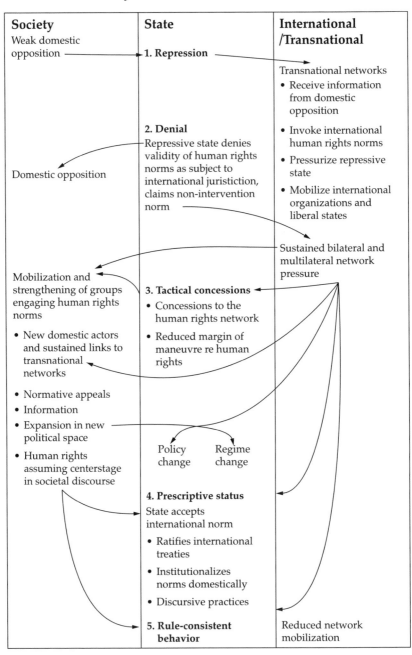

Society	State	International /Transnational
Weak domestic opposition ———	1. Repression ———	
		Transnational networks • Receive information from domestic opposition
Domestic opposition	2. Denial Repressive state denies validity of human rights norms as subject to international juristiction, claims non-intervention norm	• Invoke international human rights norms • Pressurize repressive state • Mobilize international organizations and liberal states
		Sustained bilateral and multilateral network pressure
Mobilization and strengthening of groups engaging human rights norms • New domestic actors and sustained links to transnational networks • Normative appeals • Information • Expansion in new political space • Human rights assuming centerstage in societal discourse	3. Tactical concessions • Concessions to the human rights network • Reduced margin of maneuvre re human rights Policy change Regime change	
	4. Prescriptive status State accepts international norm • Ratifies international treaties • Institutionalizes norms domestically • Discursive practices	
	5. Rule-consistent behavior	Reduced network mobilization

Figure 1.3   The "spiral model" of human rights change

of transnational advocacy networks composed of INGOs and foundations which are loosely connected to officials working for human rights IOs as well as for national governments (the norm-promoting agents). The international institutions are primarily the human rights bodies of the United Nations, and the various human rights treaties that have been drafted and ratified under UN auspices, but also include some regional institutions, such as the Inter-American Commission and Court of Human Rights. The human rights networks include international and domestic NGOs, foundations, and some governmental and inter-governmental officials who share collective understandings and a collective identity with regard to human rights norms. Other authors have described and explained the origins and growth of these institutions and networks (Donnelly 1991; Forsythe 1991); we explore what role they play in our case studies.

The existence and strength of human rights institutions, norms, and networks, however, increased signficantly over time, and thus the cases take place at different moments in "world time." Prior to 1973, international human rights treaties had not yet entered into force and the strength of international human rights norms and institutions was much weaker. No country had yet adopted an explicit bilateral human rights policy, and fewer human rights NGOs existed. The cases of Chile and South Africa are important in this period since both cases begin prior to the existence of strong international networks and institutions, and these cases actually contribute to the growth of the network, to the emergence of human rights foreign policies, and to more activist orientations by international organizations, as Ropp and Sikkink discuss in chapter 6.

Between 1973 and 1985, transnational human rights NGOs and advocacy networks expanded and states and networks built the international social structure of human rights norms and institutions. In 1976, the international human rights covenants came into effect, and new institutions, such as the United Nations Human Rights Committee, emerge. Between 1973 and 1990, most Western countries developed some form of explicit bilateral and multilateral human rights policies. After 1985, we can say that the world began a process of a genuine international "norms cascade," as the influence of international human rights norms spread rapidly (on norms cascades, see Sunstein 1997). Country cases that begin before the norms cascade will take longer to move through the phases than cases of repression that begin after the norms cascade has taken place. A completed norms cascade leads to a point where norms are internalized and gain a "taken for granted quality" (Finnemore and Sikkink 1998; see also concluding chapter). If the international human rights norms cascade is sustained, states are less likely to engage in a lengthy "denial" stage, since human rights norms become increasingly accepted.

Phase 1: repression and activation of network

The starting point for our research is a repressive situation in the state under investigation – the "target" – where domestic societal opposition is too weak and/or too oppressed to present a significant challenge to the government. The levels of repression vary greatly among the countries in the volume, from extreme repression bordering on genocide (as in the case of Guatemala) to much lower levels of repression as in the case of Tunisia.

This phase of repression might last for a long time, since many oppressive states never make it on to the agenda of the transnational advocacy network. Moreover, the degree of repression unfortunately determines to some degree whether transnational networks can even acquire information about human rights conditions in the country. Very oppressive governments sometimes do not become the subject of international campaigns by the advocacy networks, because information gathering requires at least some minimal links between the domestic opposition and the transnational networks if the latter is to gain access to the norm-violating state. Only if and when the transnational advocacy network succeeds in gathering sufficient information on the repression in the "target state," can it put the norm-violating state on the international agenda moving the situation to phase 2 (hypothesis 1).

Phase 2: denial

This phase of the "spiral model" puts the norm-violating state on the international agenda of the human rights network and serves to raise the level of international public attention toward the "target state." The initial activation of the transnational network often results from a particularly awesome violation of human rights such as a massacre and leads to the mobilization of the international human rights community. This stage is characterized first by the production and dissemination of information about human rights practices in the target state. Such information is often compiled with the cooperation of human rights organizations in the target state. The transnational network then starts lobbying international human rights organizations as well as Western states – from public opinion to policy makers and national governments. This "lobbying" usually involves some discursive activities in terms of moral persuasion. Western governments and publics, for example, are reminded of their own identity as promoters of human rights. Human rights organizations frequently remind Western states of their own standards in this area and demand that they live up to them. Network activists often point to inconsistencies in Western state behavior, stressing that they had condemned human rights violations in one state, but not another, where violations are just as egregious. This also typically involves some "shaming." So moral persuasion takes place during the first phase, but it involves networks persuading Western states to join network attempts to change human rights practices in target states. These lobbying activities might lead to some initial pressure on the target state to improve its human rights conditions.

The initial reaction of the norm-violating state in the cases considered here is almost always one of denial. "Denial" means that the norm-violating government refuses to accept the validity of international human rights norms themselves and that it opposes the suggestion that its national practices in this area are subject to international jurisdiction. Thus, denial goes further than simply objecting to particular accusations. The norm-violating government charges that the criticism constitutes an illegitimate intervention in the internal affairs of the country. The government may even succeed in mobilizing some nationalist sentiment against foreign intervention and criticism. Thus the initial "boomerang throw" often appears to be counterproductive because it allows the state to solidify domestic support. The presence of a significant armed insurgent movement in the target country can dramatically extend this stage, by heightening domestic perceptions of threat and fear. Any insurgent movement success appears to validate the government's claim that the order or the very integrity of the nation is at stake, and thus isolates domestic human rights organization and international pressures by identifying these groups as conscious or unconscious accomplices of terrorism.

We count the denial stage as part of the socialization process because the fact that the state feels compelled to deny charges demonstrates that a process of international socialization is already under way. If socialization were not yet under way, the state would feel no need to deny the accusations that are made. Governments which publicly deny the validity of international human rights norms as interference in internal affairs, are at least implicitly aware that they face a problem in terms of their international reputation. It is interesting to note in this context that denial of the norm almost never takes the form of open rejection of human rights, but is mostly expressed in terms of reference to an allegedly more valid international norm, in this case national sovereignty. Nevertheless, the denial stage can also last for quite a long time. Some repressive governments care little about international pressures. Moreover, they might kill off or buy off the domestic opposition.

Because of changes in "world time" it is possible that denial and backlash is a normative phase particular to a period in which new international norms have emerged, but when they are still strongly contested internationally. Governments, through their denial, engage in this contestation. If this is the case, we would expect the denial stage to disappear in cases of more fully institutionalized norms. The timing of the disappearance of the denial phase may differ from one region to another. For example, no state in Western Europe has denied the prescriptive status of human rights norms since the military junta in Greece in the late 1960s. In Latin America, it is possible that the historical limits to the denial phase are being reached in the mid-1990s, but we would expect this contestation to continue much longer in Asia and Africa.

In sum, however, norm-violating governments still have many strategies at their disposal to fight off international and transnational pressure. The domestic opposition is still too weak to be able to mount a major challenge to the regime. Therefore, the transition to the *third phase* constitutes the biggest challenge for the transnational human rights network. This transition primarily depends on the strength and mobilization of the *transnational* network in conjunction with the vulnerability of the norm-violating government to international pressures (hypothesis 2; see Keck and Sikkink 1998; Klotz 1995; Sikkink 1993a, b).

Almost all human rights campaigns involve particular kinds of material pressures, for example, when aid becomes conditional on human rights performance, and these pressures are indisputably important for understanding the early stages of influence. But target vulnerability may also come from prior normative commitments. Vulnerability may simply represent a desire to maintain good standing in valued international groupings (Klotz 1995). To the degree that a nation values its membership in an emerging community of liberal states, it will be more vulnerable to pressures than a state that does not value such membership. We would expect that countries receiving large military and economic aid flows will be more vulnerable to human rights pressures than those not receiving such flows.

24

Phase 3: tactical concessions

If international pressures continue and escalate, the norm-violating state seeks cosmetic changes to pacify international criticism. Although the norm-violating government might then temporarily improve the situation – for example, by releasing prisoners – we do not expect a stable amelioration of human rights conditions. This more sustained period of international concern, however, may allow the initial "rally around the flag" effect of phase 2 to wear off. The minor cosmetic changes, such as the release of prisoners, or greater permissiveness about domestic protest activities, may allow the repressed domestic opposition to gain courage and space to mount its own campaign of criticism against the government. At this point the repressive government is usually acting almost solely from an instrumental or strategic position, trying to use concessions to regain military or economic assistance, or to lessen international isolation.

The most important effect of this second phase of transnational mobilization is, therefore, not so much to change the behavior of the government as to faciliate social mobilization in the target country. In other words, if the transnational network succeeds in forcing the norm-violating state to make tactical concessions, the focus of activities is likely to shift from the transnational to the domestic level. The increased international attention serves to create and/or strengthen local networks of human rights activists whose demands are empowered and legitimated by the transnational/international network, and whose physical integrity may be protected by international linkages and attention. In this sense the transnational network serves to help creating space for the domestic groups and to amplify their demands in the international arena.

This is the most precarious phase of the spiral model, since it might move the process forward toward enduring change in human rights conditions, but can also result in a backlash (see chapter 4 on Tunisia). If a government responds with unrelenting repression of activists, it can temporarily break the upward spiral process. At the beginning of phase 3, the domestic human rights movement is often relatively small and dependent on a handful of key leaders. Arresting or killing these leaders decapitates the movement and the resulting fear paralyzes it. This, for example, is what happened in the case of the repression of the demonstrations in Tiananmen Square in China, and the initial response of the Guatemalan government to human rights pressures in the late

1970s (see chapter 6). While such actions can temporarily nip an incipient domestic opposition in the bud, this rarely suspends the spiral indefinitely, but mostly delays it. The additional repression is costly to the government in terms of its domestic legitimacy, and may validate international criticism by revealing more clearly the coercive power of the state.

If the cycle is not delayed, the domestic opposition is likely to gain strength. The fully mobilized domestic NGO networks linked to the global human rights polity can then be activated at any time. Toward the end of the tactical concession phase, norm-violating governments are no longer in control of the domestic situation. Whenever they commit another serious violation of human rights, the domestic-transnational network is activated and now pressures the government "from above" and "from below" (Brysk 1993). "From above," donor countries are now likely to coordinate foreign aid, making it contingent on human rights improvements. "From below," repression gradually ceases to serve its purpose of suppressing opposition. People start losing their fears.

In this phase of the socialization process, we expect the two ideal types of instrumental and of argumentative rationality to matter, with the latter gaining in significance. First, on the level of domestic society, human rights claims are likely to serve as the main principled idea around which an opposition coalition can be formed (see chapter 5 on the Philippines, and chapter 2 on Uganda). We expect argumentation and deliberation to become important in the coalition-building processes of the domestic opposition. Some domestic groups, however, recognizing that human rights claims have more international support and legitimacy, may take up the human rights banner because it is an easier way to criticize the government rather than because they profoundly believe in human rights principles. Thus, we assume a mix of instrumental and argumentative rationality in this crucial phase of domestic network formation.

Second and equally important, norm-violating governments no longer deny the validity of the international human rights norms when they start making tactical concessions. In the beginning, these concessions can mostly be explained on the grounds of instrumental interests. At this stage of the process, "shaming" of norm-violating governments becomes a particularly effective communicative tool of the transnational advocacy network. As argued above, human rights "persuasion" creates ingroups and outgroups (human rights norm supporters, or

26

liberal democratic states versus human rights norm violators). States are subject to a normative process of shaming, and relegation to an outgroup, which they often resent, and sometimes feel is sufficiently disturbing for either their international image or their domestic legitimacy that they are willing to make human rights concessions (see chapter 4 on Morocco). That shaming is usually reinforced by material sanctions of some sort strengthens the move to make minor changes.

When they make these minor concessions, states almost uniformly underestimate the impact of these changes, and overestimate their own support among their population. They think the changes are less costly than they are, and they anticipate that they have greater control over international and domestic processes. Leaders of authoritarian states (like many political scientists) tend to believe that "talk is cheap" and do not understand the degree to which they can become "entrapped" in their own rhetoric. As a result, states are often taken by surprise by the impact their initial changes create – in terms of both international processes and domestic mobilization. By the time they realize their mistakes, they have already unleashed forces of opposition beyond the expectations of the regime, and the situation is often out of their control.

"World time" may provide part of the explanation for this entrapment. Since human rights networks and policies were growing and changing rapidly at the time when many governments entered the tactical concessions phase, they can not be expected to know the extent of pressures and policies they would face. Governments reasoning from the past (when human rights regimes and networks were relatively weak) would understandably underestimate the impact of tactical changes in a new world context.

A similar process is likely to happen on the level of rhetoric and communicative action. Governments no longer deny the validity of the norm and start "talking the human rights talk." Initially, they usually reject any concrete allegations of violations and denounce their critics as "foreign agents" or simply as ignorant. By doing so, they nevertheless start engaging in a public controversy with their critics who usually respond by justifying their accusations. This process of arguing over human rights violations takes place both in public and in international organizations such as the UN Human Rights Commission (for evidence see chapter 2 on Kenya and Uganda, chapter 5 on Indonesia and the Philippines, and chapter 6 on Chile and Guatemala). In the beginning of such a process, the arguments on both sides resemble the logic of rhetorical action (Schimmelfennig 1995, 1997) whereby justifications are used to further one's interests without being prepared to really challenge the validity claims inherent in these interests. Slowly but surely, governments become entrapped in their own rhetoric and the logic of arguing takes over. The more norm-violating governments argue with their critics, the more likely they are to make argumentative concessions and to specify their justifications and the less likely they are to leave the arguing mode by openly denouncing their critics. At this stage then, reputational concerns keep governments in a dialogical mode of arguing. Instrumental reasons and argumentative rationality reinforce each other. At the same time, critics of human rights violations such as INGOs increasingly take the justifications of governments for their behavior more seriously and start engaging in a true dialogue with them concerning how to improve the human rights situation. In other words, a process which began for instrumental reasons, with arguments being used merely rhetorically, increasingly becomes a true dialogue over specific human rights allegations in the "target state." We expect this to be increasingly the case in the later stages of the "tactical concessions" phase.

This process of "self-entrapment" into argumentative behavior also implies that norm-violating governments take the transnational advocacy networks and the domestic opposition more seriously and start treating them as valid interlocutors which in turn only serves to further strengthen and empower them. Faced with a fully mobilized domestic opposition linked up with transnational networks for whom human rights have achieved consensual status, norm-violating governments no longer have many choices. Some rulers start a process of "controlled liberalization" (O'Donnell and Schmitter 1986: 7ff; Przeworski 1986; Wurfel 1990; see chapter 4 on Morocco) and begin implementing human rights norms domestically. Other leaders seriously miscalculate the situation, increase the level of repression which – at this stage – only serves to strengthen the domestic opposition and to annoy their last remaining international supporters (see chapters 2 and 5 on Uganda and the Philippines). As a consequence, they are likely to be thrown out of power (see also chapter 7 on Poland and the former Czechoslovakia and chapter 3 on South Africa). Resulting either from a regime change or from "controlled liberalization," this stage in the socialization process marks the transition to "prescriptive status" (hypothesis 3).

Phase 4: "prescriptive status"

"Prescriptive status" means that the actors involved regularly refer to the human rights norm to describe and comment on their own behavior and that of others (Rittberger 1993: 10–11); the validity claims of the norm are no longer controversial, even if the actual behavior continues violating the rules. We argue that the process by which principled ideas gain "prescriptive status" should be decisive for their sustained impact on political and social change. In this stage of the process, argumentative behavior matters most. But how can we differentiate between prescriptive status achieved through discursive processes of argumentation and persuasion, on the one hand, and purely instrumental or rhetorical support for a principled idea, on the other? National governments may, for example, refer to human rights norms instrumentally when dealing with the UN Human Rights Commission in order to achieve Western goodwill or economic benefits. It is ultimately impossible, of course, to establish without doubt that actors believe in what they say. We are not that interested in the "true beliefs" of actors, as long as they are consistent in their verbal utterances and their words and deeds ultimately match. For the purpose of this book, we use the following indicators for "prescriptive status"; governments are considered as accepting the validity of human rights norms if and when:

1 they ratify the respective international human rights conventions including the optional protocols;
2 the norms are institutionalized in the constitution and/or domestic law;
3 there is some institutionalized mechanism for citizens to complain about human rights violations;
4 the discursive practices of the government acknowledge the validity of the human rights norms irrespective of the (domestic or international) audience, no longer denounce criticism as "interference in internal affairs," and engage in a dialogue with their critics.

As to these discursive practices, we adopt the following criteria:

- Prescriptive status in the sense of recognizing the validity claims of a normative idea implies argumentative consistency, independent of the audience. Actors who change their arguments with regard to the idea depending on with whom they are dealing, become suspect.

29

- Prescriptive status can be particularly well investigated in those circumstances in which material and power-related interests ought to shift, but actors nevertheless continue adhering to the validity of the norm. Do governments who have engaged in controlled liberalization, stick to their words even though the domestic and transnational pressures for change have decreased (cf. chapter 4 on Morocco)? Alternatively, what happens after a regime change? Does the opposition who gained new power stick to the human rights discourse over a sustained period of time even after it has fully consolidated its rule (cf. chapters 3 on South Africa, 2 on Uganda, 5 on the Philippines, and 7 on Eastern Europe)?
- Prescriptive status of a norm can also be well examined in situations in which the actual behavior is still partly inconsistent with it. How do national governments treat accusations by the transnational networks and others of continued violations of human rights? If they engage in a dialogue with their critics, try to legitimize their behavior by referring to the norm, apologize, or promise and deliver compensation, the normative validity of the idea can be inferred.
- Last but not least, of course, words need to be matched by deeds. Prescriptive status of international human rights norms implies that governments make a sustained effort to improve the human rights conditions. In other words, we expect the "prescriptive status" phase to be followed over time by the ultimate phase of our socialization model, "rule-consistent behavior" (see, however, the case of Guatemala, described in chapter 6).

What mode of social action and interaction dominates the phase of prescriptive status? As argued above, we expect the communicative behavior between the national governments and their domestic and international critics to closely resemble notions of dialogue, of argumentation and justification. At the same time, the institutionalization of the norms into domestic law and ensuing domestic practices begins in this phase of the process. New institutions to protect human rights are created, public officials including police forces are trained, and procedures for individual complaints are instituted.

We operationalize prescriptive status as a country-level variable. If prescriptive status were the result of primarily domestic factors, we would expect human rights norms to achieve prescriptive status in different countries at very different times. And yet, in most of the countries investigated in this volume, human rights norms received prescriptive status around the same period – in the decade from 1985 to 1995. Our case countries are so different as regards all other aspects of domestic structures that the convergence around the dating of prescriptive status is puzzling unless there is an international process of socialization underway. Yet, why does international norm learning appear in the period 1985 to 1995? There is no obvious reason for this – the basic norms in the UDHR and the main international institution, the UN Human Rights Commission, have been around since 1948; the main treaties have been in force since 1976. One possible explanation is that norm socialization requires time; it is for the most part a communicative process, and takes time to engage in the kind of dialogue and contestation inherent to communication. Another is that norm socialization required all the pieces of the relevant social structure to be in place for the process to be effective. The relevant social structures include not only the norms, but also a range of international institutions to oversee compliance with the norms, and the network to monitor norm compliance and norm breaking. Not until the mid-1980s were all the parts of this structure fully formed and dense – with the increasing number of human rights treaties, institutions, NGOs, increased foundation funding for human rights work – and human rights had become a part of foreign policy of key countries. We will further explore this aspect which points to some sort of "world time" and to developments on the global level in the concluding chapter of this volume (see concluding chapter 8).

Phase 5: rule-consistent behavior

"Prescriptive status" is a necessary step toward, but not identical with, rule-consistent behavior. Governments might accept the validity of human rights norms, but still continue to torture prisoners or detain people without trial and so on. Sometimes, national governments are not fully in control of their police and military forces, who commit the human rights violations. In any case, it is crucial for this phase of the spiral model that the domestic–transnational–international networks keep up the pressure in order to achieve sustainable improvements of human rights conditions. The particular difficulty in this phase is that gross violations of fundamental human rights might actually decrease in the target state and that, therefore, international attention might

31

Table 1.1. *The spiral model, dominant actors, and dominant interactions modes*

Phase	1. Repression	2. Denial	3. Tactical concessions	4. Prescriptive status	5. Rule-consistent behavior
Dominant actors moving process to next phase	Transnational human rights networks	Transnational human rights networks	Transnational networks and domestic opposition	National governments and domestic society	National governments and domestic society
Dominant mode of interaction	Instrumental rationality	Instrumental rationality	Instrumental rationality → rhetorial action → argumentative rationality	Argumentative rationality and institutionalization	Institutionalization and habitualization

decline, too. While many INGOs have acknowledged the problem in the meantime, international institutions and Western states are sometimes satisfied when rulers start accepting the validity of human rights claims in the sense of prescriptive status. This is particularly problematic when there has been a regime change bringing the opposing coalition into power, including human rights activists. Nevertheless, we argue that sustainable change in human rights conditions will only be achieved at this stage of the process when national governments are continuously pushed to live up to their claims and when the pressure "from below" and "from above" continues (hypothesis 4). Only then can the final stage in the socialization process be reached, whereby international human rights norms are fully institutionalized domestically and norm compliance becomes a habitual practice of actors and is enforced by the rule of law. At this point, we can safely assume that the human rights norms are internalized.

During this phase of the process, we may see a "two-level game" dynamic evolve, in which domestic leaders who believe in the human rights norms take power, but may lack strength *vis-à-vis* their domestic opponents (especially in the military) to implement those norms. These leaders may then use international human rights pressures to gain influence against their domestic opponents. As Putnam has suggested, international human rights pressures may allow foreign leaders to shift the balance of power in their domestic game in favor of a policy they preferred for exogenous reasons (Evans, Jacobson, and Putnam 1993; Putnam 1988). This appears to be a dynamic in the case of the Aquino government in the Philippines, and in the case of the de Leon Carpio administration in Guatemala in the period 1993 to 1996 (cf. chapters 5 and 6).

This is a short description of the "spiral model" of human rights change establishing the causal mechanisms and the process by which internationally established norms affect domestic structural change through the activities of principled-issue networks linking domestic NGOs, transnationally operating INGOs, international institutions, and national governments. Table 1.1 summarizes the spiral model with regard to (a) the dominant actors whose efforts are crucial to move the socialization process from one phase to the next, and (b) the dominant mode of social interaction across the various levels.

We posit, first, that the transnational human rights networks – in conjunction with international regimes and organizations as well as Western powers – are crucial in the early phases in terms of:

33

- putting the repressive regimes on the international agenda;
- starting a process of "shaming" and moral consciousness-raising;
- empowering and strengthening the initially weak domestic opposition.

During later stages of the model, activities of the internal networks and of the domestic opposition become increasingly significant, the crucial transition taking place during the "tactical concessions" phase. Only if and when the domestic opposition fully mobilizes and supplements the pressure "from above" by pressure "from below" can the transition toward prescriptive status and sustained improvement of human rights conditions be achieved.

Second, we claim that the dominant modes of social interaction also change during different phases of the model. In the initial phases, most of the actions can be easily explained by instrumental reasons. Norm-violating governments, for example, want to remain in power, (re-)gain foreign aid etc., and, therefore, deny the validity of norms and/or make tactical concessions. Toward later stages of the socialization process, argumentative rationality increasingly takes over. Governments under transnational and domestic pressure for change are increasingly forced to argue with the opposition and to enter into a true dialogue (cf., for example, chapter 3 on South Africa). Once human rights norms have gained prescriptive status in the "target state," institutionalization and habitualization processes become the dominant mode of social action.

In conclusion, we need to address one more point: our spiral model does not assume evolutionary progress toward norm implementation, but claims to explain variation and lack of progress. What are the conditions under which the spiral model can be interrupted resulting in a stabilization of the status quo of norm violation? First, as discussed above, regimes might return to oppression after some tactical concessions in phase 3 when international pressures have decreased. Moreover, rulers of the target state might not care about transnational and international opposition to their behavior and simply increase repression in order to effectively prevent the emergence of local NGO networks. The less dependent national governments are on the outside world – in terms of both material and ideational resources – the less they should be concerned. In other words, oppressive rulers have some leeway during the initial stages of the spiral model when both the domestic opposition and the domestic-transnational linkages are rather weak. Once tactical concessions have led to a fully mobilized domestic opposition with transnational links, however, there is not much which oppressive rulers can do to fight off the pressure and to continue the violation of human rights. The second critical moment comes in phase 4 when human rights have gained prescriptive status on the national level, but actual behavior still lags behind. In this instance, the strength of the domestic opposition and the local NGO network is no longer a primary problem, but the difficulty of keeping up the international pressure is. This is especially acute where a country avoids human rights violations of high-profile opposition leaders, but continues endemic and low-level human rights abuses, such as routine use of torture for common criminals. The co-existence of relatively high levels of political participation and competition with human rights abuses can erode international attention. Cases such as Mexico, Brazil, and Turkey come to mind.

Alternative explanations

There are two major alternative explanations to our model of norm internalization induced by principled-issue networks operating on the domestic and transnational levels. The first alternative account is compatible with (neo-)realist or (neo-)Marxist approaches according to which principled ideas matter if they are backed by superior economic and/or military power, or if they conform to materially defined actors' interests relating to their international environment. Stephen Krasner has argued, for example, that human rights are promoted and implemented resulting from the interests, pressures and capabilities of great powers (Krasner 1993). This approach would need to explain, however, why great powers change their positions on which norms they choose to back. For example, why did the United States move from a position, before 1973, in which human rights were seen as an inappropriate part of foreign policy to a position in which human rights formed an important pillar of US policy by the 1990s?

With regard to Third World countries, one could also assume that human rights conditions improve resulting from pressures by the World Bank and/or donor countries employing "good governance" criteria. State actors in Third World countries might enact liberalizing measures in order to get financial and economic development aid from the West or from multilateral institutions such as the World Bank and the International Monetary Fund (IMF). These approaches would need to explain why these "good governance" criteria were added relatively recently to conditionality requirements of multilateral institutions, often over the resistance of more technical staff who felt they were unrelated to the core tasks of the institutions. Moreover, exogenous shock waves in international politics such as the end of the Cold War leading to changes in the international distribution of power might also improve human rights conditions through some sort of snowball effect (Huntington 1991; Kitschelt 1992).

This account is already included in our spiral model to the extent that some individuals in international financial institutions and in the governments of Western great powers form part of the transnational human rights advocacy network. But this book investigates and problematizes the preferences of these actors rather than simply assuming them. If Western donors start coordinating foreign aid or the World Bank attaches "good governance" criteria to their structural adjustment programs, these changes in policies might well result from network and INGO activities. Insofar as the spiral model does not assume the absence of coercive power in the process of inducing domestic change in the human rights area, it accommodates this explanation. Only if it can be shown empirically that pressures generated by great powers and/or international financial institutions are the most significant factors in the domestic–transnational–international link to induce sustainable human rights improvements, or if any changes in state human rights practices end as soon as external material pressures end, would this constitute a challenge to our model.

The second alternative proposition to our model also denies significant independent causal value to principled ideas, but explains it with the "primacy of domestic politics" (Kehr 1970) in the sense of changes in the economic structure of the target state. This alternative account condenses insights from modernization theories (Przeworski and Limongi 1997; for a thorough critique see Schmitz 1997a). These arguments can be divided into the economic perspective claiming a direct correlation between economic growth and democratization, on the one hand, and the social system approach emphasizing *inter alia* urbanization, literacy and the role of mass media, on the other (Brachet-Márquez 1992: 96). Emerging new social strata (middle classes) are expected to become agents of change (M. Robinson 1995: 73). The creation of economic interests not linked with state activities necessitates the implementation of rational and impartial political institutions which secure expanding market exchanges through the rule of law.

"Therefore, this hypothesis asserts that countries with the fastest growing middle class will experience the greatest political liberalization"
(Wilson 1994: 266).

There is no question that those who become active and mobilize in
domestic human rights networks and in NGOs overwhelmingly belong
to urbanized middle classes. The issue is not the social and class origins
of NGO activists, but whether changes in socio-economic conditions
lead to political mobilization processes. If this were indeed the case, we
would not have to bother about complicated processes of linking domestic actors with transnational INGOs and international institutions
to explain sustainable human rights improvements. But approaches
stemming from modernization theory must confront the dilemma that
only two decades ago the political development literature made exactly
the opposite argument – that the processes and necessities of economic
development for more advanced developing states required an authoritarian form of government (Collier 1979; O'Donnell 1973). The bureaucratic authoritarian model was developed to try to explain the puzzle of
why the most developed states in Latin America with the largest
middle classes – Brazil, Argentina, Chile, and Uruguay – in the 1960s
and 1970s experienced the most repressive forms of authoritarian rule
in their history. The idea of some automatic correlation between market
economy and democracy, or between a particular stage of economic
development and a particular regime type needs to confront this kind
of confounding evidence. The empirical chapters will each assess the
alternative accounts.

Conclusions

This book investigates the conditions under which international human
rights ideas and norms contribute to domestic political change. Norms
influence political change through a socialization process that combines
instrumental interests, material pressures, argumentation, persuasion,
institutionalization, and habitualization. We attempt to explore the
particular mix of material pressures with communicative processes.

But even if material leverage is available, the target country must be
sensitive to the pressures, and it is often the communicative dimension
that heightens the sensitivity to pressures. As the case of economic
sanctions against Haiti in 1993 and 1994 and Guatemala in the 1970s
made clear, some governments can resist pressures successfully for
long periods. Countries most sensitive to pressure are not those that are

economically weakest, but those that care about their international image. Linking human rights practices to money, trade, or prestige is not a sufficient condition for effectiveness. Haiti's military rulers chose to hang on to power in the face of universal moral censure and economic collapse. Only the threat of military invasion led to a last-minute agreement to step down from power.

It is this dimension that is most difficult to capture in research. Scholars have long recognized that even repressive regimes depend on a combination of coercion and consent to stay in power, and that consensus is the basis from which the state derives its legitimation. But in addition to securing domestic consent and legitimacy, states also seek international legitimacy. This book suggests that some states are keenly aware of the approval of other states. Through processes of persuasion and socialization, states communicate the emergent norms of international society, create ingroups and outgroups as normative communities, and may convince norm-violating states that the benefits of membership in the in-group outweigh the costs. The cases where network campaigns have been most successful are those countries that have internalized the discourse of liberalism to a greater degree.

Our book has wider implications for the literature on democratization, which has tended to neglect the international dimension of democratization, despite the "wave-like" quality of global trends in democratization (Huntington 1991) suggesting that some international factors are at work. We do not argue that international factors are the only factors responsible for democratization, but rather that international norms and networks may provide key support for democratization processes at crucial stages, and that they have been a necessary, though far from sufficient, condition for the most recent wave of democratization.We will explore this theme further in the concluding chapter.

2 Transnational activism and political change in Kenya and Uganda

Hans Peter Schmitz

Introduction

Kenya and Uganda were both subject to intensive global human rights campaigns by international non-governmental organizations (INGOs). Alarming reports on the Ugandan human rights situation appeared in the early 1970s shortly after Idi Amin had staged a successful military coup. The human rights situation worsened throughout Amin's dictatorship and hardly improved after he was himself removed from power by violent means in 1979. Until early 1986 a civil war between government troops and various rebel groups led to continued gross violations of human rights. The situation slowly improved after the National Resistance Movement (NRM) as the main rebel organization took control of the main capital Kampala in January 1986.

Kenya came into the limelight of international attention in the mid-1980s. In contrast to Uganda, increased human rights abuses were not a result of the militarization of politics and subsequent civil war. Moreover, the extent of human rights abuses was never comparable to the atrocities perpetrated in Uganda during the 1970s and early 1980s. Instead, human rights conditions deteriorated in Kenya because an increasingly powerful executive showed declining tolerance for political dissent and developed a personal and paternalistic style of rule. This development began under the independence president Jomo Kenyatta and continued until his death in 1978. During the 1980s, it was perfected by his successor Daniel arap Moi. After considerable transnational

For comments on earlier drafts I thank various contributors to this volume, the anonymous referees from Cambridge University Press, Gilbert Khadiagala, and Tom Ofcansky. Some of the evidence presented here is based on field research in Kenya, Uganda, the United Kingdom, and the United States.

mobilization against the Kenyan government and subsequent domestic turbulence in 1991/1992, the executive was forced into a fragile political and constitutional reform process.

This chapter is about the role of transnational human rights organizations in the political development of Kenya and Uganda during the last twenty years. It shows how these organizations initially brought human rights violations in both countries to the attention of the international public. Confronted with the accusations, the respective governments denied all knowledge and responsibility, while donor governments remained reluctant to adopt the views of the nongovernmental organizations. However, the continued transnational mobilization eventually had important effects on governmental foreign and domestic policy decisions. The work of organizations such as Amnesty International transformed the international image of human rights violating regimes in Kenya and Uganda. This induced donors to review their aid policies and the accused governments to use tactical concessions in an attempt to undermine international mobilization. Moreover, international mobilization was an effective means of protecting and strengthening domestic human rights activists. While inter-governmental pressure for human rights was often reluctant and erratic, transnational human rights groups consistently legitimated a domestic opposition which also advocated respect for human rights. Once governments mixed their strategy of complete denial with some tactical concessions, domestic and international human rights actors used this as another window of opportunity for intensified mobilization. Eventually, human rights issues became part of the domestic discourse.

In this chapter, I argue that Kenya has nearly completed phase 3 of the model outlined in the introductory chapter, while Uganda has moved towards the completion of the fourth phase. A comparison of overall societal mobilization for human rights leads to the expectation that the modest positive changes in Kenya are more likely to be sustainable than the predominantly "top-down" approach taken in Uganda. While Kenya is relatively isolated from regional developments, the Ugandan human rights situation is more directly linked to the political developments in neighboring countries such as the Democratic Republic of Congo, Rwanda, and Sudan.

Phase 1: deteriorating human rights conditions

Human rights conditions deteriorated in Kenya and Uganda as a result of intensified domestic competition for the control of state power. Democratic and federal conflict-mediating mechanisms which had been hastily put into place on the eve of independence by the outgoing British colonial authorities failed to take root in the domestic arena and gave way to centralization and executive preponderance in the name of nation-building. In both cases, deteriorating human rights conditions were preceded by a process of excluding dominant sections of society (the Baganda in Uganda and the Kikuyu in Kenya) from national politics. In Uganda, this became already apparent shortly after independence on October 9, 1962, while in Kenya a similar process occurred after the death of independence leader Jomo Kenyatta in 1978. In both countries, the executive branch of government won the power struggle for domestic control, permanently sidelined other democratic institutions, and increasingly defied limits set by the existing constitutional framework and the rule of law.

Uganda

In 1966/1967, the first Ugandan Prime Minister Milton Obote suspended the independence constitution and created a single-party state. He misused the military to end an ongoing dispute between the central government and the wealthiest region, Buganda, whose king Mutesa II was deposed as the president of the country (Ofcansky 1996: 41). As an unintended consequence of Obote's successful efforts to undermine Buganda's special position in Ugandan politics, an increasingly autonomous military emerged as an even greater threat to his government and the country as a whole. "The victory over Mutesa II institutionalized violence as the main instrument of political control" (Kasozi 1994: 88).

On January 25, 1971, army general Idi Amin Dada deposed Milton Obote while the latter was attending the Commonwealth Summit in Singapore.[1] Apart from the military, Amin could initially rely on support from his home area West-Nile and the disenfranchised Baganda, and the open support of Western governments, especially Israel and Great Britain. The latter welcomed the coup because the deposed Obote had recently developed socialist-leaning economic policies and attacked

---

[1] For the pertinent details of Ugandan history see Furley 1989; Kasozi 1994; Mutibwa 1992; Omara-Otunnu 1987.

41

the British government for alleged arms deliveries to the South African apartheid regime.[2] Even Amnesty International had little to complain about, because Amin immediately released more than 1,000 political prisoners including all prisoners of conscience adopted by Amnesty groups. However, not long after his coup Amin ordered the systematic killing of former supporters and tribal kinsmen of Obote, starting within the Ugandan army and the police forces. Idi Amin ignored even minimal formal safeguards of human rights, assumed dictatorial powers, and began to rule by decree. In September 1972, Amin ordered the expulsion of the Asian community living in Uganda. Tens of thousands of Asians with British passports fled to the United Kingdom. Under the euphemism of "nationalizing the Ugandan economy" the Asian businesses were expropriated and reallocated to Amin's friends and supporters. The British government harshly protested the decision and stopped all aid programs, but maintained diplomatic relations. Within the following two years, international human rights organizations and journalists informed the United Nations and the Western public about the dramatically deteriorating human rights situation in the country (Amnesty Inernational 1978b; International Commission of Jurists 1977b). In 1974, the *Observer* correspondent David Martin published his detailed account of the ongoing gross human rights violations in his book *General Amin* (D. Martin 1974). By 1975, detailed and irrefutable information about the true nature of the Amin regime was widely available in Western media and public.[3] Hence it is puzzling that it took so long for these widely available reports to affect a significant change of Uganda's international image. Despite the continuous non-governmental mobilization, the Amin dictatorship was only ended in the aftermath of Amin's military attack on Tanzania in 1978/1979.

Kenya

After the death of Jomo Kenyatta in 1978 the constitution provided that Vice-President Daniel arap Moi took over powers for an initial period of

---

[2] The British press was full of chauvinist praise for the coup. The *Daily Telegraph* wrote on January 26, 1971, that "one good reason that might be advanced for holding Commonwealth conferences more often is that the number of undesirable rulers overthrown as a result of their temporary absence, as has now happened to Dr. Obote in Uganda, would thereby be increased." The *Spectator* held on January 30 that "if a choice is to be made between quiet military men and noisy civil dictators then I prefer, in Africa at least, the military" (D. Martin 1974: 61).

[3] The last sentence of Martin's book was prophetic: "Uganda has suffered the most and will continue to suffer until the removal of the man who holds the bloodstained knife at her throat – General Idi Amin Dada" (D. Martin 1974: 249).

three months. In the same way as in Uganda, federal provisions in the constitution and the multi-party system had been effectively curtailed shortly after independence. The original two-party system consisting of the leading Kenya African National Union (KANU) and the smaller Kenya African Democratic Union (KADU) disappeared when most of the KADU leadership, including Daniel arap Moi, joined KANU's ranks in November 1964 and were rewarded with public offices (Ahluwalia and Steeves 1986: 98). Personal rule by Kenyatta rather than rivalry between a democratic government and an opposition dominated national politics, while some political competition was tolerated within the ruling party. Until the early 1980s, this justified the overall characterization of the political system as "semi-competitive" (Barkan 1992: 168). The situation changed when the Kalenjin Daniel arap Moi was able to exploit divisions within the dominant Kikuyu elite to consolidate his presidency beyond the three-month period. Despite this political success, arap Moi did not command the same kind of authority as Kenyatta, mainly because he was not a member of the dominant Kikuyu tribe and was still associated with KADU, which had been supported by white settlers and the colonial authorities.[4] Although arap Moi was able to outmaneuver his political opponents, this situation created the conditions for a further increase of executive powers and the substantive enlargement of the security apparatus. At the same time, arap Moi systematically replaced the old political and military elite with personnel from his own ethnic group and other loyal ethnicities.

When discontented opposition politicians announced in early 1982 the creation of a new party to challenge KANU, arap Moi directed parliament to outlaw such a move by converting Kenya from a *de facto* into a *de jure* one-party state. On August 1, 1982, air force officers staged an unsuccessful coup, which served as another pretext for an intensified government-led campaign against the political opposition. In the following years, political detention without trial and systematic torture and mistreatment became standard operating procedures of the security forces (African Watch/Human Righs Watch 1991; Andreassen 1993; Howard 1991). The executive and KANU increased their direct control

---

[4] In the 1950s and 1960s, KANU represented not only the nationalist independence struggle, but also the larger and domestically dominant Kikuyu, Luo, and related tribes (Embu, Meru, Kamba, and Kisii). As a counterweight, KADU was created to represent the smaller, pastoral tribes (mainly Kalenjin, Luhya, and Maasai) and their preferences for federalism (*majimbo*) and local autonomy. The white settlers' minority in Kenya favored the latter coalition because it represented a smaller threat to the status quo of land distribution after independence.

over parliament,[5] the judiciary,[6] and relevant societal organizations (unions, women's groups, etc.). Between 1984 and 1986, international human rights organizations began to alert the international public about deteriorating human rights conditions in the country.

Phase 2: initial mobilization and governmental denial

The initial mobilization of the international human rights network occurred in Uganda in 1973/1974 and in Kenya about ten years later. Uganda remained in this phase until early 1986, Kenya until 1989/1990. In both cases, Amnesty International had been active on individual cases before the transnational mobilization expanded, but during the indicated time periods human rights violations became systematic in character and, consequently, the involvement of other international human rights organizations led to a qualitative change of the mobilization patterns. All three repressive governments (under Amin, Obote, and arap Moi) did not deny in principle that the selected human rights norms applied to their countries. However, they initially denied all knowledge and responsibility for human rights abuses. Official statements accused human rights critics of intervening in the internal affairs of the country.

Uganda

Amnesty International and the International Commission of Jurists (ICJ) channeled their concerns about deteriorating human rights conditions in Uganda towards the United Nations' system. In 1974 the ICJ presented information about "systematic and gross violations of human rights" to the United Nations Human Rights Commission (International Commission of Jurists 1977: 1977b). Based on resolution 1503 the UN body began a confidential examination of the Ugandan situation. The Ugandan government denied the allegations and threatened to expel all British nationals, if the international media continued to report on these issues (Tolley Jr. 1994: 207). Amin mobilized additional support within the African continent. In August 1975,

---

[5] "Increasingly, the leaders of the party owed their offices to the President, and, by 1989, half of the members elected to Parliament occupied ministerial posts" (Widner 1992: 32).
[6] The executive interference in judicial affairs was covered by a great number of publications (African Rights 1996; Days *et al*. 1992; International Bar Association 1997; Kibwana 1992; Nowrojee 1995; Ross 1992).

the Organization of African Unity (OAU) Heads of States met in Kampala and elected Amin as their chairman for 1975/1976. This represented a major diplomatic success for Amin, who took the occasion to promote himself to the rank of 'Field Marshal'. In order to counter mounting human rights criticism, Amin also appointed a Commission of Inquiry to whitewash his domestic actions. Although the commission could not find "hard evidence indicating Amin's direct involvement ... there was evidence in plenty showing that his various terror units had killed wantonly" (Lule 1977: 5). When Amin was told by his Minister of Justice, Godfrey Lule, that the commission had not followed his directions, he tried to suppress the unexpected findings. On October 1, 1975, Amin declared in front of the United Nations General Assembly that Amnesty International relied on "rumors" provided by "criminals and exiles" (Amnesty International 1976: 104).

Meanwhile, Amin had dropped his former allies Israel and Great Britain in favour of Libya and other Arabic countries, which were much more generous in supplying military and financial aid. When the Palestinian Liberation Front (PLO) hijacked an Air France airplane originating in Tel Aviv, the plane was redirected to Entebbe airport. During the stand-off with the Israeli government, Amin collaborated with the hijackers, who were all eventually killed during a surprise raid by an Israeli anti-terrorist unit (Kyemba 1977: 166–178). As a result of the episode, which also involved a highly publicized revenge murder of the hostage Dora Bloch by Amin's henchmen, Britain broke off diplomatic but not trade relations with Uganda on July 28, 1976. The UN Human Rights Commission continued its inquiry in February 1977 and planned to discuss the evidence presented by Amin's own Commission of Inquiry. Meanwhile, gross and systematic violations of human rights continued unabated in Uganda. On February 17, 1977, Archbishop Janani Luwum and two ministers were killed, probably at the hands of Amin himself (Kyemba 1977: 179–192).[7] However, subsequent growing international outrage had little measurable effect. During the same week, Godfrey Lule, as the Head of the Ugandan delegation, had to defend his country's human rights record in Geneva. According to Lule's accounts, Amin called him

---

[7] Henry Kyemba served from 1972 to 1977 as a minister under Amin. After 1974 he was Minister of Health. In 1977 he did not return from an international conference and fled into exile to London where he immediately published his "inside story of Idi Amin's reign of fear." Godfrey Lule wrote the foreword for the book.

twice during that time. On one occasion he informed Lule about the death of the archbishop and the ministers adding that "God has punished them." With regard to the UN investigation Amin told Lule to deny all knowledge about the accusations. Lule himself knew that he could not follow these directions and simply deny the burgeoning evidence, because "I would not have been taken seriously." Instead he tried to further delay the procedures and told the UN Commission that more time should be given for the consideration of the allegations. Moreover, Uganda had just been elected a member of the Human Rights Commission for the period from 1977 to 1979.[8] After the end of the Commission's proceedings, Lule fled into exile in London.

For the first time, in June 1977 the Commonwealth Summit issued a warning of possible further action against the Ugandan government. "Cognizant of the accumulated evidence of sustained disregard for the sanctity of life and of massive violation of basic human rights in Uganda, it was the overwhelming view of Commonwealth leaders that these excesses were so gross as to warrant the world's concern and to evoke condemnation by the heads of governments in strong and unequivocal terms" (Kyemba 1977: 237). However, no action was taken. The same month, the US ambassador to the United Nations, Andrew Young, compared Amin's murderous regime to Hitler's genocide of the Jews. As a reaction to the ongoing killings, groups of exiles in Kenya, Tanzania, Great Britain, and the United States formed an umbrella coalition and finally met in Lusaka in August 1977 (Omara-Otunnu 1987: 139). Amnesty International representatives made several attempts to visit the country, but their requests were never answered. Instead, the Ugandan government successfully countered growing international mobilization by using its diplomatic leverage within the Organization of African Unity and the United Nations. Despite Godfrey Lule's and others' narrow escape into exile, the UN Human Rights Commission decided in March 1978 to take no further action, but to merely continue its observation of the Ugandan situation (Tolley Jr. 1994: 208). On April 3, 1978, Amin announced the creation of a national human rights committee composed of members of the security forces and other government agencies. It was charged with overseeing all contacts between the United Nations Human

---

[8] In retrospect, it seems surprising that Uganda was elected as a member of the Human Rights Commission even though reports about systematic torture and killings had been presented by human rights NGOs since 1974. However, as head of the Organization of African Unity Idi Amin enjoyed considerable diplomatic support at that time.

Rights Commission and the people of Uganda (Amnesty International 1979: 166).[9]

At the very end of Amin's rule, there were only a few significant official responses to the human rights reports. Following a hearing on the situation in Uganda in June 1978 (Committee on Foreign Relations 1978), the United States Congress finally demanded a trade embargo against the country. However, a majority of votes was only secured after three communist countries (Cambodia, Cuba, and Vietnam) had also been added to the list (Forsythe 1988: 78). The embargo was never implemented. Great Britain and other Commonwealth countries planned to ban Amin from attending the Summit to be held in London in June 1979 (Omara-Otunnu 1987: 138). However, the United States remained the main purchaser of Ugandan coffee until the last days of the Amin dictatorship. More importantly, airplanes used by Amin for his travels and to bring in luxury goods were still serviced in the United States. Twice a week, US pilots flew crucial supplies (so called "whisky runs") for Amin from London to Entebbe (Kyemba 1977: 254). Not surprisingly, the OAU and the Arab states never came forward to condemn the human rights violations in Uganda. Hence, it was Amin's decision to attack Tanzania in 1978 which became the catalyst for his downfall. On April 11, 1979, regular Tanzanian troops aided by Ugandan rebels captured Kampala.

Following three short-lived governments[10] and manipulated elections on December 10, 1980 (Bwengye 1985: ch. 5), Milton Obote returned to the presidency. Yoweri Museveni and parts of the disgruntled political opposition, which had already fought the Amin dictatorship, announced that they would not accept the election results and continued their violent rebellion in the bush. Within only a few months, human rights conditions deteriorated again as a result of the ensuing civil war and a further disintegration of state institutions. New army personnel were enlisted to fight the rebellion but were scarcely trained, controlled, or paid. As a result, these troops perpetrated some of the worst massacres in Ugandan history. In 1982, Obote invited a delegation from Amnesty International to visit the country. Government officials denied allegations of "systematic human rights abuses" and answered 350 individual cases highlighted by Amnesty (Amnesty International 1983:

[9] See also the statement of Whitney Elsworth, former Chairman of the Board, US section of Amnesty International at a US Senate hearing in 1978 (Committee on Foreign Relations 1978: 25).

[10] In one of those governments under Yusufu Lule, Yoweri Museveni served as a minister of state in the defense department (Omara-Otunnu 1987: 147).

124). In response to Amnesty's continued criticism the Ugandan government accused the organization in September 1983 of "hostile criticism"
and "rude behavior". The government further claimed that rebels in
army uniforms committed most of the alleged abuses (Amnesty International 1984: 124). At the same time, tens of thousands of civilians were
killed by rampaging army personnel in the infamous "Luwero Tri-
angle," where rebels had found support among the indigenous population (Amnesty International 1985b; Ofcansky 1996: 55). New technologies such as video cameras were increasingly used to document the
atrocities committed by the Ugandan army (Kasozi 1994: 172). As a
result, international mobilization against the Obote regime intensified.

In contrast to the rampaging government troops, Yoweri Museveni
enforced a code of conduct for his rebel army which included the death
penalty for his own soldiers if they were found guilty of committing
serious human rights abuses against civilians. Although the rebels did
also engage in "questionable activities" (Ofcansky 1996: 54) during the
course of military operations, the growing domestic support for them
can only be explained by their significantly higher respect for basic
human rights. Indeed, Museveni's rebel army was the first in Ugandan
history which did not operate from bases outside the country (e.g.
former Zaire and Sudan) but established itself close to the capital
Kampala in the center of the country. Grass-roots (and international)
support for Museveni increased with every new attempt of government
troops to break the local support for the rebels by randomly burning
entire villages and executing their inhabitants. The main reason for the
rebels' success was the replacement of the chiefs' system by democratically elected resistance councils which finally brought the idea of
(popular) democracy to the local level (Mamdani 1996: 200–203). This
resulted in a "unprecedented degree of village level participation in
decision-making" (de Waal 1997) and reinforced growing international
recognition of Museveni. Over time the rebel leadership was positively
integrated into the transnational human rights network, or as Mamdani
chose to put it, "bathed as it was in global ideological influences"
(Mamdani 1996: 207).[11]

---

[11] Museveni and other leaders made several semi-official visits to European countries in
preparation of their likely future role in Uganda and had continuous contacts with
international human rights groups. In December 1985, Museveni visited several European countries, where he met with parliamentarians, members of the ministerial
bureaucracy, and non-governmental groups (Weyel 1995: 555). At the same time,
Museveni created local coalitions and, most importantly, integrated the disgruntled
Baganda in his fight against the Obote government (Mamdani 1996: 207–210).

Despite the evidence of gross violations of human rights provided to the international public, official reactions from foreign governments were hardly more decisive than during the Amin era. One reason for this was Obote's willingness to distance himself from his earlier socialist ideas and to fulfil all major economic measures imposed by the donor community. Indeed, measured in terms of inflation and decreasing government spending, Obote's second presidency was a success story until 1984 (Henstridge 1994: 53). Even Great Britain returned as the main source of financial and military aid. Well-intentioned diplomatic efforts to continue a bilateral dialogue with the Ugandan government on the human rights situation were conducted without decisive follow-up. In 1983, Obote invited the Australian, British, and Canadian High Commissioners to a tour of newly established detention camps. During the visit he declared that "the people who had got displaced due to bandit activities were voluntarily returning to certain centers such as police stations, army posts, administrative headquarters and schools" (Kasozi 1994: 184). In an interview with the *Financial Times* the same year, Obote accused Amnesty International of not being able to distinguish between political prisoners and common criminals (quoted in Sathyamurthy 1986: 673). The international response to Amnesty International's continued lobbying efforts for human rights in Uganda was slow and ambiguous. Only in May 1984 did the US Assistant Secretary of State for Human Rights Elliott Abrams and the Ambassador Allen Davis publicly accuse the Obote regime of systematic killings and torture.

While Germany, Denmark, and the Netherlands soon adopted the critical US position and finally began to distance themselves from Obote, the British government continued its military and financial support. The latter declared in the middle of 1984 that it would launch its own investigations into the situation before any measures were taken. However, only when Amnesty International published its report *Six Years after Amin: Torture, Killings, Disappearances* in June 1985 (Amnesty International 1985b) did the Minister of State for African Affairs in the Foreign and Commonwealth Office, Malcom Rifkind, threaten that Britain might terminate its assistance if human rights conditions did not improve. "This was quite a switch, and he was responding to strong criticism from the Cambridge group of Amnesty International, which had accused the Foreign Office of being 'craven' and 'pussy footing' in its response to the Abrams claims" (Furley 1989: 290). Finally, the efforts of the human rights network to socialize the international public by means of moral consciousness-raising and persuasion had some effect even on reluctant governments such as Great Britain and the United States. But again, it was a domestic catalyst which ended Obote's second presidency. On July 27, 1985, parts of the increasingly disgruntled Ugandan army staged a coup against Obote. Subsequently, two military officers, Basilio and Tito Lutwa Okello, began negotiations with the rebels. A peace accord mediated by Kenyan President Daniel arap Moi went into effect on December 17, but was not respected by either side. Museveni's rebels seized Kampala on January 26, 1986.

Kenya

Kenya became a target of the international human rights community around 1984. Two years after the unsuccessful coup attempt by air force officers, the internal security situation was increasingly marked by open repression. Critical intellectuals in Nairobi and minorities in the border regions became the first visible victims. Human rights organizations informed the international public of hundreds of killings and detentions as part of "security operations" against the Somali minority in the North-Eastern Province of Kenya (Africa Watch/Human Rights Watch 1991: xi; Amnesty International 1985a: 66). "Three Norwegian volunteers stationed in the area had witnessed the aftermath of a massacre of ethnic Somalis on the airstrip at Wagalla near the provincial capital of Wajir. Very upset about what they had seen, they reported the incident to the Norwegian ambassador to Kenya. His muted reaction, which they interpreted as hushing the matter up, disgusted them" (Baehr, Selbervik, and Tostensen 1995: 64). At the same time, Amnesty International demanded the creation of an independent commission to investigate the massacre. After returning to Norway, the volunteers contacted the foreign ministry and the issue was raised in the Norwegian parliament.

In 1985 and 1986, Kenyan security forces used exceptional amounts of force to clamp down on student riots at the main universities of the country. Declared as part of security operations against MwaKenya, an alleged clandestine Kikuyu-based organization, several hundred people were arrested, mistreated, and disappeared temporarily (Anonymous 1987). In September 1986, Norway granted political asylum to the former Member of Parliament and Cornell University student Koigi wa Wamwere, who was one of the first victims of the repression. With his charisma he became a crucial figure in the process of moral consciousness-raising and redefinition of Kenya's image abroad. "Arguably, he was the most important opinion leader in Kenyan affairs in Norway in the late 1980s" (Baehr, Selbervik, and Tostensen 1995: 68). The bilateral relations between Norway and Kenya slowly deteriorated as sections of the Norwegian public began to criticize the foreign ministry and the Norwegian embassy in Nairobi for allegedly suppressing information about human rights abuses in Kenya. Thus, Norway became the first Western donor country which was profoundly affected by the activities of the human rights network on Kenya. From there, long-held perceptions of Kenya changed in concentric circles starting in neighboring Scandinavian countries and moving to Continental Europe and the United States. For two reasons, Norway and Scandinavia as a whole became the catalysts for international human rights mobilization on Kenya. First, Scandinavian countries were traditionally more open to a human rights discourse because it was already part of their international agenda in the United Nations and they had no strategic interests in the region. Second, Scandinavian aid agencies had chosen Eastern Africa as one of their main geographic areas of activities. By the mid-1980s these agencies were in the process of re-evaluating their aid programs because many had failed to realize their development goals. This situation served as an opportunity for human rights activists to put Kenya on the domestic and international agenda.

On December 2, 1986, the Kenyan parliament further strengthened executive powers by curtailing the right to bail (24th amendment) and by abolishing constitutionally guaranteed tenure for the Attorney General and other high-ranking bureaucrats (23rd amendment). At this point, Kenyan lawyers and church officials began to raise concerns about the overwhelming powers of the executive. However, only when Daniel arap Moi announced two state visits to Europe and the United States for 1987 did the transnational network find a stage for concerted international mobilization against repression in Kenya. Prior to the visit to the United States in March, Amnesty International published the report *Kenya: Torture, Political Detention and Unfair Trials* (Amnesty International 1987b). At the same time, Gibson Kamau Kuria, a defense lawyer in the MwaKenya trials, filed a lawsuit against the security organs accusing them of torturing the suspects. In anticipation of the likely consequences, Kuria provided Blaine Harden, the *Washington Post* correspondent in Nairobi, with the compiled evidence. On February 26, 1987, Kuria disappeared.

On March 12, one day before arap Moi met with President Reagan in

Washington, the government announced Kuria's arrest under the Preservation of Public Security Act and accused him of "disrespect for the Head of State." The day after the talks between arap Moi and Reagan, the *Washington Post* subtitled a picture of both politicians on the front page with "Police Torture is Charged in Kenya." The same day, State Department officials and members of Congress demanded a full explanation and an impartial investigation of the allegations (Africa Watch/ Human Rights Watch 1991: 374). Arap Moi cancelled his planned visit to New York and a meeting with the Secretary General of the United Nations and flew directly to less hostile Great Britain. Upon his return to Nairobi,[12] arap Moi declared that all torture allegations against his government were false.[13] Pressure by the human rights network continued throughout the rest of the year and peaked again in the autumn, when arap Moi planned to travel to a number of European countries. Contrary to his original plans, arap Moi only visited Finland and Romania, but decided to skip Sweden and Norway because of the negative press coverage prior to his visit (Baehr, Selbervik, and Tostensen 1995: 69). In Finland members of his delegation met with representatives from Amnesty International, while arap Moi declared back in Nairobi that the human rights community should target South Africa and not his country.[14] In his Independence Day speech on December 12, 1987, arap Moi called Amnesty International a "South African agent," promised to "arrest all members of Amnesty International found in Kenya" and advised them "to go to hell" (Amnesty International 1988a: 86, my translation).

Domestically, the international mobilization supported the creation and strengthening of opposition coalitions. In the virtual absence of independent societal organizations, individual lawyers and church officials from both Roman Catholic and Protestant denominations, became the first outspoken human rights critics of the regime (Peters 1996: 20–23). In September 1987, the first issue of the *Nairobi Law Monthly* was published by Gitobu Imanyara, soon to be one of the most important and influential independent journals devoted to human rights and the administration of justice. Despite the growing pressure on the Kenyan

---

[12] On the day of Moi's return, Blaine Harden was notified that he had to leave Kenya within forty-eight hours. After protests from the US embassy and a personal meeting, arap Moi agreed to extend his license for another two years (Harden 1990: 256).

[13] Foreign Broadcast Information Service/Daily Reports, March 17, 1987 (FBIS-MEA, vol. V, no. 051, p. R1).

[14] Foreign Broadcast Information Service/Daily Reports, September 4, 1987 (FBIS-WEU, no. 87–172, p. 8/9).

government, repression levels tended to increase for the time being. In January 1988, several visiting members of foreign NGOs, including the Lawyers' Committee on Human Rights and the American Association for the Advancement of Science (AAAS) were temporarily detained in Nairobi. The government-critical journal *Beyond*, published by the National Council of Churches of Kenya (NCCK) was banned in March, because it had criticized the partial abolishment of secret voting procedures for KANU primary elections (Widner 1992: 191). In August 1988 new amendments to the constitution removed tenure for judges and extended the period a capital-offence suspect could be held before being charged in a court from twenty-four hours to fourteen days (25th amendment). The same year, the Kenyan government hired the London-based PR-agency Raitt Orr Associates to improve its international image. In the United States, two agencies were later specifically hired to vilify US ambassador Smith Hempstone after he had become one of the most important critics of the Kenyan government (see pp. 55–59) during the crucial 1990/1991 period (Hempstone 1997: 131).

Members of the human rights network answered these measures by intensifying their transnational activities. The Robert F. Kennedy Memorial Center for Human Rights honored Gibson Kamau Kuria in March 1989 with its Human Rights Award during a ceremony held in Nairobi. During the visit, the non-governmental organization delegation also held a meeting with President arap Moi (Nairobi Law Monthly 1989), which led to no immediate consequences, but further contributed to the growing prominence of the issue domestically and abroad. Later, arap Moi denounced the demands for greater respect for human rights by the delegation and accused the members of interfering in the internal affairs of Kenya. In an address to the KANU Delegates Conference at Nyayo Stadium on June 16, 1989, he read an urgent action letter from Amnesty International in full and commented that "this shows that all those people with all their lies, write filthy and nonexisting stories. And when you hear all that they write, like those that run away, they are *self-inflicted*. They go into *self-exile*."[15]

Nonetheless, by early 1990, the continuous efforts of the human rights network to reframe the domestic and international image of the Kenyan government through moral consciousness-raising and the provision of detailed information on the human rights situation showed considerable effects. Targets of these efforts, such as other state actors

---

[15] Foreign Broadcast Information Service/Daily Reports, June 19, 1990 (FBIS-AFR-89-116, p. 4). The speech was held in Swahili. Words in italics were spoken in English.

and the general public within and outside Kenya were increasingly willing to filter information coming from Kenya through the interpretative framework provided by transnational human rights organizations. As a result, on several occasions throughout the year almost instantaneous mobilization against the government occurred on the international and the domestic level. The violent deaths of Foreign Minister Robert Ouko in February 1990 and government-critical Bishop Alexander Muge in mid-August outraged the Kenyan public and many donors (Nairobi Law Monthly 1990). Although there was no immediate and compelling evidence that the government was directly involved in the deaths, dominant interpretations of the events focused almost exclusively on the alleged responsibility of government officials. Additionally, the changes in Eastern Europe provided another mechanism which reinforced the image of a Kenyan government that was no longer sharing the emerging global consensus on human rights. As a result, the gap between the outside perceptions of Kenya and the Western-leaning self-image promoted by Kenyan government officials widened considerably. The Kenyan government now announced a number of tactical concessions to reconfirm the basic commitment to the Western community and to appease international and domestic critics.

Phase 3: tactical concessions and increased domestic mobilization

Kenya entered the third phase in 1989/1990 while the civil war in Uganda after 1981 prevented the emergence of a typical domestic mobilization pattern followed by tactical concessions. Although such concessions were made by Amin and the second Obote regime, the ever-increasing number of killings and torture cases justify the general categorization of the country in the second phase of the model until the end of 1985. This period was marked by the progressive breakdown of executive capacities to control the security forces. International human rights groups succeeded in putting human rights, understood as freedom from torture and arbitrary death, on the international agenda. In a situation of civil war, the domestic mobilization for human rights did not translate into the typical creation of new human rights groups or the expansion of societal space, but into an increased grassroots support for the comparatively more disciplined rebel forces.

With regard to Kenya, the transnational human rights network con-

54

tinuously provided new information on the deteriorating Kenyan human rights situation since 1984. The network successfully applied techniques of moral consciousness-raising and persuasion to replace the previously dominant perceptions of stability (Berg-Schlosser and Siegler 1990) with a discourse that linked Kenya to systematic abuses of basic human rights. After 1989/1990 this had two major consequences. First, within the previously rather quiet and supportive international donor community voices critical of the Kenyan government's human rights record increased significantly in number and strength. Cracks within the previously relatively closed ranks of donor countries emerged as individual countries and their representatives-in-charge adjusted their images of Kenya at different speeds. Second, the domestic playing field became increasingly inseparable from the international arena. Domestic and international mobilization reinforced each other in critical ways.

Kenya

In October 1989, the conservative Republican and former journalist Smith Hempstone arrived as the new US Ambassador in Kenya. He was a political appointee and had no incentives to follow the beaten (and rather quiet) path of a life as a career diplomat. During the next four years he became an outspoken supporter of democratic change and was joined by his German counterpart Berndt Mützelburg in 1991. For Smith Hempstone this meant not only constant personal attacks by Kenyan government newspapers and KANU officials for allegedly defying the norm of diplomatic neutrality. Moreover, even within the US State Department he became soon isolated, because of his "undiplomatic" efforts to go beyond rhetorical support for democracy and match words with deeds (Hempstone 1997: 166). Indeed, Hempstone and Mützelburg behaved as if they were part of the human rights network while their own governments and most of the other donors only slowly questioned their unequivocal support for arap Moi.[16]

At the end of 1989, arap Moi planned to make another official state visit to the United States in order to secure further international support. The White House and the State Department rebuffed this request

---

[16] Hempstone was regularly accused of favoring the opposition by inviting them to his house. During one occasion in Kisumu on August 11, 1991, he allegedly called opposition members "my very close friends" (Foreign Broadcast Information Service/Daily Reports, August 14, 1990, FBIS-AFR-90-157, p. 9). In defending his neutral diplomatic status, Hempstone later clarified that the term he actually used was: "everyone present is my friend" (Hempstone 1997: 123).

and arap Moi was forced to declare his visit a private affair. Nonetheless, arap Moi traveled with his usual large entourage including his Foreign Minister Robert Ouko. The United States government had made clear for some time now that current circumstances in Kenya made it impossible to welcome Kenyan government officials in good faith. The foreign minister and staunch supporter of arap Moi, Robert Ouko, was the only exception to that position and rumors had it that the United States government favored him as a possible successor of the current President. Ouko had distinguished himself with a relatively moderate position within the Kenyan government and had just begun to confront some of his Cabinet colleagues on the issue of corruption. Two weeks after Moi returned from his state visit, Ouko was found murdered not far from his home.[17] Immediately, rumors developed that Ouko died because he became a threat to some of his Cabinet colleagues and even the president. In the aftermath, members of Ouko's ethnic group (the Luo) rioted for several days.

The government continued to arrest and harass opposition figures and close newspapers and, thus, provoked another spiral of violence on the streets. However, encouraged by the global demise of authoritarianism, the opposition answered the repression with growing defiance. On May 3, Charles Rubia and Kenneth Matiba announced the creation of the Foundation for the Restoration of Democracy (FORD), an umbrella organization of political dissidents. Incidentally, Smith Hempstone was invited to address the Rotary Club in Nairobi the same day on economic issues. Hempstone largely stuck to the original theme of his address, but made a few remarks on the overall political situation towards the end of the speech. He reminded the audience that "a strong political tide is flowing in our Congress . . . to concentrate our economic assistance on those of the world's nations that nourish democratic institutions, defend human rights, and practice multiparty politics" (Hempstone 1997: 91). The Kenyan government and its media subsequently alleged that there was a previous collusion between Hempstone and the opposition. In his reaction to the creation of FORD, President arap Moi denounced Matiba and Rubia as traitors who were paid by foreign sources. Hempstone maintained that the whole affair

---

[17] Based on her interviews, Widner wrote that "upon his return [from the United States] arap Moi was so furious with Ouko that he ordered his assassination" (Widner 1992: 193). Hempstone even discussed accounts of the events which described a direct participation of the President in the torture and subsequent death of Ouko (Hempstone 1997: 66–70).

was a mere coincidence. Two weeks later the US Assistant Secretary of State for African Affairs Hank Cohen reassured Moi in Nairobi that the US government did not intend to make multi-partyism a condition for aid.[18] He also refused to meet opposition leaders and left the impression that Hempstone was isolated within his own government (Clough 1992: 100). "From then on it was the Kenyan government's position that relations between the United States and Kenya were fine ... but Hempstone was a maverick acting on his own" (Hempstone 1997: 95).

However, the unintended consequences of the coincidence between Hempstone's speech and the announcement of the opposition created the conditions for intensified domestic mobilization for democratic change. On July 4, the Kenyan police detained Matiba, Rubia, and others. Gibson Kamau Kuria asked for asylum at the US embassy. Demonstrations in the capital Nairobi and provincial centers culminated on July 7, 1990, when at least twenty-nine civilians were killed. Subsequently, the International Bar Association canceled its biannual meeting to be held in Nairobi in September (Muthoga 1990). Hank Cohen was back in Nairobi in August to meet President arap Moi again. At the request of arap Moi, this time Hempstone was not even allowed to attend the talks. In October 1990, the Norwegian ambassador, Niels Dahl, along with other international observers, attended another trial against Koigi wa Wamwere, who had been allegedly abducted from Uganda by Kenyan security forces. The Moi regime interpreted the actions of the ambassador as another unfriendly act and severed diplomatic relations with Norway on October 22 (Baehr, Selbervik, and Tostensen 1995: 69). The outside relationships of the Kenyan government became increasingly strained as representatives from Western donor countries had to choose how to react to the diplomatic stand-off between Kenya and Norway. For the first time, in October 1990, the US Congress attached human rights issues to foreign-aid appropriations for Kenya.[19] Within five years the transnational network had successfully completed its task of "re-mapping"(Brysk 1993: 268) Western

---

[18] However, a significant shift in US aid to Kenya had already occurred since the late 1980s. Between 1962 and 1988 Kenya received a total of about one billion US dollars in aid. Thus, it was the third largest recipient country following Sudan and Zaire. 63 percent of the aid went directly to government sources (Clough 1992: 78). After 1990 aid packages were generally cut and redirected to the non-governmental sector.

[19] The United States Congress asked the Kenyan government to "charge and try or release all prisoners, including detainees, stop the mistreatment of prisoners, restore the independence of the judiciary and permit freedom of expression" (Human Rights Watch 1991: 42). However, Kenya continued to receive unconditional military aid from the United States (1991: US $5 million; 1993: US $3,73 million).

perceptions of Kenya. The global discourse now associated the country with issues like corruption, torture, and insecurity instead of stability and economic development. The international public was socialized into a particular view of the Kenyan domestic situation by means of moral consciousness-raising and persuasion.

However, the change in perceptions did not have uniform effects on everyone. Whereas the US Congress became an advocate for aid cuts, the Reagan and Bush administrations remained reluctant to support such measures. With regard to Great Britain the impact could even be called negligible until late 1992,[20] when modest official criticism of the Kenyan human rights record finally picked up some of the arguments made by organizations such as Amnesty International. The main reason for this reluctance was the Western dependence on Kenya for furthering its military-strategic interests. The Gulf War in 1990 and two failed interventions in Chad in 1991 and in Somalia in 1992 give ample evidence of the predicament the United States government found itself in during this crucial period of Kenyan domestic politics. In Chad, US-trained Libyan dissidents (the "Haftar Force") were about to lose the ongoing war against Libyan-backed forces. Originally, the US government planned to establish a pro-Western regime in Chad and to use its territory to infiltrate neighboring Libya. After it became clear that this plan did not succeed, the responsible agencies decided to evacuate about four hundred of the surviving soldiers. Initially, Zaire's President Mobutu agreed to give them temporary refuge, although Libyan leader Muammar-el-Qadhafi never missed an opportunity to threaten everyone involved in the operation with serious consequences. Hence, the US government became worried about possible Libyan attacks on the refugee camp and a weakening of Mobutu's support (Clough 1992: 100). At this point, the State Department asked Smith Hempstone to approach the Kenyan President on the issue. More concretely, the US government wanted to airlift all the dissidents to Kenya, before bringing them to the United States after ninety days. Within one hour after the call from the State Department, Hempstone met President arap Moi and asked him to provide safe haven for the mercenaries in Kenya. Hempstone promised that the United States government would cover all costs and that all the equipment left behind would go to the Kenyans.

[20] The general attitude here was aptly described by Africa Watch as "what comes next may be worse" (Africa Watch/Human Rights Watch 1991: 362). Two parliamentary delegations visiting Kenya in the second half of 1990 concluded that there was "no evidence of political repression" (ibid.: 365).

Without much ado, arap Moi agreed to the deal and in early February 1991 operation "Magic Carpet" went ahead (Hempstone 1997: 136–141). During a period of domestic upheavals in Kenya, and after the Gulf War, this was the second time that the United States government requested (and was granted) strategic support from its long-time ally. In August 1992 the US government had to rely again on crucial Kenyan support when US troops were sent on a humanitarian relief operation in neighboring Somalia (Hempstone 1997: 214–231). As a result, the US government pursued an inconsistent policy toward its Kenyan counterpart and the domestic opposition during the crucial period between 1990 and 1992. On the one hand, the activities of the human rights network had significant impact even beyond individual members of the US government and particularly within Congress. On the other hand, strategic interests were continuously used to push human rights off the agenda.

Despite inconsistent donor policies, the crucial period between the end of 1989 and 1991 was marked by a significant increase of societal autonomy. The press and opposition voices became more courageous in their government criticism. A whole array of new non-governmental organizations sprang up and began to reclaim political space. Most of them survived on funding by outside donors. During this period the Kenyan government modified its previously consistent repressive domestic policy and moved towards an inconsistent mix of isolated measures of liberalization and continued oppression. One of the first victims of this new domestic situation was the Attorney General Matthew Greg Muli. On March 22, 1991, Hempstone presented the recently released US State Department Report on the Kenyan human rights situation and an Amnesty report to the Attorney General. He complained to Muli about the prison conditions of recently detained opposition activists and the allegedly restricted access for visitors. Specifically, Hempstone demanded a list of prison visits to the three most prominent detainees (Charles Rubia, Kenneth Matiba, and Oginga Odinga) for the last nine months. The Attorney General promised improvements and provided the US embassy with the requested information, but generally held that "all nations at one time or another in their history had employed detention without trial" (Hempstone 1997: 163). Subsequently, the government-owned Kenyan press mounted its usual attacks on Hempstone and accused him of interfering in the internal affairs of Kenya. However, more independent Kenyan newspapers used the opportunity to attack Muli for his alleged dismal performance (*Weekly*

Review, April 12, 1991). Only two weeks later, Amos Wako, an internationally known human rights lawyer, replaced Muli as Attorney General.[21] Other liberalizing measures included the reinstatement of tenure for judges a few months earlier, in December 1990 (Gathii 1994: 19) and the reintroduction of multipartyism in December 1991 (Chege 1994; Mair 1994: 87–90). At the same time, arap Moi continued to ridicule the human rights network and claimed in a speech that "Europeans are fools. When a lone African cries, they say he is being oppressed. They do not know the secrets of the African. There are others who go abroad and *demonstrate how people can be tortured* using the television in those countries, and then take it to Europe claiming that Kenyans are being tortured. So they see people being tortured; however, this is not happening here."[22]

The decision to legalize opposition parties came only two weeks after the donor community had suspended aid to Kenya on November 26 and in the midst of a *de facto* breakdown of diplomatic channels. A few weeks earlier Africa Watch had published the first comprehensive human rights report (400 pages) on Kenya (Africa Watch/Human Rights Watch 1991). After the joint declaration on democratic governance at the Harare Commonwealth Summit in October 1991, even Great Britain finally joined the critical voices, although its ambassador Tomkys was still reluctant to carry out the new directives.[23] At the same time, Smith Hempstone brokered talks between the Kenyan government and the opposition in order to avoid further confrontation. However, the talks finally broke down on November 14 and several members of the opposition were arrested by Kenyan security personnel during the following night. The next day the opposition called for street demonstrations and the US and German ambassadors lodged their protests at a meeting with the Permanent Secretary of the Foreign Ministry Bethuel Kiplagat. When the demonstrations turned violent

[21] Amos Wako was appointed Special Rapporteur for summary and arbitrary executions at the United Nations in 1982. He was a member of the Executive Committee of the International Commission of Jurists and was elected deputy chairman of the United Nations Human Rights Committee shortly before his appointment as Kenyan Attorney General. In defying these credentials, he declared in his inaugural speech at parliament, that "no one, save for the President, was above the law" (African Rights 1996: 226, Kiai 1993).
[22] Foreign Broadcast Information Service/Daily Reports, May 6, 1991 (FBIS-AFR-91-087, p. 4).
[23] "Tomkys confessed that he had lost the battle over the direction of British policy towards Kenya when he visited London the week of November 16–23... He said he had delivered a list of steps to Moi on his return to Nairobi" (Hempstone 1997: 256).

again, the group of the most critical ambassadors (Canada, Denmark, Germany, Finland, Sweden, and United States) was summoned to the Foreign Ministry on November 18. They were accused of organizing the demonstrations and of interference in the internal affairs of the country. Hempstone was personally accused by the Foreign Minister Ayah of being a "racist" and "trying to overthrow the Kenyan government" (Hempstone 1997: 252). The German foreign ministry recalled Mützelburg for consultations and instructed him to issue "the strongest of protests in the Foreign Ministry in Nairobi" on the human rights situation in the country.[24]

Last-minute efforts by the Kenyan government to avert the coming disaster failed. Most importantly, these included the arrest of Nicholas Biwott, one of the president's closest advisers, who was accused of being involved in the Ouko murder (Mair 1994: 35).[25] Four days after the donor decision, on November 30, Hempstone and the visiting US Deputy Assistant Secretary of State for African Affairs, Bob Houdek, met with President arap Moi and Foreign Minister Ayah. Houdek said that he had been instructed to pursue two essential issues. First, he wanted to know a precise date when the opposition could hold its first legal public meeting. Second, he asked arap Moi to announce publicly elections with non-KANU candidates. Arap Moi, who complained about the alleged misconduct of donors and embassy personnel, flatly rejected both demands. He asked the US to "detach itself from the dissidents and follow diplomatic conventions" (Hempstone 1997: 257). On December 2, however, arap Moi announced the end of the one-party era in Kenya.

As it turned out, by calling the first multi-party elections for December 1992, Moi regained control of the domestic situation. The mobilization for human rights and constitutional reform was pushed into the background as long as the opposition was mainly occupied with positioning itself for the electoral race. Despite governmental concessions to outside and domestic pressure, the regime continued to use repression against domestic critics. Indeed, some of the methods were ad-

[24] Foreign Broadcast Information Service/Daily Reports, November 18, 1991 (FBIS-WEU-91-222, p. 17).
[25] A detective from Scotland Yard named Biwott as one of two prime suspects in the murder case. Shortly before his death Ouko had challenged Biwott and other cabinet ministers, because of alleged misappropriation of foreign aid (including the total Swedish aid package of 1989) for their private use (Widner 1992: 196). Biwott was released after two weeks and lost his position in the cabinet. He returned as Minister in the Office of the President in January 1997 (*Daily Nation* and *Financial Times*, January 16, 1997, p. 1 and p. 4).

justed in order to avoid immediate international condemnation. Court cases of prominent opposition figures were moved far away from Nairobi in order to avoid media attention. Critics were no longer detained without trial or charged with political offences, but evidence for capital crimes like murder was fabricated and, thus, suspects could "legally" be kept away from the public as long as the government deemed it necessary (African Rights 1996: 131; Amnesty International 1995; Article 19 1995).

In December 1992, arap Moi and KANU won the first multi-party elections of his presidency, although opposition forces accounted for about 64 percent of the votes. Election rules set by the KANU government, manipulation of the results, and the fact that the opposition failed to agree on a single candidate enabled arap Moi to cling to power. Secret attempts by Hempstone, Mützelburg, and other donor representatives to unite the opposition behind one candidate had ultimately failed (Hempstone 1997: 304). When the opposition initially refused to accept the election results, Western governments openly pressed them to accept the defeat. During the preparations for the elections and in the aftermath about 2,000 Kenyans were killed and tens of thousands displaced by "ethnic violence" (Amisi 1997; Haugerud 1995; 38). Although government officials denied any role in the violence, the coincidence with the election date was all too apparent (Africa Watch/Human Rights Watch 1993). Even a parliamentary investigation (Kiliku report) implicated prominent KANU politicians, including Nicholas Biwott, as possible instigators of the violence (Republic of Kenya 1992: 9/19).

Between 1992 and the second multi-party elections in December 1997 the social pressure exerted by the transnational human rights network grew again in strength. The Kenyan government reacted with a continued mix of repression and liberalization. While well-known opposition figures by now enjoyed heightened international protection, the general harassment of the public only slowly decreased. But even activists were still not safe from attacks. In September 1994, several members of various human rights organizations were briefly detained and throughout 1995 the offices of Kituo Cha Sheria (Swahili for Legal Advice Centre), a human rights NGO, were six times the target of fire-bombings. Two members of human rights organizations were killed under mysterious circumstances in 1995 and 1996. Stephen Muruli, a university student was killed in his dormitory after he had accused police officers in 1996 of torturing him. On September 22, only eight months after Koigi wa Wamwere had been released on January

19, 1993, he and five others were arrested and charged with murder.[26] By now, Koigi was not only a symbol in Norway, but also in the United States. Several NGOs, including the Kenya Human Rights Initiative, based at Cornell University, constantly lobbied the US administration, Congress, and the embassy in Nairobi. At this point opposition figures like Gitobu Imanyara or Gibson Kamau Kuria were regularly invited to London, New York, and Washington DC by international human rights organizations and met with journalists, members of Congress and their staff (Human Rights Watch 1991: 43). Despite these continued lobbying efforts, the donor community lifted its suspension of aid in November 1993 and pledged a total of $850 million US Dollars (Human Rights Watch 1995: 24).

Although the Kenyan government had now regained some control over the domestic and the international arena, it significantly changed its human rights rhetoric and showed growing respect for the concerns expressed by human rights activists. Despite instances of continued repression, there were clear signs that the country was slowly moving along the third phase of our model towards the prescriptive status of the selected human rights norms. In June 1992, the Kenyan government lifted its ban on representatives of Amnesty International visiting the country. A coalition of domestic and international NGOs had just repulsed governmental attempts to increase executive control of the NGO sector and watered down a law regulating their registration and work (Ndegwa 1996: 31–54). During the same year two domestic human rights pressure groups with strong ties to the international arena were established and received funding from foreign donors. The Kenya Human Rights Commission (KHRC) opened offices simultaneously in Nairobi and Boston/USA, while Release Political Prisoners (RPP) followed suit. KHRC became the first domestic human rights organization to regularly monitor the human rights situation in the country and publish the results in *Quarterly Repression Reports*. The emergence of these organizations crucially supplemented the activities of the churches and individual human rights activists in challenging the Kenyan government. Moreover, detailed domestic documentation of human rights abuses deprived the government of one of its favorite arguments against alleged foreign meddling in domestic affairs. Another domestic

---

[26] Following world-wide mobilization for his release, Koigi wa Wamwere was finally freed on bail on medical grounds in December 1996. In the 1997 General Elections he ran as one of fourteen presidential candidates, but attracted only 0.13 percent of the votes.

human rights actor, the International Commission of Jurists (Kenya Section) already had strong ties with the outside world. It represented a chapter of an international non-governmental organization with consultative status at the United Nations Economic and Social Council (ECOSOC) and the United Nations Educational, Scientific, and Cultural Organization (UNESCO). Thus, channels to the outside world were solidified (Widner 1992: 188). In May 1993, the Kenya Section of the International Commission of Jurists and the Swiss-based NGO World Organization against Torture/SOS (OMCT/SOS) held a joint conference presenting detailed testimonies of torture in Kenya (Ankumah 1996: 116). Despite further denial of the evidence, the government gradually listened to the demands for increased human rights protection.

The Attorney General announced in July 1993 the creation of several commissions to review the Kenyan constitution and repressive laws (see Kenya Human Rights Commission 1994: Appendix). On 22 July 1995, Daniel arap Moi announced the creation of a KANU Standing Human Rights Committee, just two days before the annual donor meeting in Paris re-tabled the issue of human rights.[27] In 1996 arap Moi appointed ten individuals to form a Standing Committee on Human Rights, which reported directly to the president. So far, both bodies have not proved that they had any significant powers to actively promote human rights issues. Still, the seemingly empty rhetoric used by the Kenyan government to appease mainly international human rights criticism gradually took on a life of its own. In a situation where a non-governmental human rights network defines what constitutes a human rights abuse, any however instrumental acceptance of the norm on the part of a government opens a number of new windows for further mobilization, consciousness-raising, and persuasion.

Indeed, for the first time, the government responded in detail to domestic critics and, thus, could no longer rely on its standard arguments against foreign intrusion. Meanwhile, another equally important argument of the Kenyan government in the human rights debate had also disappeared with the changes in South Africa. What was rhetorically left could no longer support continued refusal to change. Between 1991 and 1996 the official argumentation clearly shifted away from counter-accusations, denial of facts and praise for its own economic successes. Instead, government officials increasingly acknowledged "areas in which it is possible to effect further improvements" (Republic

---

[27] Foreign Broadcast Information Service/Daily Reports, July 26, 1995 (FBIS-AFR-95-143, p. 4).

of Kenya 1996: 40) or invited "advice by genuine NGOs on how ... human rights conditions can be improved" (ibid.: 6). The government gradually bought into some of the arguments constantly raised by the human rights network. However, emerging domestic criticism was still treated as a form of unlawful disrespect. The authors of the report wrote that

> unlike other human rights reports, which detail in what respect the State has failed to discharge its responsibilities under international human rights instruments, the KHRC Report does not approach the subject as a specialized legal subject requiring the creation of a nexus between the incidence and State culpability! It is embarrassing to the sponsors [Western donors] of the project and it is hoped that they will analyze the professionalism of KHRC.   (Republic of Kenya 1996: 2)

In February 1997, the Kenyan government acceded to the United Nations Convention against Torture and other Cruel, Inhuman or Degrading Treatment or Punishment. The transnational network continued its reporting throughout the year and published three extensive human rights reports prior to the next general elections at the end of 1997 (African Rights 1996; Human Rights Watch/Africa 1997a; Human Rights Watch/Africa 1997b). In early June, a delegation of Amnesty International held extensive talks with Kenyan government officials. In its response to the allegations the regime no longer attacked the human rights organization and declared that "all the laws that Amnesty is calling for review are actually under active review" (Amnesty International 1997b: Appendix 4). Arap Moi himself announced upon arrival of the delegation that the government would replace one of the often-criticized colonial laws (Public Order Act) by a Peaceful Assembly Bill. With respect to the excessive use of force by the police forces, the government argued that any necessary action would be taken and that it had ratified the United Nations Torture Convention (ibid.: 24). Although the government did not entirely change its position towards Amnesty International or other critics, language and policies clearly showed the impact of the continuous work of the transnational network and the pervasive character of the human rights discourse in Kenya after 1991. On July 7, 1997, exactly seven years after the infamous Saba Saba incident, riot police again dispersed street demonstrations and a total of thirteen people lost their lives. Again, "ethnic violence" followed suit and hit the coastal region around Mombasa. Arap Moi came under additional pressure as the international public drew comparisons with the ending of the Mobutu regime in Zaire and contrasted him with "enlightened" African leaders such as Yoweri Museveni in neighboring Uganda (e.g. *Time Magazine*, April 14, 1997). Parts of the strengthened political opposition formed another umbrella organization called the National Convention Executive Council (NCEC) and pressed for substantive political reforms. However, even in the aftermath of the second Saba Saba, arap Moi refused to talk to the opposition and announced that reforms had to wait until after the elections. By the end of August, the government gave up this maximum position, but continued to accuse the NCEC of "being backed by foreigners to start a revolution in Kenya" (*Daily Nation*, August 31, 1999, p. 1). Facing further societal mobilization generated by the activities of the NCEC, the executive eventually announced the creation of an Inter-Parties Parliamentary Group (IPPG) to negotiate and institute some minimal political reforms even before the elections. On 7 November 1997, parliament turned the suggestions by the IPPG into law (*Daily Nation*, November 8, 1997, p. 1). These included, *inter alia*, the abolition of detention without trial, the abolition of the requirement to obtain a license before holding a public meeting, and greater opposition participation in the Electoral Commission. For the first time, moderate members of the opposition parties were officially included in such deliberations.[28]

Human rights criticism continued largely unabated after the General Elections in December 1997. In February 1998, members of the human rights group "Article 19" repeated accusations of "endemic torture" and other human rights abuses. The organization asked the Commonwealth Ministerial Action Group "to add Kenya to its list of serious and persistent human rights offenders [currently Nigeria, Sierra Leone and the Gambia]." In early October 1998, negotiations between the government and the opposition finally led to the establishment of a Constitution Review Commission. It was agreed that about half of its members would be selected from the political parties according to their respective strength in the 1997 general elections. The other half would be nominated by respective Roman Catholic, Evangelical, Muslim, and Protestant national church organizations and the 'civil society' at large. Representatives of the NCEC refused to participate in the decision, claiming that it was still under complete control of KANU.

---

[28] Although the NCEC had contributed to these results by its continued domestic and international mobilization, it rejected the compromise as insufficient.

In sum, government rhetoric and action has changed substantially since the human rights network began to mobilize social pressure against the Kenyan executive. Although arap Moi succeeded in temporarily halting the human rights discourse by calling elections in 1991/1992 and continues to threaten domestic human rights activists, he could not reverse the effects of the mounting pressure. Soon after winning elections, the arap Moi regime had to face again the issue of human rights, which had been established in the center of the domestic arena by the various national and international non-governmental groups. Continuous demands for action voiced by the strengthened societal sector and international supporters slowly eroded the stalling tactics of the government and eventually forced it to keep some of its promises. In the end, the Kenyan government had to retract and agree to some political reforms prior to the latest elections in 1997.

The current rhetoric and actions towards human rights groups and the issue of political reform stand in clear contrast to earlier statements of arap Moi on these issues and cannot be explained with reference to material pressure. In this sense, a process of norm socialization as described in the introductory chapter not only affected parts of the Kenyan society, but also the resistant government. As of now, the government largely took the path of *instrumental adaptation* in order to appease domestic and outside critics. A process of habitualization and internalization was set in motion, as these still isolated steps of political liberalization took on a life of their own. As shown above, donors did not consistently press for human rights improvements, but acted in an inconsistent and uncoordinated way. Despite and not because of the material pressure, the Kenyan government has nearly completed phase 3 of the model during the last ten years. This development not only coincides with, but also is directly caused by, the activities of the transnational human rights network and the following empowerment of local actors.

Phases 4 and 5: prescriptive status and rule-consistent behavior

Uganda entered the fourth phase of the model with the military victory of the National Resistance Movement (NRM) under the leadership of Yoweri Museveni in January 1986. The selected human rights have prescriptive status today and the NRM government has taken several steps to ensure their application domestically. In his first speech as president at the United Nations General Assembly, Museveni declared in October 1987 that "the Ugandan government under the NRM begins in the first place with an immutable commitment to guarantee human rights and the inviolability of human life" (cited in Amnesty International 1992b: 7). This rhetoric became a consistent feature of the new government (e.g. Museveni 1992).

These words were also followed by deeds. As a result of the general commitment of the NRM government to human rights, government-sponsored violations of human rights decreased significantly after 1986 (Oloka-Onyango 1992, 1996; Pirouet 1991). The new government extended its system of *resistance councils* throughout the country and established a mixture of representative and participatory democracy. Apart from all the shortcomings due to the gradual reassertion of "control from above" (Ddungu 1994; Mamdani 1995), the new system empowered ordinary Ugandans *vis-à-vis* local authorities and conferred legitimacy upon the new regime. In the course of the last ten years, the Ugandan government acceded to the United Nations Anti-Torture Convention (November 3, 1986), the African Charter for Human and Peoples' Rights and the International Covenant on Civil and Political Rights, including the first protocol providing for individual complaint procedures. In response to foreign or domestic criticism the Ugandan government invariably affirmed that basic human rights had grown beyond the exclusive control of individual states.[29] The military code of conduct of the rebel troops became the blueprint of similar safeguards applying to the newly established Ugandan Army (Amnesty International 1989: 15). In 1987, a truth commission was established to investigate human rights abuses committed until 1986 (Republic of Uganda 1994). Furthermore, an Office of the Inspector General of Government (IGG) was created and charged with the investigation of current human rights abuses and corruption. However, the IGG generally shied away from going beyond isolated cases and avoided issues of national significance (Oloka-Onyango 1993). Additionally, forces within the NRM government successfully limited the impact of the IGG, most significantly by removing Waswa Lule, a staunch supporter of the human rights mandate, from the post of the

[29] The prescriptive status was not perfect. In a discussion with representatives of the New York Bar Association, Museveni held in 1990 that the traditional court system was corrupt and that the investigative abilities of the police were not adequate to always protect "Western-style" principles of law including the presumption of innocence. He argued that law enforcement personnel would often fail to identify and punish criminals under the present system (Busuttil *et al.* 1991: 666).

Deputy IGG in 1992. The donor community continued to apply hardly any pressure in the Ugandan case. For the United States, Museveni was a reliable ally against Islamic fundamentalism in Sudan, for the International Monetary Fund he delivered relatively stable economic conditions and exceptional growth rates, and for the rest of the Western community he simply represented a new "breed of African leadership."

Despite a consistent rhetorical commitment to human rights and some initial efforts to institutionalize human rights safeguards after 1986, the police and the military remained the main perpetrators of ongoing violations. Although the extent of abuses was nowhere near the levels of previous regimes, such problems persisted with regard to the treatment of radical opposition members and during counter-insurgency operations mainly in the northern part of the country. Although general network mobilization fell sharply after 1986, Amnesty International maintained a critical stand and engaged the new government in a continuous discourse. Several human rights reports (Amnesty International 1989, 1990d, 1991, 1994d) by the organization finally culminated in a nineteen-page report to the United Nations Human Rights Commission. Based on the information, the commission decided in 1992 to start a second investigation on the Ugandan human rights situation based on the confidential 1503 procedure.

The action taken by the United Nations body based on information by Amnesty International did not miss its sensitive target. By presidential order, President Museveni established in the middle of 1992 a Human Rights Desk in the Ministry of Justice. The government embarked on a further institutionalization of human rights safeguards which culminated in 1995 in the ratification of the International Covenant for Civil and Political Rights (Republic of Uganda 1995a), a significantly extended constitutional Bill of Rights, and the establishment of the Uganda Human Rights Commission (UHRC). In contrast to the IGG the UHRC enjoys greater formal independence and has powers equivalent to the judiciary. On its own initiative, members of the UHRC visited dozens of prisons throughout the country and processed in 1997 a total of 352 complaints mostly relating to unlawful arrests, detention, and torture. The annual report for 1997 detailed many cases of mistreatment and the measures taken by UHRC. It criticized the Ugandan army and the Internal Security Organ (ISO) for still detaining people, although the constitution explicitly banned all state agencies except for the regular police from arresting suspects. On several occasions during the year, the chairperson of UHRC, Margaret Sekaggya, openly criticized the government on human rights issues (*The Monitor*, August 25, 1998, p. 1). In contrast to Kenya, the cause of human rights in Uganda is mainly promoted by an ongoing process of "top-down" institutionalization. This does not mean that domestic non-governmental organizations such as the Foundation for Human Rights Initiative (FHRI) make no difference, but "the vast majority of NGOs in Uganda steer clear of issues they perceive as too controversial" (Oloka-Onyango 1996: 382).

With respect to the still ongoing investigation at the UN Human Rights Commission, the government finally presented in 1995 a 49-page response (Republic of Uganda 1995b). The report pointed out, that "Amnesty generally has a proper appreciation of the country's human rights situation" and had been "accorded maximum co-operation" (ibid.: 2). "Obviously, everybody of good will should support the intentions and objectives of it's [Amnesty's] work" (ibid.: 25). Furthermore, obvious abuses committed by government agencies were not denied, but compensation was promised to the victims and their families. Following the presentation of the written response the UN body was satisfied and voted to discontinue the investigation without further action.

Since 1995, the focus of the human rights network has significantly shifted away from an exclusive attention to government-sponsored human rights abuses. Increasingly, rebel groups became the target of human rights criticism (Amnesty International 1997a; Human Rights Watch/Africa 1997c). In particular, the Lord's Resistance Army (LRA) is now at the center of attention and accused of having abducted close to 10,000 children since 1994. At the same time, Amnesty International accused the Sudanese government of supporting the LRA and its war against children.[30] Again, the non-governmental network first mobilized a UN institution. Early on, UNICEF contributed financial resources to the trauma centers and repeated the accusations brought forward by Amnesty International and Human Rights Watch against the LRA and Sudan. UNICEF and World Vision claimed in a joint publication that the rebels had abducted 6,000 to 8,000 children over the last four years and were carrying out "a psychotic war on children" (Muhumuza 1997). In September 1997, the Sudanese government accused the Executive Director of UNICEF, Carol Bellamy, of going "beyond her mandate as an international servant of the United Na-

---

[30] Since 1995, the international children's NGO World Vision treated hundreds of children in its trauma centers in Gulu and Kiryandongo.

tions." On December 10, 1997, US Secretary of State Madeleine Albright visited the World Vision trauma center in Gulu and used the occasion to pledge unconditional support for Uganda's military fight against human rights violating rebels. This time, Western support was easily mobilized because the United States government was quite happy to find another cause for its fight against the Islamic fundamentalist regime in Khartoum.

In early 1998, UNICEF brought the accusations against the LRA to the United Nations Human Rights Commission. On April 22, 1998, the Human Rights Commission demanded "the immediate cessation of all abductions and attacks on all civilian populations and in particular women and children, in northern Uganda by the Lord's Resistance Army" (Resolution 1998/75; 24 in favor, 1 against, 27 abstentions). Again, the transnational human rights network was responsible for putting the issue on the international agenda in the first place. However, this much celebrated issue of child abduction has diverted international attention away from other domestic human rights issues in Uganda.

Despite today's impressive prescriptive status and progress in rule-consistent behavior, questions have to be raised about the sustainability of the positive changes. Museveni himself and the army under his control still remain as the main guarantors of peace and stability, as they did for the last ten years. On the one hand, the "benevolent dictator" Museveni controls the army and the country and, hence, guarantees general respect for human rights. Indeed, only by taking this course in 1986 did Museveni bring down human rights abuses as quickly as he did. On the other hand, the same arrangement inhibits the development of democratic institutional arrangements, which are necessary to safeguard human rights in the long term and particularly after Museveni leaves office. Thus, the most important human rights concern in Uganda today is the government's negative attitude towards political pluralism and the insurgencies in the Northern and Western parts of the country.

In light of the regional security threats, the NRM's continued promotion of human rights issues poses a challenge to theories which discount the role of norms in constituting the interests of actors. While neither the rhetoric nor the behavior completely match the content of international human rights norms, the process of domestic institutionalization and habitualization after 1986 clearly testifies to the significance of transnational human rights networks.

Conclusions: comparing the case studies and evaluating alternative explanations

Processes of political change in Uganda and Kenya during the 1980s and 1990s cannot be understood without taking into account the independent influence of international human rights norms and their active promotion by transnational networks of non-governmental actors. In both cases, these networks played a crucial role in transferring the human rights norms into a domestic context by protecting, empowering, and even creating local groups and activists. On the international level, the human rights network changed general perceptions of the target countries by means of moral-consciousness raising and persuasion. As a result, a socialization process within the target countries was set in motion that also affected the criticized governments. Despite strategic adaptation and the abundant use of empty rhetoric, we can observe processes of institutionalization and habitualization in the Kenyan case. Moreover, the recent invitation of an Amnesty International delegation and the changing human rights rhetoric of the government can not be explained with reference to an instrumentalist analytical framework. Once human rights networks get a foot in the door, they contribute to the internalization of norms because they constantly highlight perceived gaps between rhetoric and reality. I argue here that those network actors and Kenyan government officials have begun to engage in a discourse about competing truth claims rather than a mere exchange of information about their respective preferences.

For two reasons, comparing this case to neighboring Uganda is particularly instructive. First, systematic human rights violations began in Uganda ten years earlier than in Kenya. This offers an interesting variation with respect to the strength of transnational human rights NGOs. In both cases, organizations such as Amnesty International were quick in alerting the international public to the humanitarian crises. However, in the 1970s and early 1980s the international response to the reports on Uganda was generally much slower than later in the mid-1980s in the case of Kenya. Considering that the human rights abuses perpetrated by the Amin and the second Obote regime were much worse than under Kenyatta and arap Moi, we must conclude that the transnational mobilization in these earlier cases did not have the same kind of success as in Kenya in the mid- and late 1980s.

Second, between 1981 and 1985 the abuses in Uganda were mainly the result of a full-fledged civil war within the country. Between 1986 and today, ongoing insurgencies mainly in the north continued to be the main reason for human rights abuses. In contrast, the Kenyan independence governments have never experienced such large-scale armed opposition. The domestic security situation in Uganda has always been much more fragile than in Kenya simply because of strong regional interdependencies. Political events in Rwanda, former Zaire, and Sudan often have direct consequences for Ugandans, while Kenya has been more successful in maintaining domestic stability despite political turmoil in neighboring countries. In the Ugandan case, the end of a civil war in 1986 certainly improved the human rights situation dramatically. However this success was predicated on the adoption of certain minimal human rights standards by the rebels and the parallel delegitimization of the government internally and externally. After 1986, the new NRM government continued to implement human rights standards even after it had solidified its overall domestic power position. Again, this reflects a process of norm socialization where transnational human rights groups played a crucial role.

In contrast, alternative explanations based on the (neo-) realist school (great power pressure) and the modernization paradigm (socio-economic development) would not have predicted any of the changes described above. Realism explains human rights change in a given country with reference to the influence of dominant state actors in the international system (Krasner 1993). Although these actors did play some role with respect to Kenya and Uganda, a (neo-) realist explanation is ultimately misleading. First, the pressure put upon the human rights violating governments was most of the time marginal and never consistent. Second, the bilateral and multilateral pressure, which did finally materialize with respect to both countries, was in many cases preceded and caused by the activities of the human rights network. Both case studies allow for the conclusion that human rights networks have varying success in lobbying donor governments, but became generally more influential over the last twenty years. Abundant and well-researched documentation of human rights abuses was available for the Amin government since the early 1970s, the second Obote government since 1981–1982 and the arap Moi regime since 1985–1986. The main donors' responses to those facts varied widely. While Great Britain as the former colonial power remained relatively reluctant throughout the period, the United States government and other European nations were more open to the arguments advanced by non-governmental human rights lobbyists. However, the comparison also shows that donor governments themselves became socialized into the human rights discourse over a period of nearly twenty-five years. Following the increasing strength of the transnational human rights network, Western governments responded more quickly to its activities. At the very minimum, representatives from aid agencies and Foreign Offices now found themselves forced to defend their continued cooperation with human rights violating regimes throughout the world.

In the 1970s, Britain imposed sanctions against Amin not because of his human rights record, but because the British government perceived the expropriation of British and Asian businesses and the alliance with Libya as a major threat to its economic and strategic interests. A few years later, the British government changed its general attitude towards Obote only days before he was again violently removed from power. Similarly, Britain's support for Moi only crumbled in October 1991 when the Commonwealth Summit in Harare established democratic governance as a common goal of the member states.

Representatives from the United States government were usually much more outspoken when it came to gross human rights violations, but this was hardly followed by consistent pressure. In the mid-1970s the United States replaced Great Britain as the main trading partner of Amin's Uganda. Trade embargoes demanded by Congress in 1978 and 1984 never went into force. The same kind of gap between rhetoric and action became visible with respect to Kenya in the early 1990s. Here, the contradictions expressed themselves in the substantial disagreements between an outspoken ambassador and his State Department bureaucracy at home. At three crucial moments between 1990 and 1992, the US government needed Kenyan support: during the Gulf War in 1990, when Kenya hosted Libyan dissidents in early 1991, and when the US government decided to intervene in Somalia in 1992. Nonetheless, even prior to the end of the Cold War the foreign aid given by the United States was consistently shifted away from Kenyan governmental recipients to the non-governmental sector. This increasing support for civil society reflected a fundamental normative paradigm shift within the global foreign-aid establishment, which also responded to the activities of the transnational human rights network.

The evidence presented here also contradicts a distinct domestic perspective based on ideas associated with the modernization school. Modernization theorists argue that domestic political change is the ultimate result of growing incomes and functional differentiation (Lipset 1959). However, the economic situation in both countries either stagnated or deteriorated significantly during the periods under scrutiny. Both countries are consistently in the group of the poorest nations. In 1997 levels of GNP per capita were $240 for Uganda and $280 for Kenya (World Bank 1997: 214–247). Thus, both are well below any of the threshold levels favored by modernization authors (e.g. Huntington 1991: 63). Hence, there is simply no significant change in the independent variable to account for the described political changes or the certainly significant differences between Kenya and Uganda. Instead, the results could be even interpreted in support of an inverse causal relationship. Basic respect for human rights was followed by exceptional rates of economic growth in Uganda (on average 6.4 percent in GNP since 1986), while relatively deteriorating human rights conditions in Kenya were accompanied by economic decline. Certainly, the limited scope of the study can not be used to confirm either of the causal paths, but it clearly challenges claims about economic growth as a precondition for democratic change (see also Przeworski and Limongi 1997).

Finally, the question arises, whether the described changes are sustainable and whether they fundamentally affected the underlying causes of the systematic human rights abuses. Thus, a comparison between Kenya and Uganda also needs to address the fact of uneven levels of domestic and international mobilization with respect to both countries. If it is true that continued non-governmental network activities are a necessary condition for human rights improvements and their sustainability, then Kenya represents a perfect case of high internal and external mobilization. At first, this seems puzzling, because human rights conditions have never deteriorated to the level of abuses known from infamous places like Argentina, Chile, the Philippines, Guatemala, or Uganda. Thus, after an initial period of mobilization, network activities do not seem to systematically follow increasing repression levels. Instead, some other factors characterizing the situation of Kenya, apart from the systematic human rights abuses, additionally contributed to network mobilization.

First, the Kenya government never totally cut off information flows in and out of the country. Despite occasional official threats directed at foreign journalists, Nairobi always served as the base for all major international media agencies between Cairo and Cape Town. Naturally, this also contributed to comparatively higher reporting from the host country. Second, independent Kenya generally experienced political stability and comparatively positive economic development until the mid-1980s. The reservoir for politically active and Western-trained intellectuals remained intact and contributed to the sharp increase of societal mobilization from 1987 to 1991. By African standards, tourism and strategic Western interests kept the country continuously on the international agenda. Third, competition for funding became an issue when an increasing number of international human rights organizations appeared on the scene in the 1980s. In the face of limited resources, countries like Kenya became a target simply because reports on it promised to find more publicity than other, more remote countries. Only this can explain why Kenya continues to attract an exceptional amount of international attention. The very fact that Kenya was always portrayed as a reliable Western ally and stable country contributed to the success of human rights organizations' efforts to replace this picture with the opposite. The greater the contrast to dominant perceptions in the international arena, the greater the expected attention from the targeted audience. Finally, a considerable measure of path dependency with respect to network activities also contributed to the fact that Kenya moved into the limelight of international attention. Transnational human rights organizations gained mainly international recognition and prominence because they pointed their fingers at authoritarian regimes at the fringes of the Western alliance. They exploited the tension between the rhetorical claim to be part of a liberal community of states and ongoing violations of constitutive liberal values internally. Target states included Portugal and Greece in the 1960s and South American dictatorships in the 1970s. In the 1980s, Kenya became another case fitting this logic.

Most of these conditions have not been present or were less developed in the Ugandan case. Nonetheless, today Uganda clearly leads Kenya with regard to the phase model. This is explained by the later mobilization in the Kenyan case and the ability of the arap Moi government to outmaneuver the clamor for political reforms by calling multiparty elections in 1992. Thus, the donor pressure in 1991 was instrumental in allowing arap Moi to undermine the more hazardous human rights discourse and open the arena of political contestation, where donors failed to secure a level playing field. This does not mean that political conditionality as such is doomed under any circumstances, but in the Kenyan case the donor policy partly enabled the regime to identify mounting domestic pressure for reforms with the agenda of "outsiders." Still, at that point domestic actors had been established and empowered by international human rights norms and the transnational network. Having survived donor pressure, the Kenyan government is slowly losing the rhetorical battle against these principled human rights agents. Most importantly here, previous arguments labeling criticism as foreign intrusion and pointing at South Africa lost their power. True, a sophisticated neorealist might again point to the fact that these domestic NGOs largely survive on donor funding from the outside. However, only the transnational human rights network provides them with the crucial ideational framework that ultimately turns material capabilities into purposeful action.

Still, the claims made by this chapter result in more optimistic expectations concerning the future sustainability of the changes in Kenya than in Uganda.[31] Most parts of the Kenyan society have gone through many years of intensive socialization by international human rights norms and transnational networks. In contrast, the Ugandan situation is marked by the military victory of a section of society, which has promoted human rights not solely as a matter of principled belief, but also as a means to attain political power. Only afterwards, a weak process of continuous socialization from above has been set in motion. After 1986, repression, mobilization, and general attention by Western media abated and it became difficult to sustain human rights socialization on a broader scale. In contrast to the high levels of domestic and international human rights mobilization in Kenya, indigenous human rights organizations in Uganda are still relatively weak and the general societal mobilization for the issue comparatively low. In Kenya, sustainable respect for human rights is largely a matter of socializing the government. In Uganda, the government-led process of implementing a particular set of human rights still needs to be supplemented by the combination of growing societal awareness and transnational activism beyond responding to immediate crisis and violations of human rights. Even when countries have reached the final stage of our phase model, the broadening of the socialization process will continue to be a necessary condition for sustainability. In Kenya and Uganda this process has still to include large sections of the population outside of the respective capitals and the privileged elite.

---

[31] This result is in line with the argument put forward by Michael Bratton and Nicolas van de Walle who predicted that "regimes with previous experience in political rights ... commonly make less dramatic gains but end up with a greater measure of democracy" than countries with a historical experience marked by uncompromised authoritarian rule (Bratton and van de Walle 1997: 273).

3 The long and winding road: International norms and domestic political change in South Africa
David Black

Introduction

South Africa's transition from the racial authoritarianism of the apartheid era to the non-racial democratic institutions and entrenched constitutional rights of the post-1994 period is widely regarded as one of the great human rights triumphs of the post-Second World War era. There is considerable truth in this perception. Moreover, the manner in which the struggle against apartheid was prosecuted does much to support the validity and relevance of the "spiral model" of human rights socialization and change proposed by Risse and Sikkink in the introductory chapter. From a very early stage, the struggle against apartheid was internationalized. Transnational principled issue networks composed of both state and non-state actors worked with South African opposition groups at home and in exile to bring pressure to bear, through international organizations, on the apartheid state. This pressure, combined with mounting domestic resistance, ultimately precipitated the abandonment of race-based minority rule and the subsequent adoption through negotiation of a political and constitutional order firmly rooted in international standards of human rights and liberal democracy. Indeed, given the early and prolonged nature of the international struggle against apartheid, I would go further: South Africa served as a vital precedent for the processes of transnational human rights activism and advancement explored in the other cases in this book.

Yet, in several important respects, the South African case challenges and extends the spiral model. While it adds to the cumulative understanding of how transnational activism can promote change in support of human rights norms, therefore, one must be cautious in treating South Africa as an archetype. Several distinctive features of the South African case bear emphasis, including the location of agency in "Third World"

78

states and organizations versus Western ones, and in relatively small versus major Western powers. Finally, the South African case demonstrates that the process of transnational human rights socialization embodied in the spiral model can have conservative, de-radicalizing implications as well as socially progressive ones in the "target" state.

To develop these points, I will begin by discussing the ways in which the struggle against apartheid, while clearly fitting within the broader struggle to advance human rights norms in the post-Second World War world, in fact relied significantly on a narrower normative basis and a broader ideological and strategic one for purposes of transnational mobilization. In short, to understand the ultimate success of anti-apartheid mobilization, one needs to understand its roots in the norms of anti-racism and anti-colonial self-determination, as well the support it derived from states and groups with more radical – indeed revolutionary – goals. I then trace the development of pressure for change in South Africa through four historical "Acts": the prelude to and repercussions of the Sharpeville massacre in 1960; the Soweto massacre and the national rebellion which followed in 1976–1977; the developments leading up to and surrounding the insurrection of the mid-1980s; and the negotiated transition of 1990 to 1994. These Acts broadly conform to the five phases of the spiral model, although in a particularly protracted manner and with overlap between the anticipated elements of each phase. Thus, the period up to Sharpeville (Act I) was marked by escalating repression and domestic and early international mobilization, while the post-Sharpeville period was dominated by denial and, eventually, renewed mobilization; the post-Soweto period (Acts II and III) was marked by tactical concessions, leading to renewed resistance, repression, and diminished options for the South African state; and the negotiated transition (Act IV) featured the acceptance by the leading protagonists of the prescriptive status of dominant international human rights norms, with rule-consistent behavior predominating in the post-1994 (post-apartheid) period.

Why pick on apartheid? The "uniqueness" of South Africa

The year 1948 is doubly significant in the South African case: it is the year in which the Universal Declaration of Human Rights was adopted; and it is the year the National Party (NP) was elected by the white electorate of South Africa, thereby setting the country off in the opposite direction to post-war global human rights norms. The post-1948 government was responsible for a multitude of increasingly systematic human rights violations in the course of initiating, elaborating, and defending its system of apartheid. A partial list would include: arbitrary arrests and detentions without trial; the denial of basic civil and political rights to more than three-quarters of its people; systematic press censorship; denial of equal social and economic rights and opportunities to its people; and torture and extra-judicial executions, the full extent of which has been starkly revealed by the post-apartheid Truth and Reconciliation Commission (Donnelly 1993: 69–76; Ignatieff 1997). What set South Africa apart from all other human rights violators, however, and placed its domestic policies firmly on the international agenda well ahead of the other cases explored in this book, was its institutionalization of systemic, white-on-black racism. In other words, what marked South Africa off as "uniquely evil" and liable to increasing international opprobrium and isolation was its denial of equal civil, political, social, and economic rights solely on the basis of *race*.[1] Well before most human rights violations, however egregious, came to be viewed as legitimate bases for international concern over the internal affairs of a sovereign state, South Africa was marked out by many (though by no means all) in the international community as a legitimate target for external interventions on the normative grounds of anti-racism (Klotz 1995).

It is significant in this context that international criticism and isolation of apartheid South Africa was justified not simply on the basis of the Universal Declaration and the Conventions on Civil and Political and Economic and Social Rights; rather it was buttressed by discrete Conventions on the Elimination of All Forms of Racial Discrimination (1965) and the Suppression and Punishment of the Crime of Apartheid (1973). The practical consequence of this distinct normative basis for action was that the campaign against apartheid was ultimately able to mobilize a broader base of supporters than virtually any other human rights campaign to date. Predictably enough, "traditional" human rights advocates based in the West, including human rights non-governmental organizations (NGOs) and some governments, became critics and opponents of the South African government. In addition,

---

[1] Kenneth Grundy, encapsulating much anti-apartheid thinking, summarized in 1991 that "advocates of disengagement point to the uniqueness of South Africa's racial order" (Grundy 1991: 96).

however, the campaign not only incorporated but was largely spear-headed by "Third World" state and non-state actors animated by the evil of apartheid racism (Black 1997). In the case of African states and organizations, moreover, the norm of anti-racism was strongly reinforced by pan-Africanism, the single most important manifestation of which was opposition to white minority rule (Klotz 1995: 73–90).

The international campaign against apartheid was also related to, and animated by, the wider anti-colonial struggle for self-determination. When this struggle began to bear fruit, as early as 1946 but especially after 1960, South Africa was the largest and most powerful of several white-minority-ruled colonial regimes in Southern Africa. Each of its white-ruled neighbors – Rhodesia/Zimbabwe, Angola, Mozambique – became objects of prolonged internal struggles for self-determination, supported by external solidarity groups and sympathetic, often Soviet-aligned, states. As this white *cordon sanitaire* crumbled, piece by piece, international opposition increasingly focused on the settler regime in South Africa. While the latter, a self-governing dominion within the British Empire since 1910, was distinct from more conventional anti-colonial struggles, it was also widely regarded as morally equivalent – a form of "internal colonialism."

This underscores a significant difference in the stakes and issues of the South African case from many other human rights campaigns. What was at issue here was, in the perception of many Afrikaners at least, a "national question." Apartheid was constructed as a project of national self-determination for Afrikaners, while the struggle against it was seen by many of them as a zero-sum conflict in which their collective survival as a *volk* was at stake. In other words, apartheid can be understood at least in part through the prism of "identity politics" which, as more recent experiences in the former Yugoslavia and Rwanda (among others) have demonstrated, is particularly resistant to compromise and amenable to extremism. This helps to account for the particularly prolonged and determined effort of the South African government to maintain the essence of apartheid and, in the negotiation phase, their dogged (though finally unsuccessful) campaign to maintain some form of protection for "group rights" in the new South Africa.

Even less ambiguously, anti-colonial opposition to the South African regime was also mobilized around the struggle for Namibian independence. South Africa had gained control over the then German South West Africa as a League of Nations Mandate territory after the First World War. After the Second World War, it first sought unsuccessfully to annex the territory, and then refused to submit to the United Nations' successor Trusteeship system. This prompted the UN, principally through the General Assembly, to adopt an increasingly strident stand against South Africa's continued occupation of Namibia, ruled illegal in a 1971 advisory opinion of the International Court of Justice (see Mbuende 1986; Grovogni 1996). While the complex "Namibian Question" is beyond the scope of this chapter, and was always subordinate to the main game in South Africa itself, it doubtless reinforced the campaign to punish Pretoria. (Conversely, the South African government was able to gain a diplomatic respite in 1989 and 1990 by finally acquiescing to the UN-supervised transition to Namibian independence.)

Finally, the transnational coalition of forces opposed to apartheid needs to be situated in the context of the revolutionary aspirations of a good many of the South African government's opponents, both domestic and international, state and non-state. This factor is not unique to South Africa, of course, though its manifestations there were distinctive. In the first place, the anti-apartheid cause gained important support in international organizations from the Soviet Union and its East Bloc allies, and exiled South African opponents of the regime gained vital moral and material support from these countries. Especially in light of the apartheid regime's virulent anti-communism and South Africa's rich endowment of strategic minerals, this consideration greatly attenuated any anti-apartheid instincts within Western capitals – most particularly Washington. Secondly, at the transnational level, an influential minority of anti-apartheid activists in the Western world and a growing number of its opponents within South Africa were committed to a much more radical, indeed revolutionary, transformation of South Africa than that embodied in "universal" human rights norms. Their goal, in short, was socialism – however vaguely defined it might be in the South African context (Marx 1992: 223–224; Saul 1993). There were many, therefore, who saw the South Africa of the mid-1980s as ripe for revolution. Indeed, as we will argue in our discussion of the transitional period, a good many of the latter-day converts to sanctions against apartheid in Western capitals were strongly motivated by the goal of preempting a much more radical, threatening outcome through the promotion of a moderate, liberal one in keeping with basic civil and political human rights norms. In this they were largely successful.

Act I: Sharpeville and beyond

It is symptomatic of the early, precedent-setting character of the transnational campaign for change in South Africa, as well as the determination of the apartheid regime to defend its racially based social order, that it took two major "throws," or "particularly awesome violations of human rights" (introductory chapter, p. 22), for the boomerang pattern described in the spiral model to take hold. The first of these took place in the southern Transvaal African township of Sharpeville on March 21, 1960. A new opposition organization, the Pan-Africanist Congress (PAC), tried to steal a march on the more established African National Congress (ANC) by calling an anti-Pass-law rally for that day; panicky police responded by firing on unarmed demonstrators, killing sixty-nine and wounding hundreds more. Other protestors were killed in two townships outside of Cape Town. The result was massive domestic protests and widespread international outrage. Dan O'Meara recounts that the United Nations subsequently declared March 21 to be the International Day Against Racism, and that huge rallies against apartheid in London effectively launched the nascent British Anti-Apartheid Movement (AAM) (O'Meara 1996: 100–101). Sharpeville can therefore be seen as the axis between the first two phases of the spiral model: repression and early international mobilization on the one hand, and denial and enhanced international mobilization on the other.

The international outcry over Sharpeville in 1960 was not the first time South Africa's domestic racial policies had been subject to international scrutiny and criticism. As early as 1946, the Indian government raised Pretoria's treatment of Indian nationals resident in South Africa at the first session of the United Nations. India also broke off trade relations and withdrew its High Commissioner (the British Commonwealth equivalent of an Ambassador) the same year. Throughout the 1950s, South Africa's racial policies were raised in the then Western-dominated General Assembly. Despite the accumulation of increasingly draconian apartheid legislation under the NP government and mounting domestic opposition (Mandela 1994: 83–208), however, South Africa's insistence that these policies fell within its domestic jurisdiction meant that it was gently treated by the Assembly majority (Klotz 1995: 41–43; Vandenbosch 1970).

In the years following Sharpeville, international criticism sharpened and diplomatic sanctions began (Klotz forthcoming; United Nations Department of Public Information 1994). The driving force behind this growing pressure from international organizations was the newly de-colonized bloc of African states, in conjunction with other "Third World" countries and the Soviet bloc. The apartheid issue was first considered by the UN Security Council after Sharpeville, and the Council subsequently recommended an arms embargo in 1963. South Africa's membership in numerous UN organizations, including the Economic and Social Council, the World Health Organization, and even the Universal Postal Union, was either restricted or suspended. The UN also sponsored a plethora of anti-apartheid information activities through the Special Committee on Apartheid, established in 1962. Finally, in 1974, the Third World majority in the General Assembly succeeded in having South Africa suspended by rejecting the diplomatic credentials of its representatives.[2] The 1965 Convention on the Elimination of All Forms of Racial Discrimination (in force since 1969) and the 1973 Convention on the Suppression and Punishment of the Crime of Apartheid (in force from 1976) provided normative under-pinnings for these actions.

The country's diplomatic isolation grew in other fora as well. Following the white electorate's narrow ratification of republican status in a 1960 referendum, South Africa was effectively forced to withdraw from the Commonwealth in 1961. While both Britain and Australia defended the new republic's right to retain membership, African member-states in particular made it clear that they would not remain within a Commonwealth which included apartheid South Africa. The Canadian government, led by a self-conscious civil libertarian, John Diefenbaker, played an ambiguous role at the 1961 Prime Ministers' Conference, but was ultimately pivotal in precipitating Pretoria's withdrawal. Diefenbaker's role subsequently attained mythical status in the history of Canadian foreign policy and laid the groundwork for the activism of the Mulroney government in the 1980s (Tennyson 1982; Freeman 1997: 19–29 and 149–165).

Similarly, the Organization of African Unity (OAU) refused membership to South Africa and other white minority regimes from its inception in 1963, reflecting its constitutive commitment to racial equality (Klotz 1995: 74–80). Moreover, while lobbying consistently for sanctions, it extended international recognition to the ANC, PAC, and other exiled liberation movements, and provided them with material and

---

[2] See General Assembly, A/RES/3207 (XXIX), 30 September 1974, and General Assembly, A/PV.2281, November 12, 1974 in United Nations Department of Public Information 1994: 332–333.

moral support through its Liberation Committee, headquartered in Dar es Salaam.

These liberation movements, meanwhile, initiated a "diplomacy of liberation" shortly after their banning by the South African government in the wake of Sharpeville (Vale 1997: 197–205). In the developing world, and within the UN and OAU, they operated largely at the level of inter-state diplomacy. In the Western world, by contrast, they focused on working with and promoting national and transnational networks of non-governmental organizations, including churches, trade unions, and solidarity groups constituted specifically to support the struggle against minority rule in South and Southern Africa. Groups such as the AAM and the International Defense and Aid Fund (IDAF) in Britain, the Toronto Committee for the Liberation of Southern Africa (TCLSAC) in Canada, Citizens Association for Racial Equality (CARE) in New Zealand and, later, TransAfrica in the United States, to name but a few, became linchpins in the transnational anti-apartheid movement – a quintessential principled issue network. A striking early success for this network – more particularly for the sport boycott movement spearheaded by the small group of South African exiles who formed the South African Non-Racial Olympic Committee – was the expulsion of the sports-mad republic from the Olympic Movement in 1968 (Black forthcoming). Similarly, for the World Council of Churches and other Christian organizations, the South African Dutch Reformed Church's crucial role in providing a theological justification for apartheid was a profound affront, prompting early and sustained opposition. Yet partly because some anti-apartheid solidarity groups (and the liberation movements themselves) had strong leftist elements, and came to favor armed struggle against minority regimes, they had only a limited impact on most Western governments through the remainder of the 1960s and the first half of the 1970s. Countries such as the United States, Britain, West Germany, Japan, and Canada, while escalating their rhetorical criticism of apartheid, remained firmly opposed to economic or diplomatic sanctions – and thus came to be widely regarded as effective allies of the apartheid regime. The major exceptions, even at this early stage, were the governments of the Nordic countries. Most strikingly, Sweden, Norway, and Denmark developed close and supportive relationships with exiled liberation movements, providing them with direct material assistance, beginning with Sweden in 1969 (Black 1992). Similarly, the government of Sweden provided direct support to the national "non-governmental" anti-apartheid coalition, the Isolate South Africa Committee (ISAK).

Thus, the South African government was increasingly isolated within Africa and the developing world from 1960 onwards, and was the target of mounting criticism by activists in the Western world as well. Yet it retained strong economic, social, and strategic links with those countries which mattered most to white South Africans economically and socio-culturally. Indeed, to many policy makers at the core of the Western world, South Africa was seen as a bulwark against communism in a key strategic location, controlling important strategic minerals and the "Cape Route" for ocean-bound trade. South Africa responded to these early, if still limited, international and transnational pressures with a blend of denial and repression, but also reforms aimed at legitimizing apartheid policies internationally.

Outwardly, South Africa forcefully and predictably denied that the international community had any right to interfere in its domestic affairs. At this stage, the Western countries on which Pretoria relied most heavily largely accepted this view. Thus, the adoption of non-binding military sanctions by the Security Council in 1963 had to be justified on the grounds that "the situation in South Africa is seriously disturbing international peace and security" (cited in Klotz 1995: 50). Moreover, much of the rest of the international community implicitly acknowledged the force of this defense by attempting to build a normative case for the exceptional nature of the "crime of apartheid" – that is, as opposed to "normal" human rights violations.

Inwardly, the South African government's response was a harsh crackdown on all domestic opposition. Within days of the Sharpeville massacre and the massive demonstrations it triggered, the government declared a state of emergency, arresting nearly 2,000 ANC and PAC activists and outlawing the principal vehicles for domestic (especially black) opposition – the ANC, PAC and the South African Communist Party (SACP). While the ANC subsequently abandoned its policy of non-violence and launched a campaign of sabotage through its newly created armed wing, Umkhonto we Sizwe (or MK – the Spear of the Nation), this campaign was largely ineffectual. It virtually collapsed when the head of MK, Nelson Mandela, and his key co-conspirators were captured in 1962, and sentenced to life in prison in 1964 (see Grundy 1991: 155–158; Mandela 1994: 231–330). The remainder of the decade and the first few years of the 1970s seemed to testify to the success of this repressive strategy. During these "golden years of apartheid" (O'Meara 1996: 116) or "years of confidence" (Barber and Barratt 1990: 105–171), white South Africa enjoyed political calm and unprecedented rates of economic growth.

Yet even in these "golden years," and indeed prior to them, the government demonstrated some degree of sensitivity to the cries of international opposition, making several significant reforms in an effort to persuade at least its important external supporters of the legitimacy of its domestic policies. This points to a key difference between the South African government and several other of the repressive regimes examined in this book. As the government of a self-consciously "Western" or "European" polity, the National Party regime never denied the validity of key international and liberal norms such as self-determination, the rule of law, or representative democracy. Rather it sought, both through its rhetoric and its reforms, to re-interpret these norms and principles (often virtually beyond recognition) in an effort to persuade external observers that its policies in fact conformed with them.

The first and most important "reform" reflected its failure to comprehend the changing currents of world politics. The Bantu Self Government Act of May 1959 laid the groundwork for the subsequent creation of the self-governing homelands, and Prime Minister Hendrik Verwoerd's vision of "grand apartheid." Initially, Verwoerd did not foresee these homelands becoming states or even self-governing territories, but following Sharpeville and the escalation of international pressure, he announced in April 1961 the government's intention of extending self-government, with the ultimate goal of independence for these "nations." All Africans in South Africa would become citizens of some ten independent states occupying 13 percent of the country's territory. Along with its domestic implications, this scheme was conceived as a means of demonstrating the government's adherence to the post-war norm of national self-determination. Indeed, Barber and Barratt recount a meeting between Verwoerd and ambassadors and senior foreign-service officers where he outlined these plans. The officers "emerged elated, convinced that they had a policy that could be defended abroad because it offered justice to Africans" (Barber and Barratt 1990: 95). Self-government was steadily extended to the homelands and, beginning with the Transkei in 1976, several were declared "independent." But the scheme failed to win any significant international support or legitimacy and by the early 1980s was increasingly recognized as an elaborate and expensive failure (Klotz forthcoming).

In other ways, too, the government demonstrated its sensitivity to international criticism and isolation. This was especially true after Verwoerd's assassination and the emergence of the less dogmatic John Vorster as prime minister in 1966. Vorster attempted to engineer an "outward oriented" foreign policy, and limited reforms which would place a more acceptable external face on the country's apartheid policies. A symbolically important example of the latter was a number of steps taken to try to win reacceptance into international sport. With South Africa expelled from the Olympic movement and in danger of isolation in rugby and cricket – the sports white South Africans valued most – Vorster's government reversed long-standing NP policy to announce that visiting international teams would henceforth be allowed to include "non-white" members. This policy shift was the trigger for the first split between *verkrampte* (conservative) and *verligte* ("enlightened") members of the NP, with a rump of ultra-*verkrampte* members of parliament withdrawing to form the Herstigte Nasionale Party (Reconstituted Nationalist Party) in 1969. From 1971 onwards, the government introduced and gradually extended a policy of "multinational" sport, designed to foster the impression of integration abroad, while cleaving to the vision of grand apartheid at home (Black forthcoming; Guelke 1986; O'Meara 1996: 159–164). Even these small concessions, however, began to erode the ideological basis for the racialist vision of apartheid.

Thus, even during apartheid's golden age, when the government's domestic control seemed firm, the activism of South Africans in exile and the growing international and transnational anti-apartheid movement was sufficiently troubling to elicit controversial if duplicitous policy reforms. In the mid-1970s, the state was confronted with a new and more sustained challenge, responding with true tactical concessions.

Act II: Soweto and beyond

The second and ultimately decisive boomerang "throw" came in 1976–1977 with the events unleashed by the Soweto massacre of June 16, 1976, in which sixty-nine students were killed by police when converging on a demonstration against the imposition of Afrikaans as the language of mathematics instruction in black schools. Within days, violent insurrections were underway in townships across the country. Importantly, these now extended to the "Coloured" (mixed-race) areas of the Western Cape, bridging a key racial division which the state had worked hard to entrench and exploit. Despite a harsh government crackdown, the insurrection was sustained for months. As summarized by Anthony Marx,

> Before they were quelled by continued repression, protests had been staged in townships throughout South Africa, and a quarter-million students had boycotted classes, leaving one thousand dead and twenty-one thousand prosecuted for related offenses by September 1977.　　　　　　　　　　　　　　　　　　　(Marx 1992: 69)

This was by far the most extensive mobilization in South African history, and it prompted a surge of international scrutiny and condemnation. This international reaction was heightened by the death of Black Consciousness leader Steve Biko at the hands of state security forces on September 12, 1977, and the state's callous response (Barber and Barratt 1990: 213). The events sparked by Soweto both graphically illustrated and deepened the apartheid regime's growing domestic and international vulnerability. They eventually prompted the NP government to undertake significant tactical concessions, as anticipated by the spiral model. Also as anticipated, the government was unprepared for the repercussions of these concessions, and overestimated its ability to control the tempo and direction of change.

Domestically, the Soweto insurrection tapped into a well of black opposition which had been growing since the late 1960s. It had been spearheaded by the Black Consciousness Movement, originating among the growing numbers of black university students who were, ironically, the product of the needs of the buoyant economy during apartheid's "golden age" (Marx 1992: 32–72). The unprecedented depth and breadth of black opposition was indicated by the extent of the insurrection, and the time it took to quell it as compared with the events following Sharpeville. While Black Consciousness subsequently receded as a political force, both the exiled ANC and, to a lesser extent, the PAC benefited from a resurgence of interest and support within South Africa. More immediately, they benefited from the exodus of as many as 12,000 radicalized black youths to neighboring countries and beyond, where they eventually enabled the renewal of MK's armed struggle and greatly increased the international presence of the liberation movements. These movements, in turn, gained a new level of international recognition and support. According to Barber and Barratt (1990: 208), by the 1980s the ANC in exile was receiving financial assistance from friendly governments and international organizations of roughly $100 million annually, and was able to set up large training camps and a headquarters in Lusaka with an administrative complement of more than 150 persons. ANC missions in Western countries, meanwhile, became more active and effective allies of anti-apartheid organizations and coalitions therein.

The international outcry and mounting activism prompted a new set of measures from Western governments. Even prior to Soweto, South African and Western strategic calculations had been shaken by the collapse of Portuguese rule in Angola and Mozambique and the 1975 emergence in both of Marxist regimes allied to liberation movements in South Africa, Zimbabwe, and Namibia. Following the sustained resistance and repression in South Africa, and finally the outrage over the death of Biko, the Security Council, including its permanent Western members, agreed to the adoption of a mandatory arms embargo on November 4, 1977. Although these sanctions were justified by Western members on the grounds of South Africa's increasingly aggressive foreign policy rather than its domestic policies and repression, they nevertheless constituted a watershed in South Africa's international relations (United Nations' Department of Public Information 1994: 348; Klotz 1995: 50–51). They were accompanied in many Western capitals with variations on corporate codes of conduct and mild economic "measures" reducing state support for trade and investment promotion.

The state's response once again featured unprecedented repression and continued denials of the legitimacy of opposition movements and outside intervention. The repression ultimately succeeded in quieting the townships, and even enabled a brief economic resurgence in the late 1970s and early 1980s. Yet the government could no longer harbor any illusions that the status quo was sustainable. The 1977 Defence White Paper established the intellectual basis for the coercive dimension of its response, elaborating the idea of a "Total National Strategy" to combat the "Total Onslaught" of its Moscow-orchestrated enemies (Davies and O'Meara 1985; O'Meara 1996: 254–269). This set the stage for the progressive militarization of politics and policy-making during the 1980s, and the prosecution of a ruthless campaign of destabilization directed particularly against the country's more radical neighbors.

Particularly with the rise to the prime ministership of P. W. Botha in 1978, however, the government also recognized the need for more positive and ambitious measures of reform. These were aimed both at establishing a reconstituted basis for social order, and at persuading critics in the West that the government was committed to change, thereby forestalling further isolation. Yet the bottom line of reform remained entirely consistent with grand apartheid: "South Africa was a country of a 'plurality of peoples and of minority groups'; and ... 'Black peoples' were to exercise their political rights in 'independent' states" – that is, the homelands (O'Meara 1996: 274).

The key reforms included measures concerning labor markets and trade unions, urban blacks, and political institutions. They were designed fundamentally to extend limited economic, social, and political rights to groups of black South Africans, thereby entrenching and dividing privileged "insiders" from marginalized "outsiders" and thus maintaining white privilege and control.[3] The labor reforms arising from the 1979 report of the Wiehan Commission led to the 1981 Labor Relations Act, which gradually extended trade-union rights while attempting, through strict control of the trade unions, to isolate and depoliticize work place conflicts. In fact, the Act created space for the emergence of powerful trade unions and union alliances as potent political actors in the mid- to late-1980s, often promoting a radical class-based political project. The 1979 Riekert Commission on Manpower recommended giving the right of "permanent" urban residence to those blacks already established and employed in the cities (the privileged insiders), while virtually sealing off the homelands and their residents (the marginalized outsiders) from urban areas and tightening influx control. This was accompanied by measures to improve the quality of life of the urban black middle class, in hopes of making them a bulwark against revolution.

Finally, the government sought to formulate a new political dispensation which would extend political rights without surrendering white control. Its plan, unveiled in May 1982, called for the establishment of a tricameral legislature, with separate white, "Colored," and Asian chambers for "own affairs," and a subordinate role for the Colored and Asian representatives on a small range of common concerns. The political aspirations of urban Africans were to be met through the creation of elected Black Local Authorities (BLAs), with responsibility for service delivery in segregated townships. The whole scheme, which was approved by white voters in a November 1983 referendum, was premised on a consociational theory of power sharing, or "group rights," once

---

[3] The following summary is taken primarily from O'Meara 1996: 272–8.

again distorting an approach to the organization of political life in "deeply divided" societies theorized by Western scholars such as Arendt Lijphart (O'Meara 1996: 277; Price 1991: 135–136).

These reforms were by no means inconsequential – a point underscored by the fact that they precipitated a final split between *verkramptes* and *verligtes* in the National Party and the formation of the influential Conservative Party to represent those dedicated to the original vision of apartheid. It is quite conceivable that, had the political reforms met with a less hostile domestic response, they might have won acceptance from leading Western powers anxious for a "moderate" accommodation as a positive first step. Yet they utterly failed to address the fundamental inequalities and injustice of the apartheid system. Under the circumstances, the attempt to inaugurate the new political dispensation prompted a new, massive, and decisive round of domestic opposition and international pressure, effectively foreclosing virtually all relatively low-cost policy alternatives and forcing the government to contemplate more fundamental changes.

Act III: the crisis of the 1980s

The attempt to inaugurate the new tricameral parliamentary institutions and the Black Local Authorities (BLA) towards the end of 1984 sparked the most sustained uprising against the state ever. The campaigns for the Indian and Coloured Houses of Parliament were met by highly successful counter-campaigns urging a boycott: less than 20 percent of registered voters went to the polls. In November 1984, the attempt of a new BLA in the Witwatersrand (Pretoria–Johannesburg) area to raise rents provoked violent demonstrations, leading to the intervention of the army in the townships for the first time since the 1960s. This precipitated a nationwide political strike, inaugurating often-violent protests which lasted well into 1986. Robert Price (1991: 191) defines this uprising as an "insurrection" as opposed to the "rebellion" of 1976–1977, insofar as it nullified "state power in a portion of the state's territory and insert[ed] a new system of domination in its place."

Price also notes that the insurrection marked a qualitative transformation in black opposition politics, characterized by unprecedented geographic reach and social depth. As conceptualized in the spiral model, it resulted in full domestic mobilization. Its organizational impetus came from the United Democratic Front (UDF) – an extraordinarily diverse coalition which, at its founding in August 1983, linked some 575 opposition organizations. They, in turn, were the product of a "veritable explosion of associational life" in the early 1980s, "which by mid-decade honeycombed the social fabric of all but the smallest and most remote of the townships" (Price 1991: 159–160 and 178). This explosion was a paradoxical consequence of the state's reforms in two respects. First, by falling short of real change in fundamental ways, the reforms heightened widespread feelings of relative deprivation and alienation. Second, because the reforms were aimed at seeking international acceptability, they were accompanied by an amelioration of state repression which gave the new organizations space in which to organize. The founding organizations of the UDF included local civic associations, student and youth organizations, trade unions, women's, religious, political, and other groups. Many of these, and the UDF as a whole, received support from non-governmental and, increasingly, official agencies in the West – support which grew as the insurrection deepened and Western mass-media images heightened popular interest and outrage.

The UDF has been analyzed by Anthony Marx (1992: 106–146) in terms of its "Charterist" heritage, meaning that it was rooted in the nonracial, loosely nationalist, and broadly democratic ideals of the 1956 Freedom Charter and the ANC. In order to attract as broad a constituency as possible, the UDF deliberately avoided taking a clear ideological position beyond opposition to the state and the apartheid order. "Indeed," writes Marx, "unity in opposition was the ideology, seen as defining and mobilizing the nation" (1992: 130). The rise in influence of the UDF also served to bring the ANC back to the center of liberation politics, notwithstanding (or because of?) its continued exile. This trend was reinforced by the increased tempo of MK's "armed struggle," with guerrilla attacks inside the country increasing from 40 in 1984 to 228 in 1986 (Marx 1992: 157).

As a "broad church," the UDF incorporated liberal human rights advocates as well as more radical elements. Each had their counterparts in the transnational anti-apartheid movement. To accommodate them all, the Front was consistently ambiguous with regard to socialism and class struggle. Nevertheless, the revolutionary potentialities of the 1984 to 1986 insurrection were readily apparent, as avowedly socialist elements gained ground[4] and political violence accelerated. From November 1985, South Africa's expanding trade-union movement

---

[4] As O'Meara notes (1996: 328), after November 1985 the banner of the banned South African Communist Party was raised at mass rallies.

consolidated into a single powerful confederation, the Congress of South African Trade Unions (COSATU), with a predominantly "laborist" ideological orientation. As the UDF and other opposition groups succumbed to state suppression, COSATU and its leading affiliates gained prominence, becoming the leading force in mass political opposition from early 1988 (Marx 1992: 210–211). Trade unionists' enthusiastic, if somewhat vague, support for socialism added to the concerns of leading Western powers.

The now-militarized state, its carefully crafted reformist strategy in disarray, responded with unprecedented force – at first *ad hoc* and then systematic. In late August 1985, it imposed a partial state of emergency. When this failed to quell the broadly based insurrection, it imposed a nationwide state of emergency in June 1986 – part of a multi-faceted counterrevolutionary strategy. Of the strategy's four key steps, the first and most fundamental was the "annihilation" of the enemy (Price 1991: 252–253).[5] The strategy also incorporated draconian censorship measures, designed largely to end the media images of repression so damaging to the government's position abroad. In neighboring states, Pretoria continued its ruthless campaign of destabilization, aimed particularly at Angola and Mozambique (e.g. Hanlon 1986; Johnson and Martin 1989). The combined impact of these repressive measures was to dramatically weaken the hand of South Africa's international defenders, and those (such as American Under-Secretary of State for African Affairs Chester Crocker) who advocated a conciliatory approach towards the regime.

Thus, the insurrection and the state's draconian response precipitated an extraordinary confluence of forces which deepened South Africa's international isolation and prompted an array of punitive (though still partial) sanctions. It resulted, that is, in the virtually full mobilization of the international anti-apartheid movement. South Africa was entrenched as the archetype of the pariah state. Traditional anti-apartheid forces – "Third World" governments, church groups, development and human rights NGOs, solidarity groups, trade unions, and the like – redoubled their efforts, channeling increased resources to the opposition in South Africa and in exile and heightening popular awareness internationally. This broadly based principled

---

[5] The other three were: to remove the socioeconomic basis for alienation among the masses; to "win the hearts and minds of the masses"; and to create effective "counter organizations" at the community level. Not surprisingly, the government was singularly unsuccessful in these.

issue network was supplemented by new sources of popular and local opposition, including divestment campaigns on university campuses and in municipalities in the United States and Canada (Voorhes forthcoming).

Partly due to growing non-governmental interest and pressure, leading Western politicians began to reinterpret their "national interest" as being served by a more forceful response to the apartheid state. This was reflected in both bilateral and multilateral policy shifts, incorporating varying degrees of sanctions. The policies of the Nordic states again led the way, beginning with a ban on new investment in 1979 and escalating to a comprehensive trade embargo by 1987. While a relatively minor component of South Africa's foreign trade, the Nordics' actions set a compelling example which was used by activists in other Western states to bring pressure to bear on their own governments (Black 1992: 308–356). In 1985 and 1986, the Commonwealth adopted two sets of partial sanctions and in 1987, established a committee of foreign ministers chaired by the Canadian foreign minister with the professed aim of maintaining high-level scrutiny and pressure on the South African regime. Margaret Thatcher's British government dissented from all of these measures save the original 1985 package, but even it felt compelled to go along with the European Union's mild sanctions package (Klotz 1995: 112–129). It also used its anti-sanctions position to play "good cop" to the Commonwealth's "bad cop" in attempting to persuade the South African government and leading white South Africans of the need to dismantle apartheid.

Finally, the United States Congress overrode a presidential veto to impose the Comprehensive Anti-Apartheid Act in 1986. This package of partial sanctions was a sharp rebuke to the Reagan administration's (and Chester Crocker's) policy of "constructive engagement." The decisive element in bringing it about was the conversion of moderate Republicans to the cause of partial sanctions. They were concerned both with the domestic political ramifications of being perceived as "defenders of the apartheid state," and with the need to promote rapid change in South Africa in order to forestall a radical outcome hostile to American strategic interests. Seeing their own calls for partial sanctions as a warning to a "friend" rather than a threat to an "enemy", they hoped to encourage gradual reform and to prevent a more violent revolution. Demands for democracy based on racial equality were no longer seen as "communism in disguise," but vital to the protection of Western interests in the region (Klotz 1995: 106–110).

Indeed, this "enlightened capitalist" position (as labeled by John Saul) lay behind the growth of anti-apartheid sentiments and pressures in other parts of the West. For example, it was a motivating factor for the Conservative government of Brian Mulroney in Canada, and for former Australian Prime Minister Malcolm Fraser – an intensely conservative, anti-communist politician who, in his role as co-chair of the Commonwealth's Eminent Persons Group (EPG), became a forceful sanctions advocate (see *Mission to South Africa* 1986). A principal goal of Western sanctions packages, therefore, became the promotion of a moderate, liberal human rights-based resolution of the South African crisis, preempting the growing potential for a more fundamental revolutionary transformation. These moderate strategic aspirations of Western sanctioners are discussed in the next section.

Caught between mounting, increasingly punitive international pressure, a growing structural economic crisis exacerbated by private-sector-led financial sanctions (Carim *et al.* 1998), renewed anti-state opposition inside South Africa regrouped from 1988 around the Mass Democratic Movement, and the "defections" of white capital seeking a rapprochement with the ANC in exile, the South African government was forced to contemplate more fundamental changes. As early as 1987, senior officials had initiated secretive high-level contacts with the ANC's imprisoned deputy president, Nelson Mandela (Mandela 1994: 447–486). However, more decisive change became possible with the political demise of the architect of the reforms of the early 1980s, P. W. Botha, and his replacement as State President by F. W. de Klerk in 1989. An ostensible conservative, de Klerk soon disarmed his critics by unbanning the ANC, PAC, and SACP and releasing Mandela in early 1990. Shortly thereafter, his government initiated a process of negotiation with the ANC and other parties aimed at producing a definitive political alternative to apartheid. Yet the final shape of this alternative remained very much in question. Various outcomes, including a revolutionary transformation, a group-rights-based consociationalism protecting white privilege, and an anarchic "Lebanonization" as well as a moderate transition rooted in liberal human rights norms, were realistic possibilities. The final shape of the transition, in which international human rights norms achieved prescriptive status, emerged from the protracted negotiations of the 1990 to 1994 period.

Act IV: negotiated transition

Analyses of South African domestic politics usually stress the peculiarities of the apartheid system. Nationalism, militarism, and isolation appeared to be natural outgrowths of Afrikaner rule. Many activists as well as scholars stress, in turn, the importance of internal resistance to apartheid. However, while recognizing the crucial role of domestic actors, the foregoing analysis has demonstrated the interplay of domestic and international sources of pressure for change. In this section, therefore, I focus firstly on the ways in which the South African transition to non-racial democracy resulted in part from international normative pressures. I concentrate on one dimension of the way in which norms can affect states and state behavior: legitimation. While this is not the only way in which norms affect states (see Klotz 1995: 13–35), it remains an under-emphasized dimension of international influence in general, and analyses of the South African transition in particular.

Sanctioning South Africa is one example of general processes by which the international community defines and enforces international norms. The ensuing analysis of the 1990 to 1994 reform phase shows that the power of key South African actors, and the parameters of their debates and agreements, were set in part by global pressures for racial equality and a non-violent democratic process. Three distinct dimensions of legitimation are disaggregated by examining the effects of sanctions on players, processes, and principles in the South African transition.

Secondly, the analysis in this section seeks to highlight the importance of the communicative process by which negotiated agreement was reached, and the prescriptive status of liberal human rights norms was achieved. At the outset of the process, both sides "entered into negotiations to achieve original, as opposed to compromised, objectives" (Booysen 1992: 64, cited in Ohlson and Stedman 1994: 131). Important constituents of both principal protagonists – the ANC and the NP – saw the negotiations as a means of achieving victory by other means, rather than as a process of dialogue and compromise (see Adam and Moodley 1994: 39–52). Through the sometimes-troubled negotiations which followed, widely divergent initial positions were substantially modified and a moderate, liberal outcome emerged – at the expense of both institutional protections for minority privilege and the more radical socio-economic reforms which many still regard as essential to long-term stability and justice.

Players

Sanctions changed the balance of normative power among the key parties, the National Party and the ANC, at various times enhancing and/or undermining their standings in the negotiation process. Although we will not analyze Inkatha or the Conservative Party in detail here, these other parties were also affected by the normative effects of sanctions.[6]

Over time, the declining international standing of the NP encouraged opponents in the non-racial democratic movement and among non-white groups, contributing to the classic sanctions aim of subverting the authority of the target state. In the 1980s, domestic and international pressures mounted, and the NP's apartheid policies unraveled. Both inside and outside the NP, the hand of those whites who favored abolishing apartheid and entering into negotiations with the ANC (and other banned organizations) was strengthened. A string of missions by leading white South Africans making direct contacts with the exiled ANC, the "trek to Lusaka," undermined the authority of the NP government. These unofficial meetings simultaneously enhanced the status of the ANC as a central player in South Africa's future (Price 1991: 220–248). Ultimately, the more internationalist-reformist wing of the NP became convinced of the need to secure a reprieve from sanctions-related economic decline and mounting domestic insecurity.[7]

Various sanctions packages had defined steps that the South Africa government needed to follow to give clear evidence of its intent to dismantle apartheid and thus remove international restrictions. At the minimum, these conditions included: (1) repealing the state of emergency; (2) releasing all political prisoners; (3) unbanning the ANC and other political parties; (4) eliminating apartheid laws; and (5) initiating negotiations for a new political system. During 1990 to 1991, de Klerk carefully followed these steps, seizing the opportunity to proclaim bold progress towards reform.

In response to the government's move, Britain, the European Community, and the United States all moved to reward the NP by lifting their sanctions measures – prematurely in the view of the ANC, as well

---

[6] For example, Inkatha benefited prior to the transition period as a prominent black organization opposed to sanctions, thereby eliciting material and moral support from a variety of conservative domestic and international actors – including the South African government. For a preliminary analysis along these lines, see Klotz 1995: 9.

[7] So-labeled by Price (1991: ch. 8) and contrasted with the "securocrats" who predominated under P. W. Botha.

as the Commonwealth (with the exception of Britain). South Africans also began to enjoy the benefits of renewed international contacts in a variety of socio-cultural settings, most prominently sport (Black forthcoming). Lifting sanctions substantially revived the NP's standing both internationally and domestically. As a result, the balance of normative power in South Africa shifted towards the NP and away from the ANC (which had enjoyed increasing favor internationally prior to 1990).

The prospect of continued reforms and, conversely, of the threat of renewed international isolation should negotiations fail led many white South Africans to swallow their fears of majority rule. When the NP government called a whites-only referendum on the reform process in March 1992, for example, the juxtaposition of the referendum with South Africa's debut in the Cricket World Cup, graphically illustrating the potential benefits of reform, was a boon to the government's campaign. De Klerk and the NP, strongly supported by the business community, won a resounding victory with 68.7 percent of the vote. The referendum strongly legitimized NP reform initiatives domestically and internationally – although the NP subsequently overplayed its hand.

As the NP strengthened its position through the lifting of sanctions, the ANC's position weakened as it continued to advocate international restrictions. Previously, each step in the extension of the sanctions campaign had constituted a victory for the ANC's "downstairs" foreign policy, against the "upstairs" of the apartheid state (see Vale 1997). The imposition of sanctions bolstered the ANC's claim to be the leading voice of the disenfranchised majority (particularly against Inkatha's rival claims). In turn, the ANC increased its material and moral support from the international anti-apartheid movement, international organizations such as the OAU, the UN, and the Commonwealth, East Bloc states, and progressive Western countries. At its peak in the mid-1980s, the ANC's regular international contacts extended to a growing range of Western countries, establishing its status as a "government in waiting" (Klotz forthcoming).

The ANC's international role in spearheading the sanctions campaign also helped to reinforce its domestic standing. Its identification with the United Democratic Front meant that domestic activists received financial support from external allies in the anti-apartheid movement. The internal wings of the democratic movement were strengthened both materially and morally by their association with the ANC. Nelson Mandela's enormous international stature, graphically illustrated by his triumphant tours abroad after his release from prison in 1990, symbolized this convergence between international and domestic support.

But international praise for de Klerk's reform initiatives and the relatively rapid easing of sanctions in 1990 and 1991 constituted a diplomatic setback for the ANC. Not even Mandela's appeals could forestall the trend towards lifting sanctions. The notable exception was the Commonwealth, which adopted a more cautious approach that linked sanctions to "real and practical steps in the destruction of apartheid," thus keeping the specter of sanctions alive in the negotiations phase (Commonwealth News Release 1991). Although the ANC's status diminished with de Klerk's initial success it certainly did not lose all of its international support. Rather, the ANC and NP emerged more evenly balanced as they entered into negotiations to determine the post-apartheid political system.

Processes

The relative (normative) strength of the contending players is important but not sufficient for understanding the transition; their choice of negotiation for resolving their differences was not a foregone conclusion. Indeed, traditionally analysts assume that sanctions need to inflict drastic domestic costs to provoke fundamental change. The success of sanctions in encouraging a negotiated transition, therefore, is surprising and deserves greater attention.

Sanctions helped to engender and then reinforce a dominant "culture of negotiation," at least at the level of the South African elite. This point can be illustrated with reference to the Commonwealth. The mission of its Eminent Persons Group (EPG), created by the Nassau Heads of Government Meeting in 1985 and undertaken in the first part of 1986, is widely acknowledged to have been important in the subsequent escalation of international sanctions pressure (*Mission to South Africa* 1986). The main reason for the importance of the EPG mission and the influence of its subsequent report was arguably the very moderation of its approach. Its goal, explored with all major parties in South Africa including the government and the exiled ANC, was to "initiate, in the context of a suspension of violence on all sides, a process of dialogue ... with a view to establishing a non-racial and representative government" (*Commonwealth Accord* 1985). Its approach was so measured that it had to be treated seriously by all parties, including the government. Eventually, it formulated a Possible Negotiating Concept as a basis for promoting a dialogue, and in the context of the EPG mission, all parties accepted in principle the idea of negotiations as the path to transition (Anglin 1990: 360). Thus, when the South African government (or, more accurately, "securocrats" within it) effectively scuttled the mission by raiding the capitals of three of South Africa's neighbors who were Commonwealth members, the subsequent escalation of sanctions by the Commonwealth and others was integrally linked to the apparent unwillingness of the government to embark on a meaningful process of negotiation.

That negotiations were specifically identified through sanctions as the only internationally acceptable path away from apartheid helps to account for the alacrity with which the ANC agreed to return home and launch into such a process, following the dramatic opening signals by de Klerk. It also helps to explain why the leaderships of both parties ultimately maintained their commitment to the often tortuous negotiation process, in spite of the high level of mutual suspicion and provocations – particularly on the part of agents of the state. Both recognized that only a negotiated outcome would be acceptable to the international community, and both accepted the need for this international approval. Of course, other factors also facilitated the launching of negotiations and helped to ensure that the key parties eventually saw them through. Nevertheless, international normative pressure through sanctions reinforced the shared commitment to negotiations.

Once launched, the negotiations created a communicative dynamic in the context of which both parties were ultimately persuaded to abandon long-nurtured goals of victory, and to compromise on a moderate human rights-based dispensation for the country. In consolidating the prescriptive status of these principles, both international normative influence and the dynamic of the negotiations themselves were crucial.

Principles

Strengthening various actors' commitment to the negotiation concept is just one of the ideals that sanctions sought to promote, but it signals the more general need to consider the content of the goals and norms that the international community seeks to advance by adopting sanctions. In South Africa, the sanctioning process reinforced and legitimized several key ideas around which the negotiations coalesced and a settlement was eventually structured. Sanctions also did *not* reinforce other rival principles of considerable importance, thereby helping to shape the limited nature of the transition. We will take each of these effects in turn.

Among the liberal ideas to which the international sanctions process lent positive legitimacy are those of pluralism and tolerance. The notion that the goal of sanctions pressure was the initiation of "a process of dialogue across lines of color, politics, and religion," and "the establishment of civil rights for all citizens," embedded in the justifications offered for the international sanctions adopted, strongly reinforced these post-war values.[8] Moreover, in the course of the transition itself and as sanctions pressure was alleviated, much of the involvement of international actors was oriented towards supporting the creation of a "culture of tolerance," through the promotion of local political dialogue, confidence-building efforts, and the like (see Commonwealth Observer Mission 1993). Similarly, the sanctions process strongly legitimated the goal of "non-racial and representative," or broadly democratic, government.

Certainly the normative influence of the international community was not all-determining. That these principles remained shallow and fragile in the South African context is indicated most starkly by the fact that nearly 14,000 people died in incidents of political conflict during the various phases of negotiations. And although the April 1994 elections themselves constituted, at one level, a triumph for ideas of tolerance and social peace (an "act of electoral communion," in Roger Southall's evocative phrase), the outcome reflected primarily racially based voting and a clear division between "colonizers" and "colonized," thus containing the seeds of a possible reversion to authoritarianism (Southall 1994a: 86–98).

More specifically, international influence helped to delimit the boundaries of an appropriate design for a new political system. For example, the NP's initial goals included, in effect, an explicit recognition of group rights and a minority veto (Ohlson and Stedman 1994: 148). Although this goal received some international support from more conservative interests, US Under-Secretary of State for Africa Herman Cohen made clear in the middle of 1992 that a minority veto would be considered unacceptable even to the Bush administration – let alone to the majority in South Africa (Friedman 1994: 157). Such a goal was simply not acceptable to the international actors which counted most for the South African regime, and helped to seal its fate.

---

[8] The quotations are excerpts, in turn, from *The Commonwealth Accord on Southern Africa* 1985 and the Swedish Ministry of Foreign Affairs 1985 (an unofficial translation of the Swedish Government's bill on prohibition of trade with South Africa and Namibia), p. 8.

This brings us to what international sanctioners did not legitimate. In particular, official sanctions helped to structure a moderate and limited transition in which, in important respects, there was no "radical rupture with the past" (Uys 1994: 55). This is most obvious in relation to the structure of the economy and the steps a new government might take to redress South Africa's deep historic inequalities. One is reminded, in this connection, of Canadian government officials' oft-repeated phrase that the goal of sanctions was to bring the South African regime "to its senses, not its knees." International emphasis on political, rather than economic, transformation reflects the dominant global perspective on human rights generally (e.g., Vincent 1986), however, and therefore is not surprising even in the South African situation.

While most groups in the anti-apartheid movement had an expansive socioeconomic conception of the post-apartheid transformation, the official sanctions packages explicitly promoted the more narrow goals of political democratization, particularly universal suffrage. There was no focus on socioeconomic change, despite the fact that apartheid also produced a racially based interpenetration of the state with the market (Greenberg 1980). The "international community," led by its leading Western members, demanded only political reform and juridical non-racialism, as reflected in the demands of the sanctions, and welcomed South Africa back into the fold following its universal-suffrage elections.

Moreover, a variety of international economic actors, including the International Monetary Fund, the World Bank, and the Geneva-based World Economic Forum, among others, reinforced the moderate nature of the transition. Although South Africa's deep, racially structured, inequalities needed to be addressed in some form, the pace and nature of these changes were effectively limited. For example, nationalization and other more intrusive mechanisms of government control and redistribution were rejected; more moderate welfare-state and affirmative-action policies are now favored (*Weekly Mail and Guardian* 1994: 253–280). In practice, therefore, international sanctions helped to foster the kind of moderate, negotiated outcome favored by their principal enforcers – Western states generally promoting liberal democracy and capitalism.

These international influences reinforced the communicative effects of the negotiations themselves. As noted above, the NP and the ANC began this process with very different bottom lines. As summarized by Ohlson and Stedman,

> The ANC, believing it would gain a majority in a one-person, one-vote election, wanted a strong central government in order to redress societal and political inequalities forged by apartheid. The National Party wanted arrangements that would protect the economic and political interests of the white population... As Roger Southall wrote at the time, "The NP's conversion to constitutional democracy is highly situational... Its present proposals are designed to 'non-racially' entrench existing disparities of property, wealth and power"
>
> (Ohlson and Stedman 1994: 148)

Moreover, both had key factions and followers who were ill-disposed towards compromise. As Heribert Adam and Kogila Moodley (1993: 40) noted during the transition, "The secret to the growing approval for de Klerk among the dominant white minority lies in the hope that they could continue to dominate without costs attached." Similarly, the ANC's followers included, among others, grass-roots activists and militant black youth committed to the view that the state could not be trusted, and that total victory over apartheid was both possible and necessary.

The mistrust and misunderstanding which infused each side towards the other was reinforced by the continuation of violent "third force" activities orchestrated by factions within the state security apparatus to destabilize the ANC and the negotiations (Sparks 1995: 153–178). The ANC, for its part, responded to demands by the NP for an effective veto over key provisions of the constitution and, more immediately, to the apparent complicity of the government in the massacre of forty-nine people in the township of Boipatong by Inkatha-affiliated hostel-dwellers by suspending the formal negotiations in June 1992. In August, it launched a campaign of "rolling mass action" which crippled the country, leading to the temporary ascendance of hardliners within the ANC and mounting violence and disorder (Sparks 1995: 133–152).

Notwithstanding the provocations, violence, and internal opposition in both parties, however – indeed partly because of them – the mistrust between the key negotiators was slowly overcome and the need for true compromise was accepted. Even during the period in 1992 when the formal negotiations had broken down, the principal negotiators for the ANC and the NP continued their discussions in secret (Sparks 1995: 179–196). Beyond the elite level, moreover, hundreds of negotiation processes were under way at local levels, and Local Peace Committees created under the auspices of the National Peace Accord signed in 1991 worked to bring "local parties together to foster cooperation and a

104

'culture of tolerance'" (cited in Ohlson and Stedman 1994: 171). While the success of these local-level efforts in reducing the violence was limited, they reinforced a broad constituency favouring a moderate, negotiated future resting on tolerance and compromise. Significantly, there was considerable international support for these local-level confidence-building efforts from international organizations such as the UN and the Commonwealth, bilateral donors, and non-governmental organizations.

This broad communicative process ultimately yielded an outcome in which both sides made important concessions. The ANC compromised on the principles that would guide the writing of a new constitution (including the exclusion of most "second generation" social and economic rights) and the creation of relatively strong provincial and local levels of government; the NP "abandoned the idea of an executive by committee and a white veto on policy" (Ohlson and Stedman 1994: 164). And, while the outcome was clearly the product of an elite compromise, broad popular support for the forces of moderation was demonstrated by the outcome of the April 1994 all-race elections, in which the more radical parties (the Pan-Africanist Congress on the one hand and the [Afrikaner] Freedom Front on the other) were thoroughly marginalized (Southall 1994b). That the outcome also reduced the urgency and means of dealing with the socioeconomic legacies of apartheid is a consequence whose full effects have yet to be played out.

Conclusion

The "new" South Africa which has emerged since the April 1994 elections is in many respects a model of international human rights change. It also clearly illustrates the influence of the transnational networks and processes highlighted by the spiral model in fostering such change. Through a process of negotiated accommodation, the key protagonists produced a settlement based on a multi-party electoral system and parliamentary institutions. Moreover the post-apartheid government, through its socially progressive, constitutionally entrenched bill of rights and the authoritative constitutional court established to interpret it (Steenkamp 1995), has demonstrated its intent to entrench the prescriptive status of liberal human rights norms, and to adhere to rule-consistent behavior. This commitment has had politically controversial consequences domestically, including the outlawing of the death penalty in a country afflicted with some of the highest rates of violent crime in the world (Shaw 1997). Another indicator of the new government's commitment to fostering a human rights culture, and thus rule-consistent behavior, is the ambitious Truth and Reconciliation Commission created to arrive at as full a reckoning of apartheid-era abuses as possible, and to serve the educative function of "teaching" all South Africans what must never happen again. While the level of international interest in and support for this ongoing process of rule-entrenchment has receded from the high-water mark of the mid-1980s and early 1990s, it remains an important buttress to the post-apartheid transition.

Yet it is important to recall that the success of the campaign to end apartheid owes much to Third World and East Bloc governments whose concern was less with human rights writ large than with the narrower principle of anti-racism or the ideological priority of socialism. Leading Western governments were latter-day converts to the anti-apartheid cause, and were motivated as much by the desire to protect their economic and strategic interests as they were by a concern for the basic human rights of the South African majority. Moreover, their intervention, through sanctions, helped to structure a moderate, liberal transition which aided in securing civil and political rights for all South Africans, but effectively reduced the emphasis on addressing their social and economic rights through a more radical political and economic transformation. Whether the former can be secured in the medium- to long-term without more rapid progress in addressing the latter is uncertain.

Two alternative theoretical explanations for the outcome in South Africa bear consideration. The first is the realist argument that change was fundamentally the result of decisive pressure from the great powers and, more importantly, the changing global strategic balance resulting from the end of the Cold War. With regard to the influence of Great Power policy change, it is true that the critical decision phase in which the NP government moved towards acceptance of the dismantling of apartheid coincided with the post-1986 period in which the US Congress imposed the Comprehensive Anti-Apartheid Act (CAAA). Doubtless the reversal of the Reagan administration's policy of constructive engagement underscored the apartheid regime's inexorable isolation in the world, and influenced the thinking of its decision-makers. However, one cannot understand the adoption of the CAAA over a presidential veto without taking into account the growing influence of the anti-apartheid movement on American Congressional policy makers; nor were America's partial sanctions more than one element in a rising tide of pressures for change. In other words, the American policy shift, which was not in itself decisive, also reflected the transnational process of mobilization and normative change conceptualized in the spiral model.

Concerning the changing global strategic balance, there is no denying the importance of the end of the Cold War in facilitating the decisive steps taken in early 1990. "[A]bove all else, it was the change in the Soviet Union that emboldened Pretoria to unban the ANC," wrote Adam and Moodley (1993: 44; see also Giliomee 1992). Nevertheless, it is also clear that by the time the changes in the Soviet Union were clearly irreversible, thereby undercutting both the force of Pretoria's ideological anti-communism and the ANC's material and moral support from the East Bloc, key policy makers in Pretoria had been actively preparing for the possibility of negotiations for several years. Moreover, senior officials had been holding regular, secret talks with Nelson Mandela since 1987, while leading members of the elite Afrikaner Broederbond[9] began meeting senior ANC officials in London in 1986 (Adam and Moodley 1993: 42). Thus, while the end of the Cold War was crucial in providing the pretext for launching the negotiation process, the groundwork for this process had been laid over several previous years as a result of pressures from a much wider range of internal and external forces.

Secondly, it may be argued from a structuralist perspective that the principal underlying cause of the changes in South Africa is located in the demands and growing crisis of the apartheid-based political economy. That is, government policy makers were compelled by the demands of the modernizing capitalist economy to introduce liberalizing labor reforms which created the basis for mass-based political opposition. Later, as the economy sank into a sustained structural crisis during the 1980s, the white political elite ultimately saw no option but to negotiate the demise of apartheid in order to avoid economic ruin. Once again, there is some truth in this explanation. As Marx (1992) notes, periods of sustained domestic opposition were related to structural economic conditions as well as ideological mobilization. Thus, for example, the rise of Black Consciousness in the early 1970s was linked to the growth of the black university system which was, in turn, a response to the demands for more skilled labour generated by the "golden age"

---

[9] A "secret" organization of leading Afrikaner men which was enormously influential in promoting Afrikaner nationalism and in securing the NP's hegemony among white South Africans.

of apartheid capitalism. Similarly, the labor and urban policy reforms of the late 1970s and early 1980s reflected in part an acceptance by state policy makers of the need for a stable, urban-based black labor force as a necessary condition for the renewal of the country's flagging economy.

However, as with the realist explanation, this structural economic account can only partly explain the dynamics of change, and to be compelling must incorporate the insights associated with the spiral model. For one thing, the growing structural crisis of the South African economy was partly a result of mounting pressures mobilized by the transnational anti-apartheid movement. The arms embargo, for example, created the need for a domestic military-industrial complex. The development of South Africa's sophisticated arms industry, in turn, drew resources away from more economical uses and exacerbated skilled labor shortages which had the effect of weakening economic apartheid in crucial sectors (Crawford forthcoming). Later, in the mid-1980s, the growth of domestic opposition and the international anti-apartheid movement increased the costs and risks of doing business in South Africa, thereby discouraging long-term investments and encouraging divestment. It became apparent, therefore, that renewal was impossible without fundamental political change.

On the other hand, South Africa's economic crisis was never as deep as most knowledgeable observers felt it needed to be to compel the white minority to accept political change. For example, a group of sanctions experts commissioned by the Commonwealth Committee of Foreign Ministers on Southern Africa concluded in 1989 that to be effective sanctions would have to produce a sustained 30 percent cut in imports and 25 percent cut in exports (*The Sanctions Report* 1989: 114–115). The fact that within a year de Klerk had taken the decisive initial steps towards a negotiated transition implies that the political and normative pressures mobilized by the transnational anti-apartheid movement were far more influential than a narrow structural economic explanation for the changes would allow.

In sum, while other causal explanations have some force in the South African case, they cannot be dissociated from the linked process of domestic and international mobilization around international human rights norms and, more particularly, the norm of non-racialism. It is clear that in South Africa at least, change depended on the protracted efforts of state and non-state actors which, in conventional realist and structuralist accounts, are generally discounted as weak and marginal.

4 Changing discourse: transnational advocacy networks in Tunisia and Morocco

Sieglinde Gränzer

Introduction: the emergence of transnational networks and human rights discourse in the Maghreb

In the Maghreb region, human rights became an important public theme during the 1980s. Here, international human rights norms were not interpreted in opposition to the shared cultural-political understandings of Arab societies as some scholars proposed (Huntington 1996). In all Maghreb core states, Tunisia, Algeria, and Morocco, human rights were not rejected as purely Western ideas or values. Instead, these norms were interpreted as compatible with the Islamic culture. North African intellectuals even tried to relate the human rights idea to the Islamic religion (Jürgensen 1994). Insofar as human rights are well-recognized universal values they could be used as a moral reference system by societal actors in North African states to criticize norm-violating state behavior. The political background of these new political actors was their knowledge about and their reference to the international human rights regime.

Public debate over human rights started when North African state leaders responded to public demands for political participation with measures of security control and tried to deal with socioeconomic problems by increasing state repression in the 1970s and 1980s. New political actors set the question of human rights on the agenda, challenging the legitimacy of the repressive governments. These non-governmental actors did not seek political power or to overthrow the

For helpful comments on earlier versions of this paper I am grateful to Janice Bially, Michelle Everson, Liz Hodgins; Thomas Risse, Donatella Rovera; Kathryn Sikkink. Particularly I'd like to thank Tanja Börzel for her clarifying remarks.

system. Rather, they wanted to change the operating rules of national politics through public persuasion and communication processes. As Susan Waltz (1995a) pointed out, the contribution of these actors to North African politics has been substantial. The concept of "civil society" is often used to describe the variety of non-governmental political actors demanding democratization and human rights in Arab states (El-Aoufi 1992; Jürgensen 1994, Brynen, Korany, and Noble 1995a, 1995b; Norton 1995, 1996; Ibrahim 1995a, 1995b; Al-Sayyid 1995). Yet, the existence of a "civil society" in an authoritarian state does not say much about the prospects for successful political change. Societal actors in Arab civil societies do not have enough power to change the operating rules and the repressive practice of governments by pressure from inside alone (Layachi 1995; S. Waltz 1995a; Hegasy 1997). Their mobilization has to be supported from outside. By building up transnational relationships with human rights international non-governmental organizations (INGOs), domestic North African actors gained access to additional resources crucial in their political struggle for human rights change. Except in the case of Algeria, where internal conflict has obscured the possibility of effective international pressure (see Entelis 1996; Garon 1995b; S. Waltz 1995a: 75–102), national and international non-state actors have been transmitting a norm of respect for human rights to the Maghreb region through their transnational cooperation.

In both Tunisia and Morocco, state repression gave rise to the emergence of transnational human rights networks. And both regimes initiated certain institutional changes with regard to human rights. But there were significant differences in outcome. In Morocco, the change was brought about by an ongoing process of domestic and international mobilization channeled through the transnational human rights network, which finally persuaded the king to introduce institutional reforms. These reforms resulted in a significant improvement of the human rights situation in Morocco since 1991. In Tunisia, on the other hand, domestic human rights mobilization had led to a change in political leadership in 1987. The new head of state also initiated institutional human rights reforms. But these reforms have not produced any significant human rights change. Instead, the situation deteriorated.

I argue in this chapter that this variation in outcome between the two countries is to be explained by the difference in strength and quality of the two transnational human rights networks in Tunisia and

Morocco. In Morocco, the human rights network has constantly been pressing for a more sustainable human rights change from above and below for a relatively long period (more than ten years) and, as a result, has been able to build upon its experiences to professionalize its strategies after the introduction of institutional reforms. In Tunisia, the evolving efforts of Tunisian human rights activists to politicize the issue were sidetracked by initial tactical concessions made by the new president, Ben Ali, between 1987 and 1989. In the 1990s, the Ben Ali Regime initiated a series of political reforms which claimed to promote democratization but turned out to be ineffective. In this case, the quick installation of institutional reforms after the regime change was so unexpected that national and international human rights critics were surprised and, as a consequence, the evolving networking process came to a sudden end. Ben Ali was successful in instrumentalizing the moral legitimacy of the human rights idea to stabilize the existing authoritarian state apparatus. Well-known human rights activists were quickly coopted and integrated into the new government. Moreover, the political rights initially granted have been increasingly and systematically negated by restrictions placed on their actual use. The increasing state repression in the 1990s has been justified by the need to suppress Islamic fundamentalism.

The chapter is divided into two main parts. In the first part, I briefly summarize the development of human rights in Tunisia and Morocco over the last two decades which has given rise to the emergence of transnational human rights networks in both countries. In the second part, I examine the explanations for the changes in the human rights situation. Neither the improvements in Morocco nor the deterioration of human rights in Tunisia can be explained without analyzing the political influence of non-governmental actors, in particular transnational advocacy networks. This influence is best shown in the ways in which governments are reacting willingly or unwillingly toward the existence and the mobilization of these new actors. In the North African cases, the reaction of the Tunisian and the Moroccan governments to the efforts of national and international human rights activists differs considerably.

I trace the variation in outcomes back to the differing strength of the transnational human rights networks in the two countries. The phase model presented in the introduction of this book helps to explain why the two networks have disposed of a diverging capacity to promote the internalization process of human rights norms at the domestic level.

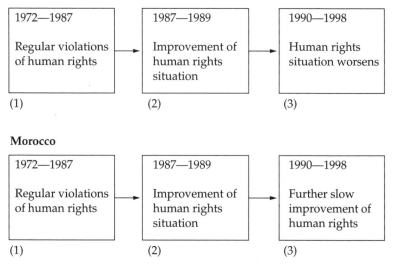

Figure 4.1   Breaking points in the human rights development

Development of human rights in Tunisia and Morocco

While both Tunisia and Morocco changed their human rights policies, the extent to which human rights norms have been internalized is quite different in each country. We can trace the development of human rights norms over time by considering the trends across four common kinds of human rights abuses: disappearances of opponents, torture, extrajudicial killings, and detentions without trial. According to the human rights abuses, one can distinguish in both countries three main time periods (see figure 4.1).

The repression which gave rise to the regular violations of human rights in the 1970s resulted in both cases from two main conflicts between state and society. First, the legitimacy of the centralist leadership of both governments was put in question. In Tunisia in 1976, 1978, and 1980, left-wing opposition groups organized demonstrations and strikes which undermined the legitimacy of the regime, while the military created this same effect in Morocco through two coup attempts in 1971 and 1972 (Damis 1992; Laurent 1996). These acts of civil and military resistance resulted in state repression. In Tunisia, the government cracked down on left-wing parties and trade unions (Amnesty International 1977b) while a whole generation of army officers and their families "disappeared" in Morocco (Amnesty International 1990a–b, 1991a–c, 1993a; Souhaili 1986). The regime in each country thus legitimized itself through a "threat of internal security." The second conflict was grounded in socioeconomic conditions; a sudden rise in the prices of staple foods as a consequence of structural adjustment measures gave rise to unorganized, "wild" rebellions and mass demonstrations in both states (Tunisia 1984, Morocco 1983; see Seddon 1989). The reactions of both state leaders to these displays of opposition was oppressive and authoritarian. Army and police forces were used to control the population with waves of arrests and widespread torture of prisoners who were held in *"garde-à-vue"* (imprisonment without court judgment) custody. Those deemed responsible for the uprisings were arrested, tortured, and, after unfair trials, disappeared to secret prisons.[1]

The majority of human rights violations in Morocco and the West Sahara concerned "disappearances" of political opponents. Reports on the human rights situation in Morocco stated that since the 1970s "disappearances" have been systematic. This practise of "disappearances" as a means of prosecuting opposition groups or individuals was extended and systematized with the occupation of the West Sahara in 1975 (Amnesty International 1994b). "Disappeared" persons were rarely killed, but certainly tortured and detained ("forgotten") for decades in secret Moroccan prisons. The conditions during long-term imprisonment of the "disappeared" have often resulted in death. Torture, occasionally to the point of fatality, was practiced systematically in both Tunisia and Morocco. Particularly during the *garde-à-vue* custody, prisoners were detained illegally for long periods of time without any contact with the outside world (Bendourou 1988; Henderson 1984). Extrajudicial executions mainly occurred in instances when torture led to killing and during violent clashes between the police and opposition groups. In both countries, the increase of repression was accompanied by intensified security measures. In Morocco, the police forces of the Ministry of the Interior were reinforced and the position of the responsible minister was strengthened by enlarging his powers and authorities (Bennani-Chraibi and Leveau 1996). In Tunisia the political conflict

---

[1] For more details on human rights conditions in both countries see the regular reports of INGOs like Amnesty International and Human Rights Watch.

113

between the government and Islamic fundamentalists also served as a pretext for enlarging governmental control in the field of security by President Bourguiba and later by President Ben Ali (Garon 1994; Macha 1994; Callies de Salies 1995).

The short period of responsiveness to the human rights ideal in Tunisia between 1987 and 1989 coincided with the regime change. The constitutional "coup" of Prime Minister Ben Ali on November 11, 1987, had been prepared by the ruling elite within the Tunisian state apparatus. Ben Ali announced institutional modifications which seemed at first glance to bring about a democratically oriented change (Toumi 1989). The constitutional amendment of July 1988 determined, for example, that the presidential office was no longer a life-long position and that succession was to be regulated by elections. But the constitution also stipulated that the executive power of the prime minister would be reduced and that the parliament would be deprived of some of its oversight capacities so that the competence of the president was greatly strengthened. Ben Ali continued to support "national pacts" in an effort to bind the opposition within a symbolic contract to the government. These pacts created the illusion of a social and political consensus and often discredited the opposition leaders. In this tradition, the pact of November 1988 resulted in a national treaty signed by all opposition parties and groups including the Islamists (Macha 1994: 41; Toumi 1989). The positive effects of the proclaimed human rights change by the new President Ben Ali were only briefly felt in the period up to 1989. In the political system, the neopatrimonial power patterns remained the same as during Bourguiba's time, only now they were concentrated on Ben Ali. The security service was systematically expanded and new laws were passed restricting the freedom of the press and media. These measures made the work of independent political organizations impossible. In 1991 at the very latest, the phase of political liberalization was over (Garon 1994; Macha 1994; Sraieb 1992; Waltz 1995: S. 176). Prior to the elections in 1994, the deputies' chamber consisted of representatives of the government party only. The other parties were forced to follow the government. Even today, any political opposition is still regarded as an assault on the state which must be repressed.[2] The government justifies this policy on the grounds that organized Islam is a potential threat to the Tunisian state and therefore the government must increase secur-

---

[2] Interviews with Tunisian human rights activists in Tunis in March 1998.

ity measures (Faath 1992a: 498f; Garon 1994; Macha 1994; S. Waltz 1995b; Ibrahimi 1997).

The serious decline in the human rights situation in Tunisia during recent years gives us reason to believe that the brief period of improvement after 1987 was tied to the state's manipulation of the norm for its own purposes. Ben Ali's human rights measures between 1987 to 1989 can therefore be judged as a successful strategy to stop any further influence and networking of the human rights movement. Thus, in the case of Tunisia, this kind of tactical concession was not accompanied by an increasingly strong and growing transnational human rights network. Instead, the transnational networking and exchange process became more and more subject to the control of the Tunisian government.

In Morocco, the human rights situation remained poor during the 1980s as described above. At the beginning of the 1990s, however, a transformation started to take place. Between 1990 and 1994 several royal acts of clemency released long-term political prisoners and so-called "disappeared persons" and announced that the secret prison at Tazmamart was to be closed down (Amnesty International 1994b: 68–83). There has since been a slow but continuous improvement in the human rights situation despite some contradictions and occasional set-backs.

Explaining the variation in human rights change: the importance of transnational human rights networks and domestic structures

The question is, what accounts for these shifts? I suggest that the variation can be explained with reference to the activities of transnational advocacy networks. These networks developed quite differently in Tunisia and Morocco according to the domestic structures of the states. The difference, as we shall see, is that the Moroccan state structure did not prevent the development of a consistently active transnational network as was the case in Tunisia.

In the case of the more pluralistic state of Morocco under the predominance of a monarch who is by definition superior to the state, a differentiated national network of human rights non-governmental organizations (NGOs) constituted the precondition for the development of a manifold and intensive transnational human rights network.

115

Through an arduous and often convoluted process, it was possible for human rights networks to have a significant impact on national politics in Morocco. It seems to be quite obvious in this case that changes in human rights conditions could be achieved as a result of coordinated action inside and outside the country.

The Tunisian government, by contrast, insulated itself from such pressure. In Tunisia, it was already impossible at the national level to constitute a diverse network of human rights NGOs. Tunisian human rights activists of different ideological backgrounds had to assemble in the only legal non-governmental human rights group, The Ligue Tunisienne des Droits de l'Homme (LTDH). The lack of a structural diversity of NGOs on the national level influenced in a negative way the development of a transnational network. The temporal strength of the only human rights NGO could be split by tactical moves of the new Tunisian government after 1987. As a consequence, international human rights critics from outside were no longer supported from and grounded in an active internal human rights movement.

By comparing the success conditions of human rights networks in each country, I show that no real change of human rights politics will be achieved without network activities from "above" and "below". In this context, I develop the causal links between the societal and state reaction towards each other in accordance with the spiral model.

The central goal of a human rights network is the implementation and real recognition of such norms in the respective states (Keck and Sikkink 1998). The institutionalization of these norms in the domestic structure is crucial as a first step toward political change. But the Tunisian case shows that this is not enough. The process of institutionalization of norms has to be accompanied by the socialization of state actors into accepting and respecting human rights. Taking into account the authoritarian nature of the North African states, it becomes clear that this socialization process could not derive only from internal communication processes between state leaders and their opposition. There needs to be support from outside. But it is nevertheless important to notice how existing national norms, identities, and institutional structures shape working conditions of non-governmental actors as well as the development of a transnational network. This will be explained in the following part.

Similarities and differences between Moroccan and Tunisian state institutions

Since the differences in the way the Moroccan and Tunisian state leaders responded to human rights demands lay in the institutional structure of their government, I will refer briefly to the political structure of each state. Morocco is a constitutional monarchy, centrally ruled by a king who is equipped with extensive powers of legislation. Tunisia is a Presidential republic. As in Morocco, the power in the Tunisian government is centralized in the President. While both the Tunisian and Moroccan constitutions provide for the legal separation of the executive, legislative, and judicial powers, there is no real division in practice. Thus, both the King of Morocco and the President of Tunisia have almost absolute power; politics are almost entirely beyond institutional control. To make matters more difficult, neither of the two constitutions preserves human rights unconditionally. Indeed respect for human rights is qualified by such clauses as "as long as the public order is not disrupted" or as long as "sacred issues" (monarchy, Islam, and country) are secure. Thus even if the constitutions were more legitimate, human rights would probably not be respected. Finally, since there is no independent judiciary or rule of law in either country victims of human rights abuse have no recourse (Faath 1986, 1987, 1992a, and 1992b).

But there is a history of differences between the two countries, despite their similarities. The neopatrimonial style of the government in Tunisia and the patrimonial tradition in Morocco derive their legitimacy from different sources. Following from his dual function as a secular and Islamic leader, the Moroccan king is not accountable to law; he is unimpeachable. Monarchy as an institution is itself regarded as "sacred" and this commitment largely determines political culture in Morocco (Damis 1992; Entelis 1989; Wolff 1993). The Moroccan king is thus supported by an institution strongly embodied in tradition. In contrast, the Tunisian President rules on the basis of a single, secularized ideology which is embodied in the constitution. Unlike the Moroccan dualism between secularism and Islam, all relevant institutions and organizations in Tunisia are obliged to follow a single political and social concept (Faath 1986, 1992a; Camau and Jellal 1987). In opposition to the more Islam-orientated Moroccan state, Tunisia has developed a more secular state identity in spite of the formally recognized state religion, Islam. This difference in national identities constructed by

117

political elites in each state after independence is reflected in the identities and norm responsiveness of the opposition movements as described below.

Another difference between the political structures of the two countries lies in the party system. Although the Tunisian political structure was taken over and nationalized by the new political ruling elite after independence, it followed the tradition of the French central colonial administration. As such, the Tunisian government is formally structured along the lines of Western democracies. In reality however, the "democracy" has developed into a socialist one-party system. Parliamentary opposition was restricted after the regime change despite some occasional openings between 1987 and 1989. The Moroccan multi-party system, however, is codified by the constitution and has been flourishing since the 1960s when the Moroccan king encouraged the founding of new parties. Compared to Tunisia, the Moroccan party system shows greater pluralism (Faath 1992b; Garon 1994; Engelhardt 1996). For a long time, the bourgeois party loyal to the king was the only party ever elected to government although an opposition party called Istiqlal (traditional trade bourgeoisie) and a number of left-wing parties existed.[3] All of them supported the monarchy as a form of government. Parliamentary opposition in Morocco has developed since the early 1990s. The king initiated a slow successive opening of the political system; party-independent members of the opposition were even included in government responsibilities at times. For the first time in Moroccan history and as a result of the last elections of 1997, the main opposition parties were in 1998 participating in the government.

State repression and initial mobilization of domestic actors in Morocco and Tunisia (phase 1)

In both Morocco and Tunisia, the starting point for the development of the human rights movement was the increasing state repression in the 1970s as described above. As a result of the continuous internal repression in the mid to late 1970s non-governmental human rights groups began to organize themselves on the domestic level. They were also using formal and informal channels to transfer information about human rights violations to foreign countries. In the case of Morocco, those channels took a long time to be built up and were much more important

---

[3] Union Nationale des Forces Populaires (UNFP) – a socialist party closely tied to the Moroccan trade union; Union Marocaine du Travail (UMT), Union Socialiste des Forces Populaires (USFP), and the Parti du Progrès et du Socialisme (PPS).

than in Tunisia. The starting point of such successful network activities among human rights actors was Moroccan domestic politics.

Morocco

As a result of its pluralist party system, Morocco has had more human rights organizations and activists than Tunisia since the 1970s. Non-governmental human rights organizations were established in the early 1970s following the attempted military coups and the subsequent arrests. Members of the Istiqlal Party founded the first human rights organization, the Ligue Marocaine pour la Défense des Droits de L'Homme (LMDDH), in 1972. At the same time, student-led left-wing groups that banded together under the auspices of the Comités de Lutte Contre la Répression au Maroc (CLCRM) acted illegally. At the end of the 1970s, the families of those arrested also began to form active human rights groups independent of the political parties (Feliu 1994). Another party-affiliated NGO, the Association Marocaine de Droits de l'Homme (AMDH) was founded on June 24, 1979, as a wing of the Union Socialiste des Forces Populaires (USFP). In contrast to the LMDDH, which focused its activities at the national level, this organization was set up particularly with the aim to uncover and to publicize human rights violations abroad. The explicit goal was to create international pressure on the Moroccan government to rectify the human rights situation (Faath 1992b: 396).

Contacts abroad played a significant role for the Moroccan human rights NGOs. Personal and informal contacts between domestic human rights groups in Morocco and Moroccan emigrant groups in Europe transmitted precise information about the human rights violations to European and international human rights organizations. Since France was the center of Moroccan exile opposition and the country with the largest Moroccan community, support committees of the CLCRM (Association de Soutien des CLCRM) and the Association of Relatives of Disappeared Persons (AFDM) were founded there. In addition to the CLCRM and the AFDM a Moroccan student group became active in the 1980s: the Association for the Protection of Human Rights in Morocco (ASDHM), which worked closely together with the Moroccan exile group ADHM (Association des Droits de l'Homme au Maroc) in Paris. Their activities concentrated on the regular publication of information brochures, the organization of public events, and occasional demonstrations in Europe. They also provided international human rights organizations like Amnesty International, the Lawyers' Committee of

119

Human Rights, and Human Rights Watch, with regular information (Sherry 1990; Sanguinetti 1991).

Throughout the 1980s, the networking process went on and resulted in a strong network density. A variety of diverse actors was involved in the transnational network over a ten-year period. Regular publications and protest campaigns in Europe against the ongoing human rights violations in Morocco showed that the transnational human rights network consisted of effective activist bases in and outside the country. Strong personal and informal links supported individual contacts between dissidents and exile groups in France and their families and friends in Morocco.

Tunisia

In Tunisia, the domestic human rights movement developed in a quite different way. In 1976, the Ligue Tunisienne des Droits de l'Homme (LTDH) was founded in reaction to growing state repression; one year later, the Tunisian government legalized this non-governmental human rights organization. Since there was no official opposition party, the LTDH could present itself as politically independent. The official acknowledgment of the universality of human rights – Tunisia had signed the international human rights convention in 1969 – was a good reference point to be raised by non-governmental actors in order to criticize the government. The Tunisian League was, therefore, in an apparently better position to voice human rights concern than Moroccan human rights organizations; the Tunisian government had to acknowledge the discourse of human rights. In the Tunisian one-party system, the official recognition of the LTDH as the only legitimate non-governmental organization bolstered its position. In the following years, the entire range of government opposition movements came together under the umbrella of the LTDH. Since there was no legal alternative voice for opposition, the LTDH became a melting-pot for political opposition for all causes – not just for human rights. To gather these different ideological groupings together was at the same time its greatest strength and its greatest weakness. Ideological differences within the organization caused many conflicts which could not be solved easily (extensively described in Dwyer 1991: 168–181).

The successful public activities of the LTDH during the early 1980s seemed to suggest that human rights norms gained greater domestic legitimacy. The Tunisian human rights movement used the fact that President Bourguiba did not reject the validity of the human rights idea, to put public pressure on the Tunisian government and force it to justify its human rights practices. This pressure from "below" seemed to be so effective that international organizations were content to take a back seat. International human rights organizations reinforced the concerns already being voiced in the Tunisian struggle over human rights in this phase rather than launching an international campaign. The human rights movement in Tunisia appeared to enjoy such a success in these early stages that its true internal impact was often overestimated, both inside and outside the country. The LTDH was cited as a successful example of human rights awareness in the Arab world (Dwyer 1991; Faath 1992a; S. Waltz 1989). But their occasional influence on government decisions remained limited and ended with the change of government tactics after the 1987 regime change. One can, therefore, conclude that the strength of the domestic human rights organization LTDH in the period just before the regime change resulted mainly from the weakness of the Tunisian government.

These differences in the way in which human rights activists in Tunisia and Morocco organized and expressed themselves were crucial for the further development of the human rights situation. Since the developments vary considerably in the two countries, I shall now describe them separately.

Morocco
Denial (Phase 2)

The first reaction of the Moroccan government to Amnesty International's reports on human rights violations was to categorically reject the accusations and to criticize Amnesty International for interfering in internal Moroccan affairs. The king of Morocco, Hassan II, reserved the right to define and interpret the idea of human rights in Morocco. This was due to his central role in government. Criticism and public debate should neither implicitly nor explicitly contest the monarchy, Islam, Morocco's territorial integrity, or the particular king himself. In 1979, Morocco signed the international human rights convention but continued to act repressively. During the 1980s, the Moroccan government continued to reject the mounting accusations of human rights violations (Amnesty International 1994b: 80, S. Waltz 1995a). At the same time and as a result of network efforts to prove that the government was lying, the Moroccan human rights network multiplied and became more diverse.

121

Pressure on the Moroccan government grew as the human rights network became more mobilized inside and outside the country. In 1985, the king rejected every single Amnesty International report on human rights violations at an international press conference. In response to the public pressure, however, Morocco signed the anti-torture convention in 1986. In the same year, Amnesty International published a short report on torture in Morocco and launched an international campaign.

In December 1988, a group of Moroccan intellectuals founded a new human rights organization that proclaimed the independence of political parties, the Organisation Marocaine de Droits de l'Homme. Instead of attempting to operate independently from the government as most opposition groups did, the OMDH recruited government officials as well as persons closely connected to the government. Towards the end of the 1980s, almost all Moroccan human rights organizations had intensified their cooperation. The political conditions in Morocco were changing and increasingly characterized by a growing social pluralism – particularly with respect to freedom of press and association.

The cooperative efforts of the various human rights groups produced a common National Charter of Human Rights in 1990. AMDH, LMDDH, and OMDH signed and activated it in Rabat on December 12 in cooperation with the Moroccan association of attorneys, and the Moroccan professional association of lawyers. On the international level, human rights organizations like the Fédération Internationale des Droits de l'Homme (FIDH) and Amnesty International supported the Moroccan non-governmental initiatives collaborating with such regional organizations as the Arab Organization of Human Rights (AOHR), various medical groups, the Lawyers Committee for Human Rights, and Middle East Watch. A regular publication of ongoing human rights violations by the transnational network raised extensive public attention (Amnesty International 1990a–c, 1991a–e, 1993a, 1994a). The publication of the book *Notre Ami le Roi* by Gilles Perrault in France in September 1990 (Perrault 1990) brought enormous attention to the human rights movement, partly because of the adverse reaction from the Moroccan government, which tried to stop publication and then bought up an entire edition. Copies of the book were smuggled to Morocco and circulated. European partner states of Morocco as well as the European Union could no longer ignore the growing criticism. Extensive mobilization against the Moroccan king during his state visits in Europe increased the pressure on Western states to act. Moroccan exile groups in France increased political pressure on President Mitterrand to express objections to the Moroccan policy. Amnesty International sponsored a demonstration against torture during King Hassan's visit to London. Exile groups and human rights activists released a report on Morocco in 1986 when King Hassan II visited the European parliament. As a result, the latter passed a resolution requiring the president of the European parliament to express the parliament's serious objections against the human rights situation in Morocco (Europa Publications 1995).

In January 1988, several demonstrations took place in Belgium, France, Germany, and the Netherlands against violations of human rights in Morocco (Faath 1992b; S. Waltz 1995a). In December 1989, King Hassan II continued to reject the supposed human rights violations during a French television interview and invited Amnesty International to a "fact-finding mission" (Amnesty International 1994b: 79). This invitation was an important breakthrough for the international human rights network. It opened a "window of opportunity" for the transnational network to have an impact. This invitation and the visit of Amnesty International in 1990 resulted from the extensive public campaign of the transnational human rights network which damaged the positive image of Morocco in the eyes of the international public. The king's public invitation to Amnesty International accompanied a political shift in his human rights discourse. By establishing official communications with a human rights INGO, he could no longer categorically reject human rights accusations. In response to the pressures of the transnational advocacy network, the Moroccan government started to react with tactical concessions.

Tactical concessions in Morocco: strengthening the transnational network (phase 3)

Between 1990 and 1992, increasing pressure by the international human rights network forced King Hassan II to undertake tactical measures in order to improve Morocco's negative image. These tactical concessions created new opportunities for communicative interactions between governmental and non-governmental actors. As a side-effect, they increasingly drew the Moroccan king into the human rights discourse. He was forced to "learn" by communicating with human rights activists that he could no longer count on traditional diplomatic rules to silence his opponents. In February 1990, the Amnesty delegation came to

Morocco and met with the Comité pour le dialogue avec Amnesty International which had been established specifically for this occasion. A report on the *garde-à-vue* custody was presented to the king who later condemned the publication as a profound violation of the diplomatic protocol. The Moroccan government attempted to save its image through an advertisement campaign which condemned the Amnesty International report. The campaign was published in Europe's most important newspapers.

The result was counter-productive. Instead of vindicating the Moroccan government, the advertisements captured public attention and focused interest ever more keenly on human rights issues in the country. The Moroccan government had originally planned to react to the Amnesty report by sending half a million collected letters of protest to France. However, with the rising tide of attention on their side, internal and international human rights groups resisted and political criticism in the international community continued to mount. Moroccan newspapers and public congresses discussed and published the criticism about human rights violations resulting in a parliamentary vote of censure against the government. This communication exchange between domestic NGOs and actors in Moroccan state institutions and the ensuing public pressure inside Morocco ultimately resulted from the activism of the transnational network outside Morocco. The successful interplay between outside and inside actions in this period exposed the Moroccan regime as a human rights violating state and forced it to react to the accusations (S. Waltz 1995a: 203–215).

The king dramatically changed his rhetoric on human rights and created a new state institution to deal with the situation. In 1990, Morocco began to set up human rights institutions in cooperation with representatives of human rights NGOs. In a most significant speech on May 8, 1990 (Saâf 1993), the king announced the creation of the Conseil Consultative des Droits de l'Homme and encouraged representatives of all human rights NGOs to participate. Each NGO was permitted to suggest two persons as representatives, one of whom the king would select. Three sub-committees were formed to respectively deal with (1) complaints regarding the police and *garde-à-vue* custody, (2) the improvement of prison conditions, and (3) contacts with international human rights organizations. The king reserved the right to meet with the committee when necessary (Saâf 1993). In accordance with suggestions by the Moroccan Conseil Consultative de Droits de l'Homme, a 6-day limitation was placed on *garde-à-vue* custody in 1991.

In November 1993, the government was restructured to include a Ministry for Human Rights. Omar Azziman, an independent human rights activist and former president of the OMDH, became its head.[4] Azziman lost his position in the ministry in 1995, but the progress to institute important measures against human rights violations from 'above' continued. In the aftermath of the 1997 elections, Azziman was named as Minister of Justice. In this new position, he could undertake even more effective measures.[5] The slow, but continuous improvement of the human rights situation that has evolved in Morocco reflected the activities of the human rights organizations and the consequences which these activities had on King Hassan II (Organisation Marocaine des Droits de l'Homme 1994a–b, 1995, 1996; Basri, Rousset, and Vedel 1994; Bensbia 1996; Hegasy 1997). The rhetorical shifts in his official speeches in Morocco and in his interviews with foreign journalists after 1990 show a successful persuasion process by the transnational network resulting in a change in human rights policy (Gränzer 1998).

According to the "spiral model," the Moroccan case can therefore be interpreted as in transition to phase 4, even though it has not yet reached full "prescriptive status."

Tunisia

First reactions of the Tunisian government: no denial (skipping of phase 2)

Since Tunisia had signed the international conventions already in 1969, the human rights norms were not denied by the Tunisian government. As a result, Tunisia did not undergo a "denial phase." This behavior of the Tunisian government is crucial for explaining the further development of the human rights situation. I shall show that the transnational human rights network could not develop its strengths as compared to Morocco in the absence of denial of the norm by the Tunisian government.

The Tunisian League for Human Rights could always refer to the international commitments of the Tunisian state in its criticism of the human rights violations. By the mid-1980s, the LTDH had become a

---

[4] Interviewed in January 1997, Omar Azziman described his enormous opportunities to build up this ministry totally outside the old bureaucratic structures of the government. He himself could choose the personnel of the ministry and put many independent intellectuals and human rights activists into strategic positions in that new ministry. Many of these people are still working there.

[5] Interview with Moroccan human rights activists in Rabat and Casablanca in January 1997, and in Tunis in March 1998.

significant political force in Tunisia which had generated a lot of domestic legitimacy through their public actions. The LTDH negotiated with the government and even intervened with the Minister of Interior in cases of suspected torture. In spring 1984, the league mounted a successful national and international campaign that led to the commutation of all death sentences after trials following the "bread riots" of January 1984. These public protests were possible because the human rights norm as such was not questioned by the Tunisian state. During the political crisis of 1987 when President Bourguiba tried to increase state repression, LTDH seemed to be the only credible opposition in Tunisia which could express criticism (Dwyer 1991).

The political elite in the state apparatus reacted to the growing national and international criticism by replacing the president. Thus, when Prime Minister Ben Ali succeeded Bourguiba in November 1987 through a "constitutional coup," he was welcomed nationally and internationally in the hope of progressive political change. The new Tunisian government now shifted directly to tactical concessions. This political move of replacing the president and introducing a new human rights rhetoric stopped immediately the further mobilization of the human rights network.

Tactical concessions in Tunisia: weakening of the transnational network (phase 3)

Tactical concessions in Tunisia occurred in the absence of significant pressure from a transnational network and have, therefore, to be judged quite differently than in the Morroccan context. The first evident change in government behavior concerned rhetoric. The new President Ben Ali declared human rights as a fundamental duty of his government. Ben Ali's government justified the replacement of Bourguiba on the basis of human rights and convincingly declared human rights to be the ideological core of the new government. Susan Waltz (1995a: 65f) pointed out that Ben Ali chose the human rights idea to secure support for his power coup. Such positive rhetoric and some institutional measures initially created the impression that the human rights situation had greatly improved (Faath 1992a). Until 1990–1991, internationally sponsored conferences on human rights, seminars disseminating information on concrete state measures and new amendments to custody and the rights of the imprisoned took place in Tunisia. Another positive measure taken by the new Tunisian government was, for example, to officially legalize the Tunisian branch of Amnesty International in April 1988 as the first Amnesty International affiliate in an Arab country. It had already existed illegally since 1981. The transformation of human rights policies by the Tunisian government under Ben Ali did not take place as a result of international pressures, but occurred "voluntarily". At first, these measures elicited a positive response in the international community among international organizations and INGOs. As a result, the change of power linked to a rhetorical turn in the human rights discourse of the Tunisian state interrupted a further mobilization inside and outside the country.

It only became clear in the 1990s that the state was violating the very legal norms it had codified (North African Students for Freedom 1991; Amnesty International 1992, 1993b, 1994c; Middle East Watch 1992; S. Waltz 1995b; Human Rights Watch 1997). The government suppressed human rights criticism by putting itself in charge of the defense of human rights. One strategy was to reduce the political influence of human rights NGOs through cooptation and integration into the government. The internal influence of the Tunisian League was limited by integrating two of their former presidents into the government. With the change of power in 1987, the LTDH had experienced a brief upturn until 1989, but by 1991 working conditions for the group had already become much less favorable (Sraieb 1993). The LTDH then dissolved itself in 1992 following a dispute with the government. It was not refounded until 1994 and then with a much more modest agenda which conformed closely with the government. With the help of the government party, the Rassemblement Constitutionnel Démocratique (RCD), the Tunisian government tried to build up another human rights organization to counterbalance the alleged "one-sided" LTDH (Faath 1992a). The state founded the Association de Défense des Droits de l'Homme et des Libertés Publiques (ADDHLP) on May 5, 1988. But the new organization rarely appeared in the public due to internal disputes. Other human rights measures by the Ben Ali government were also reversed after 1990. When the international board of Amnesty International published more and more critical reports, state authorities started to hamper the work of the Tunisian branch of Amnesty International and to harass its members. The Institut Arabe des Droits de l'Homme (IADH) which had been founded in September 1989 as a pan-Arabic human rights NGO[6] located in Tunis, ended its independent public

---

[6] Founding members of the IADH were the LTDH, the Arab Association of Lawyers, and the Arab Organization for Human Rights (AOHR). The activities of the IADH were

activities around 1993 because of the control and repression by the Tunisian government.

Yet in hindsight, Ben Ali's intentions should have been questioned much earlier. Throughout his military education and his career in the state security apparatus, Ben Ali had been part of the state when it violated human rights. At times, he himself was in positions responsible for human rights violations.[7] It thus seems plausible that he based his rise to power on the platform of human rights merely as a veil for strategic interests. The majority of political amnesties in the early years were presented as acts of mercy by the new president (S. Waltz 1995a: 55). Ben Ali's decision to appoint two founding members of the Tunisian human rights group LTDH to the cabinet after his accession illustrates the point. This move bound potential opponents of the secular human rights wing to the government and split the LTDH. As a tactical measure, this led to a weakening of the human rights community in Tunisia. The Islamic-oriented wing of the LTDH left the organization and began to act illegally at the same time as the government's persecution of Islamists was intensified.

By 1990, the Ben Ali government became more aggressive against the human rights movement; it introduced political and legal measures to reduce the activities of the national human rights groups and to limit freedom of press, association, and information (Garon 1994, 1995a–b). Since then there has been a consistent deterioration of the human rights situation. While the situation has been continuously criticized by international human rights organizations (Lawyers' Commitee for Human Rights 1993a, 1993b, 1994, 1995b), it did not lead to a successful transnational network mobilization. A major reason for this was the loss of the internal human rights structure represented in the LTDH. The splitting effect of the integration and cooptation of some of their leading members from the secular opposition was reinforced by the growing official

supported by international and Arab NGOs.
[7] At twenty-five, Zine el Abidine Ben Ali was sent to French and American military schools by the Tunisian government, where he completed his education in the military news service, security service, and the artillery. When he returned to Tunisia he was made Chief of Military Security at the age of twenty-seven. After a short time as the military attaché in Morocco, he became a member of the defense cabinet as Chief of Domestic Security. After he had proved his military capabilities in 1978 with the bloody suppression of the strikes and worker revolts, he was made a general in 1979. After serving as an ambassador in Warsaw, he was promoted from Chief of Domestic Security to Secretary of State (1984) to Home Minister in May 1987. On October 10, 1987, he also became prime minister and was therefore the natural successor of Bourguiba.

128

control and repression of all activities of national and international NGOs in Tunisia prevented it (Sraieb 1993; Callies de Salies 1995; Ibrahimi 1997).

Through a combination of tactical concessions, the Tunisian government successfully interrupted the mobilization of a transnational human rights network. The contradictory behavior of the Tunisian government – verbal support for human rights and implementation of certain human rights institutions like an ombudsman[8] together with increased political repression – prevented human rights activities in the non-governmental sector. As a result, the transnational human rights network is not visible in Tunisia; it was successfully "silenced" by the Ben Ali regime.

This case indicates that sustainable change could not be achieved without pressure from "above" and "below." Mere "external" accusations by international human rights organizations ("above") without "internal" non-governmental activities ("below") were bound to fail. Through positive rhetoric about respect for human rights and token institutional gestures to back up that talk, the Tunisian government disguised the deteriorating situation during the 1990s. Moreover, the first repressive measures were directed particularly against Islamic fundamentalists which were presented as a threat to Western values. The Tunisian government initially got away with this repression, because the secular opposition which constitutes the human rights movement in Tunisia after 1987, shares Western-oriented values and, as a result, this threat perception (Bras 1996). However, since the repression of fundamentalist activities was extended to any kind of political opposition, the Tunisian government eventually lost its internal and external credibility.

After a period of silence, the international human rights community started criticizing the Tunisian government. By 1993, the Tunisian government began to prosecute Tunisian human rights activists and to hinder the expansion of a national human rights network through restrictive political and legal measures. With freedom of the press restricted and international newspapers banned (Garon 1994), effective collaboration between national and international non-governmental

---

[8] After 1991 the Tunisian government established official institutions following heavy criticism by international human rights observers: the Comité Supérieur des Droits de l'Homme et des Libertés Fondamentales as well as a special emissary to the president regarding human rights issues and counseling offices and special human rights departments in ministries.

human rights organizations became exceedingly difficult. Monitoring human rights violations in Tunisia became next to impossible (Amnesty International 1997d; Ibrahimi 1997; US Department of State 1997; Garon 1998). Active members of human rights NGOs are today subjected to severe pressures by the police.[9] Most social activities seem to be paralyzed. The middle class seems to enjoy the advantages of the economic liberalization of the country and is, thus, not interested in openly opposing Ben Ali. This silence is reinforced by the fact that the middle class shares the government's threat description concerning Islamic fundamentalism (Bras 1996; Ibrahim 1995a). Because Islamic fundamentalism questions the basis of Western style secularism, it is considered to be a greater evil than repression. Since international human rights NGOs have begun to raise serious concerns about the deteriorating human rights situation during the last years – a fact which stands in sharp contradiction to the official human rights discourses of the Tunisian government – Ben Ali is more and more forced to justify himself abroad.

Conclusion

As the comparison of Tunisia and Morocco indicates, transnational human rights networks are crucial for the way in which international human rights norms affect the prospects of domestic political change. Alternative explanations are incapable of accounting for the developments, either in the case of Tunisia or in the case of Morocco.

Modernization theories argue, for example, that economic growth is an essential prerequisite for political change (for Tunisia see Hawkins and Tessler 1987). Empirical findings for both Arab countries contradict this assumption. During the 1980s, both countries implemented structural adjustment programs and began to overcome the economic crises they had experienced during that decade (see Hermassi 1994). Since then, both countries experienced a significant economic upturn. The increase in economic growth, however, only correlated with an improvement in human rights conditions in Morocco. In the Tunisian case, the backlash reported above cannot be accounted for by a change in economic

---

[9] The author experienced this situation herself during her stay in Tunisia in March 1998, where interviews with Tunisian human rights activists were severely hampered by the Tunisian police. Permanent supervision and "warnings" from the Tunisian secret police in order to stop contacting Tunisian opponents complicated the field research in Tunisia.

conditions. In both Tunisia and Morocco, a clientelist system secures that the middle-class interests are closely linked to state interests and, therefore, provide no serious social basis for a democratization process (Bakarat 1993; Farah and Kuroda 1987; Hermassi 1994; Perthes 1992).

An explanation of change through material pressure from Great Powers is not relevant, either, to explain positive changes in human rights policies in Morocco or Tunisia. Western partners never used serious material pressure to achieve an improvement in the human rights conditions in either country. Both North African states were regarded as politically stable and Western-oriented and, indeed, they had Western support during the Cold War. Because Morocco's and Tunisia's neighbors were socialist, the USA wanted a basis for strategic and military support in North Africa.[10] Additionally, the French maintained close economic and politico-cultural links with Tunisia and Morocco after their colonial rule ended in 1956 (Blin 1991; Clam 1988). Because of their special relationship with France, both states have been contractually involved with the European Community (EC) since the 1960s and these relationships continue to grow in scope and importance (Regelsberger 1988; Weidnitzer 1995). Since the Barcelona Conference in November 1995, the allocation of development aid has been tied to a commitment on behalf of Tunisia and Morocco to preserve human rights. But to this day, the condition of human rights in each country has never been invoked as justification for stopping the flow of development aid. As a result, the variation in the degree to which human rights conditions improved in Morocco, as compared to the increased repression in Tunisia, cannot be accounted for by simply pointing to great power pressure from abroad.

In analyzing the process of political change in each country, it becomes obvious that the absence or presence of an active transnational human rights network is playing a crucial role in the development of the human rights situation in North Africa. The discourse of human rights and the political activities to which it has given rise has altered the structure of the relationship between the state and society in the respective countries. The regimes in power in both countries had to redefine their basis of legitimacy by referring to human rights (S. Waltz 1995a, Bennani and Leveau 1996).

In the case of Morocco, a strong transnational advocacy network put

---

[10] The Reagan administration defined "security" as primarily military, and throughout 1982 to 1985 used a great deal of its "security assistance programme" to finance weapon purchases (Hubel 1988: 188).

pressure on the government from "above" and "below" and, thus, made it possible for human rights norms to take root. A protracted process of persuasion through public mediation and negotiation, ultimately had positive results; human rights norms have achieved a certain degree of "prescriptive status." In the case of Tunisia, the human rights norms were "implemented" directly by the government without much transnational network participation. By immediately responding to domestic pressure via tactical concessions, the Tunisian government was able to "silence" domestic human rights activists and to weaken the emerging transnational network. As there was no systematic pressure from "above" and "below", human rights measures were superficial and could be easily circumvented by the Tunisian government.

With regard to the "spiral model," the Tunisian case illustrates the importance of the second phase of denial. By skipping this phase, an important condition for the development of a transnational network was not fulfilled. Without the government denying international human rights norms as an intervention into their domestic affairs, the transnational network was deprived of its major political target: the non-compliance of the domestic regime with international human rights norms. By directly making tactical concessions and, at the same time, rhetorically committing itself to international human rights, the Tunisian government undermined the argumentative substance of the transnational network in the public debate, both at the domestic and international levels. The transnational network was stripped of the possibility of using its most important political resource: the power of persuasion. The ability to define political discourse is an indispensable power resource of non-governmental actors, but also of states. To a significant degree, the human rights struggle in North Africa has been a contest over political discourse. As the Tunisian case indicates, the blockade of the human rights network bears significant consequences for the internalization of international human rights norms at the domestic level.

What lessons can be drawn from this comparison? More specifically, under what conditions can we expect transnational advocacy networks to be effective in promoting and helping to institutionalize respect for human rights? First, there must be a domestic political situation conducive to the proliferation of a diversified internal human rights movement. In addition, the actors in that movement must be willing and/or able to transmit information about internal conditions to sources outside the country, even if that entails political risk. This was not possible in Tunisia where repression is on the increase; however, it did occur in Morocco during the 1980s. Second, the government must not deploy rhetoric as a smokescreen for inaction. Because the Tunisian government used a rhetoric of responsiveness, the international community was unable to perceive the government's true irresponsibility.

In Morocco, on the other hand, rhetoric has been matched with action. The human rights situation in Morocco has improved as a result of successful contacts and information exchanges between national and international human rights organizations. The intensive networking process created a snowball effect which forced the Moroccan government to take measures against human rights abuses. The international pressure which mounted on the king between 1988 and 1992 could not have been generated without the intensive cooperation of national and international NGOs. The international human rights discourse put moral pressure on Morocco. In sum, the improvement of the human rights situation in Morocco can be traced to the activities of a transnational network. The increasing pressure on authorities, both from "above" and from "below" changed the domestic political situation (S. Waltz 1995a; Amnesty International 1994b).

These empirical insights into political developments in Arab cultures contradict the arguments of Huntington (1996). In analyzing the acceptance and recognition process of human rights norms in the Maghreb states, his "clash-of-civilization" argument is empirically questionable. In the case of the more secular country, Tunisia, the human rights norms are less implemented than in the more traditional Islamic state of Morocco. King Hassan II's traditional image, combined with his strong desire to put Morocco on the list of, so-called "civilized" nations, made him more vulnerable to public pressures by the transnational network than Tunisia's president. Tunisia had already developed an image as the most Westernized Arab state before the 1987 regime change. Westerners tended to view the Tunisian republic as progressive and the Moroccan monarchy as a traditional and perhaps antiquated system. But these generalizations do injustice to the reality; the political cultures of these two countries imply the reverse. Foreign governments, Western NGOs, and researchers alike have long viewed Tunisia as a model for the Arab states in how to organize their Islamic culture into a political form. This view has to be reconsidered.

5 Linking the unlinkable? International norms and nationalism in Indonesia and the Philippines

Anja Jetschke

Introduction

The sudden change of power in Indonesia in May 1998 makes us forget that for a very long period of time it appeared as if Southeast Asian countries were "hard cases" in terms of a positive development with regard to civil and political human rights. Except in the cases of Thailand and the Philippines, democratic freedoms were and still are being severely curtailed in the entire Southeast Asian region (Hassan 1996; Mauzy 1995). The debate over the universality of international human rights standards and Asian values has influential supporters in many Southeast Asian countries such as Malaysia, Singapore, and Indonesia (see Emmerson 1996; Heinz and Pfennig 1996; Kausikan 1994). Moreover, lacking a regional mechanism for the promotion and protection of human rights, such as the European or African Human Rights Conventions, Asian countries never experienced the socialization effects that might be expected from such a regional human rights organization (see Jones 1996).

In this context, the purpose of this chapter is twofold. First, it will evaluate the spiral model presented in the editor's introduction by comparing state–society relations in the Philippines and in Indonesia from the early 1970s to the mid-1990s. I will argue that the spiral model

This is a substantially revised version of a paper I presented at the 38th Annual Convention of the International Studies Association (ISA), Toronto, Canada, March 18–22, 1997. The paper greatly profited from the comments provided by Thomas Seitz, Philip Eldridge, Wolfgang S. Heinz, Stephanie Lawson, and Richard Pierre Claude as well as Cambridge University Press's anonymous reviewers. None of these people, of course, bears any responsibility for my views or conclusions.

can be applied to the Philippines as well as to Indonesia and that in both countries, transnational human rights networks induced changes in human rights practices. The effect of these networks was more substantial in the Philippines, where according to the indicators – torture, extrajudicial killings, arbitrary arrest, and disappearances – it has led to a steady decrease in human rights violations (beginning the fifth phase of the model). Indonesia is still in an earlier stage and – at the time of writing – is in a transition phase to prescriptive status (phase 4).

Second, I will outline the differences in the two country's socialization processes which explain why the duration of the phases varies in these cases despite the general applicability of the spiral model. I will argue that due to the varying legacies of colonialism, different preconditions for human rights development can be found which shaped the process of norm internalization. I will break these differences down into the varying notions and functions of *official nationalism*, that is, the nationally varying ideologies of collective distinctiveness and purpose, as a significant part of the national discourse. The Philippine and Indonesian nationalisms reveal that far from being a residue of prerationalism or being unlinkable with civil liberties, nationalism is a highly dynamic force capable of associating itself with a human rights rhetoric in different ways.

The structure of the chapter will largely follow the five phases in the introductory chapter, describe the emergence of transnational advocacy networks, and explain how they have triggered changes in human rights policies in the Philippines and Indonesia. Later, I will evaluate whether alternative explanations can account for the observed developments. The conclusion will summarize the findings and discuss the prospects for continual progress in human rights practices in the two countries.

History and the relevance of nationalism

Indonesia and the Philippines vary greatly with respect to religion, social stratification, colonial experiences, and geographical shape. With a population of 65 million the Philippines stands out as the only predominantly Catholic country in Southeast Asia. Its long experience first of Spanish colonialism (1565–1898) and then of US colonialism (1898–1946), interrupted by Japanese occupation, left an imprint on its political culture. The resulting contact with Western culture led to a greater degree of conversion to Western values than in any of the other

Southeast Asian countries (Wurfel 1965: 679). The Philippine polity developed into a system greatly influenced by the political, economic, and military hegemony of the US.

Prior to the declaration of martial law in 1972, the Philippines had experienced continuous democratic rule since 1935. It was the oldest democracy in the region and the official rhetoric portrayed the Philippines as a modern nation-state governed by the rule-of-law (Sidel 1995: 140–142). Due to European and American influences, all Filipino constitutions since 1898 have included basic standards of human rights (Wurfel 1965: 722–742). The expansion of the educational system under American rule resulted in the emergence of an independent middle class and contributed to one of the highest literacy rates (90 percent) in Southeast Asia.

However, as a predominantly agricultural country with a marked system of landownership, economic disparities prevailed. Ownership of land through the hands of a few – a heritage of Spanish law – continued despite repeated efforts to distribute land more equally (Wurfel 1965: 692). Between the 1940s and the 1960s this unequal distribution of land led to popular uprisings (e.g. the Hukbalahap and Communist movements) aimed at overthrowing the various governments.

The Philippines' close relationship with the US significantly shaped the notion of official nationalism and helps to understand the impact which human rights norms had on the Philippines. The tight US–Philippines relationship had an almost unquestioned legitimacy among the ruling elites (Antikainen-Kokko 1996: 133; Constantino 1978; Shalom 1981: 183). As a consequence, the official nationalism in the Philippines was Western oriented. Anti-colonial nationalism played a lesser role in the legitimization of Filipino rulers than, for example, for rulers in Indonesia, but rather served as an ideational resource for various opposition groups. In such cases, nationalism had a clear anti-US agenda. Popular movements questioned the various treaties with the US, such as ones granting preferential trading status to US citizens or the unrestricted use of military facilities, and protested against the effects on the Philippines as a sovereign nation (Wurfel 1988: 59).

Indonesia is the largest Muslim country in the world. Over 80 percent out of 200 million people in Indonesia nominally belong to Islam. Indonesian nationalists declared their country's independence in 1945, which was followed by a bloody independence war against the Dutch

(1945–1949). In contrast to the Philippines, Indonesia does not have a strong democratic tradition. A short-lived parliamentary democracy (from 1950 to 1957) ended when Indonesia's first president, Sukarno, declared martial law in March 1957. He justified this measure by the political instability the democratic system had supposedly generated in the multi-religious and multi-ethnic state (Feith 1962). Sukarno thus introduced "Guided Democracy": he dissolved the parliament and reimplemented the 1945 Constitution which granted him extraordinary power. The coup attempt in September 1965, allegedly carried out by the Indonesian Communist Party (PKI), was politically maneuvred by the army in order to gain power. In 1967, General Suharto became president and instituted the "New Order," a political system based on unlimited executive power, a strong bureaucracy, and the establishment of corporatist state structures which enabled tight control of participatory organizations such as political parties, labor unions, and the media. The military's political and military role (dual function or *dwifungsi*) in society provided additional societal surveillance and gave the military extraordinary powers. In contrast to the Philippine constitutions, the current Constitution of 1945 entails only a very limited amount of human rights guarantees (Lubis 1993; Thoolen 1987).

The state philosophy Pancasila became the summation of Indonesian official nationalism (Pabottingi 1995; 233f), and has been a focus of national political discourse for both, official and non-governmental actors (see Ramage 1995: 4). It embodies five principles emphasizing the rights of the collective and thematizing unity and consensus, through the image of the "nation as a family." On a rhetorical level, two themes dominated the "New Order" regime: (1) development and particular economic growth, as the primary national goal and (2) the ("father knows best") communitarian elements of Pancasila which justified state intervention and effectively dislodged public accountability and thus the rule of law (Chua Beng Huat 1993: 155; Pabottingi 1995: 247). In contrast to the discourse in the Philippines, the anti-Western-oriented type of nationalist discourse has, since independence, been appropriated by the ruling elites, thus protecting them against Islamic political forces who challenged the secular foundations of the state as well as against the separatist movements contesting national unity. It has served as a major source of legitimization for Sukarno and later Suharto.

As I will argue, the differences between the Philippines and Indonesia in the loci and notions of nationalist discourses account for major variances in the effects of transnational networks as promoters of human rights norms. First, rather than being shaped by the severity, frequency, or range of human rights violations, it was official nationalism which influenced the strength and density of the networks and partly the strategies of the transnational networks (TN). The themes promoted by transnational networks were shaped by the issues dominating national discourses in each country. In the Philippines, the persistent "rule of law" rhetoric, with its emphasis on individual rights even under martial law, enabled a focus on a civil and political rights discourse which the TN could easily draw upon. This discourse corresponded with international non-governmental organizations (INGOs) such as Amnesty International and most NGOs in the US and contributed to the network strength right from the start. It was the anti-colonial-oriented nationalism, however, which during later stages of the spiral model (phase 3), fueled domestic mobilization. In Indonesia, the dominant anti-Western and collectivist rhetoric gave rise to a TN discourse based on economic, social, and cultural rights, which was less commensurate with the dominant international human rights discourse. It was not until the early 1990s that it switched to a civil and political human rights discourse.

Second, with regard to target governments, official nationalism shaped their ability to respond to the shaming strategies of transnational networks. The anti-Western nationalist rhetoric of the Indonesian government effectively shielded the Indonesian government from the attacks of TN and Western governments and thus prolonged the denial phase (phase 2). The Philippine orientation to and identification with – most importantly – the US and an international community shortened the denial phase, as President Marcos was not able to garner support against foreign intervention.

Phase 1: repression and emerging transnational mobilization

Despite differences in domestic structures and political culture, at the end of the 1960s and the early 1970s both countries developed into similar authoritarian states. In both cases ambitious economic programs served as the pretext for establishing authoritarian corporatist state structures which facilitated state control, lacked public accountability (Robison 1993; Stauffer 1977), and resulted in sharp curtailments of basic human rights.

Human rights violations were always more severe in Indonesia than in the Philippines and although human rights organizations formed in both countries early in the 1970s, the mobilization of a transnational network proceeded faster in the Philippines than in Indonesia. At times, the number of human rights abuses in Indonesia reached six figures. More than half a million people became victims of such abuses after an attempted coup in 1965. Human rights organizations estimate that over 200,000 people died because of food shortages and repression in East Timor after the Indonesian invasion. A wave of extrajudicial killings of petty criminals resulted in between 3,000 and 5,000 victims between 1983 and 1985; approximately 2,000 alleged members of a separatist movement in the Indonesian province of Aceh were killed during counterinsurgency campaigns between 1989 and 1991.

Philippines

In the Philippines, human rights violations dramatically increased after President Ferdinand Marcos imposed martial law on September 21, 1972. Marcos justified this measure on the grounds of the existence of a political rebellion and the disturbance of the public order caused by mass protests and an armed underground movement. As the constitution had allowed him to declare martial law under these circumstances, he accordingly called his regime "constitutional authoritarianism." Marcos abolished the legislative branch of his government, rendered political parties inactive, and demanded undated letters of resignation from members of the judiciary (Shalom 1981: 170).

In the first three months after the proclamation of martial law the government detained over 50,000 opposition figures, none of whom had the right to habeas corpus (Espiritu 1986: 71f; International Commission of Jurists 1977a). In 1973, Marcos promulgated a new constitution which contained a list of almost all civil and political rights. However, emergency laws and presidential decrees legitimating arbitrary detentions (among other things) virtually invalidated the Bill of Rights. Alleged members or sympathizers of the Communist Party of the Philippines, its armed wing the New People's Army (NPA), and members of the Muslim underground organization Moro National Liberation Front (MNLF), became main targets of human rights violations (Amnesty International 1975; US Department of State 1977).

As a reaction to this repression, two important human rights groups emerged in 1974: the Task Force Detainees of the Philippines (TFDP), founded by the church related Association of Major Religious Superiors, and the Free Legal Assistance Group (FLAG), established by

Jose W. Diokno. While FLAG concentrated on legal aid for the poor, TFDP focused on care for political detainees and a systematic but unobtrusive monitoring of human rights violations. Two peculiarities facilitated the mobilization of a transnational human rights network during this time: the Philippines' close relationship with the United States provided activists with an outstanding opportunity structure for mobilization. Most importantly, it offered a legal discourse based on civil and political rights which easily adapted to the rule-of-law rhetoric under Marcos and to salient principles of Amnesty International. Second, the TFDP could rely on a church network which covered almost the entire country and thus facilitated the documentation of individual cases related to human rights violations (Nemenzo 1995: 118). The domestic church network was connected to a great international network of church organizations such as the World Council of Churches, as well as national church organizations in the US and Western Europe.

Indonesia

In Indonesia, human rights violations multiplied after an aborted coup allegedly carried out by the Communist Party in September 1965. The coup removed President Sukarno from power and in 1967, Suharto, at the time commander of the strategic reserve, became president of Indonesia. Between 1965 and 1967, at least 250,000 supposed members and sympathizers of the Communist Party were detained, and an equal number of persons were killed in country-wide pogroms (Fealy 1995: 4f.). In 1970, as a result of repression in Indonesia, the Lawyers' Association of Indonesia founded the Lembaga Bantuan Hukum Indonesia (LBH), the Legal Aid Foundation. It started operating in Jakarta in 1971 and soon began exchanging information with international NGOs like Amnesty International, the International Commission of Jurists (ICJ), the International Committee of the Red Cross and the British Campaign for the Release of Political Prisoners in Indonesia (TAPOL).

It is interesting to note that this emerging Indonesian human rights network campaigned for the release of the approximately 35,000 to 100,000 political prisoners in the early 1970s. They managed to alert an international human rights community and pressured Indonesia to release these prisoners. The US entered into secret negotiations with the Indonesian government which resulted in the release of most of the prisoners between 1975 and 1979 (see Fealy 1995; Kivimäki 1994; Newsom 1986). The campaign made no lasting impact as the large tactical concessions were paralleled by a governmental crackdown on the domestic (student) opposition and thus eliminated the potential for further mobilization. Moreover, Indonesian officials were able to play the identity-card against international NGOs such as Amnesty International. Quasi-official statements argued that "Amnesty still suffers from a 'moral arrogance' of the West which has been deplored by the Third World at large... [A]ll their efforts and objectives will be just counterproductive" (Letters to the editor 1978). It was not until the mid-1980s, ten years later, that transnational human rights groups were able to revive this mobilization.

International attention once again focused on Indonesia in 1975, when its army invaded East Timor, and annexed the territory a year later. The United Nations Security Council immediately condemned the annexation through two resolutions – one in 1975 and one in 1976 – and never acknowledged Indonesian jurisdiction over the territory. The invasion laid the basis for a second human rights network consisting of various NGOs, in particular Australian ones, the Portuguese and parts of the Dutch governments, various other Lusophone-speaking countries, most importantly Brazil and groups linked to the Roman Catholic Church (Ramos-Horta 1987: 139). This network, together with the political resistance in East Timor, distributed information about Indonesian repression of dissent and about the severe food shortages that had killed tens of thousands of people in East Timor.

Phase 2: mobilization and governmental denial

The initial mobilization of an international human rights community for Indonesia as well as the Philippines started in 1974–1975. It is important to note, that this came at a time during which the US withdrew its troops from Vietnam and had to rely on its allies in Southeast Asia, as it feared the consequences of a Communist block in the area. Despite these counterproductive strategic interests, the transnational networks managed to fuel a continued mobilization for the Philippines, and ended phase two in 1977 to 1978. An Indonesian human rights network developed much more slowly, and the process was partially interrupted after 1975. It was not until 1986 that the network mobilized. As a result, Indonesia remained in a denial phase until 1992. In their initial reactions both governments *denied*, in that they refuted the legitimacy of international jurisdiction and resorted to arguments of noninterference. The Indonesian government, however, to a much greater extent exploited the anti-colonial sentiments in furtherance of the latter

141

argument. In the Philippines, on the other hand, for various reasons, such an exploitation was not an option for Marcos. Thus, the denial phase was much briefer in the Philippines.

Philippines

After 1975, due to the continuing flow of information about human rights abuses in the Philippines, international human rights groups were able to place the country on the international agenda. Between 1975 and 1977, the ICJ conducted three missions in the Philippines and published their first report in 1977 (International Commission of Jurists 1977a). Amnesty International visited the Philippines in 1975, and also summarized its findings in a report (Amnesty International 1975).

In its initial reactions to accusations of international human rights organizations, the Marcos government countered claims by referring to the principle of non-intervention in its domestic affairs. Human rights organizations such as Amnesty International were discredited as being instruments of the communist underground movement in the Philippines (Amnesty International 1977a). Yet, this strategy of denial was of limited use: due to the strong support for the US–Philippine relationship among the Philippine ruling elite, references to non-interference from the US or the anti-Western nationalist rhetoric did not have much credibility. Because Marcos supported an open economy and had promised to stop the flood of nationalist legislation directed against US corporations which swept into the Philippine parliament in the early 1970s (Nemenzo 1995: 115), he was unable to mobilize nationalist sentiments to support his arguments of non-interference. Moreover, the Philippines had always supported human rights in international forums. For example, the government was an active supporter of the Declaration Against Torture in the mid-1970s. Its strategy of denial sharply contrasted with the human rights image it had tried to promote internationally, thus, it was caught in its own rhetoric. Moreover, most of the criticism of the human rights performance came from organizations and solidarity groups in the US. In sum, in 1977, the Philippines shifted from a phase of denial to one of tactical concessions.

Indonesia

As mentioned, the two emerging networks regarding Indonesia initially developed relatively independently of each other. Each had comparative advantages and disadvantages which affected the international and national mobilization of NGOs. For international human rights organizations, lack of access to the territory of East Timor proved to be a fatal impediment to international and national mobilization as it limited the crucial flow of information. The United Nations (UN) became the most important forum in which the East Timor question was discussed. Yet, initially, debates strictly focused on legal matters pertaining to the right to self-determination. Negotiations between Indonesia and Portugal over the status of East Timor began in 1983 under the auspices of the UN Secretary General. However, processes of persuasion hardly made any progress at all.

Until 1988, international human rights organizations campaigned for the opening of the territory to outside observers and demanded the right to self-determination. An analysis of the UN documents between 1983 and 1989 shows that, at first, the underlying contested norm was the right of self-determination for the East Timorese people. While Indonesia's critics, particularly Portugal, argued that Indonesia had violated this right, the Indonesian government rejected such charges as unfounded. Between 1976 and 1988, the Indonesian government reacted by continually insisting that the people of East Timor had already exercised their right to self-determination in 1976, and that all that happened in East Timor had become an internal affair of Indonesia. It also rejected the UN as a legitimate arbitration forum for this conflict.[1] As a secondary argument, it used the "Asian values" argument claiming that human rights had to be seen in their social, economic, and cultural aspects. Domestically, President Suharto used both arguments in a nationalist, anti-colonial discourse against separatist elements. This strategy seemed to have been successful, as the human rights network in Indonesia was neither well-connected with the East Timor network nor with the transnational human rights networks; in other words, both networks cooperated to a limited extent. The East Timor network's regular reference to the right to self-determination as a norm was not consensual in the Indonesian NGOs. Fear of repression, lack of information, and a conflict linked to the nationalist identity of some of the Indonesian NGOs are additional explanations for this non-cooperation. A structure incorporating both networks was not effectively mobilized until 1991.

In Indonesia, the creation of a transnational network was inhibited by the domination of the military and state organizations all the way down

---

[1] Official Records of the General Assembly, Thirty-first Session, Plenary Meetings, 18th and 19th meeting.

to the village level, which resulted in a restrictive control over the work of human rights groups. These had to adhere to explicit constraints prescribed by the Indonesian military (Feith 1991). Criticism of human rights violations in the territory of East Timor and in the provinces of Irian Jaya and Aceh, the issue of political prisoners, as well as any criticism of the New Order Government were "taboos," and activists faced imprisonment for breaking them. The nationalist undercurrent of many Indonesian NGOs hindered transnationalization[2] and a closer cooperation with the East Timor network. Consequently, civil and political rights were initially not an issue (although LBH defended many political prisoners). Because of the predominantly economic governmental discourse, the network focused on economic development and human rights, advocating social justice and popular participation in development projects.[3] Thus, the issues taken up by the Indonesian networks varied greatly in comparison to the Philippine network, in which campaigns political prisoners figured prominently. In sum, the East Timor and Indonesian network faced a dilemma hindering international and domestic mobilization: the East Timor network was internationally well-connected, but lacked resonance in Indonesia. The topics taken up by the Indonesian network resonated nationally and even found supporters among the Indonesian Army (ABRI), but did not generate much international mobilization.

In the mid-1980s, these underpinnings slowly began to change. The impasse regarding East Timor broke in 1985 with the emergence of new evidence about human rights abuses. The information was gathered together by the Catholic Church in East Timor and disseminated by international non-governmental organizations such as most importantly Pax Christi, Pax Romana, and Asia Watch (Asia Watch 1989; Human Rights Watch 1990: 309; Neyer and Protz-Schwarz 1986). This information exacerbated the public demands voiced by international forums like the UN, and the Non-Aligned Movement (NAM) of which Indonesia is a member to open the territory to outside observers. In 1986, the number of NGOs asking for presentations in the UN Commission

---

[2] This can be discerned from an analysis of the topics covered e.g. by the Indonesian students' movement. According to Aspinall, in the mid-1970s student protests focused on national issues, while the ones developing in the late 1980s included demands for human rights and democracy (cited in Uhlin 1995: 112).

[3] There are several networks in the field of human rights which partly overlap in membership and functions. Riker and Eldridge provide excellent accounts for an Indonesian transnational network in the field of economic development (Riker 1997; Eldridge 1995).

on Human Rights multiplied. Specifically, they referred to "reliable information" that recently had been received "concerning the continued practice of torture" (United Nations Economic and Social Council 1986). Based on this information, the network revived activities in the United Nations and raised the consciousness of individual members of the US Congress, and the parliament of the European Community (EC), who in turn expressed their concern in letters and resolutions (Human Rights Watch 1990: 305; Taylor 1995: 242). Under pressure from the transnational advocacy networks, first the Sub-Commission on the Prevention and Discrimination of Minorities of the UN Commission on Human Rights[4] and later the Human Rights Commission itself started thematizing the human rights situation in East Timor as proof that Indonesia had ignored the Timorese right of self-determination.

At the same time, on the Indonesian side the context for mobilization changed: the positive picture of the Indonesian government's economic performance began to be domestically contested. Domestic NGOs challenged the government's emphasis on economic growth, pointed to the wide income disparities which had been generated, and to the impact of large scale economic projects on the life of ordinary citizens. The case of the Kedung Ombo Dam Project financed by the World Bank became a case in point: Indonesian NGOs took up the cases of forced resettlement of villagers and projected them as a human rights issue via the International NGO Forum on Indonesia, founded in 1985, to an international audience such as multilateral donor agencies. The issue received great media coverage in Indonesia and put even more pressure on the government to initiate reforms (Lawyers Committee for Human Rights 1995a: 83f.; Riker 1997: 5f.; Sinaga 1995: 178). The event provided a learning experience in how to utilize international pressure to influence the government. Most importantly, it raised the consciousness of Indonesian citizens regarding their rights *vis-à-vis* the state.

These developments were accompanied by the contestation and gradual re-definition of official nationalism by activists. From 1985 on, Indonesian NGOs were required by law to express in their statutes their adherence to the state ideology Pancasila. As a result, and contrary to past rejectionists (see Billah and Abdul Hakim 1989), they used the New Order's core national symbol as a reference point for criticizing

---

[4] The Sub-Commission is composed of experts nominated by governments, while government officials are the members of the Human Rights Commission itself. As a result of these institutional differences, the more serious and more honest dialogues about human rights issues usually start in the Sub-Commission.

the Suharto regime: economic disparities were attacked for contraven-
ing Pancasila's principles of social justice, and the arbitrary actions of
state agencies for working against the principle of consultation and
consensus (Chua Beng Huat 1993: 152). Since now most NGOs had at
least rhetorically accepted Pancasila, it became more difficult for the
government to denounce their activities as anti-nationalist and against
Pancasila's spirit.

While the information on East Timor and NGO activities in Indonesia
had the potential to enhance the effectiveness of the two networks, this
potential only unfolded because at this point in time Indonesian policy
makers' awareness of the importance of international opinion began to
change. Indonesia aspired to play a greater international role (Vatikiotis
1988, 1991), and a good international image was seen as prerequisite for
such a role. This aspiration made the government more vulnerable
toward international criticism. The new foreign minister, Ali Alatas, in
particular felt that inaction regarding the issue of East Timor posed a
major obstacle to an increased responsibility in the international community (Schwarz 1994: 211).

The combination of the government's desire to boost its international
prestige combined with the human rights networks' international
shaming since the mid-1980s slowly opened the window of opportunity for a socialization process between the Indonesian government and
its international critics. As a result of the persistent demands of the
transnational network, the Indonesian government opened the previously closed province of East Timor in January 1989, a decision which
was controversial within the cabinet (Feith 1992: 64; Human Rights
Watch and Lawyers' Committee for Human Rights 1989: 88; Schwarz
1994: 211). The opening backfired because (1) the enhanced accessibility
to East Timor produced more information about human rights violations, and (2) the East Timorese used every opportunity, like the
pope's visit to Dili in October 1989, to publicly protest Indonesian
integration (Pinto and Jardine 1996: ch. 6; Vatikiotis 1991). The protests
defied the Indonesian government's claims that integration had proceeded smoothly. By 1991, under the terms of the UN-sponsored Portuguese–Indonesian negotiations, the Indonesian government had
been persuaded to invite a Portuguese delegation and the UN Special
Rapporteur on Torture to the territory.

The invitations provoked the very ambivalent "breakthrough" for
the networks, the Dili massacre on November 12, 1991. Around 2,500
East Timorese were celebrating a mass for two of their fellows who had

been killed by Indonesian military a couple of days earlier in the heightened tension preceding the visits. Some of the participants began demonstrating and one Indonesian soldier was stabbed. The Indonesian military then opened fire on the participants, killing between 150 and 270 people. In the wake of the shootings, more than 200 people are believed to have disappeared (United Nations Economic and Social Council 1994: paras. 21–23). The presence of foreign journalists and the UN special rapporteur Pieter Kooijmans, made it "instant international news" and triggered an international reaction which led to temporary financial aid cuts by Denmark, the Netherlands, and Canada. The USA, Japan, and the World Bank threatened to discontinue their financial aid. Facing almost ubiquitous international criticism, President Suharto reacted speedily, and appointed a National Investigative Commission which came up with a relatively critical report within a month. Based on its findings, President Suharto retired two Indonesian generals, and prosecutions were sought against seventeen other low-ranking officers.

It is difficult to determine exactly why the National Investigative Commission did not try to make a "whitewash" of the army. According to Schwarz, there are several reasons: first, Suharto seemed to be genuinely angry at the army's mishandling of the demonstration; second, the report was meant to seize the middle ground between the earlier findings of an army investigation, which were questionable especially in regard to the number of East Timorese victims, and the considerably higher numbers of victims offered by domestic and international human rights groups. In the end, a "frank" report was seen as the only solution to lessen international pressure (Schwarz 1994: 214–215). All three explanations give ample evidence for the impact of the transnational human rights networks on the Indonesian government. The latter implicitly based its interests on a calculation of the potential international repercussions its decisions would provoke.

At this point in time, the threats of Indonesia's major aid donors, the US, Japan, and the World Bank helped to push Indonesia from the second to the third phase. After the appointment of the investigative commission, however, these actors resumed their aid disbursements (Feith 1992: 70; Schulte-Nordholt 1995: 149), and neglected to apply consistent pressure thereafter. In contrast, international human rights NGOs such as Amnesty International, backed by small donor countries including the Netherlands, continued criticizing the lack of independence of the investigating body. The Dutch threat to turn to their European partners to discuss possible consequences if Indonesia did not start negotiations with the UN general secretary over East Timor, provoked a diplomatic conflict which illustrates the *nationalist backlash* occurring in phase 2 of the editors' framework. The Indonesian government launched a diplomatic offensive and virtually singled out the government of the Netherlands, the former colonial power, to punish it for interfering in Indonesian domestic affairs (for details see Baehr, Selbervik, and Tostensen 1995; Baehr 1997; Schulte-Nordholt 1995). On April 25, 1992, the Indonesian President Suharto ended the development cooperation with the Dutch. He demanded the dissolution of the Dutch-led international donor consortium and its reconstruction under the World Bank. The gesture carried a great symbolic weight and allowed the Suharto government to mobilize nationalist sentiments in Indonesia against foreign intervention. Despite these spectacular actions, the Indonesian government now faced vehement international criticism, to which it had to respond.

Only in the context of an ongoing socialization process marked by processes of persuasion and instrumental adaption can one explain the enormous impact of an event such as the Dili massacre. Had the government not agreed to host a Portuguese delegation in the territory in October 1991 under the terms of the UN mediated negotiations, and had the government not invited the Special Rapporteur on Torture to the territory, Dili wouldn't have had this effect. After all, massacres of the sort had occurred earlier in East Timor and in Indonesia. The Dili massacre only gained significance because it congealed the nature of the Indonesian repressive practices that transnational actors had criticized for years. Videos and photographs showing the arbitrary killing of peaceful demonstrators proved that the allegations of human rights organizations were not as baseless as the Indonesian government wanted their audience to believe.

Phase 3: tactical concessions

The transnational human rights networks were able to sustain domestic and international mobilization, and thus put the governments under increasing pressure to respond to their demands. In the Philippines, this phase of growing pressure started around 1977 to 1978 and lasted until Marcos's removal from power in 1986. Indonesia entered this third phase in 1992.

Philippines

One crucial "coalition partner" of the TN became the Carter administration. Individual members of the US State Department criticized the Philippine government regularly for its human rights violations. This commitment helped to bring the Philippines from phase 2 into phase 3, as had been the case in Indonesia, even without substantial material pressure. In 1977, the Philippines was listed as a nation that violated human rights, an action that Marcos branded as "provocation" (*New York Times*, January 2, 1977: 14). The Philippines were still, however, to continue receiving American military aid. In multilateral lending agencies, the US administration abstained from voting with regard to credit for the Philippines (Stohl *et al.* 1989: 200), and it denied Marcos the privilege of an official state visit. Individual officials such as Assistant Secretary of State For Humanitarian Affairs Patricia Derian and Vice President Walter Mondale openly criticized the human rights violations. These gestures had no material consequences, yet provided crucial encouragement to Filipino activists. "Filipinos' impression of Carter was based less on concrete measures taken by his administration than on the fact that it had elevated human rights to an unprecedented level of rhetorical importance in international discourse" (Orentlicher 1991: 59). However, it is important to note that these actions only materialized after strong lobbying by members of the transnational network, individual Philippine dissidents, and the media. The US's initial position in reaction to Marcos' declaration of martial law in 1972 was that the bases were vital to American national interests and paramount to the preservation of democratic institutions in the Philippines (W. L. Robinson 1996: 121; US Senate Committee on Foreign Relations 1973).[5] As US criticism of human rights violations shows, this position had slightly changed by 1977, but the Carter administration was split over its policy in the Philippines, because to the military services (Pentagon, Department of Defense) Marcos presented himself as a reliable partner and guarantor for continued US access to the military facilities in the Philippines (Ocampo 1980: 11).

That TN activities, their shaming strategies in particular, *had* an impact on Marcos became apparent in 1977. One key event was the

---

[5] A 1972 US Senate Report on the declaration of martial law noted that "whatever U.S. interests were – or are – they apparently are not thought to be related to the preservation of the democratic process ... U.S. officials appear prepared to accept that the strengthening of presidential authority will ... enable Marcos to introduce needed stability; that these objectives are in our interests; and that military bases and a familiar government in the Philippine are more important than the preservation of democratic institutions which were imperfect at best" (cited in Schirmer and Shalom 1987: 168; US Senate Committee on Foreign Relations 1973).

World Law Congress in Manila in August 1977 which also marked the transition to a phase of tactical concessions. The ICJ had published a report in advance of the Congress, in which it argued that martial law contravened international human rights standards. Even if, in 1972, political violence had justified declaring martial law according to the rights of states under conditions of emergency, the ICJ concluded: "We are . . . unable to accept that such circumstances still exist today, so as to justify the measures taken within it, including the suspension of Parliament and all political activity, severe restrictions on all basic civil liberties, prolonged detention without trial of political opponents, and the substitution of military tribunals for the normal civilian process" (International Commission of Jurists 1977a: 12). Domestic opposition groups used the Congress to stage a People's Conference on Human Rights which was accompanied by anti-martial law demonstrations involving some 3,000 participants (Machado 1978: 205f). The whole situation completely ridiculed the rule-of-law rhetoric of Marcos. Within days, he announced a "normalization process." This would entail the lifting of restrictive measures such as the night curfew and the ban on international travel, and the release of 500 martial law prisoners. He also unveiled plans to hold elections to a transitory legislature, referred to as the Interim Batasang Pambansa (IBP), in 1978 (Corsino 1981: 239). And he pledged his "irrevocable commitment" to human rights (*New York Times*, September 10, 1977: 24).

The most important outcome of this phase of pressure on the Marcos government was the creation of a political arena in which a growing domestic opposition and a more critical media could develop (Wurfel 1990: 113). External moral pressure and Marcos' tactical concessions internally legitimized the human rights discourse and increased the human rights networks' density. Prior to this, anti-Marcos gatherings had been confronted with subversion charges and detentions without trial had had a "chilling effect" on the political opposition. As of 1977, political action was legitimated with a reference to "human rights." A Filipino attorney commented: "Since so much can now be done in the name of 'human rights' which was previously forbidden, it is not surprising that there is much curiosity about these human rights." And a sociologist observed the results: "[H]uman rights groups are springing up all over" (cited in Claude 1978: 222).

The shaming activities of the human rights networks, backed by rhetorical support from Carter, were particularly effective because the whole Philippine national identity discourse, as promoted by Marcos, presented the country as a state governed by the rule of law and a legitimate member of the international community. The transnational networks threatened this image and in contrast to the case of Indonesia, in the Philippines Marcos did not have a rhetorical "fallback" position based on anti-colonial nationalism. Thus, Marcos increasingly responded to network demands and continued with political reforms.

Observers were quick to uncover the instrumental character of Marcos's measures. For example, an observer of the *Far Eastern Economic Review* stated: "The liberalisation of the political process since 1978 is not necessarily something that Marcos wanted. But he appears to have made a virtue out of necessity: partly pressure from the United States in the days of former U.S. president Jimmy Carter's human rights policy; partly a build up of opposition steam" (Bowring 1982: 10). Martial law was revoked in 1981, shortly before the pope's visit that year. The political liberalization, however, did not result in an improvement of human rights. Rather, it modified Marcos's modes of repression. In 1982, Amnesty International reported a decline in political prisoners, yet an increase in extra-legal killings and disappearances. The removal of minimal standards for judicial processes after 1982, resulted in a sharp deterioration of human rights conditions (Amnesty International 1982: 13).

Considering the comparatively short time needed in the Philippines for the first two phases, the question arises, why the phase of tactical concessions took so long. Why did it take eight more years to remove Marcos? First, Marcos's tactical concessions successfully split the Philippine opposition which was unable to agree on a common position toward him. One dividing line among several others was the question of the future of the American bases in the Philippines. In other words, the opposition had agreed on human rights, but not on a nationalist agenda.

Second, when the Reagan administration was inaugurated in 1981, Marcos regained an important ally and source of legitimacy. Under Reagan, the US administration completely reversed the policy of the previous Carter administration, and unconditionally supported Marcos. This support was consistent with the US emphasis on military contestation of the Soviet Union. With the existence of an ever-increasing Communist underground movement in the Philippines, Marcos developed into the only guarantor for continued access to the American military facilities. In turn, the transnational network was temporarily weakened. Vice-President Bush's visit to Manila, which was characterized as "a blow to the opposition who had long dissuaded the United States from supporting Marcos" (Sodusta and Palongpalong 1982: 288), and the subsequent official state visit of Marcos to the US in 1982 were blatant signs of US support of Marcos.

The fact that, between 1975 and 1983, human rights network strength and effectiveness was dependent on the US position toward Marcos seems basically to confirm a realist explanation. The realist approach, however, ignores the fact that the transnational network was able to keep the Philippines on the international agenda, despite Reagan's open support of Marcos. In addition, it cannot explain why the Reagan administration itself began supporting change beginning in early 1983. Finally, it does not account for the growing Philippine mobilization which was increasingly anti-American in orientation, and thus cannot be portrayed as derivative of US power.

A network explanation, in contrast, is able to explain the fluctuations of the US approach. By 1983, after a period of constant lobbying by human rights groups and individual Congress members, parts of the US Administration and Congress began reconsidering the US interests in the Philippines. The US Foreign Relations Committee even discussed alternatives to the American bases in the Philippines (Ocampo-Calfors 1983). At the same time, in the Philippines, the perceived US inaction toward Marcos disappointed many activists, and spurred a domestic mobilization that was anti-American in orientation. The slogan "The US–Marcos dictatorship" became a rallying cry among the Philippine domestic opposition including some outstanding human rights figures such as Jose Diokno. In the US, this served as an argument for supporters of the military facilities in the Philippines, who were concerned that this anti-colonial, nationalist thinking among the Philippine opposition would threaten the bases once these politicians came to power.

In June 1983, the Reagan administration signaled that it would withdraw its unequivocal support of Marcos because of its doubts about the stability of Marcos's rule, and the resulting threats to the military bases (Ocampo-Calfors 1983: 17). One month later, Benigno Aquino announced his intention to return from the US to file his candidacy for the National Assembly elections scheduled for 1984. His assassination in Manila on August 21, 1983 propelled protests, which had been gathering momentum since the 1970s, to an unprecedented level and remobilized anew the entire human rights network nationally, as well as internationally.

In the Philippines, the assassination provoked a broadly based social movement, which encompassed a diverse set of social groups, including the previously more or less apolitical middle class. Mass protests following the murder of Aquino, spontaneous and unorganized first (Sacerdoti 1983), were channeled into political groupings and movements and became more organized after 1984 (Nations and Sacerdoti 1984: 22f). Human rights became the rallying cry for the opposition seeking to remove Marcos. The partly instrumental use of the human rights issue by the radical left (see below) now paid off and enabled a more-or-less effective working coalition with the middle class and the elite (Lane 1990: 7; W. L. Robinson 1996: 125f). In Manila, various political umbrella movements developed (Lane 1990: 13). Their political demands regularly included freeing all political prisoners, restoring the writ of habeas corpus, and a repeal of repressive decrees.[6]

A realist approach particularly fails to explain the crucial phase between 1983 and 1985. For the US, the assassination of Benigno Aquino had eliminated the only viable alternative to Marcos. Although the US immediately pressured Marcos to investigate the political murder, it proved to be a successful stratagem to delay his removal from power (Overholt 1986: 1157). For the US, the alternative to Marcos – a Communist government – was even more worrying. Especially for the White House, Marcos represented at the same time the political and economic problems as well as their solution. Thus, from 1983 to 1985, a deep split over the US policy in the Philippines emerged among the factions of the US executive, and led to a contradictory policy (Bello 1984; W. L. Robinson 1996: 124). As a consequence, until late 1985 the US administration largely followed events in the Philippines, rather than actively shaping them (see Karnow 1989: 406–409). It was only in Marcos's final days that the Reagan administration again provided meaningful input into the Philippine political process. It dispatched several personal envoys who tried to persuade Marcos of genuine political reforms and of early presidential elections. It was domestic mobilization from below which provided the crucial pressure that made Marcos follow this advice.

In November 1985, Marcos finally announced that he would hold snap elections the following year, and after the intervention of the Catholic Church, Cory Aquino emerged as the consensual candidate of

---

[6] See e.g. "KAAKBAY Supports Cory Aquino's Quest for Freedom and Democracy," December 9, 1985; and "BAYAN Preserve in Correct Struggles, Boycott the Sham Snap Election," both are reprinted in Schirmer and Shalom (Schirmer & Shalom 1987: 344–348).

the political opposition. The international media played a major role in providing Aquino with the recognition and legitimacy that the controlled media under Marcos denied her (Timberman 1987: 242). Aquino made human rights a key issue in the campaign leading to presidential elections. Had Marcos not manipulated the results during the elections on February 7, 1986, she would have received a majority of the votes. Aquino's call for civil disobedience led to mass protests, and on February 24, 1986, parts of the Philippine armed forces staged a coup attempt which caused the final ousting of Marcos. At this point in time, a crackdown on the military rebels was only able to be avoided through rising people power gathering outside the military camp, and because of subsequent US warnings that they would immediately cut off military aid if the rebels were attacked by troops loyal to Marcos. After the US withdrew its support and offered asylum to him and his family, Marcos finally resigned.

In sum, tactical concessions in response to pressure had become a major characteristic of Marcos's rule between 1977 and 1986. Marcos, personally, was never truly persuaded to change his human rights practices, despite the human rights rhetoric he employed. In terms of the socialization process outlined in the introductory chapter, it can be best understood as a process of instrumental adaptation to domestic and international demands. Because of the close relationship between Marcos and Reagan, the US played a key role in influencing Marcos's decisions, at distinct points in time. As has been shown, State Department support for change materialized only after constant network pressure and after the domestic mobilization had gained a momentum that threatened even the military bases in the Philippines. The overall dynamic and process at work in the Philippine situation was captured by Paul Wolfowitz, US Assistant Secretary of State at the time. During a hearing in 1985, in response to the question whether there was any hope that Marcos was going to go through a metamorphosis and pursue serious reforms, he replied: "He is obviously not going to do it just because he wakes up some day and says, 'Oh, my, this is what has to be done.' But I think there are a great deal of forces operating, and not just from the United States, and in fact, I think not principally from the United States, that push in the direction of reform."[7]

A network approach, with its emphasis on legitimation effects helps to explain the rise, between 1983 and 1986, of Corazon Aquino and the

---

[7] Statement of Mr. Wolfowitz, US Assistant Secretary of State (US Senate 1985b: 69).

relative decrease in power of the military which played a major role during the people power revolution. Corazon Aquino, a housewife, emerged as a new political actor despite lack of US support. She inherited her husband's role as leader of the anti-Marcos opposition, which can only be explained with the immense international legitimacy her husband had gained during his human rights campaigns (Timberman 1987: 241). Legitimacy seems to be also crucial in explaining why Aquino, not the military gained power after the coup. Though the army coup was welcome as the final catalyst in the overthrow of Marcos, the human rights campaigns had so much delegitimized the army as an institution that their aspirations for power were simply not feasible.

In contrast to Marcos's non-commital manner, the persuasion, and especially the consciousness-raising mode were salient among the Philippine political opposition. Human rights played a crucial role in defining political goals and legitimating domestic actors. Church groups and the Communist-affiliated New People's Army (NPA) most benefited from the domestic debate's focus on a human rights discourse, and gained more and more supporters. As indicated by several authors (Casiple 1995, 1996; Marks 1993; Sison 1995), mobilization and consciousness-raising efforts in human rights were greatly promoted by the Communist Party of the Philippines (CPP). "Human rights" as a political idea was taken up because it was internationally salient and could be conveyed to the masses more easily than more complex issues such as land reform.[8]

Indonesia

The Dili shootings marked a turning point for the transnational human rights movement, and had a profound impact on the network structure. The density and size of the network suddenly increased as the movement incorporated new supporters from among academics, students, and church leaders in and outside Indonesia. In Jakarta and other major cities, new organizations which focused on human rights and democracy, were founded (Aditjondro 1997; Uhlin 1995). International and domestic NGOs changed their strategies and brought together the two

---

[8] These features were stressed in several of the interviews which the author conducted in the Philippines with former members of the National Democratic Front (NDF), the political wing of the CPP. Starting in 1972, the CPP placed the priority of coalition-building with anti-Marcos forces over that of class struggle. "Marcos versus the people," as they phrased it, became the "primary contradiction," while "class struggle" was the "secondary contradiction." This made cooperation with parts of the Philippine elite and later the middle class possible (Marks 1993: 87).

previously weakly connected network structures of East Timor and Indonesia and finally enabled the domestic mobilization. Human rights violations in East Timor were used as a peg for criticism of repressive practices in Indonesia. As East Timorese resistance member José Ramos-Horta revealed later: "I am fully aware that the fate of East Timor and the democracy movement in Indonesia are intimately linked, each supports the other... The more pressure that is focused on Suharto about East Timor, the more space there is for the opposition to push for change in Indonesia."[9] The TN's basic points of criticism were labor rights and the role of the military in suppressing political dissent in Indonesia. These campaigns sharpened the existing disaffection in the army which had begun in reaction to Suharto's disciplinary measures against some of its members. The campaigns increased resentment within the officer corps toward him even more (Liddle 1992: 72). On a rhetorical level, "Dili" also marked the beginning of a civil and political human rights discourse in Indonesia.

In response to the increasing pressure from "above and below," tactical concessions and instrumental adaptation as response began to dominate the action repertoire of the Indonesian government in 1992 to 1993 which restricted its available options for action. For example, the government, between 1992 and 1996, openly restrained its application of the Anti-Subversion Law in regards to its domestic critics. The Anti-Subversion Law entails the maximum penalty of death and was continually criticized by domestic and international human rights organizations. Instead, the government resorted to an article forbidding the spreading of hatred (*Haatzaai Artikelen*) (YLBI 1995). It tolerated (though did not acknowledge) the formation of new political parties, an independent election monitoring body, a labor union and of an independent alliance of journalists, as well as many new NGOs. President Suharto appointed a National Commission on Human Rights in 1993. In the judiciary, despite executive intervention in its decisions, there was a trend towards more independence and an increase in prosecutions sought against human rights perpetrators (Human Rights Watch 1997a: 164). These measures were interpreted as a controled liberalization (*Keterbukaan*) initiated by Suharto (Suryadinata 1997: 275).

This positive trend was always imbued with backlashes and as the government lost control over the situation – starting in July 1997 – even with a backward trend: following a crack down on a widening opposi-

---

[9] José Ramos-Horta in an interview with Max Lane, *Green Left Weekly* (Australia), no. 251, October 23, 1996.

tion rallying around Megawati Sukarnoputri, the head of the Partai Demokrasi Indonesia (PDI), on July 27, 1996, the government's line toward the opposition hardened (Bertrand 1997: 447f; Human Rights Watch 1997a: 164; Liddle and Mallarangeng 1997: 168f). In East Timor the human rights situation worsened, according to human rights reports (Human Rights Watch 1997a; Human Rights Watch 1997b). In September 1997, the government banned all organizations affiliated with the People's Democratic Party (PRD) which was alleged to have masterminded the riots in July. Human rights organizations were also concerned about a wave of disappearances which occurred in April 1998 (SiaR 1998). It indicated Suharto's willingness to regain the control over the political situation. However, due to a firmly established network structure facilitating the gathering of information, these actions contributed even more to a rising international awareness and to a close scrutiny of Indonesian human rights practices (Associated Press 1998). The award of the Nobel Peace Prize to two East Timorese activists (José Ramos-Horta and Bishop Ximenes Belo) in December 1996 was a symbol of this increased awareness and of the success of the networks in raising the consciousness of Western states. Accordingly, the US and the European Union who were equally under network pressure, criticized the Indonesian government on a regular basis and included human rights in their bilateral relations.

One of the most far-reaching concessions of the Indonesian government which illustrates the legitimating effects of the TN was the establishment of a National Commission on Human Rights in 1993. It marked the institutionalization of human rights on the state level. The choice of timing for the announcement of its creation, in June 1993, suggested an instrumental gesture: it avoided potential international criticism in the upcoming World Conference on Human Rights scheduled one week later in Vienna. Earlier that year, the Lawyers' Committee for Human Rights had released a report concerning torture and the right to redress in Indonesia (Lawyers' Committee for Human Rights 1993c). In March the same year, the UN Human Rights Commission had issued a resolution that – for the first time – was supported by the United States (Schwarz 1994: 223).[10]

These events surely explain the timing of the announcement. Indonesia's actual receptiveness of the creation of a national human rights commission, however, was also a result of the socializing efforts

[10] UN Human Right Commission Resolution 1993/97, March 11, 1993, adopted by a roll-call vote of 22 to 12, with 15 abstentions (E/CN.4/1993/122).

of transnational actors and the United Nations. The UN had conducted two human rights seminars in Jakarta in 1992 and 1993 respectively, which were instrumental in persuading Suharto of the feasibility of such a commission. President Suharto even used the second UN workshop in 1993 to announce the establishment of Komnas-HAM (Human Rights Watch/Asia 1994; United Nations Economic and Social Council 1993).[11]

The National Commission on Human Rights (Komisi Hak Asasi Manusi di Indonesia: Komnas-HAM) began operating in January 1994.[12] Despite the constraints resulting from its dependence on the President, Komnas-HAM's stance toward the government was surprisingly critical. This was partly because of the commitment of individual Commission members, but most importantly because of pressure from domestic NGOs. In individual cases of human rights violations, it often had positions which diverged from or partially contradicted official government interpretations (Bertrand 1997: 448; Human Rights Watch 1997a: 129–134). Backed by the demands of domestic NGOs, it recommended revoking the Anti-Subversion Law ratifying the Convention against Torture, which the Indonesian Government had signed in 1985.

It is widely argued that the creation of Komnas-HAM legitimized the human rights discourse in Indonesia (see Eldridge 1996: 304). Given the still-prevalent role of anti-colonial nationalism in the governmental rhetoric, Komnas-HAM served as an important mediator between the demands of an international human rights community and their interpretation of the Indonesian government as Western and neocolonial. The commission became a point of reference for foreign countries as well as NGOs, which enhanced its otherwise delicate domestic standing. When adopting the editors' network definition, Komnas-HAM can be described as a government agency which was integrated into the transnational network. This had the effect of providing Komnas-HAM

[11] A Foreign Ministry Official emphasized that it was not international pressure that inspired the government to establish Komnas-HAM, and cited the first UN seminar (*sic!*) as having had an impact on governmental considerations. Interview, Ministry of Foreign Affairs, Jakarta, August 1996.
[12] The creation of the commission is based on the Presidential Decree No. 50, Year 1993. It comprises 25 commissioners with a staff limited to one dozen. The first commissioners were appointed by the President in December 1993, however, Komnas-HAM issued its own statutes providing for internal elections of the Commission members (US Department of State 1997: Sec. 4). It is mainly government funded. On January 24, 1996 a branch office of the Komnas-HAM was inaugurated in Dili, East Timor. Like its Philippine counterpart, the Commission does not have prosecuting powers and can only recommend specific measures to "state institutions".

with the necessary publicity, legitimacy, information, and material resources, which would make it difficult for the government to openly constrain its work (Jones 1996: 274).

A careful reader of this book might ask why the human rights commissions in Indonesia and Tunisia reacted differently, although they were certainly in similar situations. In Tunisia, the Human Rights Commission is clearly coopted by the government and has not become part of the network. I argue that in Indonesia, domestic pressure and expectations, which were non-existent in, for example, Tunisia, forced the Indonesian Komnas-HAM to be critical.

On the rhetorical and communicative level changes, similar to those that occurred on the behavioral level can be observed. Basically, in 1992, the government began to regularly respond to human rights criticism. It replied in detail to the United Nations thematic procedures,[13] and publicly commented on resolutions issued by international and inter-governmental organizations. While it almost always disputed specific violations, it openly and generally admitted that a human rights problem exists. The language used in UN human rights committees drastically changed after the shootings in Dili. The Indonesian delegates were much more cooperative, yet their arguments differed depending on the forum. To begin with, members of the Commission on Human Rights (CHR) and the Indonesian government were able to develop a common definition of the human rights situation in Indonesia. The Commission on Human Rights, between 1992 and 1997, issued "consensus statements", agreed by the Indonesian delegation, which outlined the human rights situation and suggested appropriate steps to address it. The discussion between the Indonesian government and its domestic and international critics shifted from a debate on the validity of international human rights standards (see phase 2) to one of the appropriate measures to improve the human rights situation. This change was accompanied by a dramatic change in rhetoric. At the 1992 session of the UN Human Rights Commission, the Indonesian delegate claimed that Indonesia strictly prohibited the practice of torture. He also stated that the invitation of the Special Rapporteur had been motivated by the desire "to learn and benefit from such a visit in order to minimize, if not eradicate, the practice of torture in Indonesia."[14] This statement not

---

[13] These refer to the Special Rapporteur on Torture, the Special Rapporteur on Extrajudicial Killings, the Working Group on Arbitrary Detentions, and the Working Group on Involuntary Disappearances.

[14] United Nations ECOSOC, Commission on Human Rights, 48th Session, Summary Record of the 25th meeting (E/CN.4/1992/SR.25, par. 53–54).

only acknowledged the validity of the international norm, but also constituted the first time that the Indonesian government accepted allegations of torture.

In 1996, Indonesia presented the Human Rights Commission with a list of detailed measures undertaken to deal with human rights violations, including immediate investigations of some abuses in East Timor. At first, however, government officials differentiated between valid criticisms by UN bodies and inaccurate or baseless allegations by INGOs. The discourse between the Indonesian government and its critics shifted over time from a contestation of the underlying norm – self-determination and human rights versus non-interference in internal affairs – and a complete denial of the authenticity and credibility of the respective speakers toward a situation where the underlying norm became consensual – human rights – and the speakers accepted each other as valid interlocutors. As a result, the discourse started focusing on questions of norms compliance and implementation on the ground. The statements marked a departure from earlier Indonesian responses in other ways as well: first, Indonesia was portrayed as a law-abiding state. This diverged from earlier characterizations where Indonesian policy makers rationalized the role of the state as the ultimate arbitrator that is not accountable according to the "rule of law." Second, it also diverged from statements in the 1980s in which Indonesian delegates referred to the principle of non-intervention and explicitly rejected the UN as an arbitration forum (see phase 2). To the contrary, for Indonesia, cooperation with the UN even became a yardstick by which it could demonstrate its willingness to improve the human rights situation. It only rarely invoked the nonintervention principle. Rather it argued that no country had the right to "teach" others human rights.[15]

In sum, there were observable behavioral and rhetorical changes in the Indonesian government's behavior toward allegations of human rights violations which can be traced back to the establishment of human rights networks in the mid-1980s. The Asian financial crises that erupted at the end of 1997 had a trigger effect on these developments, but crucial for any explanation are the persistent doubts about President Suharto's willingness to initiate reforms which were fueled by transnational advocacy networks. They had nourished a deep-seated crisis of legitimacy and had managed to transform to an unprecedented extent the picture of the country from one of political stability coupled

---

[15] E.g. "Alatas: RI hails European Plan to visit East Timor," *Antara*, August 30, 1997.

with economic expertise and steady growth rates, to one of lack of public accountability, systematic human rights violations, and corruption. Because Suharto's international reputation had been effectively questioned by transnational networks, the financial crisis gained a different meaning than, let's say, in Thailand and South Korea, but also in the Philippines. Consequently, in these three countries the crisis did not have such serious repercussions.

In this situation of growing political unrest, and an immense economic crisis, the "rubber stamp" appointment in March 1998 of Suharto as president for another five years proved to be the final trigger that intensified a wave of student demonstrations which spread around Indonesia. Protests escalated and involved more and more supporters of all social strata. Violent riots in Jakarta on May 14 and 15 left an estimated 500 dead and stepped up demands, backed by the US, for Suharto to resign. Great power pressure only provided the last and belated push that made Suharto topple. On the eve of May 21, 1998, he finally resigned and named Jusuf Habibie, his vice-president, as his successor. International human rights organizations immediately demanded several measures the international community would be looking for to improve the human rights situations in the long run: Human Rights Watch/Asia requested the new Indonesian government to free all political prisoners, such as Sri Bintang Pamungkas, Budiman Soedjadmiko, Muchtar Pakpahan, and Xanana Gusmao. It demanded concrete steps toward the repeal of laws and regulations that curbed dissent and prevented the formation of political parties, a timetable for a fair election, the initiation of a dialogue on reform and human rights protection with the people of East Timor, and Indonesia's signing and ratification of major international human rights treaties. Finally, it suggested the establishment of a high-level civilian–military commission to review the "dual-function" of the Indonesian military (Human Rights Watch 1998). One week after Suharto's resignation Habibie and the Justice Minister Muladi declared that the government would free selected political prisoners such as Pamungkas and Pakpahan. On June 25, 1998, the government announced a National Action Plan on Human Rights providing a five-year schedule for the ratification of major human rights instruments, such as the Anti-Torture Convention and the International Covenant on Civil and Political Rights. The plan also foresees human rights education programs. Human rights organizations, student groups, and political parties maintained their critical attitude towards Habibie and openly criticized government attempts, for example, to restrict their freedom of expression as well as the security forces severe maltreatment of demonstrators and ethnic Chinese. They successfully protested against new legislation which would have placed limits on the size and scope of demonstrations and argued that it contradicted repeated claims by Habibie that he wanted to introduce greater democratic freedom and human rights (Dow Jones Newswires 1998). In sum, with regard to the spiral model Indonesia can be situated in a transition to the prescriptive status phase.

Phase 4 and 5: prescriptive status and the development of rule-consistent behavior

The Philippines entered the phase of prescriptive status in 1986 and has since slowly developed rule-consistent behavior. Prescriptive status entails the governmental acknowledgment of the international jurisdiction regarding human rights and the implementation of the respective international legal standards. Human rights abuses have continually decreased since the early 1990s. This is largely due to increasing efforts to institutionalize human rights guarantees.

After the inauguration of Corazon Aquino, almost instantaneously, human rights gained prescriptive status. Within three years, the Aquino administration ratified the International Covenant on Civil and Political Rights (1986), the First Optional Protocol (1989), and the International Convention against Torture and Other Inhuman or Degrading Treatment (United Nations Human Rights Committee 1995). In 1987, the government created an independent agency, which dealt with individual complaints of human rights violations, the Constitutional Commission on Human Rights. Human rights provisions were also incorporated in the domestic legal structure. Legal guarantees such as habeas corpus were restored and supported by a more independent judiciary. The new constitution, ratified in a popular plebiscite on February 2, 1987, outlawed torture and all forms of secret and incommunicado detentions, protected citizens from random searches and seizures, provided for a permanent Commission on Human Rights, and called for the dismantling of private armies and paramilitary units (Green 1989: 188f.).

In 1986, after reviewing the human rights situation in the Philippines during the Aquino Administration, Amnesty International concluded that "the Aquino Government's commitment to the protection of human rights and the establishment of legal safeguards [have] led to major improvements" (Amnesty International 1992c: 3). Yet, the restoration of democratic institutions and the attack on some of the most oppressive features of the Marcos regime did not eliminate human rights abuses. Political violence escalated in 1987, with the breakdown of the peace process with the National Democratic Front, after the so-called Mendiola massacre, in which demonstrating peasants were shot by government security forces. The counterinsurgency operations of the army led to a resurgence of human rights abuses. Amnesty International observed, that "a pattern of widespread human rights violations committed by the military and paramilitary groups" had re-emerged (Amnesty International 1992c: 3). The newly created human rights institutions seemed incapable of dealing with the cases: since its creation, from 1987 to 1991, only four out of hundreds of military personnel accused of human rights abuses were convicted (Human Rights Watch 1992: 445). In sum, a gap between *prescriptive status* and *rule consistent* behavior emerged.

The movement along the spiral model and the eventual continual decrease in human rights abuses in the Philippines in the 1990s are the outcome of a combination of factors. First, personal and individual commitment to human rights played a crucial role. For example, for the Aquino Cabinet the ratification of international human rights instruments became so taken for granted that it no longer generated an internal debate. One former cabinet member, Rene Saguisag, recounted: "We tried to carry out all commitments. Otherwise, we would have lost our credibility ... I think that it did not even lead into a debate because we were all so philosophically committed to supporting any human rights initiatives."[16] The extremely committed members of the National Commission on Human Rights (currently, e.g., Mercedes Contreras) also furthered cooperation with domestic NGOs, and inspired a dialogue about measures to further improve the human rights record.

Second, the New People's Army (NPA) lost much of its legitimacy when information about internal purges and extra-legal executions of alleged governmental collaborators emerged. These actions alienated the NPA from its clientele, as it contradicted its official image as a human rights promoting force (see Casiple 1995: 84). As the number of clashes between the underground movements and the army decreased, human rights violations declined in parallel. Third, continued pressure

---

[16] Interview with Rene Saguisag, Manila, April 7, 1996.

from above and below, assured through the transnational network, guaranteed fresh incentives for human rights institutions. The strong international legitimacy of the Aquino administration actually stopped the mobilization of the transnational network and led to the defection and deactivation of some of its parts.[17] Yet, the remaining parts professionalized by creating new organizations that lobbied the parliament of the European Union and the US government (Nemenzo 1995: 122). Moreover, a free press and the creation of democratic spaces made it possible to monitor human rights practices. The latter resulted in a series of reports, which criticized the human rights violations of paramilitary groups and impunity of human rights perpetrators in general.[18] UN mechanisms were activated and provided on-going socialization in international forums. The Philippines submitted its first report, in April 1989, according to the obligations of the ICCPR (United Nations Human Rights Committee 1995). Finally, under the Aquino and later the Ramos administration, human rights were institutionalized not only in the legal and state structures (through Human Rights Commissions), but also as part of compulsory educational programs carried out in the military, the police corps, and in schools (Claude 1996).

Human rights violations do continue, albeit on a comparatively low level. The major challenges to rule-consistent behavior are the existing, yet dwindling activities of guerrilla movements such as the New People's Army and armed Muslim organizations in the south. Widespread corruption among the judiciary, and a non-professional police still pose a threat to human rights protection and are regularly criticized by international observers and domestic human rights NGOs (US Department of State 1998). So far, a tight and active network of NGOs and President Ramos's strength have been the driving force behind the institutionalization of human rights initiatives at the state level. Initiat-

---

[17] "The Aquino Mystique took its toll particularly on anti-Marcos lawyers groups such as the New York-based Filipino Lawyers' Committee on Human Rights. With some members recruited into the new government and many others convinced of Aquino's pro-human rights stance, the lawyers' committee and other groups which came together around a strictly anti-Marcos agenda were deactivated" (Legaspi 1993: 95).

[18] Between 1986 and 1992 international human rights organizations conducted twenty-five fact-finding missions in the Philippines. Amnesty International and the Lawyers' Committee on Human Rights published a substantial number of reports (e.g. Amnesty International 1988a, Amnesty International 1988b, Amnesty International 1988c, Amnesty International 1992c, Casiple 1996, Lawyers' Committee for Human Rights 1988, Lawyers' Committee for Human Rights 1990, Lawyers' Committee for Human Rights 1991, Lawyers' Committee for Human Rights & Asia Watch 1988).

ives such as the peace process between the government and two guerrilla movements[19] and the creation of a National Unification Commission suggested that the Ramos government was seeking non-violent solutions to the insurgency. These initiatives might result in further improvements in the human rights record. However, *habitualization* as a mode of socialization has been limited: for example, after 1995, the Philippines stopped replying to the requests from the UN Working Group on Involuntary Disappearances. With the Philippines' formal but imperfect adherence to the rule of law and human rights standards, an active civil society, together with partially institutionalized channels to international organizations, constitutes a necessary mechanism to provide internal checks and balances to further promote rule-consistent behavior.

Alternative explanations

A realist approach views developments in the area of human rights as a function of the extent to which great powers are willing to support the human rights regime (see Krasner 1993). The Philippines, because of the obvious hegemony of the US, thus appears to be an easy case for the realist. The connection of the strength of the network and US support also seems to confirm a realist explanation. A realist understanding, however, is misleading in several aspects: Most importantly, the US did not move the networks, rather the networks moved the US. The Carter administration's criticism of Marcos only materialized after human rights organizations had vehemently criticized the human rights situation in the Philippines. In the early 1980s, even the Reagan administration had to modify its uncritical and very supportive approach to the Philippines under pressure from the network and US public opinion. Most observers of that time agree that, under Reagan, the US's desire to contain Soviet influence in Southeast Asia increased its dependence on the military bases in the Philippines, and thus limited its ability to distance itself from Marcos (Hawes 1986; Kessler 1986). Following these interests, the Reagan administration and also the preceding Carter administration, never used military-aid cuts to show disdain for the Marcos regime. Military aid continually increased, and it was not until 1985 that the US Congress reduced military aid, yet only symbolically, transforming it into economic aid (US Senate 1985b: 42). In other words,

---

[19] The Philippine government reached a peace accord with the MNLF in September 1996, and with the NDF in March 1998.

the process is not one of material pressure. The liberal argument of a complex moral interdependence (Donnelly 1986) connecting Philippine citizens and US citizens seems to characterize this interaction process better. However, it does not offer a mechanism accounting for the process through which this moral interdependence is achieved.

No single power had such a potential impact in Indonesia. The Netherlands, the former colonial power, did, however, play a significant role. It served as an organizational base for Indonesian NGOs, and, in 1990, was among the first countries to link developmental aid to progress in human rights practices. However, the Netherlands' percentage of financial aid to Indonesia was very small and financial leverage was thus limited. In addition, individual countries reacted to the Dili killings with a temporary suspension of financial aid, yet did not consistently continue to make such aid conditional on human rights in the following years.

In the case of Indonesia a realist approach heavily underestimates the role of international and non-governmental organizations in the greater process of socialization (see also Finnemore 1996a). Transnational networks and the United Nations were the most important and consistent socializing agents in Indonesia. During the 1980s they created a dialogue between NGOs and governmental agencies and, in the 1990s, set the path for the establishment of Komnas-HAM. There is sufficient evidence that UN activities with regard to East Timor triggered the opening of East Timor and the developments which followed. Moreover, Indonesia's first experience with international human rights mobilization in the mid-1970s is the best example of Great Power pressure having no lasting impact on human rights change. It supports the claim of the editors that there can be no lasting impact on human rights practices without domestic mobilization to provide the necessary pressure from below.

Instead of material pressure, Ikenberry and Kupchan suggest a process of hegemonic socialization to account for cooperation of secondary states. Government acquiescence is achieved through the transmission of norms and the reshaping of value orientations (Ikenberry and Kupchan 1990). In the Philippines, the national rhetoric, with its emphasis on the rule of law, displayed American and European value orientations from the start and were part of the political culture. These collective values *enabled* a convergence in civil and political rights. As a constant background variable, however, they are insufficient as an explanation for changes in human rights practices. Ikenberry and Kupchan's emphasis on collective value orientations *conveyed* to political elites by the US moreover underrates the strength of anti-American and nationalist sentiments among the population, and especially, among the intelligentsia.[20] These sentiments provided activists with an ideational resource which served to mobilize the opposition as it found supporters across all social strata.

In Indonesia, nationalist sentiments equally provided an ideational base for resistance to human rights intervention. Yet, in this case they served the ruling elite. The Pancasila discourse promoted by the Suharto government was directed against the West and foreign intervention, which it portrayed as neocolonial (Pabottingi 1995). Thus, other countries' intervention or criticism of human rights practices always served to rally around a nationalist agenda. The construction of the nation-state was explicitly founded on a rejection of Western values, rather than an adoption of them. Socialization was only possible after transnational networks had eroded this construction by openly challenging the government's interpretation of Pancasila.

Another alternative explanation points to a relation between socioeconomic development and human rights progress, drawing on a diverse literature on political modernization and democratization. Democracy, this literature claims, is sequentially achieved: rising literacy expands the individual's media exposure, this leads in turn to greater economic participation and, finally, increasing demands for political participation. The most likely actors to mediate this process are members of the middle classes. In both Indonesia and the Philippines, the high proportion of NGO representatives which come from the middle classes (Sinaga 1995; Tanter and Young 1990) and, in the Philippines, their high visibility during the "people power" revolution (Anderson 1988; Timberman 1987; Wurfel 1988) seem to support this explanation.

In neither country did the major changes in the human rights area between 1980 and 1989 correlate with economic growth rates. In the Philippines, the average rate of growth of gross domestic product (GDP) was only 0.7 percent compared to 5.9 percent between 1965 and 1980. Rather than confirming the theory, this statistic points to an almost opposite effect of economic growth. Indonesia's GDP growth

---

[20] The writings of Renato Constantino and Jose Diokno are a primary example for this . Popular resentment against the US military facilities found expression in a book written by Roland G. Simbulan. It was sold out within months and was reprinted in 1985 (Simbulan 1985).

rates were always higher than the Philippine ones, but the process of norm internalization was much slower. Regarding its average GDP growth, human rights reforms in Indonesia would have been more likely to have occurred between 1965 and 1980, because it was much higher then than during the 1980–1989 period. But it actually developed during the following period (World Bank 1991). Regarding literacy rates, the statistics are indeterminate: in both Indonesia and the Philippines, literacy has continually increased since the early 1970s. The rates do not correlate with any variations on the dependent variable, human rights change.

A more actor- and process-oriented logic also fails to explain human rights change: in Indonesia, as well as in the Philippines, a majority of the middle class supported the authoritarian system for reasons of national stability and economic development. The Philippine middle class was deeply split regarding the declaration of martial law in 1972. It was not until the assassination of the opposition leader Benigno Aquino that it began to mobilize against the Marcos government. In Indonesia, analyses of middle-class development never clearly indicated the role it would play as a carrier of democratic ideas (Tanter and Young 1990). Steady economic growth rates have produced a continually growing middle class which seems, however, "unable to translate its increasing wealth, skills and economic base into an independent domain of social and economic power to impose accountability upon the state and its officials" (Robison 1992: 348; cf. Fierlbeck 1994). The predominance of student groups in political protests against Suharto in May 1998 finally contradicts claims that "the middle class" is the mover during the transition phase to democracy. Though I do not share views that describe Asian-Pacific middle classes as illiberal *per se* (see Martin Jones 1998), there is no evidence that the middle classes caused changes in human rights practices in the first place.

Conclusion

The aim of this chapter is to explain the changes in human rights practices in the Philippines and Indonesia. It has been argued that such explanations have to take into consideration the independent role of international norms and their conveyance through transnational human rights networks. International human rights norms offered an internationally salient idea which transnational networks used to protect and empower domestic actors. By establishing transnational contacts, the domestic opposition was in both cases able to overcome the constraints imposed by the domestic structure and government prohibitions. This was more evident in the Indonesian case, in which the domestic human rights discourse first wandered beyond the restrictions set by the military and openly dealt with the former "taboos" of East Timor, political prisoners, and government mismanagement, and later, after the resignation of Suharto, confronted the new government of Habibie with concrete demands to improve the human rights situation.

Moreover, I linked these network activities to official nationalism, one issue concerning discursive practices at a domestic level, in order to illustrate the various ways in which human rights issues get integrated into the domestic debate. It was more difficult to establish a national human rights discourse in Indonesia than in the Philippines. The prominent anti-colonial and collectivist rhetoric of Indonesian ruling elites posed an effective impediment to transnational actors who advocated international human rights standards. The transnational human rights network's effectiveness increased after it had effectively challenged and redefined this construction of official nationalism in Indonesia. Though it is still open what Indonesia's new official nationalism will look like, it will certainly internationalize in the sense that it will be more open to international forces and will acknowledge international human rights standards. In the Philippines, "rule of law" became a constant theme of official rhetoric in terms of characteristics of the nation-state after independence. In this case, the challenge of the TN was to redefine their version of nationalism from an opposition ideology. The new official nationalism as promoted by the state emphasizes national sovereignty and rejects close ties to the US. It has nationalized and thus mixed two supposed "unthinkables," a conservative notion of nationalism and human rights principles. The Philippines, for example, refused to extend the Military Base Agreement in 1990 and the US had to leave the military installations in 1991. At the same time, grounded in this new nationalism is the collective memory of the "Marcos dictatorship" which provides a strong incentive to further improve the human rights situation in the Philippines as well as to fight new human rights violations.

As both the overthrow of Marcos and of Suharto was accompanied by financial crises, the question remains whether these economic emergencies introduce challenges to a network explanation. Corruption charges, calls of the International Monetary Fund (IMF) and other business sectors to end monopolies, and other financial preferences which have favored the Suharto family and their closest friends in the past, reveal striking similarities with the Philippine crony capitalism under Marcos at the beginning of the 1980s. As has become clear, Marcos's as well as Suharto's overthrow had economic as well as political explanations. The changes of government in these two countries in 1986 and 1998 are overdetermined, as either one of the political or socioeconomic reasons might have toppled them in the long term (see Overholt 1986 for the Philippines). This paper, however, highlighted the specific contribution of human rights networks in facilitating such a change of power. It goes beyond explaining the ouster of repressive regimes, however, as it is interested in the conditions under which substantive positive changes in human rights situations occur.

How sustainable are the changes in human rights practices? As for the Philippines, the transnational network succeeded in bringing about a sustained decrease in human rights practices, although human rights violations continue at a low level. Silliman argues that the socioeconomic disparities within Philippine society contribute to a cycle of poverty, activism, and repression, and that breaking this cycle requires deeper societal changes (Silliman 1994). It suggests that network activities reach their limit when structural reasons account for a persistence of human rights violations. My own reading of the Philippine "case" suggests that the parameters of the domestic debate on human rights can be changed so as to effectively avoid resorting to armed activism or repression. The non-violent strategies the Ramos administration has sought against armed insurgency, as well as the public criticism the New People's Army received when it started its "internal cleansing" campaigns involving human rights violations among civilians, are illustrative of this transformation. "Human rights" have gained prescriptive status independent of political interests. Having said this, I doubt that habitualization or institutionalization at the state level have proceeded sufficiently to render pressure from societal actors futile. They still are an alternative domestic sanctioning mechanism complementing an ineffective legal structure.

In Indonesia, the road to a sustained improvement in human rights practices will be very rocky if the government does not act speedily to introduce the necessary measures to effectively avoid human rights abuses. The current Habibie government's reasons for taking further measures to combat human rights violations, in the first place, seem to be motivated by the desire to improve its international image and achieve the necessary political stability to attract foreign investments. This instrumental motivation, however, is not enough to achieve the necessary internal political legitimation and stability for any Indonesian government. It seems that guaranteeing human rights standards partly provides an answer to some of the challenges the new government faces. For example, as most secessionist movements justify their demands for self-determination with experiences of gross violations of human rights, a drastic improvement in the situation might increase the likelihood of maintaining Indonesia's territorial integrity, or – as in the Philippines – searching for non-violent solutions to the conflicts. For the political conflicts lying ahead, the adherence to human rights standards is an imperative not only for the government, but for other societal actors as well. Protecting citizens from human rights violations remains the responsibility of the state, however – a responsibility it can only take over if these standards are institutionalized properly.

6   International norms and domestic politics in Chile and Guatemala

Stephen C. Ropp and Kathryn Sikkink

Introduction

Human rights principles have long resonated in Latin America. Policy makers, legal scholars, and activists throughout the region have historically advocated regional and international human rights norms. Latin American states lobbied for human rights language in the United Nations Charter, adopted the American Declaration of the Rights and Duties of Man in 1948, and unanimously supported, later that same year, the Universal Declaration of Human Rights. But Latin Americans have also been firm advocates of principles of sovereignty and non-intervention, and when norms of sovereignty and human rights came into conflict, sovereignty usually won. By the 1980s, however, regional and international human rights regimes and networks began to have more acceptance and impact in Latin America (Sikkink 1997).

In this chapter, we examine this process through an exploration of the human rights situations in Chile and Guatemala during the period 1973 to 1998. Few countries in Latin America are as different as Chile and Guatemala. Yet despite these differences, in the 1970s and 1980s harsh authoritarian regimes in both countries unleashed more intense state terror against the population than at any previous time in their history (Medina Quiroga 1988, Figueroa Ibarra 1991). Of the two cases, repression was far more severe in Guatemala than in Chile, though the Chilean case received more international attention. By the 1990s, both countries were governed by democratic regimes, although "authoritarian enclaves" and structures remained (Garretón 1991). The transition to rule-consistent human rights behavior has been more complete in the Chilean case, while in Guatemala the process is more uncertain and still in flux. In both cases, the military negotiated its retreat from politics in a way that permitted it to maintain its autonomy and avoid legal prosecution for its role in human rights abuses.

International human rights norms/networks and attendant socialization processes are an important part of the explanation for changing human rights practices in both countries. Indeed the human rights violations in Chile contributed to growing global awareness of human rights and to the building of the transnational human rights network. Yet the transition to democracy in Chile, and the return to protection of human rights took seventeen long years. Scholars refer to Chile's "frozen transition," and to the "muted" quality of democracy there today (Frohmann 1998; Wilde 1998). Partly as a result of the failure to provide justice for victims of past violations, in October 1998 Spanish judges requested the arrest of former dictator Pinochet in Britain and his extradition to Spain to stand trial for genocide, torture and executions.

Guatemala had some of the most severe human rights violations of any country considered in this book. Human rights organizations estimate that between 1966 and 1986, some 150,000 civilians were killed, mostly by the Guatemalan military and paramilitary groups (Guatemalan Human Rights Commission/USA 1998: 7), and some 50,000 disappeared. By 1997, the country had reestablished a fragile democracy, the government and the guerrillas had negotiated an end to the civil war, and two truth commissions, one sponsored by the United Nations and one by the Roman Catholic Church, were preparing their reports. The church published its four-volume report, *Guatemala: Nunca Más*, in 1998, documenting the extent, mechanisms, and impact of state terror (Archbishopric of Guatemala, Office of Human Rights 1998).

Shortly after the publication of the report, Bishop Juan Gerardi, founder and director of the Archdiocesan Human Rights Office, and director of the project that wrote and published the Nunca Más report, was murdered in his home. Although human rights violations had declined dramatically in the late 1990s, Bishop Gerardi's murder (and the failure of the government to find and prosecute those responsible) suggested that the structures of power and impunity behind the human rights violations had not been dismantled. Guatemala appeared stalled between rhetorical support for human rights and real change in practices – between prescriptive status and behavioral change. And true to the spiral model, many Guatemalans remained convinced that the way the international community responded to the bishop's

173

murder could make a profound difference to whether human rights progress in Guatemala remained stalled or moved ahead.

Phase 1: repression and initial socialization

Before the coup in 1973, Chile had the longest tradition of democracy in the hemisphere, a well-institutionalized party system, and relatively high levels of economic development, urbanization, and industrialization for a developing country. Guatemala, on the other hand, has virtually no democratic tradition, a weak party system, and is predominantly rural and agricultural, with low levels of economic growth and very high population growth. In terms of human development, Chile ranks with Argentina, Uruguay, and Costa Rica as the most developed countries in Latin America, while Guatemala ranks with Honduras, Nicaragua, El Salvador, and Haiti as the countries with the lowest level of human development (United Nations Development Program 1996: 135–156). As our analysis of these two cases will show, these country-level differences did not fundamentally determine domestic human rights outcomes, but they did alter the general nature of the spiral socialization process in some significant ways.

Chile

In Chile, the military intervened in politics only twice between 1833 and 1973, and between 1932 and 1973 the country experienced uninterrupted democratic rule. The constitution of 1925 included significant human rights guarantees, which an independent judiciary helped to enforce (Hawkins 1996: 63–64). Although political leadership was dominated by a relatively small group of political elites, the democratic political regime prior to 1973 had gradually incorporated new groups into the political system while improving their standard of living (Garretón 1989: 3).

The coup in 1973 followed a period of intense mobilization and polarization of Chilean politics after Salvador Allende, elected president in 1970, began to implement his program for a peaceful road to socialism. Threatened social and economic elites, with the backing of the United States and several US-based corporations, worked actively together to destabilize the Allende regime (US Senate 1975; Sigmund 1993). At the same time moderate political forces were unwilling and unable to agree on compromises to save democracy (Valenzuela 1978).

In September 1973, the military, led by Commander in Chief of the Army, General Augusto Pinochet, overthrew the Allende government, and soon made clear its intention to fundamentally change the Chilean political and economic system. After the coup, the military engaged in a systematic repressive campaign against its own citizens of a kind unparalleled in Chilean history. Over half of the almost 3,000 cases of death and disappearance during the Pinochet era (1973–1989), took place during 1973 and 1974, and the months immediately following the coup were particularly violent (Ministerio Secretaria General de Gobierno 1991).

Cecilia Medina Quiroga argues that the special circumstances of the Chilean coup "riveted the eyes of the international community."

> There seemed to have been a shared feeling that some unexpressed but recognizable limit had been transgressed. Both the democratic past of Chile and the bloodiness of the coup may have accounted for this reaction... Chileans were used to having their civil and political rights respected, and no authority previously would have dared to grossly and openly violate them, since the response from the rest of the state organs and of public opinion would inevitably and promptly have called the transgressor to account. (Medina Quiroga, 1988: 261)

International network pressures and attendant socialization processes were more comprehensive and forceful toward Chile than toward any other Latin American country. Chilean intellectuals and political parties were extremely well connected to their counterparts, especially in Europe. After the coup, they were able rapidly to mobilize existing non-governmental networks, and build new ones to help exiles and to protest at the repressive policies of the regime. Only three days after the coup, Amnesty International and the International Commission of Jurists sent a cable to the Organization of American States (OAS)'s Inter-American Commission on Human Rights (IACHR) requesting its intervention. The church in Chile took a more activist stance than elsewhere in the Southern Cone (Chile, Argentina, Paraguay, and Uruguay), providing an umbrella of protection under which a sophisticated array of domestic human rights organizations coalesced. Chileans sought all the international and regional legal channels open to them to complain against the military regime, and were especially effective in the United Nations. Chile was one case where both the US (after Carter took office in 1977), and the USSR could agree that international sanctions were desirable. This convergence of Great Power interests allowed for the early use of strategic bargaining as a mode of socialization, and opened up the way for active UN involvement and for effective network pressures within the United Nations.[1]

These transnational-domestic processes of socialization are what we have called the "boomerang effect" (introductory chapter). And indeed, one can argue that the Chilean networks almost "invented" the boomerang. Shortly after the coup, various church leaders set up the first human rights organization, the Committee for Cooperation for Peace (COPACHI). The original goals of COPACHI were to gather information on the human rights situation and provide material and legal assistance to victims of human rights abuses. It soon became obvious that COPACHI could not carry on its work without international assistance, and it sought out international contacts to provide financial support, to disseminate human rights information, and to pressure the Chilean government to change its practices. The initial support for COPACHI came from international church organizations, especially the World Council of Churches (Frühling and Orellana 1991: 37). Pressures from Pinochet led the Roman Catholic Church to close COPACHI, but it replaced it with a new organization – the Vicariate of Solidarity – directly under its control and protection. The Vicariate maintained extensive international contacts. For example, the staff of the Vicariate of Solidarity was on the phone every day with Amnesty International in London throughout most of the early years of the dictatorship.[2] In addition, Chilean exiles rapidly moved to establish Chilean solidarity groups abroad, and maintained active contact with academic and political party activists. Eventually, Chile solidarity groups or groups working on human rights in Chile were active in over eighty countries around the world.

---

[1] The story of international network socializing activities on human rights in Chile has been documented more extensively than most other human rights cases. Numerous studies discuss the impact of international actors such as the Roman Catholic Church, the Ford Foundation, the Inter-American Commission on Human Rights, and NGOs on human rights practices in Chile (Hawkins 1996; Lowden 1996; Smith 1982; Medina Quiroga 1988; Orellana and Hutchinson 1991; Puryear 1994; Frühling and Orellana 1991). This chapter is based not only on the secondary literature on human rights policies in Chile, but also on interviews with human rights activists, journalists, academics, and policy makers in Santiago, Chile, in early November 1993. These interviews include: Sebastian Brett, Malcolm Coad, Hugo Frühling, Manuel Antonio Garreton, Roberto Garreton, Alejandro Gonzales, Claudio Gonzales, Santiago Larrain, Hector Ocampo, Michael Shifter, Fernando Zegers, Julio Silva Solar, and Jose Zalaquette.
[2] Interview with Roberto Garretón, Santiago, Chile, November 5, 1992.

Guatemala

Guatemala had experienced a series of authoritarian regimes with increasingly repressive practices during much of the twentieth century. The roots of Guatemala's contemporary human rights problems ultimately go back to the colonial period when the Spanish conquerors created one of the most highly stratified and brutally repressive systems of exploitation within their colonial empire (Woodward 1985). During the late nineteenth and early twentieth centuries, the position of indigenous Mayan people deteriorated even further as their highland communal village lands (*ejidos*) were rapidly dismantled to make way for coffee plantations (Castellano Cambranes 1984: 127–34).

At the end of the Second World War, a complex mix of changes within the world system and internal class transformations within Guatemala led to the emergence of a number of reform politicians and populist leaders, essentially representing the interests of urban middle-class groups. Politicians such as Dr. Juan José Arévalo (elected president in 1945) and his successor Colonel Jacobo Arbenz Guzman were advocates of a mildly socialist alternative development project that sought at one and the same time to create a more open political system and to modernize the economy through import substitution and land reform.

The period of political, social, and cultural effervescence associated with the presidencies of Arévalo and Arbenz ended in 1954 following growing confrontation between Arbenz and the Eisenhower administration. At the height of the Cold War, Arbenz made the mistake of ordering a shipment of arms from Czechoslovakia to defend his beleaguered government. The Eisenhower administration, already disturbed by the growing threat that land reform posed to the United Fruit Company, reacted in what was to become rather typical Cold War fashion. The Central Intelligence Agency provided resources and training for an exile army led by Colonel Carlos Castillo Armas that overthrew Arbenz (Woodward 1985: 239–241).

After the coup of 1954 the repression of dissident elements in society, formerly the work of a highly dispersed set of largely private groups and institutions associated with the Guatemalan land-tenure system, now became more centralized at the state level. The primary mechanism for the centralization of state control over such traditional repressive functions was the strengthening of the existing system of local military commissioners. These commissioners were former army personnel, now in the reserve system, who performed paramilitary functions in rural areas (Jonas 1991: 61). From 1954 until 1985, a succession of national civil–military coalitions used this reinforced repressive state apparatus in an attempt to reverse the political and socioeconomic processes associated with the societal effervescence of the late 1940s and early 1950s. The result of this thirty-year effort was massive (though often carefully calibrated and targeted) state-level abuse of human rights, abuse that was directed at various points in time at emerging guerrilla groups, trade-union militants, peasant organizers, and ecclesiastical base communities.

The wave of state-sponsored violence that swept the country from 1978 until 1983 was of an order of magnitude that startled even hardened observers of the Guatemalan scene. Responding to a perceived threat from the urban political opposition, newly elected President General Romeo Lucas Garcia unleashed both national security forces and their associated death squads. The worst of this state-sponsored repressive activity was aimed at stemming the tide of union organizing in the countryside as well as suppressing new guerrilla activity there. Following a coup in 1982 by General Efrain Rios Montt, military campaign strategies were adopted that aimed at stamping out such activity through well-funded and staffed rural counterinsurgency programs. A substantial portion of the highland peasant male population was forced to serve in army-run civil defense patrols and tens of thousands of civilians and guerrillas were killed (Trudeau 1993; Falla 1994; Stoll 1993).

As will be detailed below, there was very little comparable in Guatemala to the international network socialization activities that took place in authoritarian Chile, even during the most intensely repressive years. Guatemalan society was simply too closed and government policy too repressive to allow for even minimal international socialization to occur during the height of the violence (1978–1983). The Roman Catholic Church, which sheltered the human rights movement in Chile, was silent in Guatemala during this early period. Many European non-governmental organizations (NGOs), concerned for the safety of their staff, didn't maintain branch offices in Guatemala, thus severing another potential link to a transnational network.[3] From a theoretical perspective, one could say that the domestic end of the boomerang had been "sawed off" by the military regime.

---

[3] Interview with Rachel Garst, Guatemala City, May 23, 1998.

Phase 2: denial and backlash

Chile

As international criticism of Chile's human rights violations mounted, the government responded with defensive and nationalist rhetoric. But the Chilean military rarely denied the validity of human rights norms as strongly as the Guatemalans or most other authoritarian regimes discussed in this book. Given the country's historically deeply rooted democratic experience and the prior ratification of the Covenant on Civil and Political Rights, it was difficult for the government to deny prescriptive status. Instead, it criticized not the norms themselves, but the objectivity and methodology of international organizations, and the priority that should be given to human rights in the context of an alleged period of "war and disorder."

Thus, despite ongoing repression and authoritarian rule, Chilean military leaders often officially accepted international human rights norms while at the same time inventing legalistic reasons for preventing their actual implementation. For example, prior to the 1973 coup, the Allende administration had ratified the Covenant on Civil and Political Rights. When the treaty finally came into force in 1976, the Pinochet regime promulgated it through a decree which stipulated that it be put into effect in its entirety as the law of the land. But although the Chilean government had signed, ratified, and promulgated the treaty, both the regime and the Chilean courts later used the fragile excuse that it had never been published in the *Diario Oficial* (Official Journal) to argue that it was not enforceable (Detzner 1988).

Another example of this tendency to recognize the validity of human rights norms while ignoring them in practice can be seen in the military regime's response to the work of international organizations and networks on domestic human rights violations. During the early years of military rule, Chile accepted initial visits of the Inter-American Commission on Human Rights, the UN Commission on Human Rights, and even of human rights organizations like Amnesty International. Chile did not oppose the decision of the UN Commission on Human Rights to establish an ad hoc working group to look into the human rights situation in Chile. The Chilean delegation welcomed the resolution "as an attempt to seek the truth without prejudice," and promised that the government would give full support to the working group (Kamminga 1992). The Chilean government responded to the UN and IACHR requests for information on cases and comments on their reports, though such responses were usually incomplete and misleading. Later, when it stopped such collaboration, the Chilean government questioned the objectivity of the organizations and the institutional procedures they used rather than the legitimacy of international human rights norms themselves (Hawkins 1996; Medina Quiroga 1988).

In assessing the specific characteristics of Chile's denial phase, it is important to recognize that Chile is historically one of the earliest cases of attempted human rights change considered in this book. Along with the struggle against apartheid in South Africa, renewed Chilean militarism actually contributed to the construction of the international human rights regime and to the growth of the human rights network itself. Because Chile was one of the region's oldest democracies, because its efforts to pursue an electoral road to socialism were being watched with such interest internationally, and because the role of the United States in the overthrow of Allende was revealed soon after it occurred, the case took on a highly symbolic aspect that contributed to the emergence of the global human rights network and human rights policies. At the United Nations, Chile was a "watershed" case because it represented the first time that an "international threat to peace and security" was not considered a necessary precondition for the United Nations to respond to cases of human rights violations (Kamminga 1992). The Chilean case thus paved the way for future UN work on human rights. It was important because it raised international consciousness about human rights, increased membership in existing human rights organizations, and led to the creation of new human rights organizations that would become international models. The US section of Amnesty International, for example, expanded from 3,000 to 50,000 members between 1974 and 1976, an increase that has been partially attributed to the increasing interest in human rights created by the Chilean coup (*Washington Post* 1976; Hoeffel and Kornbluh 1983: 27–39).

Furthermore, Chilean organizations formed to confront government repression became models for human rights groups throughout Latin America, and sources of information and inspiration for human rights activists in the US and Europe. A handful of visionary leaders within the human rights movement – individuals like Pepe Zalaquette, the exiled Chilean lawyer who later became the Chairman of the International Executive Committee of Amnesty International, and Joseph Eldridge, the Methodist missionary who oversaw the growth and institutionalization of the Washington Office for Latin America, and later the Lawyers' Committee for Human Rights, were mobilized because of their initial experience in Chile.

When the coup in Chile occurred in 1973, there was not a single country in the world that had an explicit bilateral human rights policy. There was no legislation and no government directives instructing foreign policy elites to take human rights into account when designing coherent overseas strategies or when engaging other states. Such policies were constructed only after the coup in Chile, in part as a response to that coup and also because of other cases of human rights abuse during the same period in countries such as South Africa and Eastern Europe (Sikkink 1993a).

In other words, the transnational network, international human rights policies, and associated institutions that made global socialization processes possible were not fully operational when the bulk of the repression took place in Chile. Therefore, we need to view the period 1973 to 1976 as one during which activists working on Chile in NGOs and international organizations used their experiences to construct a human rights network that did not exist before, and to mobilize institutions such as the UN, the OAS/IACHR, and the foreign-policy apparatus of governments in the United States and some European countries to more explicitly incorporate human rights concerns into their foreign-policy agendas.

The reaction to the military coup in Chile contributed to the construction of the global human rights network, and this network in turn began to influence the attitude of the Chilean government toward human rights. This process of network gestation and growth in a country which had a historically deeply rooted democratic experience resulted in a denial phase that was somewhat unique. More specifically, it led to a kind of government schizophrenia about how to rhetorically recognize and, at the same time, continue to systematically ignore human rights norms. Otherwise, the Chilean case follows the basic logic of the spiral model, with its boomerang patterns, and interaction effects between domestic and international spheres of activity.

Guatemala

As compared to Chile, Guatemala experienced a clear and distinct denial and backlash phase during which the initial pressures of human rights networks were met with absolute rejection. During the 1970s, the military institution and civilian elites were unified in their conservative world view and opposition to the human rights pressures. They viewed the international human rights efforts as interventionist, divisive to the military as an institution, and as interfering with their pursuit of a strategy of counterinsurgency against "communist" guerrillas. They fancied themselves the upholders of free world values now that the United States was governed by the "moderate Marxists" of the Carter administration.

The denial phase was sustained in part because the Guatemalan military identified human rights pressures so strongly with Jimmy Carter. The Guatemalan government and private enterprise lobbies devoted considerable money and energies to wooing Republican politicians even before the Reagan administration took office, and they were convinced that under Ronald Reagan all the human rights pressures would disappear. A right-wing Guatemalan lobby group, Amigos del Pais (Friends of the Country) hired the influential administration-connected public relations firm of Deaver and Hannaford to improve Guatemala's international image and divert attention from its human rights record (Latin American Regional Report 1980: 3). The Chilean government had also hired public-relations firms in the United States (Schoultz 1981), but the Guatemalan efforts were more effective because the transnational human rights network on Guatemala was weaker at this time. In other words, the Guatemalan government used its own "boomerang" maneuvers more effectively than the human rights networks during this period.

During the 1970s and early 1980s, the Guatemalan government refused to permit an on-site visit by the Inter-American Commission on Human Rights, or to cooperate with any international or regional human rights organization (Buergenthal *et al.* 1986: 157–62). President Lucas Garcia summarized the general attitude: "Gringos are not going to teach us what democracy is" (Foreign Broadcast Information Service, Latin America 1980: 9). International human rights activities were denounced as part of an international campaign in support of subversion and against the government and army of Guatemala.

The upsurge in rural insurgency in Guatemala in the late 1970s served to unify the military ideologically and to focus them on the shared task of counterinsurgency, aimed at preserving the cultural and territorial integrity of the Hispanic state. The Guatemalan military was also able to use international pressures to provoke a broader nationalist backlash among the urban middle class, creating a self-image of a country able to sustain itself without outside support. After US military aid was terminated, Chief of Staff Lobos Zamora declared, "We Guatemalans can feel satisfied at being the first country in the world that has managed to inflict a substantial defeat on subversion by means of our own eminently nationalistic strategy and tactics, without outside assistance."

International NGOs first brought the case of human rights abuses in Guatemala to public attention in the late 1970s. In 1980, Amnesty International published an explosive report documenting a specialized agency, under the control of President Lucas Garcia and located in an annex to the National Palace, that coordinated the actions of various "private" death squads and regular army and policy units (Amnesty International 1981: 7). Early NGO work on Guatemala was hampered, however, because of the absence of any domestic human rights organizations in that country and because the military and elites in Guatemala were indifferent to international public opinion and sanctions.

Networks working on Guatemala were far less "dense" than in the case of Chile. Although rights violations in Guatemala were even more severe than in Chile, there were no effective local human rights NGOs there until the mid-1980s. At that time in Guatemala, no human rights organizations were functioning because two of the most prominent (the Guatemalan Commission for the Defense of Human Rights, and the Committee for Justice and Peace) had been forced to close down.

This absence of domestic human rights organizations in Guatemala, and the explicit government policy of eliminating leading members of the opposition, made the formation of transnational linkages difficult. Domestic human rights groups were formed for the first time in the 1980s, but they continued to face profound repression (Americas Watch 1989: 43). This is not to say that international socialization processes were totally absent during the late 1970s and early 1980s. But they tended to be almost exclusively the result of the half-hearted application of Great Power pressure and associated instrumental bargaining that, by itself, produced very mixed results (Martin and Sikkink 1993).

In sum, we can say then that Guatemala's denial phase was more clearly defined than Chile's due to the historically closed nature of Guatemalan society and the conservative world view of local civil–military elites and large portions of the urban middle class. This world view portrayed international human rights advocates as agents of a vast global Communist conspiracy. In a context of internal civil war, which pitted urban and rural Hispanic and Hispanicized groups against various indigenous peoples, it was relatively easy to character-ize the charges and accusations of human rights organizations as an internationally induced threat to the cultural and territorial integrity of the state. State denial of such charges and accusations was viewed as the only recourse.

Phase 3: deepening socialization processes and tactical concessions

Chile

Between 1975 and 1988, the Chilean military combined the continued use of repression (though at a lower level than before) with changes in government policy, changes that were frequently viewed as entirely cosmetic. Many of these policy changes appeared to be aimed not so much at internal constituencies as at deflecting increasing international and domestic criticism of Chile's human rights practices.

By 1981, seven main human rights organizations and six smaller groups of family members of victims of repression were operating in Chile (Orellana and Hutchinson 1991:17–20). These groups, and par-ticularly the main groups – the Vicariate of Solidarity, and the Chilean Commission for Human Rights – created an efficient and objective system for collecting and disseminating human rights information. Domestic NGOs provided a constant flow of information to interna-tional contacts, which in turn facilitated their external pressures (Frühl-ing and Orellana 1991: 53).

International organizations and states relied upon the reports of domestic human rights NGOs to justify their human rights pressures. Between eighty and ninety-five countries voted against Chile in the annual resolutions in the United Nations General Assembly condemn-ing Chile for violations of human rights (Muñoz 1986). These resol-utions sometimes explicitly recognized that they were based on infor-mation from domestic NGOs like the Vicariate and the Chilean Commission (Frühling and Orellana 1991). Except for South Africa, few other countries generated such wide-spread concern. These interna-tional groups and the international media in turn published reports of human rights abuses that states used to justify cut-offs of military and economic assistance to the Chilean government. The UN Human Rights Commission and the IACHR continued to consider Chilean human rights practices annually, and to issue reports. The reports of international organizations on human rights abuses in Chile were sometimes picked up by the Chilean media, providing ordinary Chilean citizens with one of the few sources of information on local human rights conditions.

The procedures of the United Nations Human Rights Commission and the IACHR facilitated an ongoing "dialogue" between the government and international human rights bodies about domestic human rights practices. For example, the IACHR requested information from the government on individual communications of specific cases it investigated as well as on its general country reports and country specific discussions in its annual reports. These documents provide evidence for processes of "moral discourses" discussed in the introductory chapter. In these exchanges, the actors communicate about interpretations of international human rights norms, the quality and reliability of the information that the Commission used, the correct procedures, the limits of the Commission's competence, and many other areas of disagreement. During the early period, no real process of "persuasion" was taking place. It appears that Chile's early cooperation was based on the assumption that it could persuade or influence the UN and the IACHR of its position, and convince them of the errors of their ways. In these attempts at persuasion, the Chilean government brought considerable legal and diplomatic experience, and foreign-policy staffs much larger than those of the international human rights bodies. When the Chilean government was unsuccessful in its attempts at persuasion, it then hardened its discursive position and limited cooperation and exchange. In particular, Chile stressed more extensively that it was subject to an international communist campaign, and that the IACHR had based its accusations on "false and exaggerated allegations provided by agents of this international campaign" (Medina Quiroga 1988: 281).

These communications provide significant evidence of the presence of a moral and legal discourse, but little evidence of persuasion. While the international network had as yet failed to persuade the Chilean government, its pressures did lead to tactical concessions during this period and helped open considerable space for the domestic opposition.

The efficacy of the transnational networks in influencing policy decisions of the Chilean government is evident in the minutes of the meetings of the Chilean juntas. In his review of these minutes, Darren Hawkins reports that "Junta records are filled with debate on how to counter international critics of its human rights policies, but domestic human rights groups are scarcely mentioned" (Hawkins 1996: 83–84). The juntas were quite aware that international networks helped sustain the work of domestic groups, however. In a speech to the Army Corps of Generals in 1977, Pinochet said, "Well we know that the action of our internal adversaries is connected with important political and economic centers in the international world which complicates even further the situation just described" (Hawkins 1996: 62). Junta members thus attempted to block the connections between domestic groups and their international allies, but were unwilling to encourage international protests by actually cutting off contact or closing domestic groups with strong international support.

The government, in turn, worked to deflect these pressures. For example, Hawkins notes that a key change took place in August 1977, when the government disbanded the security apparatus responsible for repression, the Dirección de Inteligencia Nacional (DINA), and replaced it with the Central Nacional de Informaciones (CNI). At the time, observers interpreted this change as purely cosmetic and designed to enhance the Chilean regime's abysmal international image in the reaction to the murder of Orlando Letelier and Ronnie Moffit in Washington DC in 1976. But whether interpreted as cosmetic or not, Hawkins suggests that the end of DINA marked an important power shift within the Chilean government, weakening the influence of the hard-liners, and leading to improved human rights practices (Hawkins 1994: 1, 21).

International socialization processes and the Chilean military regime's attendant concern with its international image also led the regime to make other tactical concessions, such as allowing some exiles to return and some opposition journals to be published. Perhaps the most successful of the tactical concessions, from the regime's point of view, was the 1980 plebiscite. The government hoped to use the plebiscite to consolidate the legitimacy and authority of the regime, by gaining support for an authoritarian constitution that gave the military a permanent constitutional role in government. In a context of considerable fear, intimidation, and fraud, the government claimed it had achieved a high level of public support for constitutional change, thus permitting Pinochet to stay in power for at least another eight years (Americas Watch 1988: 23–27). The results of the 1980 plebiscite, together with the beginning of the Reagan administration in the United States, gave the regime significant international breathing room.

The second plebiscite of 1988 can be seen as an attempt to repeat the success of the first plebiscite, but it led to very different results. Between 1983 and 1988, the domestic opposition had taken advantage of new political space to organize massive protests and demonstrations, which allowed for the revitalization of the political parties, but failed to bring a transition to democracy (Garretón 1989). It was not until political parties and civil society united in the campaign in favor of the "no" vote in the 1988 plebiscite that a true transition to democracy began. International groups provided extensive financial and technical support for intellectuals, NGOs, and political parties to carry out polling, voter registration drives, training for polling observers, and election monitoring. The increased sophistication and mobilization of the now unified domestic opposition permitted them to use a similar attempt at cosmetic change to defeat the regime at the polls, and paved the way for the transition to democracy in 1990.

Guatemala

Beginning in 1983, Guatemalans began to experience a political opening that was accompanied by a certain amount of progress in the field of human rights. In terms of political events, General Oscar Mejia Victores overthrew General Rios Montt and initiated movement toward the creation of a democratic government that would allow for substantially more political participation than those of the 1960s and 1970s. During 1984 and 1985, elections were held for a Constituent Assembly, a new constitution was written, and both presidential and congressional elections were held. Two centrist parties, the Christian Democrats and the National Center Union (UCN) in particular used the Constituent Assembly as a forum for the discussion and eventual implementation of constitutional changes relating to human rights.

In Guatemala, this democratic opening was not due to the inability of the military regime to contain pressures from below. Rather, one sector of the armed forces decided that the double effort of governing and carrying out a counterinsurgency campaign had led to an "institutional attrition" and thus advocated retreating from government but not from power (Arévalo de Leon 1997: 1). International pressures contributed to this perception of "attrition" that led to a return to civilian rule. In the early 1980s, network activities and socialization processes increased in Guatemala. Perhaps most importantly, these activities helped block attempts by the Reagan administration to reinstate economic aid during the period 1981 to 1984. When the

Guatemalan government continued to be attacked in the US Congress and by transnational networks, the country ended its denial phase and began to implement seemingly cosmetic changes.

The inauguration of Vinicio Cerezo, a Christian Democrat, as president in January 1986 was hailed as a step along the path to democracy. But President Cerezo estimated that he only exercised 30 percent of power in Guatemala during his presidency, with the rest in the hands of the military and the private sector (Arévalo de Leon 1997: 1) and he was not able to put a stop to major human rights abuses. It was not until after the failed *"auto-golpe"* (self-inflicted coup) of the elected government of Jorge Serrano in 1993 that the human rights tide began to fully turn in Guatemala, and not until after the election of President Alvaro Arzú and the 1996 Peace Accords between the government and the guerrillas that a gradual, fragile, and perhaps reversible move toward rule-governed change took place.

As in the Chilean case, the military agreed to the gradual ceding of power to civilians, in part because international socialization processes had persuaded them of the need for minimally cosmetic improvements in their international image. Though far from comprehensive, these political changes did open more space for domestic opposition to organize. During the Cerezo presidency, the consensus view appears to be that modest progress was made on human rights matters, both with regard to the movement toward prescriptive status and creation of an environment more conducive to rule-consistent behavior. In the words of Susanne Jonas, a long-time observer of human rights conditions in Guatemala: "The reduction in overt state-sponsored violence, the operation of several political parties, and the possibility of exercising constitutionally guaranteed individual rights (or minimally the expectation that such rights should be guaranteed) mitigated the purely repressive politics of the past and were greeted as improvements" (Jonas 1991: 162).

The human rights situation began to evolve and change further in the 1990s. A more diverse set of human rights organizations was now working domestically in Guatemala, and their numbers increased. Most importantly, after years of silence, the Guatemala Roman Catholic Church opened in 1990 the Archbishopric of Guatemala Office of Human Rights (ODHAG), which became the most prominent and professional human rights organization in Guatemala and developed and maintained extensive contacts with transnational network actors. At the beginning, ODHAG consisted of a room, three desks, three chairs, and three young lawyers – two Guatemalans and one from the United States. To get its work off the ground, ODHAG received crucial assistance from a handful of smaller foreign foundations and church-related organizations and from Americas Watch. The Archbishop's office developed contacts around specific prominent and paradigmatic cases of human rights abuses.[4] In 1990, members of the Guatemala military killed a young Guatemalan anthropologist, Myrna Mack, for her protests at the human rights violations of the internally displaced people in Guatemala. Myrna's sister, Helen Mack, with the help of the Archbishop's office, for the first time demanded that the Guatemalan courts address human rights issues. International groups, such as the American Association for the Advancement of Science, send high-profile delegations to investigate and pressure for accountability. After Helen Mack received an international prize for her human rights work, she used the funds to set up the Myrna Mack Foundation, which dedicated itself to human rights work.[5] These two organizations, OD-HAG and the Myrna Mack foundation, then formed the backbone of the revived domestic human rights community that galvanized the transnational network and made socialization processes more success-ful in the 1990s than they had been in the 1970s. Human rights organ-izations were also able to tentatively "link up" with newly formed state-level offices, especially the Human Rights Ombudsman's Office formed as a result of the 1985 constitution. They proved particularly effective under Ramiro de Leon Carpio, the Office's leader from 1989 to 1993.

Phase 4: prescriptive status

Chile

In Chile, the gradual movement toward granting full prescriptive status to human rights norms closely paralleled the redemocratization process. The victory of the "no" vote against Pinochet in the 1988 plebiscite opened the path towards redemocratization. The July 1989 plebiscite on constitutional reforms resulted in an amendment to the constitution that established the government's duty to act in conformity with the various international human rights instruments that had been ratified by Chile – including the Covenant on Civil and Political Rights. But the Supreme Court insisted on maintaining the fiction that Chile had not ratified the

---

[4] Interview with Daniel Saxon, Guatemala City, May 22, 1998.
[5] Interview with Helen Mack, Guatemala City, May 22, 1998.

Covenant until it had published it in the *Diario Oficial*, and thus it recognized the ratification date as April 29, 1989 for the purposes of application to national law (Americas Watch 1991: 44–45).

During the period of military rule, Chile ratified the Torture Convention in 1988, though it did so with some crippling reservations. As specified in the constitution, Chile held free presidential elections in 1990, and elected a candidate of the center-left coalition, Patricio Aylwin. The democratic government eventually withdrew Chile's reservations to the Torture Convention. However, it has not yet made the additional declaration to recognize the competence of the Committee Against Torture to receive petitions from other parties and individuals.

Individual victims in Latin America have an additional complaint procedure available to them through the Inter-American Commission on Human Rights and the Inter-American Court of Human Rights. The Inter-American Commission on Human Rights could make reports and receive complaints on all states in the region, but the Court can only take cases of countries that have ratified the American Convention of Human Rights and recognized the Court's compulsory jurisdiction. Because recognizing the compulsory jurisdiction of the Inter-American Court of Human Rights involves a potentially significant degree of international supervision of domestic human rights practices, we argue that this acceptance marks the completion of the prescriptive status phase in Chile and Guatemala. Chile ratified the American Convention and accepted the compulsory jurisdiction of the court in 1990. Two years later, the Chilean Congress also ratified the Optional Protocol to the Covenant on Civil and Political Rights, thus allowing individuals to file petitions of grievance with the UN Human Rights Committee.

Guatemala

The Guatemalan Constitution of 1985 is literally permeated with human rights norms that structure the entire document. The general importance of human rights is stressed in the Preamble and Title I of the Constitution; Title II offers a detailed bill of individual rights, including forty-two articles covering virtually all the rights in the Universal Declaration. The Constitution also contains provisions for social, cultural, and economic rights, as well as a specific section mandating the protection of indigenous communities. Finally, and most importantly, Article 46 mandates the preeminence of international law over domestic law in human rights matters (Garcia Laguardia 1996: 73–86).

The Guatemalan Constitution of 1985 is also important in that it created an independent Human Rights Ombudsman Office, with an ombudsman appointed by the Congress whose responsibility it was to investigate human rights abuses, recommend policy changes, and censure or promote legal action against human rights violators (Garcia Laguardia 1996: 167–168). Eventually the Human Rights Ombudsman became a more effective source of human rights information and advocate for human rights, especially during the period when Ramiro de Carpio Leon was its head.

Although the formal legal-institutional structures and informal principled issue networks associated with the struggle for human rights in Guatemala can be traced back to the mid-1980s, it was only in the 1990s that human rights values definitively achieved prescriptive status among a significant number of state-level actors in Guatemala. Guatemala ratified the American Convention on Human Rights in 1978, and accepted the compulsory jurisdiction of the Inter-American Court of Human Rights in March of 1987, but limited the Court's jurisdiction to violations that occurred after the date of acceptance. Thus, Guatemala completed the prescriptive status phase of our "spiral model" three years before Chile did in 1990, even though its human rights record was much more egregious.

These very small (indeed inconsequential) differences with regard to when human rights norms achieved prescriptive status in our two countries raise a very interesting question. Despite significant differences in their domestic structures and political histories, both countries completed ratification of major human rights treaties at approximately the same time. Why was this the case? This virtually simultaneous achievement of prescriptive status suggests that treaty ratification specifically, and prescriptive status more generally, may be less linked to a given country's domestic structural and historical trajectory than to global and regional normative developments. In the late 1980s and early 1990s, Latin America seems to have experienced what legal theorists have called a "norm cascade" (Sunstein 1997: 36, 38) of international human rights and democracy norms. Virtually all of the countries of the region completed ratification of major human rights treaties and accepted the compulsory jurisdiction of the Inter-American Court of Human Rights within a fairly short period of time. Therefore, the acceptance of prescriptive status of human rights norms in Guatemala and Chile do not appear to be isolated incidents, but rather part of a regional (and global) process leading to the collective acceptance of human rights norms.

Phase 5: rule-consistent behavior

Chile

The transition to electoral rule in Chile in 1990 provided a crucial turning point in human rights behavior. It contributed substantially and essentially to ending the practices of summary execution and forced disappearance that had been used for seventeen years (see table 6.2). In particular there have been no reported cases of politically motivated disappearances from 1990 through 1996.

But redemocratization did not contribute to a complete change to rule-consistent behavior. The security forces, especially the military police (Carabineros) continued to use torture and arbitrary arrests, though on a much smaller scale than in the previous period. The government announced that it would not tolerate torture, and enacted some legal reforms limiting incommunicado detention and providing for the medical examination of detainees, but these have not been sufficient to end mistreatment completely.[6] A 1996 Report by the United Nations Commission on Human Rights concluded that acts of torture still continue in Chile and that, although they are not systemic, the government has taken insufficient action to control the activities of security forces, especially the Carabineros (US Department of State, 1997b).

By 1995, all but one of the remaining prisoners convicted under the military government had been released, yet there were at least 120 people serving prison sentences or in custody awaiting trial for politically motivated offenses committed since the end of the military government (Amnesty International Reports 1994–1996). Most of the continuing human rights abuses appear to be the result of continuity of personnel associated with the old military regime in the security forces and in the judicial system.

One of the things we find most interesting about our Chilean case is the fact that prescriptive status was achieved (phase 4) and rule-consistent behavior occurred (phase 5) simultaneously in the early 1990s. Was this mere coincidence, or did Chile differ in some important fashion from the other countries that we have studied in this book? One might argue that this is one of the few examples in our book where the socialization of human rights norms into domestic practice took place in a context of redemocratization rather than initial democratization.

---

[6] This is based on a survey of Amnesty International Reports, 1991–1997, discussion of the human rights situation in Chile.

Thus, while the coup made violations of human rights possible, as soon as democracy was restored, rule-governed behavior quickly followed as a result of the strong tradition of respect for human rights associated with earlier democratic practice.

While working to quickly improve domestic human rights practices, Chile's new democratic government also moved toward ratification of the relevant treaties that would signal its full acceptance of the prescriptive status of human rights norms to the international community. Victims of past human rights abuses were able to submit their petitions to the National Commission on Truth and Reconciliation (Rettig Commission). The Commission, however, was limited to gathering and publishing information; it could neither investigate abuses nor reach conclusions as to the responsibility that individuals had for crimes. Members of the judiciary were also limited in their ability to consider cases of past human rights violations by the 1978 Amnesty Law which covered criminal acts committed by police and military between the 1973 coup and March 10, 1978. The Supreme Court has upheld the Amnesty Law, claiming that international human rights treaties ratified by Chile (which prohibit amnesties for crimes against humanity) do not override this law.

The ability of individuals to file complaints for continuing human rights abuses is also hampered by provisions inherited from the Pinochet regime giving military courts jurisdiction over most criminal acts committed by members of the military (Americas Watch 1991: 17,19). There have been a few exceptions to the pattern of judicial impunity for past human rights violations. In 1995, the Supreme Court upheld the conviction of retired general, and former head of DINA, Manuel Contreras, and Brigadier General Pedro Espinoza for their role in ordering the murder of Orlando Letelier and Ronni Moffitt by a car bomb in Washington DC in 1976. Chilean courts have also convicted and imprisoned police and military officers for a handful of human rights abuses that occurred during the military regime, but after the Amnesty Law of 1978 (Correa Sutil 1997: 142–49).

Guatemala

In contrast to Chile, the temporal gap between the granting of full prescriptive status to human rights norms and the beginnings of actual behavioral change was much greater in Guatemala. If we date prescriptive status to 1987 when Guatemala accepted the compulsory jurisdiction of the Inter-American Court of Human Rights, then the gap lasted

Table 6.1. *Complaints admitted and confirmed, by category of alleged violation, to MINUGUA, November 21, 1994 to June 30, 1997*

	November 21, 1994–May 21, 1995 Complaints admitted	May 21–December 31, 1995 Complaints admitted	January 1–June 30, 1996 Complaints admitted	July 1–December 31, 1996 Complaints admitted	January 1–June 30, 1997 Complaints admitted	As of June 30, 1997 Confirmed violations of complaints admitted during the entire period
Extrajudicial executions	76	79	61	41	23	47
Disappearance	7	4	1	1	3	1
Arbitrary arrest and detention without trial	21	60	21	72	23	171
Torture	10	14	4	3	2	1
Cruel, inhuman or degrading treatment	5	15	7	15	8	6

Note: The category "Arbitrary arrest and detention without trial" combines two categories from the Minugua report: "Arbitrary detention," and "Detention in violation of legal guarantees." Numbers for disappearances and cruel, inhuman, and degrading treatment for the period of November 21, 1994 to May 21, 1995 were not available, but were deduced by subtracting the total for May 21, 1995 to Dececember 31, 1995 from the yearly total for 1995. The final column of confirmed violations combines the "corroborated violations" category from the fifth report with the "confirmed violations" category from the sixth and seventh reports.

at least ten years (from 1987 to 1997) before significant changes to rule-consistent behavior began to occur. By the late 1990s, however, movement towards rule-governed behavior in Guatemala was indeed taking place, especially with regard to torture and disappearances.

After many fits and starts, the United Nations' brokered peace process in Guatemala finally began to make progress in 1994. One key part of the peace process between the Guatemalan government and the guerrilla movement (UNRG) was a comprehensive agreement on human rights signed in March 1994 which established the United Nations Human Rights Verification Mission (MINUGUA). The Agreement begins by recognizing the international human rights treaties and conventions that Guatemala has signed, and by the government reaffirming "its adherence to the principles and norms designed to guarantee and protect the full observance of human rights" (United Nations General Assembly 1994). MINUGUA started working in Guatemala in November 1994, and set up thirteen regional and subregional offices staffed by over 400 professional and support staff.[7] The presence of MINUGUA monitors was essential for ensuring the continuation of the peace-negotiation process and for creating human rights conditions for open elections in 1995. MINUGUA issued biannual human rights reports. Of the cases it received in its first two and a half years from November 1994 through June 1997, MINUGUA has only confirmed one actual case of disappearance and one case of torture (United Nations General Assembly 1997: 16–17).

Levels of extrajudicial executions (EJEs) remained unacceptably high, but declined from late 1994 until the middle of 1997. MINUGUA admitted twenty-three complaints of extrajudicial execution during the first six months of 1997, and confirmed forty-seven cases of EJEs during the two and a half year period that they had operated in Guatemala. If we compare this number to the thousands of people killed per year in the 1970s and 1980s, it is clear that there has been a dramatic change in human rights practices. However, arbitrary arrests and detention without trial continued to be a problem, with an average rate of about forty-five complaints admitted per six-month period (see table 6.1). In the wake of the murder of Bishop Gerardi, there is concern that human rights violations are increasing, but MINUGUA has delayed its human rights reporting, so there is not yet comparable information available to evaluate these claims.

[7] Interview with Leila Lima, Guatemala City, May 22, 1998.

Stephen C. Ropp and Kathryn Sikkink

Table 6.2. *Rule-consistent behavior: human rights conditions in Chile 1973–1996: death and disappearance*

Year	Victims
1973	1,261
1974	309
1975	119
1976	139
1977	25
1978	9
1979	13
1980	15
1981	36
1982	8
1983	82
1984	74
1985	50
1986	50
1987	34
1988	27
1989	26
1990	2
1991	0
1992	3
1993	0
1994	8
1995	0
1996	0

Note: Data for 1973 to 1990 from the Rettig Report,
summarized in Comisión Chilena de Derechos
Humanos 1991, Cuadro Resumen de Victimas, pp. 93–
94. Data for 1991 to 1996 are from Amnesty International
Reports for 1991 to 1996 for extrajudicial executions and
disappearances. The data are not strictly comparable,
because the Rettig Report data are for confirmed cases,
while the Amnesty data are for reported cases. For
example, the deaths in 1992 and 1994 are listed as cases
where people died in circumstances "suggesting they
may have been extrajudicially executed."

It is still difficult to gauge the extent to which the 1996 Peace Accords have contributed to rule-governed human rights behavior. The
decline in disappearances and in torture occurred before the Peace
Accords were signed, and there continued to be a high number of
unresolved extrajudicial executions in the aftermath of its signing.

MINUGUA officials argued that it was not the civil war itself, but impunity for past human rights abuses that blocked human rights improvements. Although a number of trials of military, police, and former government officials for human rights abuses are under way few expect – with the possible exception of the murder case of Myrna Mack – that any high level military official will be held responsible for violations of human rights.[8] An official high-level commission, the Justice Strengthening Commission, has recently issued a report making extensive recommendations for the reform of the justice system to make it more independent and effective, but it is unclear whether the government will implement most of the reforms (Comisión de Fortalecimiento de la Justicia 1998).

Complicating the picture even more is a dramatic increase in private violence in the wake of the Peace Accords. Under their terms, the government closed barracks and disbanded the Civil Patrols. It did so, however, before the new National Civilian Police Force was fully staffed and operating. As a result, large parts of the country were left without any police force, and people began taking the law into their own hands. Local communities took part in over twenty lynchings of suspected criminals in 1997 alone. Former police and military officers have been hired by private individuals to carry out assassinations for diverse social and political reasons (Guatemalan Human Rights Commission/USA, 1997). For example, street children were often killed by private policemen hired by bus owners who accused them of theft (Guatemalan Human Rights Commission/USA, 1997). The upsurge in crime led to a policy of temporarily involving Guatemala military in daily police functions. Some human rights advocates see this as a step backward in a process that had aimed at taking the military out of internal security work and focusing them solely on external defense.

Despite the setbacks and uncertainty (for example, the 1998 killing of Bishop Juan Gerardi), there can be little doubt that some minimal progress toward rule-consistent government and human rights behavior has been made in Guatemala. At this moment Guatemala seems poised between prescriptive status and rule-governed behavior. How the government, the international community, and domestic civil society responds to the challenges in the next few years will determine whether Guatemala stays stalled or moves ahead to genuine change. Particularly important will be the government's willingness and ability

---

[8] Interview with Helen Mack, Guatemala City, May 22, 1998.

to implement fully the various agreements under the Peace Accords, and to investigate and punish perpetrators of some of the most visible and symbolic human rights cases.

Conclusions

Other than the one proposed in this book, there are several other theoretical perspectives that might be used in an attempt to explain the course of human rights change in our two Latin American cases. The first proposition that we wish to examine is whether changes in Chilean and Guatemalan domestic policies and practices with regard to human rights from 1978 to 1998 might have been primarily the result of Great Power pressures. Perhaps ideas did matter, but only to the extent that they reflected the material power of large and regionally influential state actors.

Past United States policy bears responsibility for contributing to the emergence of authoritarian regimes in both Chile and Guatemala. US covert operations helped to overthrow the democratically elected government of Jacobo Arbenz in Guatemala in 1954, thus initiating the sequence of increasingly repressive regimes that culminated in the early 1980s. Likewise, Paul Sigmund characterizes the US role in Chile the 1970s as one that "includes an effort to prevent a freely elected president from taking office by fomenting a military coup; the assassination of a Chilean general, for which the United States was indirectly responsible; authorization, although not execution, of efforts to bribe the Chilean Congress; subsidization of a quasi-fascist extreme rightist group, and an improperly close relationship between the U.S. government and a major corporation" (Sigmund 1993: 48).

So when the US Congress introduced a new human rights policy in the mid-1970s, in part as a response to its distaste with past US policy towards Chile, it constituted a major shift in US policy towards the region. It was during the administration of President Jimmy Carter (1977–1980) that US human rights policy toward both Guatemala and Chile became most forceful. In Guatemala, however, Carter's human rights policy had no discernible immediate impact on victims of repression; to the contrary, human rights abuses actually escalated during the period 1978 to 1983, compared to the previous five years. In Chile, there was an improvement in human rights practices after Carter's election in 1976, but abuses continued throughout this period. Nevertheless, during the seventeen years of the Pinochet regime, the period during which there were fewest deaths and disappearances coincided with the four years (1977–1980) of the Carter administration (see table 6.2).

The Reagan administration was initially very explicit about its support for authoritarian allies such as Guatemala and Chile. The Assistant Secretary of State John Bushnell told Congress in 1981, "There is a major insurgency under way in Guatemala. I think given the extent of the insurgency and the strong Communist worldwide support for it, the administration is disposed to support Guatemala" (Brown 1985: 190). After meeting with President Efrain Rios Montt in 1982, President Reagan declared the Guatemalan government had received "a bum rap," on human rights and that military aid to Guatemala should be renewed (Brown 1985: 199).

It seems quite likely that this permissive position of the Reagan administration (in the context of a still relatively weak transnational network) provided a green light for increasing human rights violations in Guatemala. The most recent and careful research on human rights in Guatemala points to 1981 and 1982 (the first two years of the Reagan administration) as the years of greatest repression in Guatemala. The report *Guatemala: Nunca Más* shows that 80 percent of the 165 rural massacres they documented took place in the years 1981 and 1982 (Archbishopric of Guatemala Office of Human Rights 1998, volume II: 3). A detailed study by the Forensic Anthropology Team of Guatemala based on exhumation of graves of victims of massacres in the Rabinal region also showed that all the victims were killed in the period 1980 to 1983 (Forensic Anthropology Team of Guatemala 1995). It is probably not a coincidence that the upsurge of violence took place at the same time as the Reagan administration expressed support for the regime. Although the US Congress did not reinstate military assistance during this period, the Reagan administration sent numerous signals to the Guatemalan government of its support and validation. It was this unusual mix of lack of open military ties to the US combined with positive signals emanating from the Reagan administration that seems to have provided the Guatemalan government with a degree of "relative autonomy" from the United States that other governments in the region (such as that of El Salvador) did not have (Jonas 1991: 200).

In this sense, US policies appear significant in contributing to a worsening of the human rights situation in Guatemala in the early 1980s. But we would argue that changes in US policy cannot be seen as the most important factor leading to the improvement of human rights in these cases. Susan Burgerman reached a similar conclusion regarding US policy influence on human rights in Guatemala. Because of the relative independence of the Guatemalan armed forces after the military aid cut-offs in the late 1970s, she argues that US policy change was not a sufficient explanation but only an "enabling factor" to bringing about human rights change and the peace agreement (Burgerman 1997).

International factors played an important role in the Guatemalan case in particular, but these were not primarily the "big power pressures" that are most consistent with a realist explanation. Smaller regionally influential countries moved during the late 1980s to end Central America's bloody civil wars, first through the Contadora process and later through the signing of the Central American Peace Accords in 1987. The United States was initially marginal to the peace process in Central America, and this process was well under way before the United States became a major supporter. By the late 1980s, both the National Revolutionary Unity guerillas (URNG) and broad sectors of civilian society had reached the conclusion that Guatemala's civil war had reached a stalemate. As a consequence, a political space for dialogue and negotiation had opened by 1989. The new space was progressively occupied by diplomatic representatives of the Bush administration, the Guatemalan Roman Catholic Church, and in 1994 by the United Nations (Jonas, forthcoming).

The United Nations played an important role in promoting and enhancing the legitimacy of human rights norms at the state level, largely through its increasing participation in the peace process. First included in the peace negotiations as an observer during the presidency of Jorge Serrano (1991–1993), the UN moved to center stage as moderator in January 1994, following Serrano's self-inflicted coup. The United Nations' central role as moderator affected the Guatemalan human rights environment in many ways. It created new forums within which both transnational and state-level actors could articulate ideas and exchange information about existing conditions. It also helped expand the domestic "communicative arena" (i.e. space independent of more traditional and controlled channels of communication such as Congress) where domestic human rights groups could operate. Finally, and most importantly, UN involvement led directly to negotiation of a Comprehensive Agreement on Human Rights (March 1994) in which both sides in the civil war pledged to allow for UN verification of human rights compliance. Deployment of the

United Nations Verification Mission represented a critical step, both in the general peace process and with regard to human rights, because it was the UN's first "on-the-ground" operation in Guatemala. Historically, there had been only two institutions with a broad regional presence in the countryside – the Roman Catholic Church and the Guatemalan army. Now, there was a third (Jonas forthcoming).

Within this global context, the general proposition that Great Power influence alone can account for the improvement in human rights practices in either Guatemala or Chile seems highly problematical. While some amorphous great power pressure for change may have been a necessary condition for movement in the direction of democratization, it appears to have had an extremely tenuous connection to the subsequent human rights opening. Moreover, realism cannot explain why the United States and West European countries began to incorporate human rights concerns into their respective foreign policy agendas toward Latin America in the first place.

The second proposition we examined was whether the pressures which are generated by changes in Chilean and Guatemalan domestic material structures brought about human rights change in these two cases. More specifically, there is a long tradition of scholarship concerning Latin America that views economic modernization as a necessary (if not sufficient) condition for democratization and associated changes in domestic human rights regimes. A newly emerging socioeconomic stratum, often referred to as the "middle class," is viewed as having a more urban and educated view of human relationships. Thus, it is believed that the growth of this middle class will eventually lead to the emergence of policies at the state level emphasizing political liberalization and broader interpretations of human rights.

The Chilean case directly contradicts this linear modernization proposition. A long democratic tradition, relatively high levels of per capita income, adequate income distribution, and a strong and politically active middle class did not insulate Chile against authoritarian rule, and a large part of Chile's educated middle class was initially supportive of Pinochet's coup. Some of the most important theoretical accounts of coups in the Latin America in the 1960s and 1970s, found in the so-called bureaucratic–authoritarian regime literature, suggest that it was precisely the higher level of development and the corresponding growth of the middle classes in these countries that may account for the turn towards authoritarianism (O'Donnell 1973). Feeling threatened by mobilization from below by civilian populist politicians, they looked to the military for implementation of a specific type of exclusionary economic modernization model.

It is not easy to evaluate this modernization proposition as it might apply to Guatemala because it is much more difficult to obtain reliable data on wealth distribution than is the case in neighboring countries (Booth and Walker 1989: 87). The same domestic structures that long impeded progress with regard to human rights implementation make it difficult to evaluate whether socioeconomic changes took place that in turn led to class-based changes in human rights values. What we do know, however, is that the economic condition of all groups was seriously eroded during the 1980s by declining commodity prices, regional patterns of political unrest, and capital flight. While it is quite conceivable that these deteriorating economic conditions led the military government of Mejia Victores (1983–1986) to the conclusion that a civilian political opening was necessary, it seems unlikely that Guatemala's fragile middle classes, threatened as they were by ongoing guerrilla war, could have served as much of a base for democratization in the mid-1980s, much less for human rights change.

In contrast to studies of human rights change that are exclusively based on the theoretical perspectives of international realism and/or economic modernization, our study of these two Latin American cases concludes that international norms and associated networks played a significant role in transforming state-level perspectives on human rights and in moving Chilean and Guatemalan societies toward rule-consistent behavior. Our "spiral model," with its stress on phased socialization processes involving a wide variety of different modes, proved useful for understanding the process of human rights change in both countries, although there was some variation in terms of exact sequence and timing.

The Guatemalan case fits the model particularly well in terms of its specific phases (particularly the denial phase), though it is still not clear whether the country will experience true rule-consistent change in its human rights practices. Although Guatemala experienced a long and virulent denial phase, and a significant gap between the granting of full prescriptive status to human rights norms (1987) and any significant change with regard to rule-consistent behavior (1997), these are well within the average range of other cases in this volume (see the concluding chapter 8).

The impact of Guatemala's civil war, the longest-lasting such war in the world before it ended in 1996, created a siege mentality among civil-military elites and many middle-class Guatemalans that led them to deny with great conviction and endurance the charges emanating from human rights networks that the Guatemalan state was systematically violating human rights. Furthermore, the civil war created large pockets of resistance in a decentralized "reactionary despotic" society to the imposition of human rights values (prescriptive norms) by leaders of the state itself. Such societal resistance in a context of ongoing civil war largely accounts for the decade-long gap between achievement of prescriptive status and the onset of minimal rule-consistent behavior.

The presence of civil war appears in general to have such a blocking effect on human rights progress. Members of transnational networks have proven less effective in gaining domestic allies and in undermining the legitimacy of repressive regimes in these circumstances. This view is supported by the human rights progress that has been made elsewhere in Central America following the end of internal conflict (for example, El Salvador), as well as elsewhere in South America. Circumstantial evidence from Peru and Colombia, two countries that are experiencing ongoing situations of civil war, suggests that these wars have contributed substantially to the large gaps between prescriptive status and actual behavioral human rights change. These observations are also consistent with the findings of quantitative research to the effect that civil war is one of the main factors correlated with high levels of human rights violations globally (Poe and Tate 1994: 863–64).

The Chilean case differs from the model in some important ways. First, in Chile, the tactical concessions phase associated with deepening socialization processes was quite long. Second, even as it violated human rights during the 1970s and 1980s, the Chilean government didn't deny the legitimacy of human rights norms as forcefully as did Guatemala's military regimes. Finally, the move toward granting full prescriptive status to human rights norms and the achievement of rule-consistent behavior happened almost simultaneously in the early 1990s.

We note in this chapter that there are some good explanations why Chile does not exactly fit our "spiral model." Aside from South Africa and the East European countries, Chile provides one of the earliest cases of international socialization processes as applied to a norm-violating regime. Since a "complete" international human rights regime and network was not in place at the time, it should come as no surprise that the tactical concessions phase lasted for some time. Moreover, both the military regime's apparent "schizophrenia" concerning human rights norms and the simultaneous achievement of prescriptive status and rule-consistent behavior can be understood as related to redemocratization processes that were absent in most of the other cases examined in this volume.

Yet in spite of these points of divergence from our "spiral model," we are more impressed by its general fit. In both cases, the various modes of socialization that we identify played important roles at different points in time in transforming domestic structures. Also, we found significance in the fact that Chile and Guatemala completed the prescriptive status phase at roughly the same time. Given that these two Latin American countries have quite different domestic structures, regime types, and political histories, this suggests that powerful regional and global socialization processes may be transforming domestic human rights values and practices at a historically unprecedented rate.

7 The Helsinki Accords and Political Change in Eastern Europe

Daniel C. Thomas

Introduction

The overthrow of repressive Communist regimes across Eastern Europe in 1989 to 1990 represents one of the most significant advances for civil and political rights in the twentieth century. This chapter's interpretation of the demise of Communism focuses on the societal effects of the Helsinki Final Act of 1975, which established human rights as a norm binding on all the states of Europe, and as a legitimate issue in relations between them. The point is not to reduce the complex sources of "1989" to any single cause, but to trace the ways in which international human rights norms, and the transnational activist networks which emerged around them, contributed to this outcome. The Helsinki Final Act's transformation of the normative structure of East–West relations encouraged the mobilization of independent groups, justified transnational networks with sympathetic activists and sub-state actors in the West, and thereby enabled societal forces in the East to mount unprecedented challenges to regimes which had long monopolized social and political space. Though the depth and duration of this "Helsinki effect" was not equal in all countries of the region, it substantially re-shaped state–society relations throughout the Communist bloc and paved the way for the radical changes of the late 1980s. Beyond their historical significance, the Helsinki cases improve our general understanding of the processes by which the norms of international society transform the identity, interests, and behavior of states (Thomas forthcoming).

In particular, this chapter compares developments in state–society relations in Poland and Czechoslovakia from the mid-1970s through 1989 in terms of the theory that human rights norms socialize states by replacing repression with a "spiral" of social mobilization and transnational networking (phase 1), followed by regime denial of the applicability of international norms (phase 2), tactical concessions (phase 3), and expanded mobilization and transnational pressure, until the regime accepts the prescriptive validity of the norms, embedding them in its rhetoric and institutions (phase 4), and finally implements them through consistent practice (phase 5). The conclusion explores differences between the two countries, and evaluates the implications of the broader Helsinki case for the spiral model of human rights change.[1]

Opposition and repression before Helsinki

The significance of the Helsinki Final Act and the political changes which it set in motion can only be understood in comparison to domestic and international conditions in the region before 1975. As they had for decades, Communist party-states monopolized social and political space in Eastern Europe and the Soviet Union during the early 1970s. Living standards were slowly improving, but the legacy of Stalinist terror from the 1950s, Moscow's use of force in Hungary in 1956 and Czechoslovakia in 1968, and the Polish regime's bloody response to worker protests in 1970 had convinced nearly everybody in the region that political opposition was futile. And lest anybody hope that improved relations ("détente") with the West during this period would itself result in a lightening of repression, most governments in the region launched a renewed crackdown on independent social and political activity in 1972 to 1973. Those few individuals who dared challenge the status or practices of the Communist party state were quickly imprisoned or lost their jobs, while family members lost opportunities for higher education or travel. In Czechoslovakia, the post-1968 purges continued, with virtually every sector of society subjected to loyalty tests. Across the bloc, isolated dissident intellectuals despaired that they would ever find an alternative to violent revolution or party-generated reforms, which had failed, respectively, in 1956 and 1968 (Michnik 1985). Eastern Europe in the early 1970s thus clearly exhibits the political repression identified as a background condition for the spiral model.

---

[1] In contrast to most other contributions to this volume, which focus on the effects of norms against torture and disappearances, this chapter is concerned primarily with norms relating to the freedom of expression and assembly.

In fact, the broader international environment in the early 1970s was not conducive either to independent political activity or to reforms which would protect human rights in Eastern Europe. Most states had formally committed themselves to ensure a broad list of individual rights when they signed the Universal Declaration of Human Rights in 1948. However, the Universal Declaration made no provisions for monitoring or enforcement, and failed to link the human rights commitment to the practice of diplomacy, including the long-standing and fundamental norm of non-interference in domestic or internal affairs. As a result, governments East and West generally ignored the Universal Declaration in their diplomatic relations.

In fact, this practice achieved formal normative status with the UN General Assembly's 1970 Declaration on Principles of Friendly Relations Among States, and the superpowers' 1972 Agreement on Basic Principles of Relations Between the United States and the Soviet Union, both of which repeated the principle of non-interference in domestic affairs while making no mention of human rights. The Soviet Union and its allies were contented with this situation, while the United States and most of its allies were more committed to the strategic advantages of détente than to linking East–West relations to improved human rights conditions. In sum, whether one defines norms in terms of formal agreements or convergent expectations, it is clear that the protection of human rights was not a norm of East–West or European international relations through the early 1970s.

Rewriting European norms

The norms or standards of appropriate behavior for relations among European states were substantially revised through the deliberations of the 35-nation Conference on Security and Cooperation in Europe (CSCE) between 1972 and 1975. The Soviet Union and their East European allies had called throughout the 1960s for an all-European conference to legitimize the postwar territorial and political status quo and to expand economic contacts between East and West. The West delayed agreement for years, until the Soviet Union made a number of concessions: to normalize the status of Berlin to begin talks on reducing conventional arms, and to accept the United States and Canada as full participants in the proposed conference. When negotiations finally began in 1972, the European Community states placed an unprecedented issue on the agenda: human rights. The East Bloc states did all they could to block recognition of human rights as a legitimate issue in international and East–West relations, but the West Europeans refused to yield. Determined to realize their gains in other areas of the talks, the Soviet Union and its allies finally agreed to much of the West's proposed text on human rights. On August 1, 1975, thirty-five heads of state and government signed the Helsinki Final Act, including Principle 7, which established "respect for human rights and other fundamental freedoms, including freedom of thought, conscience, religion or belief" as one of ten Guiding Principles for Relations Among European States. The Final Act also linked this commitment to the "purposes and principles" of the UN Charter, the Universal Declaration of Human Rights and the two international covenants on human rights, and explicitly recognized the right of individuals to "think and act" in pursuit of these rights.

How then does the spiral model of human rights change relate to the East Bloc's position on European norms, particularly Principle 7 in the Helsinki Final Act? One possibility is to view the East's formal acceptance of the human rights principle as the opening of tactical concessions, or phase 3 of the spiral model. By this logic, phase 1 would begin with the emergence of social protest against human rights abuses in 1968, including the Prague Spring in Czechoslovakia, student demonstrations in Warsaw, and the birth of the Soviet human rights movement in Moscow; phase 2 would be then reflected in the Communist regimes' subsequent crackdown plus denial of the validity of international human rights norms, which they dismissed as "bourgeois" values through the early 1970s.

Though plausible, this interpretation has two significant drawbacks. Empirically, it forces us to condense too many distinct historical developments from the mid-1970s through the mid-late 1980s into the space between the regimes' initial tactical concessions (the beginning of phase 3) and their acceptance of the prescriptive validity of human rights norms (phase 4). More important, it defeats the purpose of the five-phase spiral model as a way of thinking about how international human rights norms socialize states through the transformation of domestic practices. If the five-phase spiral model is to be helpful, then the norms at least have to come at the beginning of the model!

It thus makes more sense to treat the inclusion of human rights in the Helsinki Final Act as a prior, inter-state bargain which the East Bloc leadership accepted in hopes of gaining economic resources and political legitimacy. Speaking to the Soviet Politburo, Foreign Minister Andrei Gromyko emphasized Principle 6 of the Helsinki Final Act, which gave equal priority to "non-intervention in internal affairs," and re-minded his colleagues that, regardless of what international pressures might be felt, "We are masters in our own house" (cited in Dobrynin 1995: 346). Likewise, Czechoslovak Premier Gustav Husak celebrated Helsinki's contribution to "the foundations of new international rela-tions based on the peaceful coexistence of states with different social systems" (Husak 1986). Even senior Western diplomats committed to human rights did not expect the Final Act to unleash significant politi-cal changes in the East.[2]

In fact, Communist authorities across Eastern Europe maintained tight control on domestic distribution of the actual text of the Final Act. For example, the Polish government published only 500 copies, along with Premier Edward Gierek's speech at the Helsinki summit, and then reserved them for regime elites or propaganda use abroad (Spasowski 1986: 548–9). In Czechoslovakia, thousands of copies of the Helsinki Final Act were published, but never distributed. These efforts notwith-standing, news of the Final Act did spread, setting in motion a domestic and transnational spiral of political change, beginning with social mo-bilization (phase 1) and regime denial of the validity (later only the applicability) of international norms (phase 2).

Initial responses: social mobilization and regime denial

Whether through word-of-mouth, samizdat publications, or Western radio broadcasts, Soviet and East European citizens gradually learned about the real content of the Helsinki agreement. Activists among them began to see the Final Act not as a ratification of the status quo, as the Communist regimes were portraying it, but as a promising and un-precedented opportunity to challenge the repressiveness of those re-gimes. Whatever the Communist authorities had intended by the signa-ture on the Final Act, these activists would invoke their official commitments to human rights as if they had been sincere.

As the CSCE negotiations were winding down in the late spring 1975, a Prague intellectual wrote to a friend in the West: "Everyone here has his own reaction to this: we, the people from the ghetto, feel a cautious hope; the secret police feel an increased nervousness" (Anonymous 1975). On June 17, democratic activists from Estonia and Latvia issued a

---

[2] Interview with Max van der Stoel (Netherlands Foreign Ministry), The Hague, March 18, 1994. (All affiliations cited for interviewees are for identification only.)

joint appeal to all governments scheduled to participate in the CSCE summit to publicize the fact that many rights guaranteed in the Universal Declaration of Human Rights were systematically violated by Soviet authorities in the Baltic republics (Krepp and Veem 1980: 25). Deeper within the Soviet Union, political prisoners in Perm Labor Camp 36 held a one-day hunger strike on July 31, the first day of the Helsinki summit, to call international attention to the violation of human rights in their country (Strokata 1986: 99). But this was just the beginning.

In Czechoslovakia, activists silenced by the policy of "normalization" which followed the Soviet invasion of 1968 interpreted the Final Act's principle of non-intervention as an open repudiation of the Soviet invasion, and the human rights components, particularly Principle 7, as the starting point for a campaign to reduce political repression (Hajek 1978). In an interview with Swedish television one month after the signing of the Helsinki Final Act, Jiri Hajek and Zdenek Mlynar explained,

> Helsinki represents a recognition of what is common to Europe... It is contrary to the script and spirit of the Helsinki conference if certain European nations and states keep alive practices conflicting with the European civilization and cultural background... We are not in favor of external meddling either, we only want the holders of power to abide by what they themselves have solemnly promised and signed.
>
> (Kusin 1979: 47, 49)

Hoping to tighten the international normative constraints on their government, Frantisek Kriegel, Gertruda Sekaninova-Carktova and Frantisek Vodslon (all former Communists) called publicly on the Czechoslovak Federal Assembly to ratify the two international human rights covenants of the United Nations, which Czechoslovakia had signed in 1968 (Kusin 1978: 295). This focus on the state's compliance with its own international normative commitments became the theme of East European opposition discourse over the following fourteen years.

European churches, including those in the East, were also quick to respond to the Helsinki Final Act. At a special meeting of the Conference of European Churches, held in East Berlin in October 1975 to discuss the implications of Helsinki, the opening sermon by Bishop Albrecht Schonherr of the Federation of Evangelical Churches in the GDR issued a clear, if implicit, criticism of the Communist authorities' tendency to emphasize status quo norms such as non-intervention: "Among the ten principles in the first part of the Final Act there are

three negations, four affirmations of the status quo and three obligations for a better future. It will depend on us, with others, to see that the
emphasis shifts more and more towards the better future" (Conference
of European Churches 1976). Meanwhile, media, religious, and human
rights groups in the West began to take notice of the grassroots focus on
Helsinki norms in the East, and to pressure the Communist authorities
to implement their Helsinki commitments.

Confronted with this unexpected domestic and transnational insistence on Helsinki compliance, the East Bloc gradually adopted a new
position on human rights norms, shifting from denying the validity of
international human rights oversight to denying the applicability of
human rights norms in particular contexts. On November 11, 1975, the
Czechoslovak Federal Assembly ratified the two international covenants, in full knowledge that this would provide the number of ratifica-
tions necessary for the International Covenant on Civil and Political
Rights to take effect. Ninety days later (as stipulated in the Covenant),
Czechoslovakia and the rest of the Communist bloc were legally bound
not only by the Helsinki Final Act, but by the Covenant as well. As these
governments would soon discover, this attempt to defend themselves
from unexpected political pressure in the aftermath of Helsinki only
entangled them more deeply in their own international normative
commitments, and thus rendered them more vulnerable to future
pressure from below and from abroad.

In Poland, opposition activists first viewed Helsinki as an opportunity to focus attention on the state's failure to implement the relatively
liberal provisions of the Polish Constitution (Lipski 1985: 24–25). In
early December, fifty-nine of Poland's most prominent intellectuals,
artists, writers, and scientists delivered an open letter to the government demanding that fundamental rights already contained in the
Constitution be implemented in practice. Their manifesto was filled
with references to human rights commitments undertaken at Helsinki.

When word spread the following month that the government intended instead to amend the Constitution to enshrine the country's
"unshakeable and fraternal bonds with the Soviet Union," leading
intellectuals and the Episcopate of the Roman Catholic Church responded with separate but parallel declarations that any constitutional
amendments must be consistent with Helsinki norms (Association of
Polish Students and Graduates in Exile 1979: 12–17; Raina 1978: 224–
228). This was just the start of a tacit but historically crucial alliance
between the Polish Church and opposition which was consolidated

under the human rights banner over the next couple of years.

The International Covenant on Civil and Political Rights came into effect worldwide on March 23, 1976, reinforcing the human rights norms around which East European activists were rapidly mobilizing. When the official media in Czechoslovakia publicized the Husak regime's special role in reaching the ratification threshold, fourteen prominent participants in the Prague Spring reforms responded with a joint letter to the parliament demanding that imprisoned supporters of Dubcek's reforms be released because their incarceration violated the principles laid down at the Helsinki conference.[3] Neither the Polish nor the Czechoslovak government was yet ready to respond positively to such petitions, but in contrast to recent years, the petitioners themselves seemed newly immune to repression. The tactical concessions of phase 3 were beginning to appear. Additional social mobilization, plus transnational networking to engage international pressure, were required, however, before phase 3 concessions would truly reshape state–society relations in the East Bloc.

Transnational networking and international pressure

As Czechoslovak and Polish (as well as Soviet) activists mobilized around Helsinki norms, governments and private groups in the West reevaluated their early skepticism about the Helsinki Final Act and began to apply diplomatic pressure on Prague, Warsaw, and Moscow to comply with their human rights commitments. Elite and grassroots voices in the West had initially condemned the Final Act as a concession to Soviet totalitarianism and regional hegemony. As President Ford prepared to go to Helsinki to sign the Final Act, the White House was inundated by angry letters, many of them from East European emigrants. A *Wall Street Journal* editorial headline screamed, "Jerry, Don't Go," while *The New York Times* declared, "nothing signed in Helsinki will in any way save courageous free thinkers in the Soviet empire from the prospect of incarceration in forced labor camps, or in insane asylums, or from being subjected to involuntary exile."[4] Similarly, the Christian Democratic Party in the West German Bundestag called on the government not to sign the Final Act.

---

[3] CNR/Reuters/AFP/RFE Special newswire item, Vienna, April 6, 1976.
[4] *Wall Street Journal*, July 23, 1975; *New York Times*, August 1, 1975.

Following the Helsinki summit, the US State Department continued with its implicit policy that the CSCE should be tolerated, but not emphasized in East–West relations. When a US diplomat returned to the State Department after the summit, and initiated measures to monitor compliance with the Helsinki Final Act, he was instructed by senior officials that the CSCE was over and no longer required attention.[5] Nor was there much reason to expect that the US Congress would take a substantially different position. Most members viewed the CSCE negotiations in Geneva, at best, as a necessary evil for the maintenance of détente, and at worst, as a concession to continued Soviet hegemony. Except for the politically powerful issue of emigration, which catalyzed the Jackson–Vanik amendment of 1973, the US Congress was not especially engaged with human rights issues in the East Bloc during the early to mid-1970s (Franck and Weisband 1979: 83–97).

Nonetheless, the first significant direct appeal for Western attention to the Helsinki process from within the East Bloc came only a few weeks after the Helsinki summit, during a US Congressional delegation's visit to Moscow. Working through a sympathetic American newspaper correspondent, several Moscow-based human rights activists approached Millicent Fenwick, a member of the delegation, and urged her to pressure the Congress for greater attention to the Helsinki process (Albright and Friendly 1986: 291). Representative Fenwick had no prior experience in foreign policy, and did not have many East Europeans in her district, but these encounters in Russia had a powerful effect on her. Before the delegation left Moscow, she pressed Leonid Brezhnev hard on several humanitarian cases – so hard that Brezhnev later described her as "obsessive" (Korey 1993: 23) More important, she returned to Washington committed to using the Helsinki Accords and American influence on behalf of those whom she had met.

On September 5, within days of her return, Fenwick introduced a bill proposing that the US Congress establish a Commission on Security and Cooperation in Europe, which would monitor compliance with the Helsinki Final Act, particularly in the human rights field. The White House and State Department resisted the initiative, but eventually bowed to lobbying pressure from human rights and ethnic groups whose own transnational contacts in the East had persuaded them of the value of the Helsinki process. In late May 1976, a week after news

---

[5] Anonymous interview (US State Department), Washington, DC, March 31, 1994.

reached Washington that Soviet dissidents had created a Helsinki Watch Group in Moscow, legislation to create the US Helsinki Commission passed both houses of Congress (Goldberg 1988). When the bill became law on June 3, the emerging transnational network of Helsinki activists in the East and West gained a bureaucratic ally within the US government. This accomplishment accelerated the reorientation of US policy begun in late 1975 in response to the unexpected grassroots mobilization within the East Bloc around Helsinki compliance. In the coming months, the issue of compliance with international human rights norms became more and more prominent in US policy toward the East. But diplomatic pressure from Western governments was not the only international force for Helsinki compliance.

Leaders of Communist parties in Western Europe saw that their political legitimacy was threatened by mounting reports of human rights violations and the repression of independent monitoring groups in the East. In order to maintain their democratic credibility, Communist parties in the West had to avoid appearing "soft" on human rights violations by socialist regimes. At a high-profile conference of twenty-nine Communist and Workers' parties held in East Berlin in June 1976, the Spanish and Italian Communist parties proposed a resolution praising the Helsinki process and explicitly committing all the parties to work for the implementation of the Final Act and the international human rights covenants. The Kremlin and its allies could have blocked the resolution, but were still under pressure to demonstrate their commitment to international human rights norms. As a result, the resolution was approved and included in the final declaration of the conference, which in turn was published in newspapers across the East Bloc.

Less than a year after the Helsinki Final Act, the combination of domestic mobilization and transnational networking had rendered the international normative environment inhospitable to the political status quo in Eastern Europe – precisely the opposite of what the Warsaw Pact elites intended when they called for a European security conference. The Soviet Union and its allies were thus caught between trying to create the impression of compliance with Helsinki norms and denying the legitimacy of Western pressure for human rights improvements. On February 24, 1976, Leonid Brezhnev's report to the 25th Congress of the CPSU acknowledged "certain difficulties in our relations with a number of capitalist European states" during the seven months since the signing of the Final Act. In response to the unexpected salience of

214

human rights, Brezhnev emphasized the principle of non-intervention in internal affairs, which had also been enshrined at Helsinki:

> Certain quarters are trying to emasculate and distort the very substance of the Final Act adopted in Helsinki, and to use this document as a screen for interfering in the internal affairs of the socialist countries, for anti-Communist and anti-Soviet demagogy in cold-war style.[6]   (Brezhnev 1979: 106)

Likewise, in September 1976, the Polish Ministry of Foreign Affairs' counselor Jerzy Nowak warned that "For the good of all-European cooperation the capitalist states should cease trying to force the socialist side to accept a different interpretation of some concepts" (Nowak 1976: 12).

Notwithstanding these frustrations, the states of the East Bloc continued to view the Helsinki process as essential to the political legitimacy and economic benefits they sought from the West. The Czechoslovak government was especially interested in gaining recognition as a normal European state, which they had been denied since the Soviet invasion of 1968. The Polish government hoped that improved relations with the West would bring access to the technology and credits which their failing economy so sorely needed. But as discussed above, the United States and other Western states were beginning to monitor the East's implementation of the Helsinki Final Act. For example, at the September 1976 meeting of the UN General Assembly in New York, West German Foreign Minister Hans Dietrich Genscher told his Soviet counterpart that promoting compliance with the Helsinki Final Act would be a major priority in Bonn's foreign policy (Genscher 1995: 329–330). Official monitoring of Helsinki implementation was particularly acute before and during the CSCE follow-on meetings (known as "review meetings" in the West), held in Belgrade in 1977–1978 and Madrid 1980–1983. This overall situation created strong incentives for the Communist regimes to adjust their rhetoric and behavior to suit Helsinki norms. The following sections compare the domestic effects of these political and normative pressures in Poland and Czechoslovakia.

[6] In the Russian text of the Final Act, principle 6 uses a Russian word generally translated into English as "non-interference." In the equally binding English text, though, principle 6 is titled "non-intervention in internal affairs," which the explanatory paragraphs interpret as a prohibition on tampering with all matters "falling within the domestic jurisdiction of another participating State." Western commentators argued strongly that since the UN Charter and international covenants, human rights practices are not protected by the shield of domestic jurisdiction. See Henkin 1977.

Poland: social mobilization, regime concessions, and reaction

As discussed above, Warsaw intellectuals and the Episcopate of the Roman Catholic Church introduced Helsinki norms into debates on reforming the Polish Constitution in late 1975. By the following spring, news of the Moscow Helsinki Group, the Berlin re-commitment to Helsinki norms and the US government's growing interest in Helsinki compliance had convinced disparate members of the Polish opposition that the time was right for a sustained and organized focus on human rights conditions in Poland. Several dozen intellectuals created the Workers' Defense Committee (KOR), an independent group to provide legal and material aid to workers imprisoned after the June 1976 strikes in Ursus and Radom. As one of its leading members recalls, the political identity and strategy of KOR was intimately tied to the international normative environment of the period:

> They issued a challenge to the Communist bureaucracy saying, "You signed the Helsinki Declaration on Human Rights, and we want to and will make practical use of your signature. Here it is: here is our Workers' Defense Committee." (Michnik 1990: 242)

The strategy appeared to work: KOR was not subjected to the usual crackdown against independent groups, and the workers were freed within a few months. The regime had clearly decided that in the post-Helsinki political environment, both domestically and transnationally, the best way to consolidate control was through significant tactical concessions (phase 3). Meanwhile, more and more Poles concluded that the Helsinki human rights frame could undermine the government's ability to discredit and then crush organized dissent, while serving the interests of both workers and intellectuals. "We managed to use the law to protect people," said one activist, remarking how unprecedented this was in a state generally not beholden to its own laws.[7]

In March 1977, seeking to exploit this same opportunity, a number of other dissidents created the Movement for the Defense of Human and Civil Rights (ROPCiO). Much of ROPCiO's energies were devoted to Helsinki monitoring functions, including public statements about rights violations and publication of an underground periodical on human rights and opposition issues. While ROPCiO's membership was

[7] Interview with Barbara Rozycka (KOR), Warsaw, June 24, 1991.

drawn largely from nationalist and center-right circles, and KOR's from leftist and social-democratic circles, both groups used the human rights banner to build alliances with workers in industrial and farming areas across Poland. Both also established underground newspapers – KOR's *Robotnik* ("The Worker") and ROPCiO's *Opinia* – which informed tens of thousands of working-class readers about political and economic developments and disseminated tactical advice for the expansion of independent groups.

The expansion of KOR and ROPCiO activity during the spring and summer of 1977, including their human rights monitoring functions, coincided with the Polish government's preparations for the CSCE meeting in Belgrade, which would review implementation of the Helsinki commitments and consider future measures. As the Belgrade preparatory talks opened in June, KOR issued a statement that the Helsinki Final Act's human rights norms were not being respected in Poland, and cited its own repression as an example (Lipski 1985: 166–167). Fearing more adverse publicity, the Polish authorities stopped the occasional arrests and beatings of opposition members which they had relied upon to deter any further expansion of independent activism (Amnesty International 1978a: 223–225).

Though 1978 and 1979, KOR and ROPCiO activists found that workers were greatly encouraged to learn that international pacts recognized and signed by the government actually guaranteed the right to free association and specifically to form independent trade unions.[8] Walesa himself remembers, "One of the central freedoms at stake was freedom of expression (a direct corollary of the Helsinki Agreement). Without this basic freedom, human life becomes meaningless; and once the truth of this hit me, it became part of my whole way of thinking." In fact, he says, it was these human rights groups who "gave rise to the idea of an independent trade union . . . to defend the rights of workers" (Walesa 1987: 97).

The first unofficial trade-union cell was established in Radom in November 1977 by a dismissed worker with ties to KOR. Five months later, Walesa and other KOR-affiliated workers from Gdansk formed the Committee for Free Trade Unions of the Baltic Seacoast. Before long, they launched their own edition of the KOR newspaper, Robotnik Wybrzeza ("The Coastal Worker"). Other independent industrial and farmers' organizations created the same year included the Katowice

---

[8] Interviews with Henryk and Luwika Wujec (KOR), Warsaw, June 17 and 18, 1991.

Committee for Free Trade Unions (February 1978); the Lublin Region Farmers' Self-Defense Committee (July 1978); the Grojec Region Farmers' Self-Defense Committee (September 1978); Pomorze Region Committee for Free Trade Unions (October 1978); and the Rzeszow Region Farmers' Self-Defense Committee (November 1978). The election of Cardinal Karol Wojtyla as Pope John Paul II in October 1978 and his repeated references to human rights during his visit to Poland early the following year accelerated the awakening of Polish society.

References to Helsinki and human rights remained central to opposition platforms across the ideological spectrum, while the taboo against linking human rights implementation to political change began to break down. In May 1979, the independent National Committee of Polish Socialists declared that the "most concrete and urgent task" in any campaign for political change in Poland was "the struggle to carry into effect the political and economic rights of the citizen, guaranteed by the Polish People's Republic, in the Final Act of the Helsinki Conference and the International Conventions on Human Rights."[9] Four months later, believing that Helsinki norms and the détente process had fundamentally constrained the authorities in Warsaw and Moscow, a number of radical nationalists abandoned the gradual, civil society strategy of KOR and ROPCiO and established the Confederation for an Independent Poland (KPN) to demand Soviet withdrawal and overthrow of the Polish United Workers' Party.[10]

Meanwhile, the Polish economy continued to deteriorate. The government had turned to the West in the early 1970s for investment and loans to reverse the technological obsolescence of Polish industry. However, the government's failure to simultaneously decentralize the economy deterred most foreign investors, while public pressure for improvements in the quality of life caused the government to divert most of its hard currency loans from capital improvements to present consumption. The result, not surprisingly, was a steady decline in industrial productivity and an increase in foreign debt through the late 1970s. The Polish government was thus trapped between an inefficient economy, an increasingly well-organized and demanding society, and growing pressure from the West for the protection of human rights.

In September 1979, Robotnik Wybrzeza published a Charter of

---

[9] *Labour Focus on Eastern Europe*, 3:5 (November 1979–January 1980), 9–11.
[10] KPN founder Leszek Moczulski discusses the Helsinki connection in Moczulski 1977, and in an interview with the author in Warsaw on June 24, 1991. See also Radio Free Europe/Radio Liberty, "Polish Situation Report," 20 (September 13, 1979): 1–4.

Workers' Rights, signed by sixty-five workers, technicians, engineers, and intellectuals from the KOR and ROPCiO-affiliated free trade-union cells, demanding better wages, shorter working hours, improved safety precautions, promotions by merit, abolition of special privileges, and above all, independent trade unions: "Only independent trades unions, which have the backing of the workers whom they represent, have a chance of challenging the authorities; only they can represent a power the authorities will have to take into account and with whom they will have to deal on equal terms" (Ash 1983: 24). The Charter buttressed these claims with relevant clauses from the International Labour Organization Convention and the International Covenant on Economic, Social, and Cultural Rights.

By late 1979, then, Polish society was far more assertive and the opposition far more organized than it had been only a few years earlier. By framing its challenge to the status quo in terms of internationally recognized human rights, the opposition had restrained the repressive capacities of the regime. Moreover, the workers' growing insistence on the creation of independent, self-governing unions represented a significant advance on their 1970 platforms, which in most cases had only demanded elections within the official trade unions. The regime's post-Helsinki strategy of consolidation-through-tactical-concessions (phase 3) had reached its limits, yet organized opposition continued to mount.

Workers and intellectuals from these same KOR and ROPCiO circles, free trade unions and self-defense committees were among the leaders of the strikes which erupted in Gdansk and Szczecin in August 1980 and quickly spread nationwide. Fearful of the costs of reversing their earlier concessions, both domestically and internationally, and hopeful that one more concession might restore order, the regime agreed to recognize the independent trade union Solidarity. Before long, 10 million industrial, agricultural, and professional workers (nearly a third of Poland's population) had joined Solidarity, the East Bloc's first significant mass organization outside the Communist party structure. In fact, Solidarity quickly assumed a leading role in Polish society, including dialogue with the regime on the country's economic and social problems. This was obviously more than a tactical concession by the regime: the unprecedented freedom of expression and independent social organization evident in Poland by late 1980 suggest that human rights norms were finally being incorporated into the institutions which actually determine relations between state and society. In terms of the spiral model, Poland was entering phase 4.

Looking back on this period, Lech Walesa concluded that the emergence of the human rights movement after Helsinki had been a "turning point on the road to Gdansk," the symbolic birthplace of Solidarity (Walesa 1987: 97). This is not to say that the Helsinki-focused human rights movement was alone responsible for the emergence of Solidarity. But the Helsinki process and the human rights activists who focused on it clearly contributed substantially to the creation and strategy of the national alliance of workers, intellectuals, and the church, which became Solidarity (Kubik 1994). As if to confirm this connection, one of the ten demands of the Szczecin strikers in August 1980 was that the government publish and distribute 50,000 copies of the international human rights covenants and the Helsinki Final Act (Mason 1985: 99).

Both ideologically and politically, the Polish government's decision to legalize Solidarity, and thus concede that it did not represent the interests of workers or the society as a whole, was a major defeat for Communist rule. In fact, it sent shock waves throughout the Communist bloc, delegitimizing the political monopoly of the Communist party, legitimizing independent grassroots initiatives, and causing many elites throughout Eastern Europe and the Soviet Union to question whether the political and economic status quo could be sustained. In the short term, though, conservative elites still had a firm grip on power, and international norms could not prevent them from taking whatever action they deemed necessary to maintain control.

As the Polish economy continued to deteriorate through 1981, Solidarity pressed the regime to institute fundamental economic reforms; meanwhile, Warsaw's Soviet and East European allies demanded that the union be eliminated. The first signs of a hardline response to these pressures came in October, when Minister of Defense General Wojciech Jaruzelski was appointed both prime minister and secretary general of the party. Finally, on December 12, 1981, Jaruzelski declared martial law, outlawed Solidarity, arrested most of its leaders and drove the rest underground. Yet while martial law remained in place until 1984, Jaruzelski recognized that the party was too weak to return to a pre-Solidarity era. After a five-month campaign of arrests and purges to destroy Solidarity as a viable opposition, Jaruzelski reinstituted a policy of tactical concessions, both real and symbolic, designed to maintain popular support. Despite martial law, the period in Poland from 1982 through 1987 is thus best characterized as a return to phase 3 of the spiral model.

In the context of this chapter, it bears noting that Helsinki norms remained on the agenda of independent activists throughout the martial-law period. In early 1982, underground activists announced the creation of a Polish Helsinki Committee to monitor human rights abuses during martial law. Once the regime lifted the initial crackdown, a renamed Helsinki Committee in Poland emerged publicly to investigate reports of human rights abuses and convey such information to international organizations, including the CSCE, the United Nations, and the International Labour Organization. In a preface to one of these reports, issued in 1983, Solidarity's underground Temporary Coordinating Committee declared. "We consider it our civic duty to monitor our country's compliance with the Helsinki agreements and international covenants on human rights" (Polish Helsinki Committee 1983: ix). Given Jaruzelski's desire to rebuild contacts with the West ruptured by martial law, one can only guess that such monitoring contributed in some measure to staying the hand of more reactionary elements within the regime.[11]

Czechoslovakia: normative pressure and selective repression

The Helsinki Final Act had a very significant impact in Czechoslovakia. Nonetheless, the differences between this and the Polish case shed light on the processes and conditions under which international human rights norms affect domestic change. To begin with, unlike Poland, Czechoslovakia did not have a history of organized opposition or grassroots resistance to Communism. Even the famous cultural and political awakening of 1968, known as the "Prague Spring," resulted not from opposition activity but from the Czechoslovak Communist Party's internally generated moves to liberalize the system. Moreover, the Czechoslovak people were effectively demobilized by the brutality of the Soviet invasion in August 1968, and the ensuing "normalization" policy, which purged all reform-minded people from government, industry, media, and educational institutions, denied educational opportunities to their children, and generally made life miserable for "non-conformists." Finally, but just as important, Czechoslovakia was

---

[11] The 1984 disappearance and murder of activist priest Father Jerzy Popieluszko, apparently by a rogue faction of the secret police, is notable politically both for its uniqueness and for the resulting trial and conviction of four police officers. See Stokes 1993: 112–115.

far less dependent than Poland on trade and credits from the West, and thus less restrained by diplomatic pressure from that direction. As a result, through the early to mid-1970s, few dared criticize the regime or organize any activity outside official channels.

On the other hand, Prague's responsibility to support the Soviet commitment to détente, and the Husak regime's own desire to end the international isolation imposed after the invasion of 1968, did make the government sensitive to charges of noncompliance with its Helsinki commitments. As a result, news of the Helsinki Final Act provoked an almost immediate reaction (phase 1 of the spiral model) among disaffected intellectuals and some former Communist officials in Czechoslovakia. Through late 1975 and early 1976 (as discussed earlier), these individuals issued a series of public appeals to the authorities to lift the repressive policy of "normalization" and reconsider the aborted Prague Spring reforms. These appeals failed to break through official denials of the applicability of international human rights norms, or even to engage the authorities in a dialogue with society. In this sense, the regime was secure in its "phase 2" strategy.

It was nonetheless notable that these appeals did not provoke additional repression. Given the total intolerance of public dissent in previous years, this minor opening was attributed by the new dissidents to the government's commitment to the Helsinki process and the West's growing interest in Helsinki compliance. By identifying their cause with the implementation of international human rights norms, dissidents in Czechoslovakia thus became the subject of international oversight, and thus gained some measure of protection from official repression. In this sense, state–society relations in Czechoslovakia were beginning to incorporate the denials of phase 2 and the limited tactical concessions of phase 3 – at least with regard to those regime critics publicly identified with international norms.

In the early autumn of 1976, an *ad hoc* alliance of theologians, artists, lawyers, and ex-Communists formed to protest the arrest of an underground rock band. None of these intellectuals was previously familiar with the band or its music, yet they all regarded the case as symbolic of broader violations of human rights in Czechoslovakia. As KOR had done two months earlier in Poland, a number of these activists attended and publicized the trial. Ten former lawyers also wrote an open letter labeling the trial "the latest in a series of administrative interventions limiting and invalidating civil rights and freedoms, especially freedom of artistic creation, scientific research, and freedom of expression"

(Skilling 1981: 13). But the situation in Czechoslovakia was different from Poland: the imprisonment of nonconformist musicians was far less likely to provoke widespread domestic opposition than the imprisonment of workers; the economy was healthier and the government in Prague less dependent on economic ties to the West. As a result, the protests failed to gain the release of the imprisoned musicians. Prague dissidents wondered whether disparate social forces could ever be transformed into a coherent and viable opposition movement.

At the same time, though, the new US Helsinki Commission was gradually raising the salience of human rights in East–West relations. Bit by bit, evidence accumulated within Czechoslovakia that the Husak regime was indeed sensitive to foreign criticism of its record on compliance with Helsinki norms. The international human rights covenants which Czechoslovakia had ratified almost a year earlier were released to bookstores in early November (Prečan 1983: 58). Several weeks later, four political prisoners who had been the subject of earlier Helsinki-based appeals were released before their prison terms had expired, confirming the activists' growing sense that public appeals for the Czechoslovak government to honor its Helsinki commitments could be effective.[12] The tactical concessions of phase 3 were beginning to accumulate. If random appeals and publicity could bring minor concessions, the activists reasoned, then an organized independent mechanism to monitor Czechoslovakia's compliance with its human rights obligations might cause the government to substantially improve its behavior. Reflecting on the text of the international covenants (few copies of which were actually made available to the public), the Prague dissidents concluded, "we must do something with this" ("Un chartiste" 1977). In short, escalating social mobilization and transnational networking might provoke serious dialogue and ever more fundamental concessions by the regime.

The Charter 77 movement was born on January 1, 1977, with the appearance of 242 signatures on a four-page document chronicling the denial of human rights in Czechoslovakia and appealing for dialogue with state authorities on how those rights could be protected. The Charter declared itself to be a "free informal, open community of people of different convictions, different faiths and different professions" devoted to protecting fundamental human rights – "rights accorded to all men by the two mentioned international covenants, by

---

[12] RFE Research, Czechoslovak Situation Report/2, January 19, 1977.

the Final Act of the Helsinki conference and by numerous other international documents opposing war, violence and social or spiritual oppression, and which are comprehensively laid down in the United Nations Universal Declaration of Human Rights." But this was not merely a matter of principle: as noted in the concluding paragraph of the Charter, "it has come into being at the start of a year proclaimed as the Year of Political Prisoners – a year in which a conference in Belgrade is due to review the implementation of the obligations assumed at Helsinki." As such, Charter 77 posed a serious challenge to the regime's preferred "phase 2" strategy of responding to domestic and foreign critics by denying the applicability of human rights norms.

In fact, Charter 77's intention to monitor human rights conditions threatened not only the regime's ability to hide the abuses committed under the guise of "normalization," but also its effort to pacify Czechoslovak society by eliminating all means of self-organization. Like its Polish counterparts, the Charter trapped the regime between its domestic illegitimacy and its international commitments. The Communist authorities were under no illusions about their popularity: Minister of the Interior Jaromir Obzina estimated that 90 percent of the public would sympathize with the Charter if it were published openly (Kusin 1979: 52). Nonetheless, an exiled activist observed,

> [O]ne should not be under any illusion that the government can actually grant these rights. If the government were to implement that law, it would really be its own swansong... The present structure of government would be unable to defend itself against open discontent and criticism.[13]

As a result, the regime set out to eliminate the Charter movement before it could spread domestically or gain international support.

The regime's first campaign to eliminate the Charter combined mild repression and a massive propaganda campaign, labeling Charter signatories as tools of Western imperialism, bourgeois reactionaries, and moral degenerates. Leading signatories were interrogated by the police and several were arrested; dozens of signatories were fired from their jobs, including many whose professional careers had already been aborted by the purges of the early 1970s. Eventually, almost all signatories were denied employment except as window-washers, furnace-stokers, and in other low-status positions. Still more citizens were fired

---

[13] "Czechoslovakia in the Wake of Charter 77," *Labour Focus on Eastern Europe* 1:1 (March–April 1977), 5–6.

from their jobs merely for refusing to participate in public condemnations of the Charter. Up to this point, state–society relations in Czechoslovakia combined phase 2 of the spiral model – social protests against human rights abuses, regime denial, and continued repression – with very limited "phase 3" concessions.

But given the Charter's explicit connection to Helsinki, this policy provoked a loud outcry from abroad. On January 26, the US State Department criticized the Czechoslovak government's response to Charter 77 as a violation of its Helsinki commitments. Similar criticisms were voiced in following weeks by the Austrian, British, and Swedish Foreign Ministers, the British Labour Party, and the Italian Socialist and Communist parties, among others.[14] The Czechoslovak Foreign Ministry understood what had provoked such international criticism, and reported frequently to the Central Committee about the negative impact of domestic repression on relations with the West.[15] Yet regardless of this international pressure, the regime was concerned primarily by the internal political challenge posed by Charter 77. As the number of Charter signatories approached 1,000, the Interior Ministry estimated that 2 million people would sign if given a free choice (Kusin 1979: 52). With KOR and ROPCiO mobilizing across the border in Poland, the Czechoslovak government resolved to contain Charter 77.

The result of these pressures was a new, three-part policy: a propaganda campaign to discredit the Charter by rebutting its claims; isolation and harassment of well-known dissidents; and harsher repression against lesser-known individuals who dared to sign the Charter or participate in any such "anti-social" activities. On April 5, following a debate within the Federal Assembly on "socialist legality" and a special report by the Procurator General on the functioning of the court system, the government asserted that human rights were duly protected in Czechoslovakia:

> [T]he social achievements of the Czechoslovak people were in fact their rights and freedoms. Everyone had the right to work, to receive a decent wage, to have paid holidays, to enjoy free medicine and to draw a pension. Through the good offices of social and political organisations of the National Front, the citizens could also put to use freedom of speech and assembly.　　　　(Kusin 1978: 313–314)

---

[14] *New York Times*, January 27, 1977; Special/McGill newswire item, London, January 28, 1977; Reuter newswire item, Vienna, January 29, 1977; UPI newswire item, Stockholm, February 15, 1977.

[15] Interviews with Ivan Busniak and Zdenek Matejka (Czechoslovak Foreign Ministry), Prague, July 27, 1992.

Apart from the four signatories arrested in the initial crackdown, well-known members of Charter 77 were generally free from repression except for routine harassment. One Chartist was actually told by his Secret Police "tail" that the Interior Ministry was prepared to arrest the entire Charter 77 leadership, but was being restrained by the Foreign Ministry.[16]

The limitations of these tactical concessions were evident in the fact that lesser-known individuals who signed or contacted Charter 77 were still subjected to intimidation, beatings, and arrests, often on false charges. The message was clear: the partial protection afforded by Charter 77's identification with international norms would not extend to individuals unknown in the West. Diplomatic preparations for the Belgrade CSCE review conference through the late spring and summer of 1977 created some political space for dissent, but when the conference became deadlocked in late autumn, the crackdown was reapplied, but even more harshly than before. In the process, the regime made clear that it would not respond to continued societal pressure with ever-expanding concessions. Not even the informal pluralism beginning to take hold in Poland would be permitted. In short, phase 3 would go no further than minor protections for those members of Charter 77 best known abroad.

The following April, frustrated with Charter 77's informal structure and commitment to dialogue with the regime, a number of Chartists created a parallel organization which could more directly challenge the status quo: the Committee for the Defense of the Unjustly Prosecuted (VONS). The new organization was dedicated to monitoring arrests and imprisonments which violated the Czechoslovak legal code, the Constitution, and the International Covenant on Civil and Political Rights, which had been legally binding since March 1976. In particular, it would seek to check the arbitrary exercise of state power which left all citizens vulnerable (Havel 1991: 109–116). As a direct challenge to the justice of the Czechoslovak legal and political system, VONS was the most significant (and risky) societal development since the creation of Charter 77.

Though VONS generally referred only to legally binding commitments (rather than the non-binding Helsinki Accords) in its communiqués, its members remained hopeful that Charter 77's attention to the Helsinki process would offer them some protection from

---

[16] Interview with Martin Palous (Charter 77), Prague, July 31, 1992.

reprisal.[17] This strategy seemed to work for a year, until the regime (and perhaps its allies in the Kremlin) concluded that more drastic action was necessary to combat the still-growing opposition. Ironically, VONS offered a convenient target to the regime: unlike Charter 77, which remained within the law, VONS was an unregistered formal organiz-ation, and thus a clear violation of the law. In May 1979, the authorities arrested five leading members of VONS, who were also leading Chart-ists. Four months later, all five were tried and sentenced to prison (Skilling 1981: 145–149, 321). The Czechoslovak regime's tentative ex-periment with tactical concessions to domestic and foreign critics (phase 3) was essentially over. Henceforth, the regime would seek to consolidate its power only through continued repression.

Charter 77 and VONS never became or aspired to be a broad grass-roots movement, but they did survive through the 1980s as moral and legal critics of the regime, both at home and abroad. Whenever a spokesperson was jailed, new signatories took their place. Their com-muniqués were distributed clandestinely among those willing to risk being caught with dissident materials, and were regularly broadcast back into Czechoslovakia by Radio Free Europe, giving millions access to frank criticisms of their government. Few dared act on this informa-tion, but given the state's total monopoly of other media, it did provide people with some critical perspective on the status quo. The two groups also provided regular documentation of human rights violations in Czechoslovakia to interested parties in the West, including private Helsinki watch groups, the US Helsinki Commission and the second major CSCE review conference, held in Madrid from 1980 to 1983.

The relationship between state and opposition in Czechoslovakia was thus fairly stable through most of the 1980s. Knowing that it lacked popular legitimacy, the regime relied on repression to maintain its monopoly of political space, and thus defend the status quo. Where possible, this repression was applied selectively, granting somewhat greater leniency to activists known in the West while targeting lesser-known individuals in order to intimidate the broader society. Mean-while, knowing that it lacked the broad social network which Polish human rights groups were able to create, Charter 77 continued to rely on international normative pressure in its campaign to highlight and criticize human rights violations by the regime. This identification with international norms was sufficiently powerful to shield Charter 77 from

---

[17] Interviews with Jiri Dienstbier (Charter 77), New Haven, CT, April 14, 1991 and Vaclav Maly (Charter 77), Prague, August 5, 1992.

being completely eliminated, but not powerful enough to seriously challenge the regime, as long as the economy remained reasonably productive and Moscow supported the status quo.

Constructing rights-protective states in Eastern Europe

As seen above, the human rights norms of the Helsinki Final Act catalyzed significant changes in state–society relations in Eastern Europe. Yet by the early 1980s, the human rights and opposition movements which emerged in Poland and Czechoslovakia after Helsinki had failed to overthrow the political hegemony of the Communist party-state or to bring about real compliance with the Final Act. There are a number of reasons why, but most are related to the on-going political and military hegemony of the Soviet Union: as long as a conservative Communist regime held sway in Moscow, and believed that maintaining allied regimes in Eastern Europe was necessary for its security, no substantial change would be permitted. The Soviet use of force to defend Communist rule in Hungary in 1956 and Czechoslovakia in 1968 had made the limitations on political change clear to elites and non-elites alike. Soviet pressure on Warsaw to destroy Solidarity in 1980 to 1981, including threats of invasion, confirmed that this limitation had not been eliminated by the Helsinki Final Act's commitment to human rights and national self-determination.

Recognition of Soviet hegemony does not mean, however, that the post-Helsinki movements had no long-term effects on the viability of Communist rule. In the short term, for largely internal reasons, Solidarity and Charter 77 had pushed their respective regimes in opposite directions: once the initial crackdown of martial law was complete, Jaruzelski sought to consolidate Communist rule in Poland through "permissible pluralism"; in contrast, Husak retreated to a rigid policy of repression and confrontation with Czechoslovak society (Stokes 1993). Nonetheless, the existence of Solidarity followed by martial law had fundamentally delegitimated Communist rule in Poland and throughout the bloc, while the harsh repression in Czechoslovakia only aggravated that country's social and economic sclerosis.

The ultimate linchpin of real political change in Eastern Europe, including substantial improvements in human rights conditions, was the accession of a reform-minded leadership in Moscow. Mikhail Gorbachev's rise to power in February 1985 was thus the beginning of

Communism's end-game in Eastern Europe. His government's initiatives for political and economic reform within the Soviet Union beginning in 1986, and simultaneous rethinking of the international requirements for Soviet security, signaled to East European opposition activists and regime elites alike that familiar limitations on political discourse and change were gradually breaking down. At this point, the opposition and human rights movements of the 1975 to 1981 period re-emerged and led the final assault on Communist rule.

Yet notwithstanding the importance of leadership, Helsinki norms did contribute substantially to political developments in the Gorbachev era. First of all, the emergence and persistence of human rights movements across the Soviet Union and Eastern Europe after Helsinki, culminating in the spectacular rise of Solidarity, had already delegitimated Communist rule in popular eyes, and forced elites across the bloc to question how long the status quo could be maintained. In fact, many within the party leadership in the Soviet Union and Eastern Europe had "quietly digested a lot of dissident thinking during the Brezhnev years," and their commitment to greater openness reflected this exposure (Crouch 1989:101). This is especially true of the generation of Soviet party intellectuals who supported Gorbachev's reforms (Cohen and Heuvel 1989; Herman 1994).

Second, the expanded salience of human rights in East–West relations – which resulted directly from transnational networking between Charter 77, KOR, and other private "Helsinki watch" groups and governmental agencies in the West, especially the US Helsinki Commission – had created an environment in which the international contacts necessary for economic reform in the East bloc could not be achieved without improvements in human rights. In fact, Gorbachev and his advisors understood that normalizing relations with the West would require an improved human rights situation in the East. As Georgi Arbatov, director of the official Institute for the Study of the United States and Canada and later a close advisor to Mikhail Gorbachev, remarked in 1983, "How can one be against human rights nowadays? It's the same as to be against motherhood" (Arbatov and Oltmans 1983:144). In April 1985, just two months after taking power, Gorbachev specifically told the Central Committee that improved economic relations with the West would depend upon progress in the Helsinki process (Gorbachev 1986: 35–44). Ten years after the Final Act, even the most conservative Communist elites understood that progress in the Helsinki process meant loosening up on domestic opposition across the bloc.

Politically and socially, the Poland of the mid to late 1980s was very different from a decade earlier: "[c]onstant pressure applied by the opposition since the days of KOR, coupled with Jaruzelski's willingness to respond to that pressure, had produced a real opening of the public space" (Stokes 1993: 121). Meanwhile, winds of reform blowing from Moscow coincided with increasing evidence of economic crisis. Renewed strikes forced the government to reopen talks with Solidarity in late 1988. With the union insisting that the country's crisis could not be resolved without some power-sharing arrangement, formal roundtable negotiations between the government, the ruling party and its allies, Solidarity, and the church opened in February 1989. Agreement was announced nine weeks later: Solidarity would be re-legalized and permitted to field candidates in partly free parliamentary elections; economic reforms would be implemented and civil liberties would be expanded. Once again, Poland was entering phase 4, with fundamental principles of human rights accepted as the basis for political and social reconstruction. Only this time, with the threat of Soviet invasion removed, the slope toward real change was far more slippery.

When the elections were held in June, Solidarity candidates won every freely contested seat. Thirty-three of the thirty-five leading ruling-party candidates actually failed to secure the required majority for seats which had been shielded from real competition. The installation in late August of a Solidarity-dominated government headed by Tadeusz Mazowiecki, Eastern Europe's first non-Communist prime minister in almost forty years, was the first step toward a new political system (phase 5) constitutionally and ideologically committed to the protection of human rights in Poland.

The collapse of the Czechoslovak Communist Party also began in 1988, during Mikhail Gorbachev's visit to Prague, when his spokesman publicly acknowledged that the only difference between the Prague Spring and contemporary Soviet reforms was "twenty years." With Charter 77 shielding them from a still-hardline regime, young people in Prague formed new independent associations dedicated to peace, the environment, music, and other issues. Charter 77 also organized a series of public demonstrations to protest the continued repressiveness of the regime and to accustom the wider population to asserting its rights. Each demonstration attracted a larger crowd, while the authorities' heavy-handed responses further alienated the population. In the summer of 1989, tens of thousands of citizens signed "A Few Sentences," an unprecedented petition for political liberalization and dialogue drafted by Charter 77 veterans (US Helsinki Watch Committee, 1989). By this point, though, developments in Czechoslovakia were increasingly swept along by events elsewhere in the bloc.

Just as its emergence had in August 1980, Solidarity's political success in June 1989 sent shock waves across Eastern Europe. In Hungary, summer-long roundtable talks between the ruling party and opposition groups resulted in an agreement to hold free and direct presidential elections in late November, and parliamentary elections ninety days later. Beginning in September, thousands of demonstrators gathered regularly in Leipzig, East Berlin, and provincial cities to demand political change in East Germany. With tens of thousands of refugees crossing from East Germany into Hungary, the Hungarian leadership's September 11 decision to open the border to Austria deepened the regional crisis. Erich Honecker stepped down as East German party leader in mid-October. Hoping to stem the tide of unrest, his replacement announced on November 9 that East Germans would be allowed to travel freely to the West.

The collapse of the Berlin Wall terrified the government in Czechoslovakia, increasingly besieged by demonstrators yet unwilling to entertain proposals for reform. The end-game of Czechoslovakia's "velvet revolution" began one week later, on November 17, when a student demonstration in Prague was attacked by the police. As student leaders fanned out to organize a public strike, opposition veterans of the Charter 77 generation formed Civic Forum to coordinate protest activities and negotiate with the regime. Demonstrators now numbering in the hundreds of thousands cheered the appearance of Vaclav Havel, Vaclav Maly, and other Charter 77 leaders known previously only by name. Four days later, Havel stood on a balcony overlooking Prague's Wenceslas Square, and announced to the crowds assembled below that the Communist authorities had begun negotiations with the opposition (see Ash 1990).

On December 10, following the opposition's assurances that peaceful abdication would not be followed by criminal prosecution or vendettas, the Communist government handed power to a coalition dominated by Civic Forum. Vaclav Havel was immediately elected president. The ranks of the new government, diplomatic service, educational, cultural, and media institutions were filled with Charter 77 veterans, and the transition to a rights-protective regime in Czechoslovakia was underway. State–society relations in Czechoslovakia were thus catapulted in a matter of days from the denials and repression of phase 2 to the institutionalization of human rights principles of phases 4–5.

Conclusions

The impact of the 1975 Helsinki Final Act on Eastern European politics is perhaps the paradigmatic case of international human rights norms contributing to the transformation of domestic practice and regime type – not because Helsinki norms alone caused the demise of Communism, but because of how much they contributed to that end despite the coercive power and relative international isolation of the regimes in question. As seen in both the Polish and Czechoslovak cases, dissident forces responded to the inclusion of human rights norms within the Helsinki Final Act by creating social movement organizations which could use the norms to challenge repressive state practices. These movements also used the international legitimacy of the norms to build networks or alliances with sympathetic forces in the West, both state and non-state, whose oversight and pressure would further expand the political space available at home. Both the Polish and Czechoslovak states responded to this unprecedented domestic and international challenge by denying the claim that they were violating human rights, yet by tacitly granting greater political space to those groups clearly identified with Helsinki norms. At this point, though, developments in the two cases diverged.

Despite its initial, limited concessions, the Czechoslovak party-state proved unwilling to tolerate any significant challenge to its monopoly on politics and public discourse: as soon as the CSCE review conference in Belgrade was over, the Czech authorities cracked down on Charter 77, especially on those members not well known in the West. In contrast, the Polish party-state granted far greater space to KOR and ROPCiO, allowing them to play a major role in the creation of a nationwide, independent trade union, Solidarity. In this case, the crackdown did not come until Solidarity had gained legal recognition, asserted itself in Polish life, and thereby called the entire Communist system into question. Just as the first half-decade after Helsinki had demonstrated the unforeseen power of international norms, the declaration of martial law in Poland in December 1981 demonstrated their limitations as a catalyst for domestic change. This "reversal" of the spiral model reminds us that while norms can transform geopolitics, especially in the long term, they can also be trumped by geopolitics (in this case the political, ideological, economic, and military hegemony of the Soviet Union) in the short term.

Attention to regime vulnerability and opposition strategy help us to understand the differences and similarities in the impact of Helsinki norms on state–society relations evident in these two cases. First, the Czechoslovak economy was far more productive and less dependent than its Polish counterpart on Western economic assistance, so the regime in Prague was less constrained by the threat of Western sanctions in response to a domestic crackdown. Related but not reducible to this fact, the members of Charter 77 attempted to use international human rights norms to engage the regime in a discussion of political reform, while the Polish activists used the same norms to strengthen civil society by bringing together religious and secular, socialist and nationalist, intellectual and worker constituencies. This comparison demonstrates that the strategies and tactics chosen by non-state actors do matter politically, while also reminding us that such choices are not made in a vacuum. The strategic choices made by non-state actors in response to changes in international norms depend in large part on the opportunities provided by the domestic structures and vulnerabilities of the states they face.

On the other hand, none of the states of Eastern Europe before 1989 was a "normal" member of international society – not even in the sense of a "normal" repressive state. Though legally sovereign, they were inextricably part of an ideological, political, economic, and military bloc, dominated by a neighboring superpower, which controlled their internal structure and terms of political discourse, as well as their external relations. Whatever the preferences of the individual East European regimes, the overwhelming presence of this hegemonic bloc severely constrained their freedom to make concessions to societal challengers. It is thus not surprising that the potential impact of Helsinki norms was interrupted (albeit temporarily) by renewed repression in both Czechoslovakia and Poland. In fact, given this strategic context, it is remarkable both how much influence Helsinki norms exerted on state–society relations and diplomatic practice, and that this legacy contributed in so many ways to the demise of Communist rule in Eastern Europe. Contrary to the claims of skeptics, international human rights norms are clearly worth far more than the paper on which they are printed.

8   International human rights norms and domestic change: conclusions

Thomas Risse and Stephen C. Ropp

Introduction

In adopting the Universal Declaration of Human Rights on December 10, 1948, the delegates to the United Nations General Assembly established a common set of principles against which the human rights practices of individual member states could be measured. Although these principles were not initially binding on UN member states, they included the seeds of an international legal system in the realm of human rights. In the meantime and following the Universal Declaration, a global human rights regime has emerged consisting of numerous international conventions, specific international organizations to monitor compliance, and regional human rights arrangements (see Alston 1992; Donnelly 1986; Forsythe 1991). Moreover, the global human rights regime has led to the emergence of a huge network of transnationally operating advocacy coalitions and international non-governmental organizations (INGOs; see Brysk forthcoming; Keck and Sikkink 1998; Smith, Chatfield, and Pagnucco 1997; Smith, Pagnucco, and Lopez 1998). As a result, some have argued that human rights have increasingly become part of the shared knowledge and collective understandings informing a "world polity" (Boli and Thomas 1997, 1998). International human rights, thus, have become constitutive elements of modern and "civilized" statehood.

But it is one thing to argue that there is a global human rights polity composed of international regimes, organizations, and supportive

We thank Sieglinde Gränzer, Anja Jetschke, Hans-Peter Schmitz, and Kathryn Sikkink for critical suggestions and comments.

advocacy coalitions. It is quite another to claim that these global norms have made a real difference in the daily practices of national governments toward their citizens. On the fiftieth anniversary of the Universal Declaration, we thought it appropriate to evaluate the processes by which human rights principles and norms found their way from the international into the domestic political arena. To what extent had these principles and norms brought about changes in the behavior of states toward their citizens? And if they had brought about such changes, what kind of models for the transfer of ideas and domestic socialization processes made sense? Finally, to the extent that international human rights principles and norms appeared to be having minimal impact on certain states, why was this the case?

In this book, we have not attempted to provide a comprehensive evaluation of the effectiveness of all existing international human rights norms. Rather, we concentrated on an important subset of such norms which are enshrined in the International Covenant on Political and Civil Rights, the International Convention Against Torture and Other Cruel, Inhuman or Degrading Treatment, and in particular the so-called "freedom from" rights (freedom from torture, from detention without trial, from disappearance, etc.). We chose to focus on this central core of rights for mostly practical and measurability reasons, not because we consider other human rights less important.

In this final chapter, we begin by briefly summarizing our theoretical framework as presented in the introductory chapter. Second, we evaluate the findings of the empirical case studies in light of the theoretical propositions, and offer some preliminary observations concerning factors that may explain variation among our cases. Third, we consider potential alternative explanations. We then proceed to show how our findings contribute to larger academic debates about the impact of norms as a general phenomenon of theoretical interest, as well as to more specific academic debates among comparativists concerning various kinds of domestic socio-political change. Finally, we conclude with some observations regarding how transnational human rights networks can be most effective and what Western governments can do to best promote human rights.

What we sought to learn about the socialization of human rights norms into domestic practices: theoretical departures

As elaborated throughout this book, our basic argument has been that international norms, defined as "collective expectations about proper behavior for a given identity" (Jepperson, Wendt, and Katzenstein 1996, 54), matter. But in light of the recent ideational turn in comparative politics and international relations (for reviews see Jacobson 1995; Laffey and Weldes 1997; Yee 1996), the simple finding that ideas matter no longer lies on the cutting edge of theory or empirical research. Research on the effects of ideas including norms needs to show *which* ideas matter, *why*, and *how*. We need to specify the causal mechanisms through which ideas affect actors' identities, interests, and behavior. We also need to account for the *variation* in the impact of principled ideas and norms on domestic actors.

In this study of human rights, we adopted a view of the relationship between ideas and social processes that draws on the work of social constructivists (Adler 1997; Checkel 1998; Katzenstein 1996a, b; Kratochwil 1989; Wendt 1992, forthcoming). The interests and preferences of actors involved in protecting or violating human rights cannot simply be treated as externally given by objectified material or instrumental power interests. Rather, we argue that conflicts over human rights almost always involve the social identities of actors. International human rights norms have become constitutive for modern statehood; they increasingly define what it means to be a "state" thereby placing growing limits on another constitutive element of modern statehood, "national sovereignty" (see Biersteker and Weber 1996). As a result, the struggles and contestations reported in this book concern almost by definition the identities of actors.

Our reliance on the insights of social constructivism as a point of theoretical departure means that our model of human rights change differs considerably from that used by rational choice theorists. We argue that bargaining on the basis of given preferences and instrumental adaptation to external pressures only constitute one mode of social interaction observable in the human rights area (see introductory chapter by Thomas Risse and Kathryn Sikkink). Actors' identities may also be reshaped through discursive processes of argumentation and persuasion. Transnational advocacy coalitions frequently engage norm-violating governments in an argumentative process whereby truth

236

claims have to be justified and moral convictions are challenged. Finally, we claim that the sustained improvement of domestic human rights conditions requires the domestic institutionalization of international norms so that norm compliance becomes a habitualized practice. In sum, this book tried to investigate the mix of the three processes of bargaining and adaptation, of arguing and moral consciousness-raising, and of institutionalization and habitualization thought necessary for the enduring domestic implementation of human rights norms.

We conceived of these three modes of social interaction as components of an overall *socialization process* by which domestic actors increasingly internalize international human rights norms. We investigated socialization processes by looking at the interactions among actors on four levels:

- interactions between norm-violating governments and their domestic society including the opposition;
- interactions between the norm-violating state's domestic opposition and the transnationally operating human rights networks;
- interactions between transnational advocacy networks and international organizations as well as Western powers;
- interactions between the transnational advocacy networks, international organizations as well as Western powers, on the one hand, and the norm-violating governments, on the other.

To capture the dynamics of the socialization processes and to identify the causal mechanisms by which international human rights become embedded in domestic practices, we developed a "spiral model" of human rights change which builds upon earlier concepts known as the "boomerang effect" (see introductory chapter by Thomas Risse and Kathryn Sikkink; see also Keck and Sikkink 1998). The initial phase in our "spiral model" is one of state *repression*, repression that is severe enough to disallow any serious opposition challenge to the state's violation of international human rights norms. If the transnational human rights networks succeed in gathering sufficient information on the norm-violating state, it can put it on the international agenda which marks the transition to the second phase of the model. The norm-violating government almost always reacts by *denying* not just the charges, but the validity of the international human rights norms themselves and by claiming the principle of non-interference in domestic affairs. The "denial stage" might be quite long in duration.

If the transnational advocacy network is sufficiently mobilized to keep the norm-violating government on the international agenda and if that government is vulnerable to such international pressures, the third phase in our "spiral model" is eventually reached. The norm-violating government is now forced to make *tactical concessions* to the international human rights community. This permits the domestic opposition to gain courage and to start its own process of social mobilization. If it increases its strength and links up with the transnational networks, the government is under pressure "from above" and "from below" (see Brysk 1993, forthcoming). At this stage, some national leaders start a process of "controlled liberalization." Others, however, continue to miscalculate the situation as a result of which a regime change is likely to happen.

The outcome of either controlled liberalization or a regime change is the transition to the fourth phase of our model during which international human rights norms gain *prescriptive status* in the target state. The validity of the international norms is no longer contested and governments start to institutionalize them domestically. If the domestic-transnational advocacy networks keep up the pressure, *prescriptive status* is followed by full implementation of human rights norms which marks the final stage in our model, "rule-consistent behavior."

To evaluate the explanatory power of our model and to examine the manner in which international human rights norms become embedded in domestic practices, we chose a variety of paired country cases from different regions of the world. In the following, we discuss and compare the evidence of the eleven country cases reported in this book.

Evaluating the evidence: what our case studies tell us about the socialization of human rights norms into domestic practice

The general applicability of the "spiral model"

Our most important finding is that socialization processes are effective across a strikingly diverse range of regions, countries, socio-economic systems, cultures, and types of political regimes. The socialization processes captured by our "spiral model" are truly universal and generalizable across regions and domestic structures. Indonesia under Suharto was a multi-ethnic state with an authoritarian government whose right to rule has been historically tied to so-called "performance legitimacy." It was representative of a whole genre of repressive authoritarian regimes that began to emerge in the Third World during the 1950s and which used developmental themes to promote national unity (see chapter 5). Kenya and Chile offer variations on this theme of developmental authoritarianism (see chapters 2 and 6). In the Kenyan case, Daniel arap Moi used developmental motifs and increasingly practised exclusionary politics. The "bureaucratic authoritarian" regime established in Chile after the 1973 military coup was a more highly modernized version of developmental authoritarianism associated with a later stage of national economic development. Yet, in spite of some major differences in the bases of legitimacy and structure of these various developmental authoritarian regimes, our case studies show that all of them were subject to effective network socialization.

Even more surprising is the fact that network socialization processes were effective in several entirely different types of political regime settings. In the case of Morocco, King Hassan II practised a neo-patrimonial style of government in which his legitimacy derived from his dual function as both a secular and Islamic leader of his people (see chapter 4). And in Guatemala, there was an extremely decentralized pattern of state–society relations that led to the creation of "reactionary despotic" regimes based on semi-feudal coalitional groupings (see chapter 6).

Similar processes of effective network socialization can also be seen in former Communist states such as Poland and Czechoslovakia[1] (see chapter 7) where we again find completely different economic and political systems. Finally, in the case of South Africa, an industrialized state was subjected to intense domestic and transnational network pressure which finally overcame the apartheid regime (see chapter 3). What is most significant in all of these diverse cases is a common movement (albeit at different speeds) along the general trajectory of our "spiral model."[2] This general finding effectively disconfirms the notion that certain types of political, economic, or social systems cannot be subjected to change and that international human rights are fundamentally alien to particular cultures or regions of the world (Huntington 1996).

---

[1] Chapter 7, on Eastern Europe, examines the transition of Czechoslovakia when Slovakia and the Czech Republic were still one state. In the meantime, the country split up.

[2] We do not argue, though, that variation in domestic economic, social, political, and cultural structures is completely irrelevant. As we suggest later in this chapter, these differences mostly account for the timing of changes rather than their substance.

Phase	3. Tactical concessions	4. Prescriptive status	5. Rule-consistant behavior
States investigated in this book	Indonesia → Kenya → ←Tunisia Morocco →	Uganda → Philippines → Guatemala →	Poland Czechoslovakia South Africa Chile

Figure 8.1   Phases and country cases.
Note: The arrows denote the current estimates by the individual authors as to where the individual countries are moving

In general then, our cases fit well within the phases of the "spiral model," although at different points (see figure 8.1). Each of the eleven countries investigated in this book started the socialization process in a phase of repression, even though the degree of human rights abuses varied considerably (from the genocide in Uganda to the comparatively mild repression in Communist Poland). Nine of the eleven countries also went through a period of "denial" when the norm-violating governments strongly rejected the notion that their domestic order was subject to international human rights jurisdiction. The exceptions are Tunisia and Chile which "skipped" the denial phase, although for different reasons and with different results. Moreover, Uganda is the only case which moved directly toward prescriptive status without going through an extended period of tactical concessions, after Yoweri Museveni had won the civil war (see chapter 2). These exceptions are worth mentioning because the fact that they do not belong to one single category of socioeconomic or political system suggests to us that no particular group of countries systematically skips stages in our "spiral model."

All countries investigated have moved by now toward at least the phase of tactical concessions. Other than that, they remain at various stages in the socialization process. Our four "success stories" of mostly completed internalization of human rights norms and sustained improvement of human rights conditions are Poland, Czechoslovakia (now Slovakia and the Czech Republic), South Africa, and Chile. It is noteworthy that these countries are now all liberal democracies, even though they reached this stage from very different starting points (Communist regimes in Poland and Czechoslovakia, white minority rule in South Africa, and bureaucratic authoritarianism in Chile). Thus, while it is clear that democracies can sometimes create human rights problems when they erode or collapse (e.g. Chile in 1973) and that democratizing processes can lead to major human rights abuses (e.g. Algeria after 1991), democratic consolidation is closely associated with human rights progress (see the elegant analysis in Linz 1978).

Three more countries – Uganda, the Philippines, and most recently Guatemala – have institutionalized human rights norms to a very large degree ("prescriptive status" phase) and have moved quite far toward rule-consistent behavior. If we add these three countries to the four most complete success cases, another finding is striking: in each of these seven cases (and in Indonesia most recently), a regime change preceded the dramatic improvement of human rights conditions and in many cases brought the domestic human rights network into power. Moreover, these regime changes came about through a peaceful and/or negotiated transition process – with only one exception (Uganda). In the cases of Poland and Czechoslovakia, the Communist rulers gave up power peacefully, when they realized that they had lost all domestic legitimacy and that Soviet tanks were no longer available to crush the opposition. In the South African case, the white minority rulers, who were increasingly isolated in the international community, started a secret dialogue with the African National Congress (ANC) in the late 1980s, a process which culminated in the famous public turnaround by President F. W. de Klerk and the ensuing negotiated end of the apartheid system. Uganda is our only "success story" in which the change came about through a bloody civil war.

The exception to the rule of regime change as a precondition for human rights improvements is Morocco. As Sieglinde Gränzer shows in chapter 4, King Hassan II started to modify his human rights policies and practices, both because he faced a serious international image problem and because his domestic self-image (and even identity) as an enlightened monarch was at stake.

But we have also included three countries in our case studies where the human rights conditions are still far from satisfactory. Two of these cases, Indonesia and Kenya (see chapters 4 and 2), exhibited similar characteristics of increasing domestic mobilization and sustained transnational network pressures which are both typical of the "tactical concessions" phase. As a result, the rulers – Daniel arap Moi in Kenya and President Suharto in Indonesia – were forced to institute some changes in the human rights area. Both governments also changed their rhetoric considerably in the international arena. In other words, progress has been made even in these two cases.

The only country in our case studies which moved toward the tactical concession phase and then experienced a backlash without further progress is Tunisia (see chapter 4). Despite general government rhetoric in support of human rights (President Ben Ali was even awarded some human rights prizes), repression has increased in recent years. But as we will argue below, Tunisia is the exception which proves the rule, that is, a case which generally confirms rather than challenges our propositions concerning the "spiral model."

Specific phases in the spiral process
From repression to denial

Let us now turn to our case material and the extent to which it supports our views concerning the conditions under which we expect progress to be made along the various phases of the "spiral model" (see introductory chapter by Thomas Risse and Kathryn Sikkink). Concerning the first transition from the repression to the denial stage, we found confirming evidence that transnational networks of human rights activists are indeed the single most important group of actors to put a norm-violating government on the international agenda through a process of moral consciousness-raising. Human rights violations in South Africa during the 1960s and in Chile and the Philippines during the 1970s created an environment in which such consciousness-raising could take place, and were thus "constitutive" for the very emergence of transnational advocacy coalitions in the human rights area. These networks could then be re-activated in the other cases analyzed in this book, mostly during the early 1980s, when network members started lobbying Western powers and international organizations. Even in Poland and Czechoslovakia where the repression under Communism had always been a concern for Western governments, transnational network pressure put human rights on the Western agenda in the 1970s.

The empirical evidence also confirms our expectation that the first reaction of most governments accused of violations of human rights is one of denial. Repressive governments almost universally tried to fight off the international opposition by claiming national sovereignty and challenging the validity of international human rights norms. At the same time, many Third World governments attempted to use nationalist and anti-colonialist rhetoric in order to increase their domestic legitimacy in the face of international criticism. For example, Indonesia's Suharto and Kenya's arap Moi used similar anti-colonial rhetoric to reject charges of human rights violations made by Amnesty International.

However, two countries (Chile and Tunisia) skipped the denial phase and moved directly toward tactical concessions in response to international network activities. But the reasons for this were very different. In the Chilean case (see chapter by Steve C. Ropp and Kathryn Sikkink; also Hawkins 1997), denying the validity of human rights norms was not an option available to General Pinochet, given Chile's democratic tradition. In this case, the process of institutionalizing human rights norms domestically dates back as far as the 1925 constitution, which contained a variety of personal guarantees enforced by an independent judiciary. Even during the period of military dictatorship, Chile continued to institutionalize human rights. General Pinochet used the signing of international human rights agreements such as the Covenant on Civil and Political Rights in 1976 as tactical concessions in a domestic culture in which human rights had long before gained prescriptive status.

The Tunisian case is altogether different (see chapter 4). When Prime Minister Ben Ali became president in 1987, he immediately moved toward tactical concessions and declared human rights a supreme goal of the state. He restored Tunisia's international reputation and, at the same time, considerably weakened the domestic opposition. In the absence of a fully mobilized domestic human rights coalition with ties to the transnational networks, his human rights supporting rhetoric effectively silenced Western criticism, while the domestic opposition was further weakened due to increased repression. Skipping the denial phase turned out to be a clever move by a norm-violating government. The full mobilization of the domestic opposition and of the transnational advocacy networks which we assume to be necessary for moving the situation toward prescriptive status and rule-consistent behavior, never materialized. The absence of change in the Tunisian case, therefore, confirms our model and its causal mechanisms.

From denial to tactical concessions

In the introductory chapter (Risse and Sikkink), we argue that a transition to the third phase of tactical concessions is the more likely the stronger the transnational advocacy network becomes and the more vulnerable the norm-violating government is to external pressures. With the exceptions of Tunisia (discussed above), Uganda, and Eastern Europe, we can confirm this hypothesis for the remaining seven cases. In each of these countries, transnational network pressure turned out to be the single most important cause of change toward initial concessions by the norm-violating government. In some cases – Indonesia, Kenya, Guatemala, Chile, and the Philippines (to a lesser extent) –, the advocacy coalitions managed to convince some Western governments to institute sanctions which further helped to bring about change.

But Great Power pressure was by no means a necessary enabling condition for change in this stage of the process. In the Moroccan case, the country's major ally, France, did not do much to force King Hassan II to change course. In South Africa, which entered the tactical concessions stage after the Soweto massacre in 1976, the international sanctions regime only gradually emerged in response to the massacre and was not fully effective until the mid-1980s. Guatemala also offers an illustrative example of a case where Great Power pressure was not particularly effective. During the late 1970s, the Carter administration applied a great deal of pressure to the military government, pressure that was explicitly designed to alter Guatemala's egregious human rights record. This pressure did not result in an improvement in human rights practices there but rather in a highly nationalistic elite reaction to external great power interference. The Reagan administration then changed course and signaled to Guatemala that Carter's human rights policy was not enduring. This turnaround preceded one of the worst periods of human rights abuse in that country's history (see chapter 6).

In the East European cases, the acceptance of a human rights provision within the 1975 Helsinki Final Act was a concession in a bargaining process with the West, but network pressure was not involved at this stage. The Soviet Union and its allies agreed to the human rights norm as a *quid pro quo* for Western recognition of the territorial status quo in Europe. The peculiar Cold War situation in Europe is responsible for this aberration from our general pattern. It should also be noted that the US did not take the Helsinki Final Act very seriously when it was signed in 1975. Only later, when a transnational network focused attention on Helsinki's human rights norms, did they recognize what the Final Act meant as a window of opportunity for dissidents.

Uganda constitutes the final exception regarding the transition to the third phase (see chapter 2). A bloody civil war was fought between the norm-violating government and a rebel group which included human rights advocates under Yoweri Museveni's leadership. Museveni's guerrilla army became immensely popular in the country, not only because it liberated the people from a most oppressive dictatorship, but also because it respected human rights standards toward the civilian population even during the war. When Museveni assumed power in 1986, he immediately institutionalized human rights norms, thus moving toward the phase of "prescriptive status."

Our second assumption, concerning the conditions under which a move toward tactical concessions is likely, pointed to the vulnerability of norm-violating governments to external pressures. The case studies reveal that "regime vulnerability" constitutes a multifaceted variable. In some cases, Third World governments indeed depend materially on outside assistance (foreign aid, for example). The most prominent case in our sample is probably Kenya, where the suspension of foreign aid in 1991 led to some significant tactical concessions. In the case of Indonesia, the threat of sanctions had the desired result, but also led to a nationalist backlash when President Suharto froze the Dutch–Indonesian economic cooperation program in 1992 (see chapter 5).

More important, however, our case studies show that "regime vulnerability" also implies vulnerability to moral pressures. States do care about their international reputation and image as "normal" members of the international community. We find that shaming as a mechanism of moral consciousness-raising works in many cases. Very few norm-violating governments are prepared to live with the image of a pariah for a long period of time. The Moroccan king, for example, almost completely changed his rhetoric when faced with increasing external criticism (see chapter 4). His self-image as a benign patriarch who cares about his people was shattered by the domestic and international networks. In response, he indicated his desire to belong to the community of civilized ("European") nations. Similar examples can be reported from Indonesia under Suharto, the Philippines under Marcos, Kenya during the 1990s, South Africa during the early 1980s, Chile, Guatemala, and Communist Eastern Europe. In most of these cases, transnational advocacy networks used the moral power of human rights norms which had become consensual in the international community, both to persuade Western states to apply additional political and economic pressures against the norm-violating governments, and to "shame" these states directly in terms of their reputational concerns.

As to the effects of this stage of the "spiral model," we posited that tactical concessions most importantly serve to open up space for the domestic opposition in the "target state." We can confirm this argument almost universally across our cases – with Tunisia and Uganda being the only two outliers, for the reasons already discussed. In each of the nine other countries, the most important effect of the tactical concession phase was to empower, strengthen, and mobilize the domestic opposition. Domestic non-governmental organizations (NGOs) started to spread and to link up with the transnationally operating advocacy networks. The five "success stories" – Poland, Czechoslovakia, South Africa, Chile, and the Philippines – which managed the transition to prescriptive status and rule-consistent behavior were all characterized by a lively, widespread, and fully mobilized domestic opposition toward the later stages of the tactical concessions phase. Human rights had acquired consensual status in the domestic society which was also fully linked to the transnational networks.

But the road toward prescriptive status was bumpy for these opposition groups. Tactical concessions by norm-violating governments were often accompanied by increased repression and rights violations. The South African government, for example, instituted reforms of the labor market and of political institutions during the late 1970s and early 1980s, while embarking on a "Total National Strategy" to combat the "Total Onslaught" of its alleged Moscow-orchestrated enemies at the same time (see chapter 3). In Guatemala, tactical concessions began just after some of the worst human rights violations during the early 1980s (see chapter 6).

In sum, then, the phase of tactical concessions indeed turned out to be the most crucial with regard to achieving sustainable human rights improvements in our empirical case studies. This stage of the "spiral model" is remarkably Janus-faced. On the one hand, there are some real human rights improvements which in turn empower and strengthen the domestic opposition. On the other hand, norm-violating governments increasingly struggle to remain in power and, therefore, may quickly change from making concessions to increased repression.

From tactical concessions to prescriptive status and rule-consistent behavior

Our "spiral model" posits that norm-violating governments are faced with fully mobilized domestic opposition groups and transnational advocacy networks toward the end of phase 3. At this point, we argue, either a process of controlled liberalization or a regime change is likely to occur which then moves the process toward prescriptive status. The empirical evidence mostly confirms our expectations. Except for Uganda, the move toward enduring human rights improvements in the seven remaining cases (Poland, Czechoslovakia, South Africa, Chile, Guatemala, Philippines, and Morocco) resulted from the pressures of a full-fledged and well-organized domestic opposition linked up with the transnational advocacy coalitions. In the cases of South Africa, Chile, Guatemala, and the Philippines, Western powers and major allies of the respective states finally joined the transnational networks in their opposition against the norm-violating regimes and helped to move them "over the top." But they almost always followed rather than led the opposition. The Philippines and Indonesia are cases in point (see chapter 5). The Reagan administration only ceased supporting the Marcos regime when it had convinced itself that he would be toppled anyway. The same holds true for the Clinton administration's decision to cease supporting Suharto one day before he resigned.

The final stages of reaching "prescriptive status" always preceded the sustained improvements in actual behavior. The process by which human rights norms achieved prescriptive status in the various countries turned out to be more gradual in many cases than we had originally assumed. Only for Uganda, the Philippines, and South Africa can one argue that full prescriptive status was reached immediately after the regime change when the new governments began ratifying international agreements, institutionalizing them into domestic law, and fully embracing human rights norms in their communicative behavior. In the Latin American and Eastern European cases (see chapters 6 and 2), however, this change took place more incrementally and over an extended period of time. Guatemala instituted an independent Human Rights Ombudsman Office in 1985 and accepted the jurisdiction of the Inter-American Court of Human Rights in 1987, while severe human rights violations continued. Czechoslovakia had already ratified the two International Human Rights Covenants by 1976. Poland is the only case in our sample which entered the phase of "prescriptive status" and then moved back to earlier phases of the model when martial law was instituted in 1981.

While none of these "early" developments with regard to legally recognizing the importance of human rights as such justify placing the respective country in the prescriptive status phase, they do suggest that the first steps toward this stage are usually made during earlier phases of the "spiral model." Ratification of this or that international human rights agreement may constitute a tactical concession rather than full acceptance of its precise normative content. Nevertheless, our empirical case studies provide ample evidence that the acceptance of international norms through treaty ratification is not inconsequential. Governments entangle themselves in an international and domestic legal process which they subsequently find harder and harder to escape. The Helsinki human rights norm and its consequences for domestic change in Eastern Europe is a particularly striking example (see chapter 7).

The outlier again is Tunisia (see chapter 4). In this case, President Ben Ali ratified the Anti-Torture Convention, instituted a domestic Human Rights Commission and even an individual complaint procedure as tactical concessions when faced with international pressures. By doing so, he effectively silenced his domestic and international critics, even though the repression increased during the early 1990s. In this case, then, changes in rhetoric had no subsequent consequences for behavioral changes; they even became a substitute for real change.

But Tunisia is the exception to the rule. Each of the seven countries which reached full prescriptive status as defined by our model also experienced a subsequent, sustained, and drastic improvement of human rights conditions. Poland, Czechoslovakia, South Africa, Chile, Uganda, the Philippines, and Guatemala all matched words with deeds eventually. While the human rights record of Uganda, the Philippines, and Guatemala remains far from perfect, the progress has been dramatic and sustained. Our findings also suggest that the move from full prescriptive status toward sustained rule-consistent behavior is very likely. The Guatemalan case, which seems to be temporarily stalled between prescriptive status and rule-consistent behavior, indicates that continuing international pressure is crucial, even during these later stages of the socialization process.

Modes of socialization and social interaction

We stated in the introduction of this book that we expected three modes of social interaction to operate in our phased socialization process, leading to the domestic internalization of human rights norms. We distinguished between institutionalization and habitualization, strategic bargaining and instrumental rationality, as well as arguing and persuasion. The presence of the first of these three modes of social interaction (institutionalization and habitualization) can be most easily confirmed throughout our case studies.

Institutionalization and habitualization

Institutionalization as a form of socialization is a universal phenomenon in our cases. But institutionalization does vary a great deal from country to country with regard to when human rights norms were incorporated into domestic law, the types of rights recognized, and the degree to which they are protected. A common feature of our seven "success stories" is the presence of institutionalization as a socializing mechanism for implementing human rights norms in domestic practice. There is not a single case in which a sustained improvement of human rights conditions was not preceded by the country's move toward the rule of law. The incorporation of international human rights norms into domestic institutions and law is, of course, most pronounced in cases where democratic governments with fully functioning multi-party systems have been installed or restored – the Philippines, Poland, Czechoslovakia, South Africa, Chile, and Guatemala. But we also find that institutionalization forms part of the "socializing landscape" in one-party systems (Uganda), a monarchy (Morocco), and various types of secular authoritarian states (Indonesia under Suharto and Tunisia). Even Indonesia, which has not yet signed the International Convention on Civil and Political Rights or ratified the Convention against Torture, established a National Commission on Human Rights in 1993 which has become surprisingly independent.

This finding regarding the nearly universal presence of domestically institutionalized human rights norms is quite encouraging since the incorporation of international human rights norms into domestic institutions and law is a necessary precondition for the eventual establishment of fully rule-consistent domestic behavior. It might even suggest that the world is moving toward a point in human history where the historical post-Second World War "debate" between the contested norms of universal human rights, on the one hand, and sovereignty, on the other, will have ended through universal institutionalization of human rights values.

We do not mean to suggest, however, that the incorporation of international human rights norms into domestic institutions and law is sufficient in and of itself to ensure adherence to these norms by state leaders. To date, this process of incorporation has been far too uneven and potentially reversible to warrant such a suggestion. But we do believe that widespread institutionalization of these norms across an extremely broad range of regime types is a socializing "precursor" that has helped prepare the domestic human rights terrain in most countries for the eventual comprehensive socialization of human rights norms into domestic practice.

Finally, it is particularly noteworthy that most states investigated in this volume showed a surprising appreciation for international law. With only a few exceptions (Tunisia and Czechoslovakia, to some degree), national governments only ratified international human rights conventions including the optional protocols if they were prepared to live up to these standards domestically. On the one hand, ratification of international agreements usually went hand in hand with the institutionalization of these standards in domestic law. On the other hand, norm-violating governments were careful not to ratify international conventions through which they could be held legally accountable to the world human rights community. This finding might not come as a surprise to international lawyers, but it certainly is significant for political scientists who usually treat international law as somehow epiphenomenal to the power realities of world politics.

Instrumental vs. argumentative rationality

Compared to institutionalization mechanisms, it is harder to identify empirically the extent to which movement along the socialization path of our "spiral model" can be accounted for by referring to instrumental interests and strategic bargaining among actors, on the one hand, as compared with argumentative rationality and processes of persuasion, on the other. The communications between norm-violating governments and transnational as well as domestic advocacy networks resemble a public discourse which is carried out in front of international as well as domestic audiences in the target state. The international audiences include Western states, Western publics, and international organizations, while the domestic audiences mainly consist of various groups within the civil society of the "target state." In general, our empirical findings confirm the expectation that instrumental interests and strategic rationality tend to dominate the early phases of the controversy, while argumentative behavior becomes more relevant later on (see introductory chapter, table 1.1).

It is self-evident that the transition from the repression to the denial phase is dominated by instrumental interests on both sides. The very fact that norm-violating governments deny the validity of international human rights norms implies that they are not interested in engaging in a serious dialogue with their critics at that stage. At the same time, the efforts at moral consciousness-raising by the transnational networks do not entail much arguing about the validity of the norms, either, but primarily serve to put the norm-violating state on the international agenda. At this stage of the process, both sides engage in rhetorical action (Schimmelfennig 1995, 1997, 1998). They use arguments, not to convince each other, but to persuade the international and/or domestic audiences of their respective points of view. Transnational advocacy networks use strategies of moral consciousness-raising and shaming to blame the norm-violating governments, while such governments tend to stress the Westphalian norm of state sovereignty in their attempt to garner domestic and international support.

If moral persuasion plays any role at this stage, it concerns the process by which members of transnational networks try to convince Western governments and public opinion to pay attention to the situation in the norm-violating state and to act accordingly. The moral arguing here is mainly about identity politics, that is, Western governments and their societies are reminded of their own values as liberal democracies and of the need to act upon them in their foreign policies. This process of moral consciousness-raising can take quite a long time. In the case of South Africa, for example, the transnational anti-apartheid networks tried to persuade Western governments for almost twenty years that South Africa was to be treated as a pariah state rather than an ally in the fight against Communism (see chapter 3).

At this stage of the process, then, the two sides do not accept each other as valid and truthful interlocutors. The advocacy coalition treats the norm-violating state as an international pariah, as an outsider to the community of civilized nations. At the same time and in response, norm-violating governments not only tend to deny the validity of the international norms, but also to ridicule their accusers as ignorant "foreigners." Their main target audience is usually the domestic society, in an attempt to fight off the challenges to their legitimacy. Many Third-World governments engage in an anti-colonial and anti-imperialist as well as a nationalist discourse at this stage.

The transition from the denial stage to tactical concessions can also be explained mostly by instrumental interests and strategic bargaining. Under increasing international pressures, norm-violating governments feel that they must make some concessions in order to increase their domestic and international room to maneuver, to increase their legitimacy, or simply to regain foreign aid. The Soviet Union and Eastern Europe signed the human rights provisions in the Helsinki Final Act as a quid pro quo for Western acceptance of the political and territorial status quo in the détente period. South Africa and Indonesia needed to make some concessions in order to repair their international reputation after the Soweto and the Dili massacres, respectively. Chile's Pinochet could never deny the validity of international human rights and, therefore, had to respond to the international outcry with some tactical moves almost from the beginning of his repressive dictatorship. At this stage, norm-violating governments no longer deny the validity of the international norm, but they continue to ridicule their critics and to reject specific allegations of norm violations.

Argumentative rationality might have played a bigger role in the process of convincing King Hassan II of Morocco that he faced a reputational problem. In the relatively "open" political context created by Morocco's multi-party system, argumentative forms of socialization had some domestic impact during the long gestation period when human rights groups were attempting to convince King Hassan II to change repressive government practices. Moroccan emigrant groups in Europe, which maintained strong personal and informal links with activists at home, were able to use these channels to publicize violations and thus keep human rights issues visible until the king began to institutionalize human rights norms. Sieglinde Gränzer cites a classic example of consciousness-raising that resulted from publication of *Notre Ami le Roi* ("Our Friend the King") by French author Gilles Perault in 1990. In this particular case, the legitimacy of the king's rule was not challenged by his critics, but he was reminded of his own identity as a "benign monarch" who cares about his people. The king's speeches at the time document that argumentation might have played a role in changing his behavior (for evidence see Gränzer 1998). Precisely because King Hassan II was a monarch, and almost by definition "above criticism," he was much more sensitive to criticism through processes of argumentative rationality than leaders of other types of ideologically or bureaucratically grounded regimes might be. It is important to recognize this fact because the general policy approach best suited to altering the domestic behavior of the few remaining world monarchies might vary from our standard phased socialization "script."

As a general rule, though, arguing rather than strategic adaptation to external and domestic pressures becomes more important during later stages of the tactical concessions phase. While argumentative processes of deliberation among the opposition groups in domestic society appear to vary depending on the general openness of the system, we found a striking trend toward more use of argumentative rationality in the later stages of this phase. The more norm-violating governments accept the validity of international norms, the more they start arguing with their critics over specific accusations (see also introductory chapter by Thomas Risse and Kathryn Sikkink). This process usually begins with the denial of any wrongdoing and with outraged denunciations of the transnational and domestic network actors as "traitors," "ignorant foreigners," or as agents of "imperialism" and "communism." Kenya's arap Moi, Indonesia's Suharto, as well as the Communist leaders in Eastern Europe and the white minority in South Africa used very similar rhetoric in this regard (see the respective chapters). Argumentative concessions are part of a larger picture of tactical concessions at this stage. There is no dialogue between norm-violating governments and their critics, but their arguments are directed at various audiences, both in domestic society and abroad. Both sides attempt to win over their audiences, to increase international pressures on norm-violating governments, for example, or to rally one's domestic society around a nationalist discourse.

If the transnational and domestic pressure grows stronger, however, norm-violating governments increasingly engage in a public dialogue with their critics and the logic of argumentative rationality incrementally takes over. The Kenyan and Indonesian governments as well as the Philippines under Marcos, for example, started acknowledging that some minor human rights violations had in fact occurred and promised to punish the perpetrators. The human rights international non-governmental organizations responded by arguing that violations in these countries were not isolated incidents, but fairly widespread and systematic (for details see Jetschke 1997; Schmitz 1998). At this point, the two sides started arguing about how to measure systematic human rights abuses and how to prevent them in the future. Norm-violating governments such as those in Kenya, Indonesia, Guatemala, and also Morocco (see chapters 2, 5, 6, and 4) then promised to create independent human rights commissions and other institutions. At this point during the tactical concession phase, both sides' arguments became more and more detailed and also more and more legalistic. It was no longer a discourse about the validity of the norm, but about the situation on the ground. It was about the interpretation of the law of the land, but no longer about its validity.

At the same time, the two sides also gradually accepted each other as valid interlocutors and abandoned the inflammatory rhetoric of the past. Amnesty International and other organizations within the transnational network, for example, no longer branded the governments of the "target state" as inhuman oppressors, but rather put forward concrete proposals for human rights improvements. In the end, then, a true dialogue emerged between the previously norm-violating government and its domestic and international critics. Finally, the argumentative consistency of actors irrespective of the audience increased dramatically. Toward the beginning of the tactical concession phase, norm-violating governments might "talk the talk" at the UN and toward the Western donor community, but adopt an entirely different language when making statements targeted at a domestic audience. Later on, we observe that the argumentative consistency increased.

How can one explain this process of argumentative "self-entrapment" theoretically? It certainly does not resemble an "ideal speech situation" in the Habermasian sense, since governments rarely enter the process of arguing voluntarily, but are forced into it by the pressure of a fully mobilized domestic and transnational network. At the same time, however, the dialogue no longer resembles rhetorical exchanges, either, by which both sides use arguments to justify their given interests and behavior, but are unprepared to change and to reconsider their preferences. Even these "forced dialogues" have all the characteristics of a true argumentative exchange. Both sides accept each other as valid interlocutors, try to establish some common definition of the human rights situation, and to agree on the norms to be used in guiding subsequent action. In other words, they behave "as if" they were engaged in a true moral discourse. This is precisely what Jürgen Habermas calls communicative rationality in the sense of a counterfactual presupposition of the ideal speech situation (Habermas 1981, 1992, 1995a, b; Müller 1994; Risse 1997).

Finally, if either side violates the rules of the dialogue and falls back on earlier harsh rhetoric, it is immediately obvious to everybody else that he or she is not serious. One could argue that this is precisely what happened in the cases of the Philippines, Uganda, and most recently in Indonesia (see chapters 5 and 2). President Marcos of the Philippines had moved a long way on the path of tactical concessions and was forced to engage in a dialogue with the opposition. He then violated the rules by murdering opposition leader Benigno Aquino. This only strengthened the domestic and transnational opposition further. Finally, the US forced Marcos to accept early presidential elections. When it became clear that the results were fraudulent, he had to resign, and the opposition took over. Similarly, Uganda's Milton Obote had also started making some tactical concessions including a change in rhetoric, but then reverted to repression. At this point, the domestic opposition rallied around human rights norms under the leadership of Yoweri Museveni, who then fought a guerilla war against the government. He won the war, partly because his troops obeyed human rights norms toward the civilian population which greatly increased his legitimacy. The recent events in Indonesia also seem to follow this pattern. President Suharto and his government had changed their human rights rhetoric quite considerably and had instituted some changes in domestic law. When the economic crisis hit the country, he was forced to violate the "rules" of the tactical concession phase and was eventually forced by the domestic opposition to resign.

In the cases of Poland, Czechoslovakia, South Africa, and Chile, a negotiated and peaceful transition toward prescriptive status and rule-consistent behavior took place (see chapters 7, 3, and 6). The governments did not enter these negotiations with the opposition voluntarily, of course, but were forced by international and domestic pressures. Nevertheless, the Polish roundtable in late 1988, the Czechoslovak negotiations following the "Velvet Revolution" one year later, and the South African negotiated transition starting in 1990 are remarkable cases of peaceful regime change. While each of these negotiations ultimately brought the opposition into power, they also resulted in reassurances for the previous rulers that there would be no vendettas even though justice to the victims of human rights violations was to be done. We need more empirical evidence from these negotiations in order to establish to what extent they resembled true dialogues and argumentative processes as opposed to strategic bargaining.

In sum, the empirical evidence suggests that "talk is not cheap," particularly during the latter phases of our spiral model's socialization process. Once they have entrapped themselves in such a discourse, governments which choose to violate the rules of argumentative rationality and dialogue are very likely to be thrown out of power, as was the case in the Philippines, Uganda, and Eastern Europe. And in these above-mentioned cases, the new governments that replaced them engaged in a similar moral dialogue with the international human rights networks soon after assuming power. They invited human rights INGOs and other actors to help with the further institutionalization of human rights norms into domestic practice.

The necessity of both argumentation and institutionalization

Our analysis of general patterns suggests that both habitualizing forms of socialization such as institutionalization and argumentative forms such as moral consciousness-raising are necessary to ensure enduring human rights change. The necessity of such "across-the-board" socialization is revealed through a comparison of four of our cases, two in which the socialization of human rights norms would appear to be fairly deep and enduring (Chile and the Philippines), and two where it would appear to be still somewhat problematic (Morocco and Uganda).

In Chile, both argumentative and habitualizing processes of socialization were widespread. As Steve Ropp and Kathryn Sikkink point out, for example, the staff of the Vicariate of Solidarity was in almost constant contact with Amnesty International in London throughout the early years of the Pinochet dictatorship. Reports by the UN Commission on Human Rights as well as the Inter-American Commission on Human Rights were often picked up by the international and local Chilean media, providing local human rights activists with "ammunition" in the internal "argumentative wars" within Chile. Somewhat later in the dictatorship, more habitualizing and institutionalized forms of socialization became increasingly common.

We find a similar reliance on both argumentative processes and institutionalization in the Philippine case. As previously discussed, socializing processes or argumentation and moral consciousness-raising were introduced by US NGOs in a favorable context where Philippine ruling elites had been conditioned to be responsive to US values (see chapter 5). These argumentative discourse processes were particularly important during the late 1970s in facilitating a shift in the stance of the Marcos regime on human rights and contributed to the change of government in 1986. It was at this point that socialization of the Marcos regime through instrumental adaptation and NGO/opposition argumentation began to be reinforced by processes that led to the institutionalization of human rights norms.

Both the Chilean and Philippine cases of human rights change thus demonstrate how different modes of socialization can be effective at different points in time in our "spiral model." On the other hand, the Moroccan and Ugandan cases reveal some of the difficulties for positive movement along our "spiral model" that are associated with unbalanced and partial socialization processes. Uganda has reached the fifth and final phase, but in a somewhat unbalanced fashion that placed President Yoweri Museveni at the center of the process before and after his military victory in 1986. Given the centrality of Museveni to the process, there were few successful attempts by actors either at the international or state level to engage members of Ugandan civil society in a socializing discourse about human rights. As Hans Peter Schmitz points out, Museveni personified the human rights debate for Ugandan citizens, and the institutionalization of human rights norms into domestic practice occurred simultaneously with his accession to power.

In the case of Morocco, emigrant groups in Europe extensively used argumentative and persuasive forms of socialization to move King Hassan II in the direction of meaningful human rights change, as Sieglinde Gränzer suggests in chapter 4. Also, the institutionalization of human rights has proceeded apace for some two decades in Morocco. The International Convention on Civil and Political Rights was signed in 1979 and the Convention against Torture in 1986. The king took further major steps in the direction of institutionalizing human rights norms with the establishment of a Consultative Council on Human Rights in 1990, and a Ministry for Human Rights in 1993.

But the highly personalistic nature of leadership in both countries renders sustainable human rights change more problematic than in the Chilean and Philippine cases. Indeed, with regard to the socialization of human rights norms into domestic practice, we need to recognize that there is a great paradox associated with personalist rule. On the one hand, such rule can result in more rapid short-term progress along the course of our "spiral model," precisely because an influential leader can quickly institute human rights norms from the top down. However, personalist rule has the great disadvantage of "short-circuiting" the socialization process at the level of civil society. Under such conditions, it is likely that deep and internalized support for human rights norms will take longer to develop.

In sum, then, our model seems to have general applicability across a wide variety of regions, cultures, and different types of political and economic systems. The case material supports our views concerning the conditions under which we would expect change in the domestic behavior of states to occur along various points in our "spiral model." While our three modes of socialization can be found throughout the various phases of human rights transition in most of our cases, our data seem to support the general view that instrumental interests and strategic rationality tend to dominate the early phases with argumentative processes coming to the fore later on.

Observations concerning the variation among the cases

Our case-study evidence strongly suggests that the spiral model has applicability in strikingly diverse domestic circumstances, and generally supports our conclusions concerning specific phases in the spiral process and modes of socialization. However, we also note that there are individual differences in our country cases with regard to both the time horizons for moving from one phase to another and the scope of the ultimate change. Since our primary focus in this book has been on the nature of the socialization process itself and the development of a causal model that can explain the dynamics of this process, we chose to pay less attention to political and social "contextual" factors. Nonetheless, we feel that the topic of variation among cases deserves more attention (see table 8.1).

We have at least four cases where it took an exceptionally long time to move the country from the denial phase to prescriptive status and rule-consistent behavior. South Africa, Poland, and Czechoslovakia entered the denial phase roughly during the 1960s, moved toward tactical concessions in the mid to late 1970s, while the regime change resulting in drastically improved human rights conditions occurred in 1989 and the early 1990s, respectively. In other words, each of these three countries denied the validity of human rights norms for roughly fifteen years and then moved toward tactical concessions for another fifteen years, with the change from denial to rule-consistent behavior, thus taking more than thirty years altogether. Indonesia under Suharto stayed in the denial phase for roughly twenty years, and the path of change through the tactical concessions phase has only recently accelerated quite dramatically leading to the overthrow of Suharto.

In stark contrast to these four cases of "slow" transition, the neigh-

Table 8.1. *Timing and phases of human rights change*

Phase	Denial	Tactical concessions	Prescriptive status rule-consistent behavior
1960s	South Africa		
Early 1970s	Guatemala Indonesia Philippines Uganda Poland Czechoslovakia	Chile	
Late 1970s		Poland Czechoslovakia South Africa Philippines	
Early 1980s	Kenya	Guatemala	
Late 1980s	Morocco	Tunisia	Philippines Uganda Poland Czechoslovakia
Early 1990s		Morocco Kenya Indonesia	South Africa Guatemala Chile

boring Philippines needed only a little more than ten years to move from denial to the institutionalization of human rights norms. The same holds true for Uganda where the civil war had the counter-intuitive effect of speeding up the transition from denial to prescriptive status. The Moroccan monarchy was also exceptionally fast in moving from an initial denial of the norms' validity to the current situation of transition between tactical concessions and prescriptive status. The two Latin American countries are located somewhere in between our "slow" and "fast" cases. Chile needed almost twenty years to overcome the military dictatorship and to institute enduring human rights norms. It took Guatemala more than twenty years to move from denial to prescriptive status and most recently rule-consistent behavior.

The scope of the political and institutional changes accompanying the improvement in human rights conditions also varies enormously across our cases. Morocco is the only country in our sample in which human rights improved considerably, while the political regime – the monarchy under King Hassan II – remained stable. In contrast, Poland

and Czechoslovakia probably traveled the longest distance in terms of regime change – from Communist one-party rule and Stalinist oppression to liberal democracy. South Africa is a unique example of a country moving from white minority rule to a multi-racial democracy. Chile and the Philippines transited from military dictatorships to liberal democracies, while Uganda changed from a genocide committing dictatorship to a quite liberal one-man rule. So far, Tunisia and Kenya have not experienced a change in their regimes, but improvements in human rights conditions are also lacking.

What accounts for these variations in timing and scope of change? While the original intent of our study was not to provide an answer to this question, we feel that the emerging evidence points toward three major factors which will be briefly discussed below. They are:

1 The presence or absence of class-based, ethno-national, or religious forces threatening either the territorial integrity or the internal cohesion of the state ("blocking factors");
2 The degree of societal "openness" to external processes of argumentation and persuasion;
3 "world time," that is, the increasing strength and robustness of both the international human rights regime and the transnational advocacy networks.

The presence or absence of internal "blocking factors"

Our case studies point to a number of "blocking factors" which may operate at the domestic societal level and are frequently viewed as posing serious threats to elite, middle-class, or even more broadly defined "national" interests. Ropp and Sikkink's analysis of Chile shows how the threat to elite interests in that country was viewed strictly in class terms, and as coming from "hyper-activated" and increasingly politically empowered lower classes. In reaction to changing class dynamics during the 1960s and early 1970s, the Chilean military (with the support of the United States and the tacit approval of large portions of the middle class) overthrew the Socialist government of Salvador Allende in 1973 and installed a brutal authoritarian regime. Although network socialization processes and Great Power pressure resulted in a "chipping away" at the new regime's bases of legitimacy over the next decade and a half, progress along the course of our "spiral model" was slowed down considerably.

Many additional examples of blocking phenomena can be found in other case studies. Anja Jetschke's discussion of Indonesia shows how popular nationalism and nationalist undercurrents within many Indonesian NGOs imposed severe limitations on the effectiveness of human rights socialization processes during the crisis in East Timor. From 1976 through 1991, network effectiveness was limited by countervailing national norms and value structures which emphasized sovereignty and domestic cohesion more than human rights principles. Similar constraining appeals to a narrowly defined sense of cultural and territorial nationalism were made by Hispanic elites in Guatemala when they felt threatened by network influence. These appeals rallied the country's largely Hispanic urban and rural middle classes around the human rights-violating internal war that the Guatemalan army waged for more than three decades against rural indigenous Mayan peoples (see chapter 6).

In both the Indonesian and Guatemalan cases, the major blocking factors with regard to network expansion were, thus, threats perceived by the elites to the cultural and territorial integrity of the state. In other words, norm-violating governments were able to use perceived threats to the territorial integrity of the state to increase their own legitimacy and to orchestrate a nationalist response to the increasing transnational network pressures. These two cases are, therefore, consistent with quantitative findings according to which international and civil war is identified as a significant factor correlated with high levels of human rights violations (Poe and Tate 1994; Poe, Tate, and Camp Keith 1997).

The Ugandan case would, at first glance, appear to be the exception that proves the rule in that a civil war accelerated rather than blocked human rights progress (see chapter 2). In this case, the domestic opposition started a civil war against the norm-violating regime and instituted human rights change after its victory. However, as we argue above, this "acceleration" of human rights progress through civil war was associated with only partial socialization processes which render true consolidation of a human rights regime there problematical. Thus, the Ugandan case does not seem to invalidate our general conclusion that civil wars tend to have a negative impact on human rights change, and seldom (if ever) have a positive impact with regard to the enduring socialization of human rights norms into domestic behavior.

While the alleged threat of secessionist forces might be used to increase the *domestic* legitimacy of norm-violating governments resulting in a nationalist backlash, some governments are equally successful in stabilizing their *international* legitimacy by pointing to perceived threats to their states. The South African government, for example, successfully claimed for a long time that it was the Western strategic bulwark at the southern tip of Africa during the Cold War. It took the transnational networks decades to convince Western publics and governments that anti-Communism is no legitimate excuse for severe human rights abuses associated with apartheid (see chapter 3).

Today, the perceived threat of Islamic fundamentalism to Western security interests (e.g. oil supplies) might serve a similar function as did the threat of Communism during the Cold War. The alleged threat due to the rise of Islamic fundamentalism in Tunisia has all but halted domestic mobilization and has severely hampered transnational network activities. Chapter 4 demonstrates how the increasing repression and human rights violations of the Ben-Ali regime were legitimized domestically and internationally by the need to suppress Islamic fundamentalism. Ben Ali could always point to the situation in neighboring Algeria. Because Tunisia's human rights organizations were overwhelmingly secular, their criticism of human rights abuses committed against fundamentalists was muted. The tragic irony of this situation is that Tunisian Islamic fundamentalists are among the strongest supporters of human rights in the Western sense.

The examples of Tunisia and South Africa point out that these "blocking factors," when used in a state's international discourse, cannot always be treated as quasi-objective conditions which are necessarily preventing domestic human rights improvements. Rather, they can also be viewed as arguments put forward by norm-violating governments in a public discourse with their critics during the phases of denial or tactical concessions. To the extent that the domestic or international audiences find these arguments persuasive, governments might temporarily be able to fight off transnational pressures. However, our empirical case studies reveal that most of these arguments in defense of domestic human rights violations lose credibility over time. This happened with regard to the "Communist threat" in South Africa, and in many cases where the "threat" of terrorism has been used to justify continued human rights abuses.

Societal openness to external processes of argumentation and persuasion

Our case studies demonstrate that network socialization works particularly well where domestic societies are relatively "open." By "open" societies, we do not necessarily mean democratic ones. Rather, we refer to societies that for a variety of historical reasons have developed cultures and institutions that are responsive to and can accommodate some meaningful degree of internal debate and external influence. Morocco, Chile, Kenya, and the Philippines provide good examples of the importance of relative societal openness. At first glance, Morocco would appear to be a closed traditional monarchy. Yet, as Sieglinde Gränzer points out, it established a pluralistic system of political parties beginning in the 1970s which provided some space for domestic human rights organizations. In fact, Morocco's first human rights group was founded by members of the Istiqlal Party, and party contacts were maintained with emigrant groups in Europe such that network linkages could expand abroad. This might explain to some degree the speed of the change in Morocco. Similarly, Anja Jetschke uses the Philippine case to highlight the importance of relative societal openness. Marcos was not able to sustain the denial phase very long following his 1972 imposition of martial law because of the elite's relative openness to policy suggestions coming from its traditional ally, the United States.

Chile provides an example of the importance of pluralistic party systems in providing for communicative space. Before the 1973 military coup, Chile had the longest tradition of democracy in the hemisphere and well-institutionalized political parties. Thus, even following the onset of harsh authoritarian rule and abolition of existing parties, communicative channels were preserved between party members in Chile and affiliated groups abroad which could continue to denounce human rights violations. And in the Kenyan case, Hans Peter Schmitz points to the importance of the country's relative cultural and social openness in determining the trajectory of human rights reform. In spite of the increasingly repressive practices of arap Moi's government after 1978, information flows supportive of continued domestic debate over human rights continued due to Western economic interests and tourism.

In contrast, the two East European countries investigated in this volume (see chapter 7) remained quite closed to outside pressures during the first twenty years of the Cold War. It was the détente period of the 1970s which not only led to the Helsinki process of the Conference on Security and Cooperation in Europe (CSCE) establishing the human rights norms, but also enabled transnational contacts between dissident groups and Western human rights networks to be established in the first place (see also Chilton 1995; Evangelista 1998). In this case, then, international conditions, in particularly the US–Soviet relationship, but also the European détente led by the Federal Republic of Germany, served to open up the previously closed Communist societies.

Our case studies, thus, seem to confirm our observation that transnational actors are more likely to influence state behavior, the better their access to the domestic societies of the affected state (Risse-Kappen 1995). However, this is not to say that we view domestic social structures as more causally consequential in explaining human rights change than are international networks and their associated socialization processes. Indeed, the degree of societal "openness" in any particular case needs to be viewed at least partly as the product of international and transnational forces. In other words, "openness" has to be viewed as partly *cause* and partly *effect* of human rights networks.

"World time" and the increasing strength of international regimes and advocacy coalitions

Finally, there are probably additional factors that can help explain variation across our cases despite striking similarities with regard to the socialization process itself. We suspect that the growing robustness of the human rights regime itself in combination with the increasing strength of transnational advocacy coalitions (see Keck and Sikkink 1998) may have led to a process of "deepening," similar in some ways to that found in the process of global democratization.

Our "spiral model" treats the existence of global human rights norms and transnational advocacy networks as a given, as a constant rather than a variable. However, as Steve Ropp and Kathryn Sikkink point out in chapter 6, the international and regional normative context was much weaker in the 1970s than in the 1990s. Norm robustness and specificity, both preconditions for norm effectiveness (Checkel 1997b; Legro 1997) increased gradually in Latin America and elsewhere over time. The same holds true for the strength of the transnational advocacy coalitions in the human rights area as well as their ability to mobilize quickly (Keck and Sikkink 1998; Smith, Chatfield, and Pagnucco 1997; Smith, Pagnucco, and Lopez 1998). This mobilization potential has, of course, been affected enormously by the recent revolution in information technologies, from the fax to the internet.

Moreover, international norm robustness and transnational network strength have themselves been affected by developments in some of our country case studies. The human rights violations by the apartheid

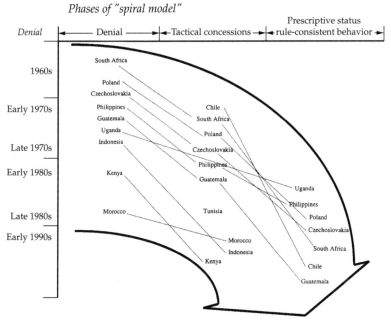

Figure 8.2 "World time and norms cascade"

regime in South Africa during the 1960s and 1970s contributed quite substantially to changes and to the increasing specificity of international human rights norms (Klotz 1995) and, in parallel, to the emergence of transnational advocacy networks. The same holds true for Pinochet's military dictatorship in Chile which led to one of the first truly global mobilization campaigns of human rights networks. A similar case is the Greek military junta whose human rights violations led to one of the first anti-torture campaigns by Amnesty International and, subsequently, to the Anti-Torture Convention (for evidence see Schmitz 1997). In other words, international norms and transnational advocacy networks had to be created first, rather than simply invoked or mobilized in some of our cases, as a result of which it took much longer for these countries to move through the phases of the "spiral model."

Figure 8.2 reveals two striking developments during the past several decades which might be ascribed to the "world time" phenomenon. First, norm denial only occurred in two of our eleven cases (Kenya and Morocco) during the 1980s, and this number decreased to zero during the 1990s. By the late 1990s, even the People's Republic of China no longer denies the validity of international human rights norms, although it continues to violate them in practice. We suggest that human rights norms have reached consensual ("prescriptive") status on the international level by now. Moreover, the international community also appears to agree today that the principle of national sovereignty can no longer be invoked to fight off accusations of severe human rights violations. As a result, norm denial might no longer be a viable option for norm violating regimes in their argumentative battles with the transnational networks.

Figure 8.2 also reveals a gradual narrowing of the time span covered by individual phases of our "spiral model," a narrowing that is expressed through the progressively diminishing width of the arrow. The "denial phase" for our eleven cases lasted at least three decades (from the 1960s through the 1980s). By comparison, figure 8.2 shows that the subsequent "tactical concessions" phase covered roughly two decades during the 1970s and 1980s. The collective "prescriptive status" and "rule-consistent behavior" phases are even shorter, lasting roughly a decade and a half from the mid-1980s until the late 1990s. In other words, there appears to have been a progressively more pronounced "compression" of these socialization processes over time.

Of course, one explanation of this phenomenon might simply be unintended biases built into our case selection. However, the growing temporal "compression" of our phases does correlate with the growing robustness of international human rights norms and increasing strength of transnational advocacy networks. If our figure 8.2 accurately reflects larger global realities, we are seeing here in our eleven cases what Martha Finnemore and Kathryn Sikkink have called an international "norms cascade" (Finnemore and Sikkink 1998). They argue that international norms undergo a "life cycle" which starts with principled ideas pushed forward by (transnational) actors. The more these principled ideas become norms in the sense of being less contested and increasingly shared, the more international actors and states sign up to them. A "norms cascade" develops, at which point the international norm is no longer disputed, but has reached prescriptive status. Thus, while the intent of our book is not to explain the evolution of international normative structures, our case studies seem to collectively suggest their growing domestic impact (see, for example, Boli and Thomas 1997; Mayer *et al.* 1997).

In sum, while we do not have a sufficient amount of aggregate data to support such a conclusion, we suspect that there are factors at work, including an increasingly robust global human rights regime, that can be used to explain some of the variation with regard to both the pace at which various individual states proceed along the human rights path toward prescriptive status, and the overall pace at which some states collectively internalize human rights norms.

Alternative explanations: Great Power politics and theories of modernization

Our rather complicated "spiral model," which incorporates five phases of transition toward rule-consistent behavior, four levels of interactions, and three different modes of social interaction, needs to be evaluated against two alternative explanations which are based on only one decisive variable each (see the introductory chapter by Thomas Risse and Kathryn Sikkink).

The first account is taken from international relations theories, in particular (neo-)realism (Gilpin 1981; Morgenthau 1948; K. Waltz 1979; Krasner 1995a, 1995b). This explanation emphasizes much more strongly than assumed in our "spiral model" the involvement of great powers in processes of human rights change. In the cases of the Philippines and South Africa, US pressure was significant in the final stages of moving the country from tactical concessions to prescriptive status by way of regime change. US power also insured that the transition process took place peacefully through negotiations. In the cases of Poland and Czechoslovakia, the story must include the dramatic turnaround of Soviet foreign policy under Mikhail Gorbachev culminating in the "Sinatra" rather than the Brezhnev doctrine ("I did it my way!"). The transition to democracy in both countries was only possible when Soviet tanks were no longer available to back the Communist governments.

Mobilization and expansion of the human rights network in Kenya during the late 1980s and early 1990s took place during a period when the German and US ambassadors gave more support to the political opposition. The US Congress became increasingly concerned about human rights developments in Kenya and aid resources were shifted from the public to the private sector. In a similar way, foreign-aid donor pressure helped move Indonesia from denial to tactical concessions (see chapters 2 and 5). As to Eastern Europe, the signing of the Helsinki Final Act's human rights provisions was a concession to the West by the Soviet Union and its allies.

While our case studies demonstrate that Great Power pressure is frequently supportive and enabling of domestic human rights change, they also demonstrate that it is seldom crucial in this regard. There was not much Great Power pressure in the cases of Uganda, Morocco, and Guatemala, which all moved considerably toward human rights improvements. Moreover, Western Great Powers rarely pursue consistent human rights policies and sustain them over time. In the cases of Guatemala and Chile, for example, there was a dramatic shift from the human rights endorsing policies of the Carter administration to the Reagan administration which looked the other way and confirmed its alliance with the two states, at least initially. In the Guatemalan and Chilean cases, US policies changed once again during the Bush administration.

Most importantly, our case studies confirm that Great Power pressure toward compliance with human rights norms was almost always the result of shaming and lobbying activities by the transnational advocacy networks. In the case of South Africa, for example, it was the transnational anti-apartheid movement which worked for years to persuade Western states, the US and Great Britain in particular, to institute the sanctions regime (see chapter 3; also Klotz 1995). As Anja Jetschke argues in chapter 5, the Reagan administration was deeply split over policies toward the Philippines during the early 1980s. It only backed the opposition against Marcos when Washington concluded that this was the only way to preserve its strategic alliance with that country. In this case, then, "people power" moved the US government, which subsequently aided in toppling the dictator. We find a similar presence of network activities behind the coordination of foreign aid donors in pressuring Kenya and Indonesia toward norm compliance during the early 1990s.

In Eastern Europe, the turnaround of Soviet foreign policy as an enabling condition for the peaceful revolutions of 1989 resulted at least partly from the fact that the Gorbachev leadership was itself heavily influenced by Western liberal ideas spread through transnational actors and coalitions (Checkel 1997a; Evangelista 1998; Herman 1996; Risse-Kappen 1994). Moreover, Gorbachev's move only provided an enabling condition for the change; the peaceful transformation itself was brought about by the dissident groups in Poland and Czechoslovakia with the transnational human rights networks empowering and strengthening their claims.

In sum then, what looks like a "realist" account at first quickly turns into a "liberal" explanation once we no longer treat states as unitary actors and endogenize their preferences (for an attempt to synthesize liberal theories of international relations see Moravcsik 1997). Our empirical case studies provide ample evidence to suggest that great powers and their resources are only used to promote international human rights norms to the extent that shaming and lobbying activities of transnational advocacy networks are successful (see also Keck and Sikkink). As shown above, Great Power pressure in the human rights area varies, and this variation results from differing degrees of network strengths and activities. In other words, human rights policies of the US or the European Union members can be easily integrated into our "spiral model" which consists of several transnational–international "boomerang throws" (see the introductory chapter by Thomas Risse and Kathryn Sikkink).

The second alternative account to our model of human rights change stresses the primacy of the domestic domain. This account argues essentially that economic growth will be largely determinative of positive or negative outcomes with regard to socio-political changes such as democratization and human rights. As we suggested in the introduction, this particular variant of modernization theory has difficulty explaining why many of the most developed states in the Third World with the largest middle classes (e.g. Argentina) had some of the most brutal dictatorships and worst human rights records during the 1960s and 1970s.

Moreover, our own empirical findings hardly support the view that there is a direct correlation between economic growth and improvement with regard to human rights. With the possible exception of Guatemala, none of our seven "success stories" fits the argument and, if anything, the opposite argument might be made. The regime changes leading to prescriptive status and rule-consistent behavior in the Philippines, Poland, Czechoslovakia, South Africa, and Chile, were all preceded by severe economic crises rather than by periods of growth. In the case of South Africa, this economic crisis was partly brought about by the international sanctions that resulted from the efforts of the transnational human rights networks and the domestic opposition. In addition, our two most problematic countries which did not move very much along the path of the "spiral model" – Kenya and Tunisia – have all experienced sustained periods of economic growth.

Based on our empirical findings then, one could even reverse the causality between political liberalization and positive human rights change, on the one hand, and economic development, on the other. Except for South Africa and Guatemala, the remaining five successful cases – the Philippines, Uganda, Poland, Czechoslovakia, and Chile – all experienced high economic growth rates *after* a political regime change and after they had largely institutionalized human rights reforms. In sum, our empirical findings support the most recent quantitative studies establishing that the link between domestic socio-political change and economic growth is much weaker than previously assumed (Hadenius 1992; Przeworski and Limongi 1997; Arat 1991; see also Rueschemeyer, Huber Stephens, and Stephens 1992).

In the final analysis, both of these alternative explanations (international realism and modernization theory) fail to fully explain human rights change in our cases for much the same reason. What is missing in both is a sense of the independent causal importance of international principled ideas and norms. Realism ignores international norms as constitutive of changing "material interests" of powerful states. Modernization theories, stressing the role of domestic middle classes, ignore international norms as constitutive of changing "material interests" of these classes within a larger society of civilized nations. Thus, these two alternative explanations exhibit the same basic flaw at two different levels of analysis.

The contribution of our findings to debates in international relations and comparative politics

Our empirical findings contribute to at least two larger scholarly debates in international relations and comparative politics. First, our case studies add to the growing literature on the domestic impact of international norms as a general phenomenon of theoretical and empirical interest. Second, we also contribute to the debate concerning how one best explains certain specific kinds of domestic socio-political change, such as those related to processes of democratization, identity politics, economic liberalization, and environmentalism.

The domestic impact of international norms

Scholarship on the domestic effects of international norms originated from two theoretical departures in recent years. First, rationalist regime analysis and neoliberal institutionalism became increasingly interested in exploring the implementation of and compliance with regime norms

270

and rules (overview in Hasenclever, Mayer, and Rittberger 1997). Empirical work on these matters has grown considerably, particularly with regard to international environmental regimes (see, for example, Young 1997; Schreurs and Economy 1997; for security policy see Müller 1993). Second, the new constructivist literature in international relations has increasingly taken up the challenge to develop an empirical research program (see Keohane 1989) and, in particular, to identify the precise causal mechanisms by which principled ideas and norms influence the identities, preferences, and ultimately the behavior of actors (Checkel 1998; Yee 1996). Research in this area concentrates increasingly on the domestic impact of international norms (see Checkel 1997b; Cortell and Davis 1996; Finnemore 1996a; Finnemore and Sikkink 1998; Katzenstein 1996a, b; Klotz 1995; Ulbert 1997a, b; Thomas forthcoming).

This book contributes to both literatures. As to work on international regimes, we have developed a socialization model to explain the conditions under which domestic actors internalize the rules and norms emanating from international human rights regimes. While Martha Finnemore has argued that international (governmental) organizations might serve as "teachers" of norms (Finnemore 1993), we also focus on non-state actors and transnational networks. Transnational advocacy networks fulfill two tasks in this respect. They remind Western states of their own collective identities as liberal democracies and urge them to act upon these identities in the human rights area. And they also teach human rights norms to norm-violating governments. More broadly, the "spiral model" specifies and details causal mechanisms through which international norms are transmitted into the domestic arena and ultimately lead to domestic institutional change. In other words, our contribution moves beyond merely correlational arguments about norm compliance in the human rights area that simply take note of the "convergence" of international norms and improved domestic human rights behavior (see, for example, Poe and Tate 1994; Poe, Tate, and Camp Keith 1997).

As to the debates within the constructivist literature, there seems to be increasing convergence around the following proposition (see, for example, Checkel 1997b; Cortell and Davis 1996; Ulbert 1997b): international norms are more likely to be implemented and complied with in the domestic context, if they resonate or fit with existing collective understandings embedded in domestic institutions and political cultures. The theoretical background of this argument can be found in sociological institutionalism which argued that institutions tend to

271

converge through isomorphic adaptation (Powell and DiMaggio 1991; Jepperson 1991; Finnemore 1996b).

On the one hand, our empirical findings tend to confirm the "resonance" proposition. The more open a society and culture to Western ideas and the more a country had a liberal past which included the recognition of human rights, the less likely it was that norm-violating governments would deny the validity of the international norms (Chile, Tunisia) and the faster the country moved through the stages of our "spiral model" (the Philippines and Morocco versus Kenya, Indonesia). But on the other hand, our argument goes further than just claiming "norm resonance." The "spiral model" and the eleven cases investigated in this book start with situations of utmost norm violation. Most repressive governments in our cases were not only not complying with international legal norms, but were actually denying the validity of these norms themselves. In many cases, they had not even signed or ratified the respective international agreements. In other words, a severe "misfit" between the international norm and the domestic institutional setting is the starting point of our socialization model.

Moreover, in the beginning of the socialization process, norm-violating governments did not really perceive any pressure to comply with the norms. Rather, it was the task of the transnational advocacy network to create such adaptational pressure in the first place. Only in later stages of the "spiral model" do the international human rights norms start resonating with domestic audiences. This is the case if the transnational coalition succeeds in keeping the norm-violating government on the international agenda and if domestic opposition becomes fully mobilized during the tactical concessions phase. In sum, our model incorporates the recent findings about "norm resonance" as a precondition for norm institutionalization and implementation. But it also theorizes more comprehensively the stages through which a "fit" between international norms and domestic understandings and institutions can eventually be achieved.

We also contribute to the larger general theoretical debate in international relations between rational choice and constructivist approaches (see, for example, Checkel 1998; Finnemore and Sikkink 1998; Adler 1997). Our socialization model attempts to incorporate insights from each camp into one causal argument about the domestic impact of international norms. We have identified three modes of social action and included them in the various stages of the "spiral model." During the early phases of denial and tactical concessions, the logic of action largely resembles instrumental and strategic reasoning of actors. Norm-violating governments tactically adjust to the new international discourse in order to stay in power, receive foreign aid, and the like. This process can be easily modeled by rational-choice approaches. Later on, however, we find that a different logic of interaction incrementally takes over and at least supplements strategic behavior. This logic emphasizes communicative rationality, argumentation, and persuasion, on the one hand, and norm institutionalization and habitualization, on the other. We feel that social constructivism, which endogenizes identities and interests of actors, can accommodate this logic more easily, in conjunction with sociological institutionalism (on the various institutionalisms see Hall and Taylor 1996).

We thus view our main contribution to the general literature on the domestic impact of international norms as being our attempt to integrate rational choice and constructivist approaches by building on the respective strengths of each. In particular, the "spiral model" tries to specify the transition points between the logic of instrumental rationality and strategic behavior, on the one hand, and of argumentative rationality, moral discourse, and the like, on the other.

Domestic socio-political processes

Our book reminds scholars in comparative politics once again that they have an increasingly hard time to explain domestic change if they leave out the international dimension. Beyond this general contribution, we believe that our "spiral model" might possibly help explain domestic socio-political change processes, where such change involves norms other than human rights. The model should be applicable under any conditions where (1) a given state is adhering to a particular set of public norms that have become embedded in its laws, institutions, and policies; *and* (2) these state norms are increasingly being challenged by a contradictory set of international norms promoted by emerging transnational issue networks. Two such processes to which our model might be applied are *democratization* and *identity politics*. In each of these cases of socio-political change, states that long adhered to certain domestically dominant (and often internationally or regionally reinforced) norms, have seen these norms increasingly challenged.

Take, for example, processes of democratization. There are, of course, many different aspects of these processes, but one of the most fundamental is the question of how states regard and discursively represent

273

their relationship to their people. Historically, "authoritarian" represen-tations have evoked factors such as higher religious authority, national-ism, and (more recently) bureaucratic rationality and economic effi-ciency (Huntington 1991). Our "spiral model" might help those studying processes of democratization to better specify the transition points at which such authoritarian discursive representations of the state and state–society relations are increasingly challenged by interna-tional norms stressing the procedural aspects of democratic governance.

Democratization would, thus, be at least partially represented as a discursive process of transnational socialization in which authoritarian regimes at first deny the legitimacy of democratic norms, later make tactical concessions, and finally move toward the institutionalization of prescriptive status. To be sure, those studying global processes of democratization have long noted so-called international "demonstra-tion effects" or "snowballing." But the precise mechanisms and transi-tion points through which these global processes alter domestic prac-tice are seldom discussed in much detail. Moreover, the analysis of global impacts on domestic processes tends to be state-centered, and inferences concerning the probable existence of socialization processes are often simply based upon supportive aggregate data (for example, Huntington 1991).

Identity politics provides a second example of a field of study where our "spiral model" may have some potential applicability. In the case of democratization, the issue is the way in which states discursively represent their political relationship to their own people. With identity politics, the issue is which "people" (or peoples) states will decide to base their sense of identity upon. Does the state represent itself as embodying a single common people (a unitary cultural representation) or does it adopt a pluralistic identity (multi-culturalism)? Does it make claims to be the embodiment of a particular transnational class (as in the case of classical Marxist states), a particular religious group (Islamic states), and so forth. Whenever a state makes a discursive claim to a particular identity, and that identity is being challenged by groups making different identity claims from within or without, we ought to be able to apply our "spiral model" (Duara 1996; Dagnino 1998).

For example, our phase model might be of some help to those studying the new identity politics in regions of the world such as Latin America. There, indigenous groups are increasingly challenging the state's "monopoly of representation" and its historical willingness to identify the state either as Hispanic or as representing some unitary "cosmic race" (see Brysk forthcoming). As unitary state identities are increasingly challenged by the emerging norms of multi-culturalism associated with new transnational networks, this process might be studied as one in which states progress from denial that they have an "identity problem," through tactical concessions, and to eventual prescriptive recognition of new multi-cultural identity norms.

There are no doubt other phenomena involving the impact of international norms on domestic processes to which our "spiral model" might equally well be applied. States adhere to various norms regarding the best strategies (models) for improving the collective economic condition of their peoples (communism, state capitalism, neo-liberal capitalism, etc.). They similarly adhere to such norms with regard to the extent of their obligations to protect their people from hazards in their physical surroundings (environmentalism). These and similar socio-political processes that involve norm contestation at several levels of analysis might also benefit from application of our more highly specified model of the relationship between international norms and domestic change.

In conclusion: ten lessons for human rights practitioners

For practitioners in any field, theoretical models are often viewed with considerable skepticism. However, our "spiral model" has important practical implications that allow for more effective use of the time and resources of transnational human rights networks as well as of Western governments and international organizations:

1. Our first lesson reiterates the main point of this book: transnational human rights pressures and policies, including the activities of advocacy networks, have made a very significant difference in bringing about improvements in human rights practices in diverse countries around the world. Without the international human rights regimes and norms as well as the transnational networks that worked to make these norms meaningful, we believe that the human rights changes documented in this book would not have occurred.

2. However, we also need to be aware of the limits of external influence on human rights developments in any given "target state." While our findings stress that transnational network pressure constitutes a necessary condition for domestic change in the human rights area, it is by no means sufficient. During the "tactical concessions"

phase of our spiral model, internal developments in the "target state," in particular the mobilization of domestic societal opposition around human rights norms, become more and more significant for inducing change. Sustainable change in the human rights area can only be expected, once pressure is exerted on norm-violating governments "from above" *and* "from below."

3. This implies that the current efforts of external actors to directly help strengthen and support the domestic opposition and civil society are crucial for human rights progress to be made. However, our findings also suggest that the *indirect* effects of external pressure placed upon norm violating government can play just as important a role in strengthening the domestic opposition. Pushing governments toward making tactical concessions almost always opens up political and discursive space in the society of the "target state" during early phases of the change process.

4. External actors need to be aware that different modes of socialization are at work during different phases of the "spiral model." Blaming and shaming strategies tend to be particularly effective during the repression and denial phase. But note the caveat above: there are various points in the socialization process when instrumental rationality and the bargaining mode prevail in the interactions between norm-violating governments and their critics. Strategies stressing instrumental rationality and bargaining are also useful during later stages of the socialization process, particularly when the rulers of the "target state" revert to repressive practices. However, the further along the socialization path the process has moved, the more strategies stressing argumentation and persuasion should be used.

5. Words matter! They can even hurt, as Ernst Haas pointed out some fifteen years ago (Haas 1983). Words matter, even if they are only rhetoric. A central finding of our research suggests that involving and entangling norm violating governments in an argumentative process which then becomes self-sustained, constitutes an extremely powerful socializing tool, particularly during the "tactical concessions" phase. It might seem hopelessly naïve to attempt to "talk governments out" of human rights violations, and talk is certainly not sufficient. But transnational human rights advocacy groups should be aware that arguments are among their most powerful socializing tools.

6. The empirical evidence in this book suggests that the INGOs have been correct in placing great importance on adherence to international law. A necessary condition for sustained rule consistent behavior in the

human rights area is attainment of "prescriptive status" for the international norms, which in turn implies the signing and ratification of the relevant international human rights conventions including the optional protocols. This has been proven to be the first step toward institutionalization of human rights provisions into domestic law in most of our cases. And the rule of law is a crucial precondition for sustained human rights change and for habitualized practices. But prescriptive status is inadequate in and of itself, and domestic and international human rights pressures need to be applied in many cases even after prescriptive status is achieved in order to assure that countries move beyond prescriptive status toward rule-consistent behavior.

7. This latter point concerning the rule of law has important implications that run counter to some of the implicit anti-statist orientations of many advocacy networks. While our findings point to transnational advocacy networks as the primary instigators of human rights change, states still play a fundamentally important role. Pressure by Western states and international organizations can greatly increase the vulnerability of norm-violating governments to external influences. More important though, the erosion or disintegration of state authority in many Third World countries – both in Africa and Latin America – was often responsible for severe human rights violations through attendant violence and/or civil war. Instituting the rule of law as a precondition for rule consistent and norm abiding behavior requires effective state authority including the domestic monopoly over the use of force. Human rights campaigns should be about transforming the state, not weakening or even abolishing it.

8. Our empirical findings point to two lessons for Western governments. First, one of the most serious problems our research revealed with regard to Western efforts to promote human rights change was that these governments rarely employ consistent human rights policies toward a given state over a long enough period of time. We do not want to suggest that human rights concerns should *always* override other economic or strategic goals in Western foreign policies. But there should be clear recognition in policy making circles that a reemphasis on economic or strategic goals after a period when human rights have been emphasized frequently created conditions where norm-violating governments were "let off the hook."

9. The other lesson for Western governments concerns the use of economic and other material sanctions against norm violators. Our findings indicate that sanctions can be crucial during certain phases of

the "spiral model," particularly in moving the norm violators from the "denial stage" toward tactical concessions. But such sanctions can be quite counterproductive during other phases. For example, if a repressive government is still sufficiently in control of its domestic environment to orchestrate a nationalist backlash movement, or a particular society is already open enough to allow for effective domestic network socialization, material sanctions can do great harm. In sum, our study suggests that it is important for Western governments to remember that sanctions should always be crafted with an eye toward both the phase of our "spiral model" during which sanctions are being implemented, and the predominant mode of socialization operating at the time.

10. This leads to our last point concerning the use of "constructive engagement" toward norm-violating states. Our data suggest that constructive engagement might indeed work, but only at the later stages of the spiral model when communicative and argumentative processes constitute the main dynamic. To use constructive engagement at the early stages of the process when a norm-violating government is working in a purely strategic and instrumental mode will almost always be taken for weakness and indecisiveness. Moreover, constructive engagement will only work at later stages of the socialization process when it communicates a consistent and enduring Western human rights policy.

List of references

Adam, Heribert, and Kogila Moodley. 1993. *The Negotiated Revolution: Society and Politics in Post-Apartheid South Africa.* Johannesburg: Jonathan Ball Publishers

Aditjondro, George J. 1997. *Challenges and Prospects of the Indonesian Pro-East Timor Movement.* Newcastle: unpublished manuscript

Adler, Emanuel. 1987. *The Power of Ideology: The Quest for Technological Autonomy in Argentina and Brazil.* Berkeley, CA: University of California Press

1991. Cognitive Evolution: A Dynamic Approach for the Study of International Relations and their Progress. In *Progress in Postwar International Relations,* edited by E. Adler. New York: Columbia University Press, 43–87

1997. Seizing the Middle Ground: Constructivism in World Politics. *European Journal of International Relations* 3 (3): 319–363

Africa Watch/Human Rights Watch. 1991. *Kenya Taking Liberties.* New York

1993. *State-Sponsored Ethnic Violence in Kenya.* New York

African Rights. 1996. *Kenya Shadow Justice.* London

Ahluwalia, Davinder Pal Singh, and Jeffrey S. Steeves. 1986. Political Power, Political Opposition, and State Coercion: The Kenyan Case. In *The Political Economy of Crime,* edited by Brian D. MacLean. Scarborough: Prentice-Hall, 93–105

Alaoui, Hicham Ben Abdallah. 1996. La Monarchie Marocaine Tentée par la Réforme, *Le Monde Diplomatique* 6 (September)

Albright, Madeleine K., and Alfred Friendly, Jr. 1986. Helsinki and Human Rights. In *The President, the Congress and Foreign Policy,* edited by E. Muskie *et al.* Lanham, MD: University Press of America, 285–310

Al-Sayyid, Mustafa Kamel. 1995. The Concept of Civil Society and the Arab World. In *Political Liberalization and Democratization in the Arab World,* edited by Rex Brynen, Baghat Korany, and Paul Noble. Vol. I. Boulder, CO: Lynne Rienner Publishers, 131–147

Alston, Philip, ed. 1992. *The United Nations and Human Rights. A Critical Appraisal.* Oxford: Clarendon Press

List of references

American Convention on Human Rights, November 22, 1969. OAS Treaty Series No. 36, at 1, OEA/Ser. L./V/II.23 doc. rev. 2

Americas Watch. 1985. *With Friends Like These: The Americas Watch Report on Human Rights and U.S. Policy in Latin America,* edited by Cynthia Brown. New York: Pantheon

1988. *Chile: Human Rights and the Plebiscite.* New York: Americas Watch

1989. *Persecuting Human Rights Monitors: The CERJ in Guatemala.* New York: Americas Watch

1991. *Human Rights and the Politics of Agreements: Chile During President Aylwin's First Year.* New York: Americas Watch

Amisi, Bertha Kadenyi. 1997. *A Crisis in the Making: Conflict in the Rift Valley and Western Kenya.* Notre Dame: University of Notre Dame

Amnesty International. 1975. *Report of an Amnesty International Mission to the Philippines 1975.* London: Amnesty International

1976. *Jahresbericht 1975/76.* Bonn: Amnesty International

1977a. *Philippinen – Stellungnahmen zum Bericht einer Mission November/Dezember 1975.* Bonn

1977b. *Tunesien im Zwielicht oder Politische Verfolgung in Tunesien.* Bonn

1978a. *Amnesty International Report.* London

1978b. *Human Rights in Uganda.* London

1979. *Jahresbericht 1978.* Baden-Baden: Nomos

1981. *Guatemala: A Government Program of Murder.* London: Amnesty International

1982. *Report of an Amnesty International Mission to the Republic of the Philippines.* London: Amnesty International

1983. *Jahresbericht 1982.* Frankfurt am Main: Fischer Verlag

1984. *Jahresbericht 1983.* Frankfurt am Main: Fischer Verlag

1985a. *Jahresbericht 1984.* Frankfurt am Main: Fischer Verlag

1985b. *Uganda. Six Years After Amin, Torture, Killings, Disappearances.* London

1987a. *Jahresbericht 1986.* Frankfurt am Main: Fischer Verlag

1987b. *Kenya. Torture, Political Detentions and Unfair Trials.* London

1988a. *Jahresbericht 1987.* Frankfurt am Main: Fischer Verlag

1988b. *Philippines: Unlawful Killings by Military and Paramilitary Forces.* London

1988c. *Philippines: Incommunicado Detention, Ill-treatment and Torture during 1988.* London

1988d. *Philippines: The Killing and Intimidation of Human Rights Lawyers.* London

1989. *Uganda. The Human Rights Record 1986–1989.* London

1990a. *Morocco: "Disappearances" of People of Western Saharan Origin, A Summary of Amnesty International's Concerns: Submission to the United Nations Human Rights Committee.* New York

1990b. Morocco: *Human Rights Violations in Garde à Vue Detention.* New York

1990c. *Menschenrechtsverletzungen in garde-à-vue-Haft in Marokko.* Cologne

1990d. *Uganda. Death in the Countryside. Killings of Civilians by the Army in 1990.* London

1991a. *Le Livre Blanc sur le Droits de l'Homme au Maroc, Etudes et Documentation Internationales: Ligue des Droits de l'Homme.* Paris

1991b. *Maroc – Torture, "Disparitions," Emprisonnement politique.* Paris

1991c. *Morocco: A Pattern of Political Imprisonment "Disappearances" and Torture.* London

1991d. *Morocco: Amnesty International Briefing.* New York

1991e. *Morocco: Amnesty International's Concerns February–June 1991.* New York

1991f. *Uganda. Human Rights Violations by the National Resistance Army.* London

1992a. *Tunisia: Prolonged Incommunicado Detention and Torture.* New York

1992b. *Uganda. Der Alptraum ist noch nicht zu Ende.* Bonn

1992c. *Philippines. The Killing Goes On.* London

1993a. *Morocco: Breaking the Wall of Silence: The "Disappeared" in Morocco.* New York

1993b. *Tunisia: Women Victims of Harassment, Torture and Imprisonment.* New York

1994a. *Marokko. Opposition hinter Gittern. Die Verfolgung Politisch Andersdenkender als System.* Bonn

1994b. Morocco: The "Disappeared" Reappear. In *"Disappearances" and Political Killings, Human Rights Crisis of the 1990s, A Manual for Action,* edited by Amnesty International. Amsterdam, 68–83

1994c. *Tunisia, Rhetoric vs. Reality: The Failure of a Human Rights Bureaucracy.* New York

1994d. *Uganda. Detentions of Suspected Government Opponents without Charge or Trial in the North.* London

1994e. *Annual Report, 1994.* London

1995. *Kenya, Tanzania, Uganda, Zambia and Zimbabwe. Attacks on Human Rights through the Misuse of Criminal Charges.* London

1997a. *"Breaking God's Commands": The Destruction of Childhood by the Lord's Resistance Army.* London

1997b. *Jahresbericht 1997.* Frankfurt am Main: Fischer Verlag

1997c. *Kenya. Violations of Human Rights. Communications between Amnesty International and the Government of Kenya.* London

1997d. *Tunisia, A Widening Circle of Repression.* New York

Anderson, Benedict. 1988. Cacique Democracy in the Philippines: Origins and Dreams. *New Left Review* 169, May/June: 3–33

Andreassen, Bård-Anders. 1993. Kenya. In *Human Rights in Developing Countries 1993,* edited by B.-A. Andreassen and T. Swinehart. Oslo: Nordic Human Rights Publications, 180–233

Anglin, Douglas. 1990. Ripe, Ripening or Overripe? Sanctions as an Inducement to Negotiations: The South African Case. *International Journal* 45 (2): 360–385

Ankumah, Evelyn A. 1996. *The African Commission on Human and Peoples' Rights. Practice and Procedures.* The Hague: Martinus Nijhoff Publishers

List of references

Anonymous. 1975. Joint Publications Research Service, Translations on Eastern Europe 64128 (19 February): 8–18. Original text in Czech, in *Listy* (Rome), December 1974

1987. Arrest and Detention in Kenya. *Index on Censorship* 16 (1): 23–28

Antikainen-Kokko, Annamari. 1996. *Cooptive Power in an International Organization: The Case of Japan–ASEAN Dialogue 1974–1992.* Turku, Finland: Turun Yliopisto Turku

Arat, Zehra F. 1991. *Democracy and Human Rights in Developing Countries.* Boulder, CO: Lynne Rienner Publishers

Arbatov, Georgi A., and William Oltmans. 1983. *Cold War or Détente? The Soviet Viewpoint.* London: Zed Books, 1983

Archbishopric of Guatemala, Office of Human Rights. 1988. *Guatemala: Nunca Más: Informe Proyecto Interdiocesano de Recuperación de la Memoria Histórica.* 4 vols. Guatemala City: ODHAG

Arévalo de Leon, Bernardo. 1997. Sociedad y ejército en Guatemala: Elementos para Una Nueva Relación. Paper presented at a seminar on Society and Armed Forces in Central America, organized by FLACSO, Guatemala City, 22 to 24 September

Article 19. 1995. *Censorship in Kenya. Government Critics Face the Death Sentence.* London

Ash, Timothy Garton. 1983. *The Polish Revolution: Solidarity.* New York: Vintage Books

1990. *The Magic Lantern: The Revolution of '89 Witnessed in Warsaw, Budapest, Berlin and Prague.* New York: Vintage Books

Asia Watch. 1989. *Human Rights in Indonesia and East-Timor, Asia Watch Report.* New York: Asia Watch

Associated Press. 1998. U.S. Urges Indonesia to Determine Fate of Missing Activists. *Dow Jones Newswires*, April 17

Association of Polish Students and Graduates in Exile. 1979. *Dissent in Poland: Reports and Documents in Translation*, December 1975–July 1977. London

Baehr, Peter R. 1997. Problems of Aid Conditionality: The Netherlands and Indonesia. *Third World Quarterly* 18 (2): 363–376

Baehr, Peter, Hilde Selbervik, and Arne Tostensen. 1995. Responses to Human Rights Criticism: Kenya–Norway and Indonesia–The Netherlands. In *Human Rights in Developing Countries Yearbook 1995*, edited by P. Baehr, H. Hey, J. Smith, and T. Swinehart. The Hague/Oslo: Kluwer International Publisher/Nordic Human Rights Publications, 57–87

Bakarat, Halim. 1993. *The Arab World. Society, Culture and State.* Berkeley: University of California Press

Barber, James, and John Barratt. 1990. *South Africa's Foreign Policy: The Search for Status and Security, 1945–88.* Cambridge: Cambridge University Press

Barkan, Joel D. 1992. The Rise and Fall of the Governance Realm in Kenya. In *Governance and Politics in Africa*, edited by G. Hyden and M. Bratton. Boulder, CO: Lynne Rienner Publishers, 167–192

Barnes, James, Marshall Carter, and Max Skidmore. 1980. *The World of Politics.*

New York: St. Martin's Press

Basri, Driss, Michel Rousset, and Georges Vedel. eds. 1994. *Le Maroc et les Droits de l'Homme: Positions, Réalisations et Perspectives.* Paris: L'Harmattan

Bello, Walden. 1984. The Pentagon and the Philippine Crisis. *Southeast Asia Chronicle* 95: 20–24

Bendourou, Omar. 1988. The Exercise of Political Freedoms in Morocco. *International Commission of Jurists* 40: 31–41

Bennani-Chraibi, Mounia, and Remy Leveau 1996. Maroc 1996: Institutions – Economie – Société, in *Acteurs et Espaces Politiques au Maroc et au Turquie,* edited by H. Borzaslan, M. Bennani-Chraîbi, and R. Leveau. Berlin: Wissenschaftzentrum, 47–104

Bensbia, Najib. 1996. *Pouvoir et Politique au Maroc. Du Rejet à l'Alternance.* Rabat: Editions Média Stratégie

Berg-Schlosser, Dirk, and Rainer Siegler. 1990. *Political Stability and Development. A Comparative Analysis of Kenya, Tanzania, and Uganda.* Boulder, CO: Lynne Rienner Publishers

Bertrand, Jacques. 1997. "Business as Usual" in Suharto's Indonesia. *Asian Survey* 37 (5) May: 441–451

Biersteker, Thomas J., and Cynthia Weber. eds. 1996. *State Sovereignty as Social Construct.* Cambridge: Cambridge University Press

Billah, M. M., and Abdul Hakim G. N. 1989. State Constraints on NGOs in Indonesia: Recent Developments. *Prisma (Jakarta)* 47: 57–66

Black, David. 1992. Australian, Canadian and Swedish Policies Toward Southern Africa: A Comparative Study of "Middle Power Internationalism." Unpublished PhD dissertation, Dalhousie University

1997. Echoes of Apartheid? Canada, Nigeria and the Politics of Norms. Paper presented to the workshop on "Human Rights, Ethics and Canadian International Security Policy." York University, November 21–22

Forthcoming. "Not Cricket": The Effects and Effectiveness of the Sport Boycott. In *How Sanctions Work: South Africa,* edited by N. Crawford and A. Klotz. Basingstoke, UK: Macmillan

Blin, Louis. 1991. Les Investissements Français au Maghreb. In *Europäische Unternehmenskooperation im Mittleren Osten und im Maghreb,* edited by G. Baugé and C. Ulig. Arbeitspapiere der Universität Bochum, 117–126

Boli, John, and George M. Thomas. 1997. World Culture in the World Polity. *American Sociological Review* 62: 171–190

eds. 1998. *World Polity Formation Since 1875.* Stanford, CA: Stanford University Press

Booth, John A., and Thomas W. Walker. *Understanding Central America.* Boulder, CO: Westview Press

Booysen, Susan. 1992. Changing Relations of Political Power in South Africa's Transition: The Politics of Conquering in Conditions of Stalemate. *Politikon* 19 (December)

Bowring, Philip. 1982. Playing a New Tune: Marcos Keeps Up with Changing Political Times. *Far Eastern Economic Review,* January 1, 10

List of references

Brachet-Márquez, Viviane. 1992. Explaining Socio-political Change in Latin America: The Case of Mexico. *Latin American Research Review* 27 (3): 91–122

Bras, Jean-Philippe. 1996. Tunisie: Ben Ali et sa classe moyenne. *Pôles*. April–June, 174–195

Bratton, Michael, and Nicolas van de Walle. 1997. *Democratic Experiments in Africa: Regime Transitions in Comparative Perspective*. Cambridge: Cambridge University Press

Brezhnev, Leonid. 1979. *Peace, Détente and Soviet–American Relations: A Collection of Public Statements*. New York: Harcourt, Brace, Jovanovich

Brown, Cynthia. ed. 1985. *With Friends Like These: The Americas Watch Report on Human Rights and U.S. Policy in Latin America*. New York: Pantheon Books

Brynen, Rex, Baghat Korany, and Paul Noble. eds. 1995a. *Political Liberalization and Democratization in the Arab World*. Vol. I. Boulder, CO: Lynne Rienner Publishers

1995b. Theoretical Perspectives on Arab Liberalization and Democratization, in Rex Brynen, Baghat Korany, and Paul Noble. eds. *Political Liberalization and Democatization in the Arab World*. Vol. I, Boulder, CO: Lynne Rienner Publishers, 3–27

Brysk, Alison. 1993. From Above and Below: Social Movements, the International System, and Human Rights in Argentina. *Comparative Political Studies* 26 (3): 259–285

Forthcoming. *From Tribal Village to Global Village: Indian Rights and International Relations in Latin America*. Stanford: Stanford University Press

Buergenthal, Thomas, *et al*. eds. 1986. *Protecting Human Rights in America: Selected Problems*. Strasbourg: N. P. Engel Publisher

Bull, Hedley. 1977. *The Anarchical Society. A Study of Order in World Politics*. New York: Columbia University Press

Burgerman, Susan. 1997. The Evolution of Compliance: The Human Rights Regime, Transnational Networks, and United Nations Peace-building. Draft PhD dissertation

Busuttil, James J., Robin L. Dahlberg, Sheldon Oliensis, and Sidney S. Rosdeitcher. 1991. Uganda at the Crossroads – A Report on Current Human Rights Conditions. *The Record of the Association of the Bar of the City of New York* 46 (6): 598–673

Bwengye, Francis A. W. 1985. *The Agony of Uganda. From Idi Amin to Obote*. London: Regency Press

Byrne, Hugh. 1997. *The First Nine Months of the Guatemalan Peace Process: High Expectations and Daunting Challenges*. Washington, DC: Washington Office on Latin America

Callies de Salies, Bruno. 1995. Tunisie: Politique Sécuritaire et Croissance Economique. *Les Cahiers de l'Orient: Revue d'Etude et de Réflexion sur le Liban et le Monde Arabe* 38: 77–97

Camau, Michel, and Abdelkefi Jellal. eds. 1987. *Tunisie au Présent: Une Modernité au-dessus de Tout Soupçon?* Centre National de la Recherche Scientifique. Paris: Editions du CNRS

Carim, Xavier, Audie Klotz, and Olivier Lebleu. Forthcoming. The Political Economy of Financial Sanctions. In *How Sanctions Work: South Africa*, edited by N. Crawford and A. Klotz. Basingstoke, UK: Macmillan

Casiple, Ramon. 1995. Questioning Human Rights. *The Human Rights Journal (Manila)* 1 (1): 82–100

1996. Fallacies Against Human Rights. *Pingkian* 1 (1): 9–29

Castellano Cambranes, Julio. 1984. Origins of the Crisis of the Established Order in Guatemala. In *Central America: Crisis and Adaptation*, edited by S. C. Ropp and J. A. Morris. Albuquerque, NM: University of New Mexico Press, 119–152

Centro de Estudios de Guatemala. 1994. *La Democracia de Armas: Gobiernos Civiles y Poder Militar*. Guatemala City: Nueva Imagen

Chaiken, Shelly, Wendy Wood, and Alice H. Eagly. 1996. Principles of Persuasion. In *Social Psychology: Handbook of Basic Principles*, edited by E. T. Higgins and A. Kruglanski. New York: Guilford Press, 702–742

Checkel, Jeffrey T. 1997a. *Ideas and International Political Change. Soviet/Russian Behavior and the End of the Cold War*. New Haven, CT: Yale University Press

1997b. International Norms and Domestic Politics: Bridging the Rationalist–Constructivist Divide. *European Journal of International Relations* 3 (4): 473–495

1998. The Constructivist Turn in International Relations Theory. *World Politics* 50 (2): 324–348

Chege, Michael. 1994. The Return of Multiparty Politics. In *Beyond Capitalism vs. Socialism in Kenya and Tanzania*, edited by J. D. Barkan. Boulder, CO: Lynne Rienner Publishers, 47–74

Chilton, Patricia. 1995. Mechanics of Change: Social Movements, Transnational Coalitions, and the Transformation Processes in Eastern Europe. In *Bringing Transnational Relations Back In*, edited by T. Risse-Kappen. Cambridge: Cambridge University Press, 189–226

Chua Beng Huat. 1993. Looking for Democratization in Post-Soeharto Indonesia. *Contemporary Southeast Asia* 15: 131–160

Clam, Jean-Josef. 1988. Frankreichs Maghreb-Politik. In *Nordafrika in der internationalen Politik*, edited by H. Hubel. Munich: Oldenbourg, 151–178

Claude, Richard Pierre. 1978. The Decline of Human Rights in the Republic of the Philippines: A Case Study. *New York Law School Law Review* 24 (1): 201–223

1996. *Educating for Human Rights: The Philippines and Beyond*. Quezon City: University of the Philippines Press

Clough, Michael. 1992. *Free at Last? US Policy toward Africa and the End of the Cold War*. New York: Council on Foreign Relations Press

Cohen, Stephen F., and Katrina Vanden Heuvel. eds. 1989. *Voices of Glasnost: Interviews with Gorbachev's Reformers*. New York: W. W. Norton

Collier, David. ed. 1979. *The New Authoritarianism in Latin America*. Princeton: Princeton University Press

List of references

Comisión Chilena de Derechosw Humanos. 1991. *Para Greer en Chile: Síntesis del Informe de la Comisión Verdad y Reconciliación.* Santiago

Comisión de Fortalecimiento de la Justicia. 1998. *Una Nueva Justicia Para La Paz: Resumen Ejecutivo.* Guatemala City: Magna Terra, April

Committee on Foreign Relations. 1978. *Uganda: The Human Rights Situation.* Hearings before the Subcommittee on Foreign Economic Policy of the Committee on Foreign Relations/US Congress, June 15, 21, 26, 1978. Washington, DC

Commonwealth Accord on Southern Africa, The. 1985. Adopted at Lyford Cay, Nassau, Bahamas, October 20

Commonwealth News Release. 1991. Commonwealth Committee of Foreign Ministers on Southern Africa, Special Session: London, February 16

Commonwealth Observer Mission to South Africa (COMSA). 1993. *Violence in South Africa.* London: Commonwealth Secretariat

Conference of European Churches. 1976. *The Conference on Security and Cooperation in Europe and the Churches.* Report of a Consultation at Buckow, G.D.R., October 27–31, 1975, Occasional Paper No. 7. Geneva

Constantino, Renato. 1978. *Neocolonial Identity and Counter-Consciousness: Essays on Cultural Decolonisation.* Edited with an Introduction by István Mészáros. London: Merlin Press

Correa Sutil, Jorge. 1997. No Victorious Army Has Ever Been Prosecuted: The Unsettled Story of Traditional Justice in Chile. In *Transitional Justice and the Rule of Law in New Democracies,* edited by A. J. McAdam. Notre Dame, IN: University of Notre Dame Press, 123–154

Corsino, MacArthur F. 1981. The Philippines in 1980 – At the Crossroads. In *Southeast Asian Affairs 1981,* edited by the Institute of Southeast Asian Studies. Singapore: Institute of Southeast Asian Studies, 235–257

Cortell, Andrew P., and James W. Jr. Davis. 1996. How Do International Institutions Matter? The Domestic Impact of International Rules and Norms. *International Studies Quarterly* 40: 451–478

Cox, Robert W. 1987. *Production, Power, and World Order.* New York: Columbia University Press

Crawford, Neta C. 1993. Decolonization as an International Norm: The Evolution of Practices, Arguments, and Beliefs. In *Emerging Norms of Justified Intervention,* edited by L. Reed and C. Kaysen. Cambridge, MA: American Academy of Arts and Sciences

Forthcoming. How Arms Embargoes Work. In *How Sanctions Work: South Africa,* edited by N. Crawford and A. Klotz. Basingstoke, UK: Macmillan

Crouch, Martin. 1989. *Revolution and Evolution: Gorbachev and Soviet Politics.* New York: Philip Allan

Dagnino, Evalina. 1998. Culture, Citizenship, and Democracy. In *Culture of Politics/Politics of Culture: Revisioning Latin American Social Movements,* edited by S. Alvarez, E. Dagnino, and A. Escobar. Boulder, CO: Westview Press, 33–63

Damis, John. 1992. Sources of Political Stability in Modernizing Regimes: Jordan and Morocco. In *Civilian Rule in the Developing World. Democracy on the March?*, edited by C. P. Danopoulos. Boulder, CO: Westview Press, 23–51

Davies, Rob, and Dan O'Meara. 1985. Total Strategy in Southern Africa: An Analysis of South African Regional Policy, *Journal of Southern African Studies* 11 (2): 254–269

Dawson, Richard E., and Kenneth Prewitt. 1969. *Political Socialization.* Boston: Little, Brown and Co.

Days, Drew S. III, Nathaniel R. Jones, Marc-René Blanchard, and Jonathan Klaaren. 1992. *Justice Enjoined. The State of the Judiciary in Kenya.* New York, NY: Robert F. Kennedy Memorial Center for Human Rights

Ddungu, Expedit. 1994. Popular Forms and the Question of Democracy. The Case of Resistance Councils in Uganda. In *Uganda. Studies in Living Conditions, Popular Movements, and Constitutionalism*, edited by M. Mamdani and J. Oloka-Onyango. Vienna: JEP, 365–404

De Waal, Alex. 1997. Democratizing the Aid Encounter in Africa. *International Affairs* 73 (4): 623–639

Detzner, John A. 1988. *Tribunales Chilenos y Derecho Internacional de Derechos Humanos: La recepción del derecho internacional de derechos humanos en el derecho interno chileno.* Santiago, Chile: Comisión Chilena de Derechos Humanos

Dobrynin, Anatoly. 1995. *In Confidence: Moscow's Ambassador to America's Six Cold War Presidents.* New York: Random House

Donnelly, Jack. 1986. International Human Rights: A Regime Analysis. *International Organisation* 40 (3): 599–642

1991. Progress in Human Rights. In *Progress in Postwar International Relations*, edited by E. Adler. New York: Columbia University Press, 312–358

1993. *International Human Rights.* Boulder, CO: Westview Press

Dow Jones Newswires. 1998. Indonesia Abandons Proposed Law to Control Demonstrations. September 29

Duara, Prasenjit. 1996. Historicizing National Identity, or Who Imagines What and When. In *Becoming National*, edited by G. Eley and R. G. Suny. New York: Oxford University Press, 151–177

Dwyer, Kevin. 1991. *Arab Voices: The Human Rights Debate in the Middle East.* London: Routledge

Eagly, Alice, and Shelly Chaiken. 1993. *The Psychology of Attitudes.* Fort Worth, TX: Harcourt Brace Jovanovich

El-Aoufi, Noureddine. ed. 1992. *La Société Civile au Maroc.* Rabat: SMER

Eldridge, Philip J. 1995. *Non-Government Organizations and Democratic Participation in Indonesia.* Oxford: Oxford University Press

1996. Human Rights and Democracy in Indonesia and Malaysia. *Contemporary Southeast Asia* 18 (3): 298–319

Emmerson, Donald K. 1996. Do "Asian Values" Exist? Paper presented at the annual meeting of the ISA at San Diego, April 16–20

Engelhardt, Kerstin. 1996. Marokko. Ein islamisches Königreich zwischen Modernisierung und Tradition. In *Afrika: Stagnation oder Neubeginn: Studien zum politischen Wandel*, edited by P. Kevenhörster and D. van den Boom. eds. Münster: Lit-Verlag, 53–68

Entelis, John P. 1989. *Culture and Counterculture in Moroccan Politics*. Boulder, CO: Westview Press

1996. Civil Society and the Authoritarian Temptation in Algerian Politics. In *Civil Society in the Middle East*, edited by Augustus R. Norton. Vol. II. Leiden: E. J. Brill, 45–86

Espiritu, Caesar. 1986. *Law and Human Rights in the Development of ASEAN. With Special Reference to the Philippines*. Singapore: Friedrich-Naumann-Stiftung

Europa Publications. eds. 1995. *The Middle East and North Africa 1995*. 41st edn. London

Evangelista, Matthew. 1998. *Taming the Bear. Transnational Relations and the Demise of the Soviet Threat*. Ithaca, NY: Cornell University Press

Evans, Peter B., Harold K. Jacobson, and Robert D. Putnam. eds. 1993. *Double-Edged Diplomacy: International Bargaining and Domestic Politics*. Berkeley, CA: University of California Press

Faath, Sigrid. 1986. *Tunesien. Die politische Entwicklung seit der Unabhängigkeit 1956–1986. Kommentar und Dokumentation*. Hamburg: Deutsches Orient-Institut

1987. *Marokko. Die innen- und aussenpolitische Entwicklung seit der Unabhängigkeit*. Hamburg: Deutsches Orient-Institut

1992a. Anspruch und Grenzen der Demokratisierungsbestrebungen in Tunesien unter Präsident Ben Ali. In *Demokratie und Menschenrechte in Nordafrika*, edited by S. Faath and H. Mattes. Hamburg: Edition Wuquf, 487–563

1992b. Rechte und Freiheiten der Staatsbürger im Hassanismus. In *Demokratie und Menschenrechte in Nordafrika*, edited by S. Faath and H. Mattes. Hamburg: Edition Wuquf, 365–432

Falla, Ricardo. 1994. *Massacres in the Jungle: Ixcan, Guatemala, 1975–1982*. Boulder, CO: Westview Press

Farah, Tawfic, and Yasumasa Kuroda. eds. 1987. *Political Socialization in the Arab States*. Boulder, CO: Lynne Rienner Publishers

Fealy, Greg. 1995. *The Release of Indonesia's Political Prisoners: Domestic Versus Foreign Policy, 1975–1979*. Melbourne

Fearon, James D. 1997. What Is Identity (As We Now Use the Word)? Draft manuscript, Stanford University

Feith, Herbert. 1962. *The Decline of Constitutional Democracy in Indonesia*. 2nd edn. Ithaca: Cornell University Press

1991. East Timor and the Indonesian Reformists: Out of the Too Hard Basket?, Department of Politics, Monash University, Melbourne

1992. East Timor: The Opening Up, the Crackdown and the Possibility of a Durable Settlement. In *Indonesia Assessment 1992: Political Perspectives on the 1990s*, edited by H. Crouch and H. Hill. Canberra: Australian National University, 63–82

Feliu, Laura. 1994. *Human Rights in Morocco: A Political Tool Beyond all Ethics*.

List of references

Working Papers. Universitat Autonoma de Barcelona

Fierlbeck, Katherine. 1994. Economic Liberalization as a Prologue to Democracy: The Case of Indonesia. *Canadian Journal of Development Studies* 15 (2): 151–169

Figueroa Ibarra, Carlos. 1991. *El Recurso del Miedo: Ensayo Sobre El Estado y El Terror en Guatemala*. San Jose, Costa Rica: EDUCA

Finnemore, Martha. 1993. International Organizations as Teachers of Norms: The United Nations Educational, Scientific, and Cultural Organization and Science Policy. *International Organization* 47 (4): 565–597

1996a. *National Interests in International Society*. Ithaca: Cornell University Press

1996b. Norms, Culture, and World Politics: Insights From Sociology's Institutionalism. *International Organization* 50 (2): 325–347

Finnemore, Martha, and Kathryn Sikkink. 1998. Norms and International Relations Theory. *International Organization* 52(4): 887–917

Foreign Broadcast Information Service, Latin America. 1980. Lucas Criticizes Carter at Rally After Bombing. September 8: 9

Forensic Anthropology Team of Guatemala. 1997. *Las Masacres en Rabinal: Estudio Histórico Antropológico de las Masacres de Plan de Sanchez, Chichupac y Rio Negro*. Guatemala City: Equipo de Antropologia Forense de Guatemala

Forsythe, David P. 1988. *Human Rights and U.S. Foreign Policy. Congress Reconsidered*. Gainesville, FL: University of Florida Press

1991. *The Internationalization of Human Rights*. Lexington, MA: Lexington Books

Franck, Thomas M. 1990. *The Power of Legitimacy Among Nations*. New York: Oxford University Press

Franck, Thomas M., and Edward Weisband. 1979. *Foreign Policy by Congress*. New York: Oxford University Press

Freeman, Linda. 1997. *The Ambiguous Champion, Canada and South Africa in the Trudeau and Mulroney Years*. Toronto: University of Toronto Press

Friedman, Steven. ed. 1994. *The Long Journey*. Johannesburg: Ravan

Frohmann, Alicia. 1998. Chile 1988–1998: The Frozen Transition. Paper presented at a conference on "Legacies of Authoritarianism," University of Wisconsin, Madison, April 3–5

Frühling, Hugo and Patricio Orellana. 1991. Organismos no gubernamentales de derechos humanos bajo regímenes autoritarios y en la transición democrática: el caso chileno desde una perspectiva comparada. In *Derechos Humanos y Democracia: La Contribución de las Organizaciones No Gubernamentales*, edited by H. Frühling. Santiago: Inter-American Institute for Human Rights

Furley, Oliver. 1989. Britain and Uganda from Amin to Museveni: Blind Eye Diplomacy. In *Conflict Resolution in Uganda*, edited by Kumar Rupesinghe. Oslo: International Peace Research Institute, 275–294

Garcia Laguardia, Jorge Mario. 1996. *Política y Constitución en Guatemala: La Constitución de 1985*. Guatemala City: Procurador de los Derechos Humanos

Garon, Lise. 1994. *North African Political Communication in Transition: The Case of*

List of references

Tunisia. Berlin: International Political Science Association

1995a. L'Islam dans l'Agenda des Droits de l'Homme, *Médiaspouvoirs*: 345–359

1995b. The Press and Democratic Transition in Arab Societies. In *Political Liberalization and Democratization in the Arab World*, edited by R. Brynen, B. Korany, and P. Noble. Vol. I. Boulder, CO: Lynne Rienner Publishers, 149–166

1998. Le Silence Tunisien. Les Alliances Dangereuses au Maghreb. Paris: L'Harmattan

Garretón, Manuel Antonio. 1989. *The Chilean Political Process*. London: Unwin-Hyman

1996. Human Rights in the Democratization Process. In *Constructing Democracy: Human Rights, Citizenship and Society in Latin America*, edited by Elizabeth Jelin and Eric Hershberg. Boulder, CO: Westview Press, 39–56

Garrett, Geoffrey, and Barry R. Weingast. 1993. Ideas, Interests, and Institutions. Constructing the European Community's Internal Market. In *Ideas and Foreign Policy*, edited by J. Goldstein and R. O. Keohane. Ithaca NY: Cornell University Press, 173–206

Gathii, James Thuo. 1994. *The Dream of Judicial Security of Tenure and the Reality of Executive Involvement in Kenya's Judicial Process*. Nairobi: Kenya Human Rights Commission

Genscher, Hans Dietrich. 1995. *Erinnerungen*. Munich: Goldman

Giliomee, Hermann. 1992. *Broedertwis*: Intra-Afrikaner Conflicts in the Transition From Apartheid, *African Affairs* 91: 339–364

Gill, Stephen. ed. 1993. *Gramsci, Historical Materialism, and International Relations*. Cambridge: Cambridge University Press

Gilpin, Robert. 1981. *War and Change in World Politics*. New York: Cambridge University Press

Goldberg, Paul. 1988. *The Final Act: The Dramatic, Revealing Story of the Moscow Helsinki Watch Group*. New York: Morrow

Goldstein, Judith, and Robert O. Keohane. 1993a. Ideas and Foreign Policy: An Analytical Framework. In *Ideas and Foreign Policy. Beliefs, Institutions and Political Change*, edited by J. Goldstein and R. O. Keohane. Ithaca, NY: Cornell University Press, 3–30

eds. 1993b. *Ideas and Foreign Policy: Beliefs, Institutions and Political Change*. Ithaca, NY: Cornell University Press

Gorbachev, Mikhail. 1986. *Mandate for Peace*. New York: Paperjacks

Green, Jennie. 1989. The Philippines: United States Policy and Allegations of Human Rights Abuses under Aquino. *Harvard Human Rights Yearbook* 2: 187–197

Greenberg, Stanley. 1980. *Legitimating the Illegitimate*. Berkeley, CA: University of California Press

Grovogni, Siba N'Zatioula. 1996. *Sovereigns, Quasi-Sovereigns, and Africans*. Minneapolis: Minnesota University Press

Grundy, Kenneth. 1991. *South Africa, Domestic Crisis and Global Challenge*. Boulder, CO: Westview Press

Gränzer, Sieglinde. 1998. Staatliche Menschenrechtsdiskurse in Marokko. Florence: European University Institute

Guatemalan Human Rights Commission/USA. 1996–1998. *Guatemala Human Rights Update*. Washington, DC: Guatemalan Human Rights Commission/USA

Guelke, Adrian. 1986. The Politicisation of South African Sport. In *The Politics of Sport*, edited by L. Allison. Manchester: Manchester University Press, 118–147

Haas, Ernst B. 1983. Words Can Hurt You; Or, Who Said What to Whom About Regimes? In *International Regimes*, edited by S. D. Krasner. Ithaca NY: Cornell University Press, 23–59

1990. *When Knowledge Is Power*. Berkeley, CA: University of California Press

Haas, Peter M. ed. 1992. Knowledge, Power and International Policy Coordination. *International Organization, Special Issue*, 46 (1)

Habermas, Jürgen. 1981. *Theorie des kommunikativen Handelns*. 2 vols. Frankfurt am Main: Suhrkamp

1992. *Faktizität und Geltung. Beiträge zur Diskurstheorie des Rechts und des demokratischen Rechtsstaats*. Frankfurt am Main: Suhrkamp

1995a. Replik auf Einwände. In J. Habermas, *Vorstudien und Ergänzungen zur Theorie des kommunikativen Handelns*, Frankfurt am Main: Suhrkamp, 475–570

1995b. *Vorstudien und Ergänzungen zur Theorie des kommunikativen Handelns*. Frankfurt am Main: Suhrkamp

Hadenius, Axel. 1992. *Democracy and Development*. Cambridge: Cambridge University Press

Hall, John A. 1993. Ideas and the Social Sciences. In *Ideas and Foreign Policy*, edited by J. Goldstein and R. Keohane. Ithaca, NY: Cornell University Press, 31–54

Hall, Peter A. ed. 1989. *The Political Power of Economic Ideas: Keynesianism Across Nations*. Princeton: Princeton University Press

Hall, Peter A., and Rosemary C. R. Taylor. 1996. Political Science and the Three New Institutionalisms. *Political Studies* 44, 952–973

Hanlon, Joseph. 1986. *Beggar Your Neighbours*. London: Catholic Institute for International Relations

Harden, Blaine. 1990. *Africa: Dispatches From a Fragile Continent*. New York: Harper Collins

Hasenclever, Andreas, Peter Mayer, and Volker Rittberger. 1997. *Theories of International Regimes*. Cambridge: Cambridge University Press

Hassan, Mohamed Jawhar. 1996. The Nexus Between Democracy and Stability: The Case of Southeast Asia. *Contemporary Southeast Asia* 18 (2) September: 163–173

Haugerud, Angelique. 1995. *The Culture of Politics in Modern Kenya 1890s to 1990s*. Cambridge: Cambridge University Press

List of references

Havel, Vaclav. 1991. *Open Letters: Selected Writings, 1965–1990*. New York: Knopf

Hawes, Gary. 1986. United States Support for the Marcos Administration and the Pressures that made for Change. *Contemporary Southeast Asia* 8 (1): 18–36

Hawkins, Darren. 1994. International Influence and Human Rights in Chile: Explaining the Disappearance of DINA in 1977. Paper delivered at the Annual Meeting of the American Political Science Association, September 1–4

— 1996. *The International and Domestic Struggle for Legitimacy in Authoritarian Chile*. PhD Thesis, University of Wisconsin-Madison

— 1997. Domestic Responses to International Pressure. Human Rights in Authoritarian Chile. *European Journal of International Relations* 3 (4): 403–434

Hawkins, Linda L., and Mark A. Tessler. 1987. Acculturation, Socioeconomic Status and Attitude Change in Tunisia: Implications for Modernization Theory. In *Political Socialization in the Arab States*, edited by T. Farah and Y. Kuroda. Boulder, CO: Lynne Rienner Publishers, 107–127

Hajek, Jiri. 1978. *Dix Ans Après: Prague 1968–1978*. Paris: Editions du Seuil

Hegasy, Sonja. 1997. *Staat, Öffentlichkeit und Zivilgesellschaft in Marokko*. Hamburg: Deutsches Orient-Institut

Heinz, Wolfgang S., and Werner Pfennig. 1996. Widerstand gegen Demokratie und Menschenrechtsintervention in ASEAN-Ländern. In *Demokratieexport in die Länder des Südens?*, edited by R. Hanisch. Hamburg: Deutsches Übersee-Institut, 339–365

Hempstone, Smith. 1997. *Rogue Ambassador. An African Memoir*. Sewanee: University of the South Press

Henderson, George. 1984. How Morocco Treats its Dissidents. *Index on Censorship* 13 (6): 30–31

Henkin, Louis. 1977. Human Rights and "Domestic Jurisdiction". In *Human Rights, International Law and the Helsinki Accord*, edited by T. Buergenthal. Montclair, NJ: Allanheld, Osmun, 21–40

Henstridge, Mark. 1994. Stabilization Policy and Structural Adjustment in Uganda,1987–1990. In *Negotiating Structural Adjustment in Africa*, edited by Willem van der Geest. London: James Currey, 47–68

Herman, Robert G. 1994. *Ideas, Identity and the Redefinition of Interests: The Political and Intellectual Origins of the Soviet Foreign Policy Revolution*. PhD dissertation, Cornell University

— 1996. Identity, Norms, and National Security: The Soviet Foreign Policy Revolution and the End of the Cold War. In *The Culture of National Security. Norms and Identity in World Politics*, edited by P. J. Katzenstein. New York: Columbia University Press, 271–316

Hermassi, Abdelbaki. 1994. Socio-Economic Change and Political Implications: The Maghreb. In *Democracy Without Democrats? The Renewal of Politics in the Muslim World*, edited by G. Salamé. London: I. B. Tauris, 227–241

Hoeffel, Paul Heath, and Peter Kornbluh. 1983. The War at Home: Chile's Legacy in the United States. *Nacla Report to the Americas* (17): 27–39

Holiday, David. 1997. Guatemala's Long Road to Peace. *Current History.* February

Howard, Rhoda E. 1991. Repression and State Terror in Kenya 1982–1988. In *State Organized Terror. The Case of Violent Internal Repression,* edited by P. T. Bushnell, V. Shlapentokh, C. K. Vanderpool, and J. Sundram. Boulder, CO: Westview Press, 77–98

Hubel, Helmut. 1988. Die USA und Nordafrika. In *Nordafrika in der internationalen Politik,* edited by H. Hubel. Munich: Oldenbourg, 179–201

Human Rights Watch. 1990. *The Bush Administration's Record on Human Rights in 1989.* New York: Human Rights Watch

1991. *Human Rights Watch World Report 1991. Events of 1990.* New York: Human Rights Watch

1992. *Human Rights Watch World Report 1992. Events of 1991.* New York: Human Rights Watch

1995. *Human Rights Watch World Report 1995. Events of 1994.* New York: Human Rights Watch

1997a. *Human Rights Watch World Report 1997. Events of 1996.* New York: Human Rights Watch

1997b. *Indonesia/East Timor: Deteriorating Human Rights in East Timor.* New York: Human Rights Watch

1997c. Tunisia. In *Human Rights Watch World Report.* New York: Human Rights Watch, 303–307

1998. Indonesia: Reforms Needed After Soeharto's Resignation. New York: Human Rights Watch

Human Rights Watch/Africa. 1997a. *Failing the Internally Displaced: The UNDP Displaced Persons Program in Kenya.* New York: Human Rights Watch

1997b. *Juvenile Injustice. Police Abuse and Detention of Street Children in Kenya.* New York: Human Rights Watch

1997c. *The Scars of Death. Children Abducted by the Lord's Resistance Army in Uganda.* New York: Human Rights Watch

Human Rights Watch/Asia. 1994. *Human Rights in Indonesia and East Timor: The Limits of Openness.* New York: Human Rights Watch

Human Rights Watch, and Lawyers' Committee for Human Rights. 1989. *Reagan Administration's Record on Human Rights in 1988.* New York: Human Rights Watch

Humphrey, John P. 1984. *Human Rights and the United Nations: A Great Adventure.* Dobbs Ferry, NY: Transnational Publishers

Huntington, Samuel P. 1991. *The Third Wave. Democratization in the Late Twentieth Century.* Norman, OK: University of Oklahoma Press

1996. *The Clash of Civilizations and the Remaking of World Order.* New York: Simon & Schuster

Husak, Gustav. 1986. *Speeches and Writings.* Oxford: Pergamon Press

Ibrahim, Saad Eddin. 1995a. Civil Society and Prospects for Democratization in the Arab World. In *Civil Society in the Middle East,* edited by A. R. Norton, Leiden: E. J. Brill, 27–54

List of references

1995b. Liberalization and Democratization in the Arab World: An Overview. In *Political Liberalization and Democatiztion in the Arab World*, edited by R. Brynen, B. Korany, and P. Noble. Vol. I. Boulder, CO: Lynne Rienner Publishers, 29–57

Ibrahimi, Hamid. 1997. Tunesien. Der Kampf gegen den Islamismus als Al-lzweckwaffe. *Le Monde Diplomatique.* February 14, 4–5

Ignatieff, Michael. 1997. Digging Up the Dead. *The New Yorker,* November 10

Ikenberry, John G., and Charles A. Kupchan. 1990. Socialization and Hegemonic Power. *International Organization* 44 (3): 283–315

International Bar Association. 1997. *Report on the Legal System and Independence of the Judiciary in Kenya (November 1996).* London

International Commission of Jurists. 1977a. *The Decline of Democracy in the Philippines.* Geneva: International Commission of Jurists

1977b. *Uganda and Human Rights. Reports to the UN Commission on Human Rights.* Geneva: International Commission of Jurists

Jacobson, John K. 1995. Much Ado About Ideas: The Cognitive Factor in Economic Policy. *World Politics* 47 (January): 283–315

Jepperson, Ronald L. 1991. Institutions, Institutional Effects and Institutionalism. In *The New Institutionalism in Organizational Theory,* edited by P. J. DiMaggio and W. P. Powell. Chicago: Chicago University Press, 143–163

Jepperson, Ronald, Alexander Wendt, and Peter J. Katzenstein. 1996. Norms, Identity, and Culture in National Security. In *The Culture of National Security: Norms and Identity in World Politics,* edited by P. J. Katzenstein. New York: Columbia University Press, 33–75

Jetschke, Anja. 1997. Government Rhetoric: Indonesia and the Philippines. Florence: European University Institute

Johnson, Phyllis, and David Martin. 1989. *Apartheid Terrorism, The Destabilization Report.* London: The Commonwealth Secretariat

Jonas, Susanne. 1991. *The Battle for Guatemala: Rebels, Death Squads, and U.S. Power.* Boulder, CO: Westview Press

Forthcoming. Between Two Worlds: The United Nations in Guatemala, in *Multilateral Approaches to Peacekeeping and Democratization in the Hemisphere,* edited by T. S. Montgomery. Miami, FL: North–South Center

Jones, Sidney. 1996. Regional Institutions for Protecting Human Rights in Asia. *Australian Journal of International Affairs* 50 (3): 269–277

Jürgensen, Carsten. 1994. *Demokratie und Menschenrechte in der arabischen Welt.* Hamburg: Deutsches Orient-Institut

Kamminga, Menno T. 1992. *Inter-State Accountability for Violations of Human Rights.* Philadelphia: University of Pennsylvania Press

Karnow, Stanley. 1989. *In Our Image: America's Empire in the Philippines.* New York: Random House

Kasozi, A. B. K. 1994. *The Social Origins of Violence in Uganda, 1964–1985.* Montreal: McGill-Queen's University Press

Katzenstein, Peter J. ed. 1996a. *The Culture of National Security. Norms and*

Identity in World Politics. New York: Columbia University Press
1996b. *Cultural Norms and National Security. Police and Military in Postwar Japan*. Ithaca, NY: Cornell University Press
Kausikan, Bilahari. 1994. Human Rights: Asia's Different Standard. *Media Asia* 21 (1): 45–51
Keck, Margret, and Kathryn Sikkink. 1998. *Activists Beyond Borders. Transnational Advocacy Networks in International Politics*. Ithaca, NY: Cornell University Press
Kehr, Eckart. 1970. *Der Primat der Innenpolitik*. Berlin: de Gruyter
Kenya Human Rights Commission. 1994. *Independence without Freedom. The Legitimization of Repressive Laws and Practices in Kenya*. Nairobi
Keohane, Robert O. 1989. International Institutions: Two Approaches. In *International Institutions and State Power*, R. O. Keohane. Boulder, CO: Westview Press, 158–179
Kessler, Richard J. 1986. Marcos and Americans. *Foreign Policy* 63 (2): 41–57
Kiai, Maina. 1993. Is Amos Wako A Fallen Angel? *Nairobi Law Monthly* 7 (48): 9–14
Kibwana, Kivutha. 1992. *Law and the Administration of Justice in Kenya*. Nairobi: International Commission of Jurists (Kenya Section)
Kitschelt, Herbert. 1992. Political Regime Change: Structure and Process-Driven Explanations? *American Political Science Review* 86 (4): 1028–1034
Kivimäki, Timo Antero. 1994. National Diplomacy for Human Rights: A Study of US Exercise of Power in Indonesia, 1974–1979. *Human Rights Quarterly* 16: 415–431
Klotz, Audie. 1995. *Norms in International Relations. The Struggle against Apartheid*. Ithaca, NY: Cornell University Press
Forthcoming. Diplomatic Isolation. In *How Sanctions Work: South Africa*, edited by N. Crawford and A. Klotz. Basingstoke, UK: Macmillan
Korey, William. 1993. *The Promises We Keep: Human Rights, The Helsinki Process, and American Foreign Policy*. New York: St. Martin's Press
Kowert, Paul, and Jeffrey Legro. 1996. Norms, Identity, and Their Limits: A Theoretical Reprise. In *The Culture of National Security: Norms and Identity in World Politics*, edited by P. J. Katzenstein. New York: Colombia University Press, 451–497
Krasner, Stephen D. 1993. Sovereignty, Regimes, and Human Rights. In *Regime Theory and International Relations*, edited by V. Rittberger and P. Mayer. Oxford: Oxford University Press, 139–167
1995a. Minority Rights and the Westphalian Model. Stanford: Department of Political Science
1995b. Power Politics, Institutions, and Transnational Relations. In *Bringing Transnational Relations Back In. Non-State Actors, Domestic Structures and International Institutions*, edited by T. Risse-Kappen: Cambridge: Cambridge University Press, 257–279
Kratochwil, Friedrich. 1989. *Rules, Norms, and Decisions*. Cambridge: Cambridge University Press

Krepp, Endel, and Konrad Veem. 1980. *Testing the Spirit of Helsinki: From Helsinki to Madrid*. Stockholm: National Committee of the Estonian Evangelical Lutheran Church

Kubik, Jan. 1994. *The Power of Symbols against the Symbols of Power: The Rise of Solidarity and the Fall of State Socialism in Poland*. University Park, PA: Pennsylvania State University Press

Kusin, Vladimir V. 1978. *From Dubcek to Charter 77: A Study of "Normalization" in Czechoslovakia*. New York: St. Martin's Press

1979. Challenge to Normalcy: Political Opposition in Czechoslovakia, 1968–77. In *Opposition in Eastern Europe*, edited by R. L. Tokes. Baltimore: The Johns Hopkins University Press, 26–59

Kyemba, Henry. 1977. *State of Blood. The Inside Story of Idi Amin's Reign of Fear*. London: Corgi Books

LaFeber, Walter. 1993. *Inevitable Revolutions: The United States in Central America*. New York: W. W. Norton

Laffey, Mark, and Jutta Weldes. 1997. Beyond Belief: Ideas and Symbolic Technologies in the Study of International Relations. *European Journal of International Relations* 3 (2): 193–237

Lane, Max. 1990. *The Urban Mass Movement in the Philippines, 1983–1987*. Canberra: Australian National University

Latin American Regional Report. 1980. Guatemala: A Sharp Twist to the Right. *Latin American Regional Report: Mexico and Central America*. November 28: 3

Laurent, Eric. 1996. *Hassan II. von Marokko. Erinnerungen eines Königs*. Berlin: edition q

Lawyers' Committee for Human Rights. 1988. *Vigilantes in the Philippines: A Threat to Democratic Rule*. New York: Lawyers' Committee for Human Rights

1990. *Out of Control. Militia Abuses in the Philippines*. Vol. I. New York: Lawyers' Committee for Human Rights

1991. *Impunity. Prosecution of Human Rights Violations in the Philippines*. New York: Lawyers' Committee for Human Rights

1993a. Critique. *Review of the US Department of State's Country Reports on Human Rights Practices 1992*. New York

1993b. *Promise Unfullfilled: Human Rights in Tunisia since 1987*. New York

1993c. *Broken Laws, Broken Bodies. Torture and the Right to Redress in Indonesia*. New York: Lawyers' Committee for Human Rights

1994. *Tunisia. Spreading the Net of Persecution*. New York

1995a. *In the Name of Development: Human Rights and the World Bank in Indonesia*. New York: Lawyers' Committee for Human Rights

1995b. *Illegal Detention and Unfair Trials in Tunisia*. New York.

Lawyers' Committee for Human Rights, and Asia Watch. 1988. *Lawyers under Fire: Attacks on Human Rights Attorneys in the Philippines*. New York: Lawyers' Committee for Human Rights

Layachi, Azzedine. 1995. *Civil Society and Democratization in Morocco*. Cairo: Ibn Khaldon Center for Development Studies and Dar Al-Ameen Publishing

Legaspi, Eileen C. 1993. The Cory Mystique and The International Community. In *Pumipiglas 3: Torment and Struggle after Marcos*, edited by B. M. Tuazon. Cubao, Quezon City: Task Force Detainees of the Philippines, 95–104

Legro, Jeffrey W. 1997. Which Norms Matter? Revisiting the "Failure" of Internationalism. *International Organization* 51 (1): 31–63

Letters to the editor. 1978. Indonesia's Political Prisoners. *Far Eastern Economic Review*, 20 January, 5–7

Liddle, R. William. 1992. Indonesia's Threefold Crisis. *Journal of Democracy* 3 (4): 60–74

Liddle, R. William, and Rizal Mallarangeng. 1997. Indonesia in 1996: Pressures from Above and Below. *Asian Survey* 37 (2) February: 167–174

Linz, Juan J. 1978. *Crisis, Breakdown, and Reequilibration*. Baltimore, MD: The Johns Hopkins University Press

Lipset, Seymour Martin. 1959. *Political Man. The Social Bases of Politics*. Garden City, NY: Doubleday

Lipski, Jan Jozef. 1985. *KOR: A History of the Workers' Defense Committee in Poland, 1976–1981*. Berkeley: University of California Press

Lowden, Pamela. 1996. *Moral Opposition to Authoritarian Rule in Chile, 1973–1990*. London: Macmillan Press

Lubis, Todung Mulya. 1993. *In Search of Human Rights. Legal Political Dilemmas of Indonesia's New Order. 1966–1990*. Jakarta: Gramedia Pustaka Utama

Lule, Godfrey. 1977. Foreword. In *State of Blood. The Inside Story of Idi Amin's Reign of Fear*, edited by Henry Kyemba. London: Corgi Books, 5–8

Macha, Carol Ann. 1994. Human Rights Abuses in Tunisia under the Ben-Ali Regime: Microcosm of a Larger Crisis. Austin. Unpublished

Machado, Kit G. 1978. The Philippines in 1977: Beginning a "Return to Normalcy"? *Asian Survey* 18 (2): 202–211

Mackie, Jamie, and Andrew MacIntyre. 1994. Politics. In *Indonesia's New Order*, edited by H. Hill. Sydney: Allen & Unwin, 1–44

Mair, Stefan. 1994. *Kenias Weg in die Mehrparteiendemokratie. Von Uhuru über Harambee und Nyayo erneut zur Uhuru*. Baden-Baden: Nomos

Mamdani, Mahmood. 1995. And Fire Does not Always Beget Ash. Critical Reflections on the NRM. Kampala: Fountain Press

1996. *Citizen and Subject. Contemporary Africa and the Legacy of Late Colonialism*. Princeton: Princeton University Press

Mandela, Nelson. 1994. *Long Walk to Freedom*. New York: Little Brown

Mansour, Fawzy. 1992. *The Arab World. Nation State and Democracy*. London: Zed Books

March, James G., and Johan P. Olsen. 1989. *Rediscovering Institutions*. New York: The Free Press

Marks, Thomas A. 1993. Maoist Insurgency: The Communist Party of the Philippines, 1968–93. *Issues and Studies* 29 (II): 80–121

Martin, David. 1974. *General Amin*. London: Faber and Faber

Martin, Lisa, and Kathryn Sikkink. 1993. U.S. Policy and Human Rights in Argentina and Guatemala, 1973–1980. In *Double-Edged Diplomacy:*

List of references

International Bargaining and Domestic Politics, edited by P. Evans, H. Jacobson, and R. Putnam. Berkeley, CA: University of California Press, 330–362

Martin Jones, David. 1998. Democratization, Civil Society, and Illiberal Middle Class Culture in Pacific Asia. *Comparative Politics* (2): 147–169

Marx, Anthony. 1992. *Lessons of Struggle, South African Internal Opposition, 1960–1990*. New York: Oxford University Press

Mason, David S. 1985. *Public Opinion and Political Change in Poland, 1980–1982*. Cambridge: Cambridge University Press

Mauzy, Diane K. 1995. Human Rights in Indonesia, Malaysia and Singapore. *The Round Table* 335: 279–296

Mauzy, Diane K., and R. S. Milne. 1995. Human Rights in ASEAN States: A Canadian Policy Perspective. In *New Challenges for ASEAN: Emerging Policy Issues*, edited by A. Acharya and R. Stubbs. Vancouver: UBC Press, 115–145

Mbuende, Kaire. 1986. *The Broken Shield: Anatomy of Imperialism and Revolution*. Malmo, Sweden: Liber

Medina Quiroga, Cecilia. 1988. *The Battle of Human Rights: Gross, Systematic Violations and the Inter-American System*. Dordrecht: Martinus Nijhoff Publishers

1990. The Inter-American Commission on Human Rights and the Inter-American Court of Human Rights: Reflections on a Joint Venture. *Human Rights Quarterly* 12

Meyer, John W., John Boli, George M. Thomas, and Francisco O. Ramirez. 1997. World Society and the Nation-State. *American Journal of Sociology* 103 (1): 144–181

Michnik, Adam. 1985. The New Evolutionism – 1976. In *Letters from Prison and Other Essays*, by A. Michnik. Berkeley, CA: University of California Press, 135–148

1990. The Moral and Spiritual Origins of Solidarity. In *Without Force or Lies: Voices from the Revolution of Central Europe in 1989–90*, edited by W. M. Brinton and A. Rinzler. San Francisco: Mercury House, 239–250

Middle East Watch, International Human Rights Law Group. 1992. *Tunisia. Military Courts That Sentenced Islamist Leaders Violating Basic Fair-Trial Norms*. 4 (9). New York/Washington

Ministerio Secretaria General de Gobierno, Secretaria de Comunicación y Cultura. 1991. *Informe Rettig: Informe de la Comisión Nacional de Verdad y Reconciliación*. Santiago, Chile: Talleres La Nación

Mission to South Africa: The Findings of the Commonwealth Eminent Persons Group on Southern Africa. 1986. Harmondsworth, UK: Penguin

Moczulski, Leszek. 1977. O Co Chodzi Z Tym Belgradem, *Opinia (Warsaw)* (2): 32–36

Moravcsik, Andrew. 1997. Taking Preferences Seriously: A Liberal Theory of International Politics. *International Organization* 51 (4): 513–553

Morgenthau, Hans J. 1948. *Politics Among Nations*. Brief edition, 1993. New York: McGraw Hill

298

Morrow, James D. 1994. Modeling the Forms of International Cooperation: Distribution versus Information. *International Organization* 48 (3): 387–423

Müller, Harald. 1993. The Internalization of Principles, Norms, and Rules by Governments: The Case of Security Regimes. In *Regime Theory and International Relations*, edited by V. Rittberger. Oxford: Clarendon Press, 361–388

— 1994. Internationale Beziehungen als kommunikatives Handeln. Zur Kritik der utilitaristischen Handlungstheorien. *Zeitschrift für Internationale Beziehungen* 1 (1): 15–44

Muhumuza, Robby. 1997. *Shattered Innocence. Testimonies of Children Abducted in Northern Uganda*. Kampala: World Vision/UNICEF

Muñoz, Heraldo. 1986. *Las Relaciones Exteriores del Gobierno Militar Chileno*. Santiago: Las Ediciones del Ornitorrinco

Museveni, Yoweri Kaguta. 1992. *What is Africa's Problem?* Kampala: NRM Publications

Mutibwa, Phares. 1992. *Uganda since Independence. A Story of Unfulfilled Hopes*. London: Hurst

Muthoga, Lee. 1990. Why the I. B. A. Conference was moved from Nairobi. *Nairobi Law Monthly* 4 (24): 8–9

Nairobi Law Monthly. 1989. Uproar Over the Kennedys' Human Rights Visit. *Nairobi Law Monthly* 14–24

— 1990. Bishop Muge's Death Shocks the Christian World. *Nairobi Law Monthly* 4 (24): 11–12

Nations, Richard, and Guy Sacerdoti. 1984. The Aquino Legacy. *Far Eastern Economic Review*, August 30, 22–29

Ndegwa, Stephen N. 1996. *The Two Faces of Civil Society. NGOs and Politics in Africa*. West Hartford: Kumarian Press

Nemenzo, Francisco. 1995. People's Diplomacy and Human Rights: The Philippine Experience. In *Human Rights and International Relations in the Asia-Pacific Region*, edited by J. T. H. Tang. London, New York: St. Martin's Press Inc., 112–124

Newsom, David. 1986. Release in Indonesia. In *The Diplomacy of Human Rights*, edited by D. Newsom. Laugham/New York/London: University Press of America, 101–109

Neyer, Harry, and Michael Protz-Schwarz. eds. 1986. *Völkermord in Südostasien: Ost-Timor 1974–1984. Hunderttausende starben seit dem Einmarsch der Indonesier*. Bonn: Deutsche Kommission Justitia et Pax

North African Students for Freedom; American Muslim Council; Muslim Public Affairs Council. 1991. *Updated Report on Human Rights Violations in Tunisia*. Washington/Los Angeles

Norton, Augustus R. ed. 1995. *Civil Society in the Middle East*, Vol. I. Leiden: E. J. Brill

— 1996. *Civil Society in the Middle East*, Vol. II. Leiden: E. J. Brill

Nowak, Jerzy M. 1976. Cooperation Between East and West on Humanitarian Issues. *Sprawy Miedzynarodowe* (9) September, from Joint Publication Research Service, *Translations on Eastern Europe* 68273 (December 3): 1–17

List of references

Nowrojee, Pherozee. 1995. Being Nobody's Darling. The Independence of the Bar. *University of Nairobi Law Journal* 2 (3): 79–85

Ocampo, Sheila. 1980. Aquino is Out, But is He Free at Last? *Far Eastern Economic Review*, May 16, 10–11

Ocampo-Calfors, Sheila. 1983. Where Aquino Dares. *Far Eastern Economic Review*, July 7: 16–17

Odell, John. 1982. *U.S. International Monetary Policy: Markets, Power, and Ideas as Sources of Change*. Princeton, NJ: Princeton University Press

O'Donnell, Guillermo. 1973. *Modernization and Bureaucratic Authoritarianism: Studies in South American Politics*. Berkeley, CA: Institute of International Studies, University of California

O'Donnell, Guillermo, and Philippe C. Schmitter. 1986. *Transitions from Authoritarian Rule. Tentative Conclusions about Uncertain Democracies*. Baltimore, MD: The Johns Hopkins University Press

Ofcansky, Thomas P. 1996. *Uganda. Tarnished Pearl of Africa*. Boulder, CO: Westview Press

Ohlson, Thomas, and Stephen John Stedman. 1994. *The New is Not Yet Born, Conflict Resolution in Southern Africa*. Washington: The Brookings Institution

Oloka-Onyango, Joe. 1992. Uganda. In *Human Rights in Developing Countries 1991, A Yearbook on Human Rights in Countries Receiving Aid from the Nordic Countries, the Netherlands and Canada*, edited by B. -A. Andreassen and T. Swinehart. Oslo: Nordic Human Rights Publications, 316–355

——— 1993. The Dynamics of Corruption Control and Human Rights Enforcement in Uganda: The Case of the Inspector General of Government. *East African Journal of Peace and Human Rights* 1 (1): 23–51

——— 1996. Uganda. In *Human Rights in Developing Countries Yearbook 1996*, edited by P. Baehr, L. Sadiwa, and J. Smith. The Hague/Oslo: Kluwer Law International/Nordic Human Rights Publications, 365–410

Omara-Otunnu, Amii. 1987. *Politics and the Military in Uganda, 1890–1985*. Houndsmills: Macmillan Press

O'Meara, Dan. 1996. *Forty Lost Years*, The Apartheid State and the Politics of the National Party. Johannesburg: Ravan

Orellana Patricio, and Elizabeth Quay Hutchinson. 1991. *El movimiento de derechos humanos en Chile, 1973–1990*. Santiago, Chile: Centro de Estudios Politicos Latinoamericanos Simon Bolivar

Orentlicher, Diane F. 1991. The Power of an Idea: The Impact of United States Human Rights Policy. *Transnational Law and Contemporary Problems* 1 (43): 44–80

Organisation Marocaine des Droits de l'Homme. 1993. *Organisation Marocaine des Droits de l'Homme , O. M. D. H., a Travers ses Communiqués et Declarations: Mai 1991–Decembre 1992*. Casablanca

——— 1994a. *Observations de l'Organisation Marocaine des Droits de l'Homme au Sujet du 3ème Rapport Gouvernemental au Comité des Droits de l'Homme des Nations Unies*. October 1994. Casablanca: Les Editions Maghrébines

1994b. *Organisation Marocaine des Droits de l'Homme , O.M.D.H., à Travers ses Communiqués et Déclarations: Décembre 1992–Mai 1994.* Casablanca: Les Editions Maghrébines

1995. *Non a la Torture au Maroc. Rapport Alternative de l'O.M.D.H. dans la Cadre de La Convention Internationale Contre la Torture et les Autres Peines ou Traitements Cruels, Inhumains ou Dégradants. Novembre 1994.* Casablanca: Les Editions Maghrébines

1996. *Rapport Annuel sur La Situation des Droits de l'Homme Au Maroc 1996.* Rabat

Osiel, Mark. 1986. The Making of Human Rights Policy in Argentina: The Impact of Ideas and Interests on a Legal Conflict. *Journal of Latin American Studies* 18: 135–178

Overholt, William H. 1986. The Rise and Fall of Ferdinand Marcos. *Asian Survey* 26 (11) November: 1137–1163

Pabottingi, Mochtar. 1995. Indonesia: Historicizing the New Order's Legitimacy Dilemma. In *Political Legitimacy in Southeast Asia: The Quest for Moral Authority*, edited by M. Alagappa. Stanford, CA: Stanford University Press, 224–256

Perrault, Gilles. 1990. *Notre Ami le Roi.* Paris: Gallimard

Perthes, Volker. 1992. The Private Sector, Economic Liberalization and the Prospects of Democratization: The Case of Syria and some other Arabian Countries. In *Democracy without Democrats*, edited by G. Salamé. London: I. B. Tauris, 242–269

Peters, Ralph-Michael. 1996. *Zivile und politische Gesellschaft in Kenya.* Hamburg: Institut für Afrikakunde

Pinto, Constancio, and Matthew Jardine. 1996. *East Timor's Unfinished Struggle: Inside the Timorese Resistance.* Boston, MA: South End Press

Pirouet, Louise. 1991. Human Rights Issues in Museveni's Uganda. In *Changing Uganda*, edited by H. B. Hansen and M. Twaddle. Kampala/London: James Currey/Fountain Press, 197–209

Poe, Steven C., and C. Neal Tate. 1994. Repression of Human Rights to Personal Integrity in the 1980s: A Global Analysis. *American Political Science Review.* 88 (4): 853–872

Poe, Steven C., C. Neal Tate, and Linda Camp Keith. 1997. Repression of the Human Right to Personal Integrity Revisited: A Global Crossnational Study Covering the Years 1976–1993. Paper presented at 38th Annual Convention of the International Studies Association, 18–22 March 1997, at Toronto, Canada

Polish Helsinki Committee. 1983. *Poland Under Martial Law.* New York: US Helsinki Watch Committee, 1983

Powell, Walter W., and Paul J. DiMaggio. eds. 1991. *The New Institutionalism in Organizational Analysis.* Chicago–London: University of Chicago Press

Preçan, Vilem. ed. 1983. *Human Rights in Czechoslovakia: A Documentation, September 1981–December 1982.* Paris: International Committee for the Support of Charter 77 in Czechoslovakia, April

List of references

Price, Robert. 1991. *The Apartheid State in Crisis*. New York: Oxford University Press

Prittwitz, Volker von. ed. 1996. *Verhandeln und Argumentieren. Dialog, Interessen und Macht in der Umweltpolitik*. Opladen: Westdeutscher Verlag

Przeworski, Adam. 1986. Some Problems in the Study of the Transition to Democracy. In *Transition from Authoritarian Rule. Prospects for Democracy*, edited by G. O'Donnell, P. C. Schmitter, and L. Whitehead. Baltimore, MD: The Johns Hopkins University Press, 47–63

Przeworski, Adam, and Fernando Limongi. 1997. Modernization: Theories and Facts. *World Politics* 49 (2): 155–183

Puryear, Jeffrey. 1994. *Thinking Politics: Intellectuals and Democracy in Chile, 1973–1988*. Baltimore, MD: The Johns Hopkins University Press

Putnam, Robert. 1988. Diplomacy and Domestic Politics. The Logic of Two-Level Games. *International Organization* 42 (2): 427–460

Raina, Peter. 1978. *Political Opposition in Poland, 1954–1977*. London: Poets & Painters Press

Ramage, Douglas E. 1995. *Politics in Indonesia: Democracy, Islam and the Ideology of Tolerance*. London: Routledge

Ramos-Horta, J. 1987. *Funu – The Unfinished Saga of East Timor*. Trenton, NY: Red Sea Press

Regelsberger, Elfriede. 1988. Die Europäische Gemeinschaft und Nordafrika. In *Nordafrika in der internationalen Politik*, edited by H. Hubel. Munich: Oldenbourg, 220–240

Republic of Kenya. 1992. *Report of the Parliamentary Select Committee to Investigate Ethnic Clashes in Western and Other Parts of Kenya 1992*. Nairobi: The National Assembly

——— 1996. *Human Rights Situation in Kenya. The Way It Is*. Nairobi: Government Press

Republic of Uganda. 1994. *The Report of The Commission of Inquiry into Violations of Human Rights. Findings, Conclusions, and Recommendations*. Kampala: Government of Uganda

——— 1995a. *Instrument of Accession to the First Optional Protocol of the International Covenant on Civil and Political Rights, 22 September 1995*. Kampala: Government of Uganda

——— 1995b. *Observations by the Government of Uganda on Communication No. 92/4/6,719 in Respect of Human Rights Violations to the United Nations by Amnesty International*. Geneva

Riker, James V. 1997. NGOs, Donor Agencies, and the Rise of Civil Society in Southeast Asia. Paper presented at the 38th Annual Convention of the International Studies Association. Unpublished Toronto, Canada.

Risse, Thomas. 1997. Let's Talk! Insights from the German Debate on Communicative Behavior and International Relations. Paper presented at Annual Convention of the American Political Science Association, Aug. 27–31, at Washington, DC

Risse-Kappen, Thomas. 1994. Ideas Do Not Float Freely: Transnational Coalitions, Domestic Structures, and the End of the Cold War. *International Organization* 48 (2): 185–214

ed. 1995. *Bringing Transnational Relations Back In: Non-State Actors, Domestic Structures, and International Institutions*. Cambridge: Cambridge University Press

Rittberger, Volker. 1993. Research on International Regimes in Germany: The Adaptive Internalization of an American Social Science Concept. In *Regime Theory and International Relations*, edited by V. Rittberger. Oxford: Clarendon Press, 3–22

Robinson, Mark. 1995. Strengthening Civil Society in Africa: The Role of Foreign Political Aid. *IDS-Bulletin* 26 (2): 70–80

Robinson, William L. 1996. *Promoting Polyarchy. Globalization, US intervention, and Hegemony*. Cambridge: Cambridge University Press

Robison, Richard. 1992. Indonesia: An Autonomous Domain of Social Power? *The Pacific Review* 5 (4): 338–349

1993. Indonesia: Tensions in State and Regime. In *Southeast Asia in the 1990s: Authoritarianism, Democracy and Capitalism*, edited by K. Hewison, R. Robison, and G. Rodan. St. Leonards/Australia: Allen & Unwin, 39–74

Ropp, Stephen C. 1992. Explaining the Long-Term Maintenance of a Military Regime: Panama Before the U.S. Invasion. *World Politics* 44: 210–234

Ross, Stanley D. 1992. The Rule of Law and Lawyers in Kenya. *Journal of Modern African Studies* 30 (3): 421–442

Rueschemeyer, Dietrich, Evelyne Huber Stephens, and John D. Stephens. 1992. *Capitalist Development and Democracy*. Oxford: Polity Press

Saâf, Abdallah. 1993. Les Droits de l'Homme au Maroc: Acteurs, Discours, Actions. Unpublished paper. Rabat/Tunis

Sacerdoti, Guy. 1983. No Birthday Surprises. *Far Eastern Economic Review* December 8: 17–18

Sanctions Report, The. 1989. Prepared for the Commonwealth Committee of Foreign Ministers on Southern Africa. Harmondsworth, UK: Penguin

Sanguinetti, Antoine. 1991. *Le Livre Blanc sur les Droits de l'Homme au Maroc, Etudes et Documentation Internationales*. Paris

Sathyamurthy, T. V. 1986. *The Political Development of Uganda: 1900–1986*. Aldershot: Gower

Saul, John S. 1993. *Recolonisation and Resistance: Southern Africa in the 1990s*. Toronto: Between the Lines

Schaber, Thomas, and Cornelia Ulbert. 1994. Reflexivität in den internationalen Beziehungen. Literaturbericht zum Beitrag kognitiver, reflexiver und interpretativer Ansätze zur dritten Theoriedebatte. *Zeitschrift für Internationale Beziehungen* 1 (1): 139–169

Schimmelfennig, Frank. 1994. Internationale Sozialisation neuer Staaten. Heuristische berlegungen zu einem Forschungsdesiderat. *Zeitschrift für Internationale Beziehungen* 1 (2): 335–355

1995. *Debatten zwischen Staaten: Eine Argumentationstheorie internationaler Systemkonflikte*. Opladen: Leske & Budrich

1997. Rhetorisches Handeln in der internationalen Politik. *Zeitschrift für internationale Beziehungen* 4 (2): 219–254

1998. Rhetorisches Handeln in internationalen Menschenrechtsdebatten. Wie menschenrechtsverletzende Regierungen sich rechtfertigen. Konstanz: Universität Konstanz

Schirmer, Daniel B., and Stephen Rosskamm Shalom. 1987. *The Philippines Reader. A History of Colonialism, Neocolonialism, Dictatorship, and Resistance.* Boston: South End Press

Schmitz, Hans Peter. 1997a. Why Structural and Agency-based Approaches Fail to Explain Democratisation – Cultural and Institutional Aspects of Political Change in Kenya and Uganda. Paper presented at 25th ECPR Joint Sessions of Workshops, February 27, 1997, at Bern

1997b. Nichtregierungsorganisationen (NRO) und internationale Menschenrechtspolitik. *Comparativ* 7 (4): 27–67

1998. Communications Between the Kenyan Government, the Human Rights Community, and United Nations Human Rights Mechanisms. Florence: European University Institute

Schneider, Gerald. 1994. Rational Choice und kommunikatives Handeln. Eine Replik auf Harald Müller. *Zeitschrift für Internationale Beziehungen* 1 (2): 357–366

Schoultz, Lars. 1981. *Human Rights and United States Policy toward Latin America.* Princeton: Princeton University Press

Schreurs, Miranda A., and Elizabeth Economy. eds. 1997. *The Internationalization of Environmental Protection.* Cambridge: Cambridge University Press

Schulte-Nordholt, Nico G. 1995. Aid and Conditionality: The Case of Dutch–Indonesian Relationships. In *Aid and Political Conditionality*, edited by O. Stokke. London: Frank Cass & Co, 129–161

Schwarz, Adam. 1994. *A Nation in Waiting: Indonesia in the 1990s.* St. Leonards: Allen & Unwin

Seddon, David. 1989. Riot and Rebellion in North Africa: Political Responses to Economic Crisis in Tunisia. In *Power and Stability in the Middle East*, edited by B. Berberoglu. London: Zed Books, 114–135

Shalom, Stephen Rosskamm. 1981. *The United States and the Philippines: A Study of Neocolonialism.* Philadelphia: Institute for the Study of Human Issues

Shaw, Mark. ed. 1997. *Policing the Transformation.* Halfway House, SA: Institute for Security Studies

Sherry, Virginia. 1990. *Cleaning the Face of Morocco: Human Rights Abuses and Recent Developments.* New York: Lawyers' Committee for Human Rights

SiaR. 1998. Since April, 50 Activists have disappeared. *SiaR (Jakarta)* 14 April

Sidel, John T. 1995. The Philippines: The Languages of Legitimation. In *Political Legitimacy in Southeast Asia: The Quest for Moral Authority*, edited by M. Alagappa. Stanford, CA: Stanford University Press, 136–169

Sigmund, Paul E. 1993. *The United States and Democracy in Chile.* Baltimore, MD: The Johns Hopkins University Press

Sikkink, Kathryn. 1977. Reconceptualizing Sovereignty in the Americas: Historical Precursors and Current Practices. *Houston Journal of International Law* 19 (3): 705–729
1991. *Ideas and Institutions: Developmentalism in Brazil and Argentina.* Ithaca, NY: Cornell University Press
1993a. Human Rights, Principled Issue Networks, and Sovereignty in Latin America. *International Organization* 47 (3): 411–441
1993b. The Power of Principled Ideas: Human Rights Policies in the United States and Western Europe. In *Ideas and Foreign Policy*, edited by J. Goldstein and R. O. Keohane. Ithaca, NY: Cornell University Press, 139–170
1997. Reconceptualizing Sovereignty in the Americas: Historical Precursors and Current Practices. *Houston Journal of International Law* 19 (3): 705–729
Silliman, G. Sidney. 1994. Human Rights and the Transition to Democracy. In *Patterns of Power and Politics in the Philippines: Implications for Development*, edited by J. F. Eder and R. L. Youngblood. Tempe, AZ: Arizona State University, 103–146
Simbulan, Roland G. 1985. *The Bases of Our Insecurity.* 2nd edn. Metro Manila: Balai Fellowship, Inc
Sinaga, Kastorius. 1995. *NGOs in Indonesia. A Study of the Role of Non-Governmental Organizations in the Development Process.* Saarbrücken: Verlag für Entwicklungspolitik
Sison, José Maria. 1995. Strengthen the Alliance for Human Rights in the National-Democratic Movement. Paper presented at the KARAPATAN Congress, Manila, April 17
Skilling, H. Gordon. 1981. *Charter 77 and Human Rights in Czechoslovakia.* London: Allen & Unwin
Slaughter, Ann-Marie. 1995. International Law in a World of Liberal States. *The European Journal of International Law* 6: 139–170
Smith, Brian H. 1982. *The Church and Politics in Chile: Challenges to Modern Catholicism.* Princeton, NJ: Princeton University Press
Smith, Jackie, Charles Chatfield, and Ron Pagnucco. eds. 1997. *Transnational Social Movements and Global Politics: Solidarity Beyond the State.* Syracuse, NY: Syracuse University Press
Smith, Jackie, Ron Pagnucco, and George A. Lopez. 1998. Globalizing Human Rights: The Work of Transnational Human Rights NGOs in the 1990s. *Human Rights Quarterly* 20 (2): 379–412
Sodusta, Jesucita, and Artemio Palongpalong. 1982. The Philippines in 1981 – Normalization and Instability. In *Southeast Asian Affairs 1981*, edited by Institute of Southeast Asian Studies. Singapore: ISEAS, 285–299
Souhaili, Mohamed. 1986. *Les Damnés du Royaume: Le Drame des Libertés au Maroc.* Paris: Etudes et Documentation Internationales
Southall, Roger. 1994a. The South African Election of 1994 in Comparative African Perspective. *Africa Insight* 24 (2): 86–98
1994b. The South African Elections of 1994: The Remaking of a Dominant-Party State, *Journal of Modern African Studies* 32 (4): 629–655

List of references

Sparks, Allister. 1995. *Tomorrow is Another Country*. London: Mandarin

Spasowski, Romuald. 1986. *The Liberation of One*. New York: Harcourt Brace Jovanovich

Sraieb, Noureddine. 1993. Tunisie: Chronique Intérieure 1993, *Annuaire de l'Afrique du Nord* 32: 590–643

Stauffer, Robert B. 1977. Philippine Corporatism: A Note on the "New Society." *Asian Survey* 17 (4): 393–407

Steenkamp, Anton. 1995. The South African Constitution of 1993 and the Bill of Rights: An Evaluation in Light of International Human Rights Norms, *Human Rights Quarterly* 17: 101–126

Steinmo, Sven, Kathleen Thelen, and Frank Longstreth. eds. 1992. *Structuring Politics. Historical Institutionalism in Comparative Analysis*. Cambridge–New York: Cambridge University Press

Stohl, Michaels, David Carlton, Mark Gibney, and Geoffrey Martin. 1989. US Foreign Policy, Human Rights and Multilateral Assistance. In *Human Rights and Developments, International Views*, edited by D. P. Forsythe. London: Macmillan, 196–211

Stokes, Gale. 1993. *The Walls Came Tumbling Down: The Collapse of Communism in Eastern Europe*. New York: Oxford University Press

Stoll, David. 1993. *Between Two Armies: In the Ixil Towns of Guatemala*. New York: Columbia University Press

Strokata, Nina. 1986. The Ukrainian Helsinki Group. In *The Fifth International Sakharov Hearing, Proceedings, April 1985*, edited by A. Wynn *et al*. London: Andrei Sakharov Campaign, André Deutsch Ltd., 99–101

Sunstein, Cass. 1997. *Free Markets and Social Justice*. New York: Oxford University Press

Suryadinata, Leo. 1997. Democratization and Political Succession in Suharto's Indonesia. *Asian Survey* 37 (3) March: 269–280

Swedish Ministry of Foreign Affairs. 1985. *Prohibition of Trade with South Africa and Namibia*. Stockholm

Tanter, Richard, and Kenneth Young. 1990. *The Politics of Middle-Class Indonesia*, Monash Papers on Southeast Asian Studies. Clayton, Australia: Monash University

Taylor, John G. 1995. East Timor: Contemporary History. A Chronology of the Main Events since 1974. In *East Timor at the Cross Roads: The Forging of a Nation*, edited by P. Carey and G. C. Bentley. New York: Social Science Research Council, 238–250

Tennyson, Brian Douglas. 1982. *Canadian Relations with South Africa*. Washington: University Press of America

Thomas, Daniel C. forthcoming. *The Helsinki Effect*. Princeton, NJ: Princeton University Press

Thomson, Janice. 1993. Norms in International Relations: A Conceptual Analysis. *International Journal of Group Tensions* 23 (2): 67–83

Thoolen, Hans. 1987. *Indonesia and the Rule of Law: Twenty Years of "New Order" Government. Published for the International Commission of Jurists and the Netherlands Institute of Human Rights*. London: Frances Pinter Publishers

Timberman, David G. 1987. Unfinished Revolution – The Philippines in 1986. In *Southeast Asian Affairs 1987*, edited by Institute of South East Asian Studies, 239–263

Tolley Jr., Howard B. 1994. *The International Commission of Jurists. Global Advocates for Human Rights*. Philadelphia: University of Pennsylvania Press

Toumi, Mohsen. 1989. *La Tunisie de Bourguiba à Ben Ali*. Paris: PUF

Trudeau, Robert. 1993. *Guatemalan Politics: The Popular Struggle for Democracy*. Boulder, CO: Lynne Rienner Publishers

Uhlin, Anders. 1995. *Democracy and Diffusion. Transnational Lesson-Drawing Among Indonesian Pro-Democracy Actors*. Lund: Department of Political Science

Ulbert, Cornelia. 1997a. *Die Konstruktion von Umwelt. Der Einfluss von Ideen, Institutionen und Kultur auf (inter-) nationale Klimapolitik in den USA und der Bundesrepublik*. Baden-Baden: Nomos

1997b. Ideen, Institutionen und Kultur. Die Konstruktion (inter-)nationaler Klimapolitik in der BRD und in den USA. *Zeitschrift für Internationale Beziehungen* 4 (1): 9–40

"Un chartiste." 1977. Conscience contre existence: Information à propos de la naissance et de l'évolution de la Charte 77. *Cahiers de l'Est* (9/10): 132–142

United Nations Department of Public Information. 1994. *The United Nations and Apartheid, 1948–94*. New York

United Nations Development Program. 1996. *Human Development Report 1996*. New York: Oxford University Press

United Nations Economic and Social Council. 1993. United Nations Workshop for the Asia-Pacific on Human Rights Issues, January 26–28, Jakarta, Indonesia

1994. *Question of the Violation of Human Rights and Fundamental Freedoms in any Part of the World, With Particular Reference to Colonial and Other Dependent Countries and Territories. Extrajudicial, Summary or Arbitrary Executions. Addendum. Report by the Special Rapporteur, Mr. Bacre Waly Ndiaye, on his mission to Indonesia and East Timor from 3 to 13 July 1994 (E/CN.4/1995/61/ Add.)*. Geneva, New York: United Nations

United Nations Economic and Social Council, and Commission on Human Rights. 1986. *The Right of Peoples to Self-Determination and its Application to Peoples under Colonial or Alien Domination or Foreign Occupation: Question of the Violation of Human Rights and Fundamental Freedoms in any Part of the World, With Particular Reference to Colonial and other Dependent Countries and Territories*. Forty-Second Session, Agenda Items 9 and 12. Geneva

United Nations General Assembly. 1994. Comprehensive Agreement Human Rights: The Situation in Central America Procedures for the Establishment of a Firm and Lasting Peace and Progress in Fashioning a Region of Peace, Freedom, Democracy, and Development. March 29, 1994 (A/48/928-S/1994/ 448, annex I)

List of references

1997. *The Situation in Central America: Procedures for the Establishment of a Firm and Lasting Peace and Progress in Fashioning a Region of Peace, Freedom, Democracy, and Development. United Nations Verification Mission in Guatemala.* Report of the Secretary General, June 30
United Nations Human Rights Committee. 1995. *Official Records of the Human Rights Committee 1988/ 89. Summary Records of the meetings of the 34 to 36 sessions (24 October 1988–28 July 1989).* 2 vols. Vol. II. New York: United Nations
US Department of State. 1977. *Country Reports on Human Rights Practices for 1976, Report Submitted to the Committee of Foreign Affairs.* Washington, DC: GPO
1997a. *Tunisia Report on Human Rights Practices for 1996.* Stockholm
1997b. *Indonesia Human Rights Practices 1996, Report Submitted to the Committee on Foreign Affairs.* Washington, DC: GPO
1997c. *Chile Human Rights Practices.* Washington, DC: Bureau of Democracy, Human Rights, and Labor
1998. *The Philippines Country Report on Human Rights Practices for 1997.* Washington, DC: Government Printing Office
Uys, Stanley. 1994. South Africa: Dividing the Spoils. *The World Today* 50 (3): 53–56
US Helsinki Watch Committee. 1989. *Toward Civil Society: Independent Initiatives in Czechoslovakia.* New York: Government Printing Office, August
US Senate. 1975. *Staff Report of the Select Committee on Intelligence Activities: Covert Action in Chile, 1963–1973.* Washington, DC: Government Printing Office
1985a. *Congressional Quarterly Almanac.* Washington: Government Printing Office
1985b. *Administration Review of U.S. Policy Toward the Philippines: Hearing before the Committee on Foreign Relations, U.S. Senate, Ninety-ninth Congress, First Session, October 30, 1985.* Washington: Government Printing Office
US Senate Committee on Foreign Relations, 93rd Congress, 1st Session. 1973. *Korea and the Philippines, November 1972.* Washington, DC: GPO
Vaky, Viron P., and Heraldo Muñoz. 1993. *The Future of the Organization of American States.* New York: Twentieth Century Fund Press
Vale, Peter. 1997. South Africa: Understanding the Upstairs and the Downstairs. In *Niche Diplomacy: Middle Power Foreign Policies After the Cold War,* edited by A. Cooper. Basingstoke, UK: Macmillan, 197–214
Valenzuela, Arturo. 1978. *The Breakdown of Democratic Regimes: Chile.* Baltimore, MD: The Johns Hopkins University Press
Vandenbosch, Amry. 1970. *South Africa and the World: The Foreign Policy of Apartheid.* Lexington, KY: University of Kentucky Press
Vatikiotis, Michael. 1988. Bidding for a Larger Role: New Foreign Minister Moves to Raise Jakarta's International Profile. *Far Eastern Economic Review,* April 14: 31–32
1991. Defusing Criticism: The Government Works on its Human Rights

Image. *Far Eastern Economic Review*, January 17: 13
Vincent, R. J. 1986. *Human Rights and International Relations*. Cambridge: Cambridge University Press
Voorhes, Meg. Forthcoming. The US Divestment Movement. In *How Sanctions Work: South Africa*, edited by N. Crawford and A. Klotz. Basingstoke, UK: Macmillan
Walesa, Lech. 1987. *A Way of Hope*. New York: Henry Holt and Company
Waltz, Kenneth. 1979. *Theory of International Politics*. Reading, MA: Addison-Wesley
Waltz, Susan. 1989. Tunisia's League and the Pursuit of Human Rights. *Maghreb Review* 14 (3–4): 214–225
1995a. *Human Rights and Reform: Changing the Face of North African Politics*. Berkeley and Los Angeles, CA: University of California Press
1995b. Les Défis de la Réforme. In *Tunisie, la Politique conomique de la Réforme*, edited by W. Zartman. Tunis: Alif-Les Editions de la Méditerranée, 45–65
Weekly Mail and Guardian. 1994. *A-Z of South African Politics*. Johannesburg: Penguin
Weidnitzer, Eva. 1995. Die Europäische Union und der Maghreb vor einer neuen Euro-Mediterranen Partnerschaft? *Wuquf: Beiträge zur Entwicklung von Staat und Gesellschaft in Nordafrika* (9): 189–206
Wendt, Alexander. 1992. Anarchy is What States Make of It: The Social Construction of Power Politics. *International Organization* 88 (2): 384–396
1995. Constructing International Politics. *International Security* 20 (1): 71–81
Forthcoming. *Social Theory of International Politics*. Cambridge: Cambridge University Press
Weyel, Volker. 1995. Uganda. In *Rüstung statt Entwicklung? Sicherheitspolitik, Militärausgaben und Rüstungskontrolle in der Dritten Welt*, edited by V. Büttner and J. Krause. Baden-Baden: Nomos, 554–572
Widner, Jennifer A. 1992. *The Rise of the One-Party-State in Kenya: From "Harambee" to "Nyayo"*. Berkeley, CA: University of California Press
Wilde, Alexander. 1998. A Conspiracy of Consensus: Chile's Transitional Democracy. Paper presented at the conference on Legacies of Authoritarianism: Cultural Production, Collective Trauma, and Global Justice, University of Wisconsin-Madison, April 3–5
Wilson, Ernest J. III. 1994. Creating a Research Agenda for the Study of Political Change in Africa. In *Economic Change and Political Liberalization in Sub-Saharan Africa*, edited by J. A. Widner. Baltimore, MD: The Johns Hopkins University Press, 253–271
Wolff, Jürgen H. 1993. Marokko, *Handbuch der Dritten Welt: Nordafrika und Naher Osten* (6): 238–260
Woodward, Ralph Lee Jr. 1985. *Central America: A Nation Divided*. New York: Oxford University Press
World Bank. 1991. *World Development Report: 1991*. Washington, DC: Oxford University Press
1997. *World Development Report 1997: The State in a Changing World*. Oxford:

List of references

Oxford University Press

Wurfel, David. 1965. The Philippines. In *Governments and Politics of Southeast Asia*, edited by G. M. Kahin. Ithaca, NY: Cornell University Press, 679–767

1988. *Filipino Politics. Development and Decay*. Ithaca/London: Cornell University Press

1990. Transition to Political Democracy in the Philippines: 1978–88. In *Democratic Transition and Consolidation in Southern Europe, Latin America, and Southeast Asia*, edited by D. Ethier. London: Macmillan, 110–135

Yee, Albert S. 1996. The Causal Effects of Ideas on Policies. *International Organization* 50 (1): 69–108

YLBI. 1995. From the Anti-Subversion Law to the Haatzaai Artikelen. *Indonesian Human Rights Forum* (9) July–December: 12–13

Young, Oran R. ed. 1997. *Global Governance: Drawing Insights from the Environmental Experience*. Cambridge, MA: MIT Press

Index

accountability for past human rights
violations, 173, 193, 197, 255
African National Congress (ANC), 83, 84,
86, 89, 90, 93, 96–105, 107, 241, *see also*
South Africa
aid
to Chile, 184, 187
economic, 24–25
foreign, 34, 74, 245
to Guatemala, 182–183, 199, 200
to Indonesia, 145, 147, 148, 166
to Kenya, 51, 55–60, 61, 63, 76
military, 24–25
to Morocco and Tunisia, 131
to the Philippines, 149, 154, 165
to Uganda, 42, 45, 49
Algeria, 109, 110
Allende, Salvador, 174, 175, 179, 180, 260,
see also Chile
alternative explanations, *see*
modernization theory explanations;
neo-Marxism; realism
Amin, Idi, 39, 41, 42, 44, 45, 46, 54, 72, *see*
also Uganda
Amnesty International, 3, 127, 141, 147
and Chile, 175, 179
and Kenya, 50– 53, 58, 59, 63, 65, 72
and Morocco, 119, 121, 122, 123, 124
and the Philippines, 138, 140, 141, 162,
163
and Uganda 40, 44, 45, 46, 47, 48, 49, 69,
70
Angola, 81, 90, 94
anti-apartheid mobilization, 79, 84, 85, 86,
94, 108
apartheid, 79, 80, 81, 82, 83, 87, 97, 98, 104
Aquino, Corazon, 154–155, 162–163, 164,
see also the Philippines

Arab Organization of Human Rights
(AOHR),122
arap Moi, Daniel, 39, 42, 43, 44, 50–60,
62–67, 72, 73, 74, 76, 239, 241, 243, 253,
see also Kenya
arbitrary detention, 235
in Chile, 192
in Czechoslovakia, 223, 224, 226,
227
in Guatemala, 195
in Indonesia, 144, 161
in Kenya, 43, 53, 59
in Tunisia and Morocco, 113
(*garde-à-vue* custody), 124
argumentative discourse, 28, 29, 236,
255
argumentative rationality, 252–253, 256,
276, *see also* communicative action;
socialization
armed insurgent movements
in Guatemala, 178, 203
in the Philippines, 163, 164, 170
see also civil war
Asia Watch, 144
Australia, 49, 84, 96
Austria, 225
authoritarianism, 9, 27, 238–239
in Chile and Guatemala, 172
in Indonesia and the Philippines, 138,
139
in South Africa, 78
see also bureaucratic authoritarian
states; norm-violating states
Aylwin, Patricio, 190, *see also* Chile

bargaining, *see* strategic bargaining;
instrumental adaptation
Belgium, 123

Index

CAMBRIDGE STUDIES IN INTERNATIONAL RELATIONS